DOUGLAS LONG has been associated with the Bentham Research Project at University College, London, and is a member of the Department of Political Science at the University of Western Ontario.

Bentham on Liberty focuses on the crucial formative years, when the English social philosopher Jeremy Bentham was in his twenties and thirties between 1770 and 1790, and draws on the unpublished manuscripts held at University College, London, to throw a new light on his early intellectual development. Using also both private correspondence and published works, it shows how Bentham's legal training and enthusiasm for Enlightenment ideas steadily broadened his horizon from criminal law to constitutional law to social theory.

Bentham's desire to create a science of man and society modelled on the physical sciences led to his systematic exposition of the conception of utilitarianism. His broad perspective came to encompass aspects of what are now called psychology, sociology, political science, moral philosophy, and jurisprudence.

A central theme of this study is the way in which, in Bentham's mind, liberty became subordinated to security as an end of social action. The arguments he used to defend this characteristic but controversial principle were novel and significant.

The common opinion of Bentham as a liberal and a democrat has been superficial, Professor Long suggests; the evolution of Bentham's thought is to be understood, not in terms of political radicalization, but rather in relation to his commitment to a particular and growing conception of social science. The implications of that conception are explored in the concluding part of the book, which compares features of Bentham's 'scientific' social theory with the ideas of a modern 'designer of cultures,' B.F. Skinner.

Douglas G. Long

BENTHAM ON LIBERTY:

Jeremy Bentham's idea
of liberty in relation
to his utilitarianism

UNIVERSITY OF TORONTO PRESS
Toronto and Buffalo

© University of Toronto Press 1977
Toronto and Buffalo
Printed in Canada

Library of Congress Cataloging in Publication Data

Long, Douglas G. 1947 -
  Bentham on liberty.

  Bibliography: p.
  1. Bentham, Jeremy, 1748-1832. 2. Liberty. 3. Utilitarianism.
  4. Law — Philosophy. I. Title.
  B1574.B34L63   323.44'01   76-45376
  ISBN 0-8020-5361-0

This book has been published during the
Sesquicentennial year of the University of Toronto

To Roberna

for faith and friendship

Contents

Preface

In June 1973 I submitted a thesis on the subject of Bentham's idea of liberty for the doctoral degree in history at the University of London. Much of that thesis has been incorporated directly into this book. Some of the original work's errors of style or substance have been corrected, the introduction expanded, and some conclusions added. In spite of the tightly focused field of vision implied by its title, this book is relevant to a variety of contemporary problems and interests. It is my hope that it will be read not only by specialists in the study of the Enlightenment or Utilitarianism or Bentham but also by anyone interested in the idea of liberty or the idea of a social science.

As my research and writing proceeded in the years 1969-73, it became increasingly clear that the study of Bentham's idea of liberty could throw much new light on the nature and genesis of his utilitarian system as a whole. I came to see, and continue to believe, that Bentham's decision to concentrate on making men happy did, as Professor Halévy suggested,[1] entail a conscious de-emphasizing of the intrinsic importance of making them free. When happiness was granted a position of pre-emptively high priority on the scale of objectives of social policy, liberty more than any other social value was thus denied its accustomed place in men's minds. My historical interest in the birth and growth of an idea in Bentham's writings was intensified by a theoretical interest in the confrontation between the idea of liberty and that of authority in the mind of an eighteenth-century advocate of a scientific approach to social theory.

The 1960s and 1970s have been years of great interest in the idea of liberty, and particularly of liberation. In this respect they resemble the 1770s, the years when Bentham first encountered rhetorical, partisan usages of the term 'liberty' in the vocabularies of English and American political radicals. Whatever one's twentieth-century opinion of its ultimate merits, Bentham's analysis of liberty does display a certain compatibility with the frame of reference used in modern-day disputes about individual and political liberty.

The 1960s also witnessed a widespread upsurge of support for the idea of scientific social studies. In this respect as well, the applicability of Bentham's perspective to present-day theoretical disputes is striking. Bentham was, in fact if not in title, a behavioural scientist. His 'logic of the will' was nothing if not a framework for a science of human (and animal) behaviour. Any suggestion that Bentham's writings hold conclusive answers to twentieth-century political problems would be suspect. Transplanting ideas in such an unqualified way is frequently anachronistic. We learn, however, by antithesis as well as by example. The very possibility of learning from Bentham's mistakes gives his writings more than historical significance. The recent appearance of the first volumes of the new *Collected Works of Jeremy Bentham* marked the beginning of a publishing programme that promises to provide the immensely strengthened foundation upon which an improved understanding of Bentham's life and thought may be built. The Bentham Committee's General Preface to the first volume of Bentham's correspondence, which launched the *Collected Works*, summarizes both the past problems and the future potentialities of Bentham scholarship. The Committee points out that an accumulation of factors has hitherto obliged or induced students of Bentham to content themselves with 'an impoverished and at times a false picture' of his thought.[2] The Bentham manuscripts themselves are frequently illegible, as disorganized as their author's interests were diverse, and above all depressingly voluminous. Nevertheless, they remain the only incontestable source of knowledge of Bentham's ideas beyond the very partial picture provided by his published works. Etienne Dumont's *Traités de Législation* (3 vols, 1803) bear witness to herculean editorial labours, but perforce represent a selective, condensed, and reorganized version of the contents of the manuscripts entrusted to him by Bentham. Translation of the *Traités* into English (1896 and 1931) simply resulted in a text *('Theory of Legislation, by Jeremy Bentham')* one step further removed from the thought of Bentham himself. J.S. Mill's *Utilitarianism* (1863) is far from being an exposition of Benthamism. Mill was well aware of this. His 'Essay on Bentham' indicates clearly that he was as much Bentham's censor as his expositor. Most important, the severe formal and substantive deficiencies of John Bowring's edition of Bentham's *Works* (1838-43) have hindered a full and accurate understanding of Bentham's views. A glance at the list of the thirty-eight volumes projected for the *Collected Works* provided by the Committee in the General Preface will show how much is now to be done that previous editors and expositors have not done.

Publication of Bentham's extensive correspondence has until now been particularly incomplete and inaccurate. The new *Collected Works* will include 'the first comprehensive presentation' of Bentham's letters, a source of essential biographical data which has hitherto been only partially available to those interested in Bentham's thought. During my years of research at University College London, three volumes of Bentham's correspondence were published as parts of the new series, and a fourth and a fifth volume reached the typescript stage. This circumstance gave me the immense benefit of access to a complete chronological record of Bentham's correspondence throughout the period primarily focused upon in this work, that is, before 1803. Much of this book's distinctive usefulness may stem from the fact that it draws upon such remarkable and previously untapped resources. The publication of Bentham's *Of Laws in General*, edited by H.L.A. Hart, in 1970 afforded yet another chance to explore Bentham's writings presented more accurately and completely than in any previous edition. In sum, the completion of the new *Collected Works of Jeremy Bentham* will place Bentham scholarship on a new and dramatically improved footing. This book ought to reflect the improvement in resource materials brought about by the publication of such volumes as have already appeared in that series. If it does not, the fault can only lie with the author.

The raw materials for successive volumes of the *Collected Works* are provided by the staff of the Bentham Research Project. They supply individual editors with complete and expert transcriptions of passages of Bentham manuscript relevant to their particular projects. Working in close proximity to and co-operation with the Bentham Research Project staff at University College London, I was generously allowed access to large quantities of typescript produced with fidelity to the manuscript original the only end in view. Thus footnotes used in this book to give sources for extracts from Bentham's 'Essay on indirect legislation,' from his study of 'The influence of place and time in matters of legislation,' and from material accumulated in the course of his attempts to produce a plan for a civil code, generally refer directly to the manuscripts. Many of the passages thus cited have not been included in any past editions of the particular work concerned. All of them, however, will form part of the text of that work when it appears as a volume in the *Collected Works*. In view of the manifold deficiencies of John Bowring's *Works of Jeremy Bentham* I have at all times preferred to cite the Bentham manuscripts rather than his volumes, and have tried not to rely upon his authority alone for any point of importance in my arguments.

A NOTE CONCERNING BENTHAM'S 'PREPARATORY MANUSCRIPTS'[3]

In the fourth chapter of the present work considerable use is made of manuscript extracts, often extremely brief, taken from Bentham manuscripts headed 'Key,' 'PPI' ('Preparatory Principles Inserenda'), or 'Crit. Jur. Crim.' The reader may be assisted in evaluating these manuscripts, as the writer has been, by a description of their form and context.

The most thorough and reliable extant account of Bentham's interests and activities during the period in which the preparatory manuscripts were written (the 1770s) has been given by Burns and Hart in the Editors' Introduction to their edition (a volume in the *Collected Works*) of the *Introduction to the Principles of Morals and Legislation*. The evidence culled from a reading of the Key, PPI, and Crit. Jur. Crim. manuscripts supports their assertion that 'Bentham's first major project as a writer was conceived originally as a treatise on the "Elements of Critical Jurisprudence" or the "Principles of Legal Polity" ' (p. ii). This work, 'probably begun in 1770,' was 'interrupted' from Autumn 1774 to autumn 1776 by Bentham's work on the *Comment on the Commentaries* and the *Fragment on Government*. By 1 October 1776, however, Bentham could write to his father: 'I am now at work upon my capital work: I mean the Critical Elements of Jurisprudence' (CW, *Correspondence*, I, p. 358).

Thereafter the story becomes more complex. Two threads of development emerge, 'the treatise was beginning to bifurcate,' the branches being Bentham's analyses of punishments and of offences. Bentham's view when he drafted a letter (unsent) to Voltaire, probably in November 1776, was that he was nearing completion of his 'Theory of Punishment,' and that it would form 'part of a work to which if ever it should be completed I intend to give some such title as Principles of Legal Policy: the object of it is to trace out a new model for the Laws: of my own country you may imagine, in the first place, but keeping those of other countries all along in view. To ascertain what the Laws ought to be, in form and tenor as well as in matter: and that elsewhere as well as here' (CW, *Correspondence*, I, 192 to Voltaire, 'November 1776' [?], pp. 367-8; p. 367). The editors tell us (p. ii) that, as the letter just cited indicates, the work in the area of 'a treatise on offences to match that on punishment' progressed more slowly than its mate. 'Punishments' dominated 1777. Work on what was conceived of as a 'Code of Criminal Law' progressed in early 1778 (*Introduction*, ed. Burns and Hart, 'Editors' Introduction,' p. ii, n. 1), spurred on by the announcement of the Berne Oeconomical Society's sponsorship of a competition for a 'Plan of legislation on criminal matters.' Was this the seed-time of Crit. Jur. Crim.? Probably not. It undoubtedly flourished in 1778, but it was born earlier.

According to one manuscript source, Crit. Jur. Crim. and the 'Principles of Legal Policy' were one and the same. UCL manuscripts Box 140, page 14 (4), gives the impression that Crit. Jur. Crim. was first conceived in broad terms (perhaps in the autumn of 1776) as a continuation of the old 'capital work,' the 'Elements of Critical Jurisprudence.' The relevant manuscript sheet is headed 'Crit. Jur. Crim.' Below this heading is the marginal heading 'Title of the Work,' and across from it appear the candidates for the office of title:

Principles of Legal Policy
Philosophy of Jurisprudence
Law as it ought to be
The Policy of Jurisprudence
Principles of Legal Policy
adapted to the Jurisprudence of all nations [nations in General] but more particularly to the English.

Part the 1st containing / comprehending / relating so much of the Penal Law as relates to offences against individuals.

With an Introduction in which is contained what is thought necessary to be premised [to the whole] relating to Law in General.

There is a hint here of an embryonic conception of what became, by 1789, the idea of a 'General view of a complete code of laws,' and more than a hint of the work recently published as *Of Laws in General*. Clearly, Crit. Jur. Crim. lies at the beginning (after 1776) of the development which led to the works described in Bentham's letter to Lord Ashburton in 1782 and, still further on, to the group of ten projects described in Bentham's Preface to the *Introduction to the Principles of Morals and Legislation* in 1789.

UCL manuscripts, 159, p. 269, headed 'Crit. Jur. Crim. 153,' contains an additional nugget of information: 'Title of the Chapter called Key — Exposition of certain fundamental terms of Universal Jurisprudence.' The subject of the Key manuscripts was to be the 'fundamental terms' of jurisprudence in general, and the definitions therein established were to provide the foundation for the Crit. Jur. Crim. work as a whole, and thus for a whole succession of works of which the *Introduction to the Principles of Morals and Legislation* is merely the best known.

The PPI ['Preparatory Principles Inserenda'], material mainly, but not exclusively, located in UCL manuscripts, Box 69, is exactly what its title implies: a collection of definitions, distinctions, and aphorisms whose importance to a full understanding of Bentham's thought can hardly be overestimated. Logically they relate equally closely to the earlier 'Critical elements of jurisprudence' or the later 'Principles of legal policy' (alias 'Crit. Jur. Crim.'). In either case their importance in the development of Bentham's thought seems clear enough. The fact that UCL manuscripts, Box 69 pp. 77-80, are headed 'Contents of Prep. Princ.' may be taken as suggesting that the 'Inserenda' headed 'PPI' are merely the tip of an iceberg. Could there once have been a larger bundle of 'Preparatory Principles' manuscripts, now lost, perhaps discarded by the author as superceded? Or was the preparatory principles idea abortive? Did Bentham find that his preparatory principles did not add up to a single printable work in themselves, but rather to an unpublishable aggregation of essential *points de départ*? We cannot say. What we can say is that the table of contents of 'Prep. Princ.' contains a number of important titles, to which some of the fragments cited in chapter 4 of the present work bear an obvious relationship:

[UCL manuscripts, Box 69, p. 79 (4)]
237, 238, 239, 240 — Liberty not in proportion to the bulk of Law — 574 [page ref.]
258 — Liberty and its four senses — 622 [see also Box 69, p. 84 (1).]
258 — Free Government or constitution. Metonymics (?) — 624

[UCL manuscripts, Box 69, p. 79 (3)]
Law of Personal Security, modal objects of — 226 — 553
Law of Personal Liberty, modal objects of — 226 — 556
Law of Property. Moral field of Dominion it leaves untouched — 227 — 558

It seems likely that the PPI manuscripts are the earliest of the three groups. A strange redundancy would seem to exist if they are in fact to be construed as contemporary with the Crit. Jur. Crim. and Key manuscripts, and it is most unlikely that the PPI are later than the others. However, although there may be some doubt as to the precise chronology involved here, there can be no doubt of the importance of the contents of these manuscripts as evidence of the nature of Bentham's thought process during a formative intellectual period unlike any other similar span of years in his long life.

No decision has yet been made as to how Bentham's preparatory manuscripts may be presented in print. My study of them leaves me convinced that they merit inclusion in the *Collected Works*. Information drawn from them has been of central importance to the development of my arguments. I leave the reader to make his own estimate of the importance of their contents as indicated by their role in this book.

Acknowledgments

Canada Council Doctoral Fellowships provided the financial support which enabled me to research and write my doctoral thesis on this subject in the years 1969-73. I am most profoundly grateful to the Canada Council for having made what I hope is a valuable piece of work possible.

Without the wise, patient, and conscientious tutelage of my thesis supervisor, Professor J.H. Burns, I could never have charted a course of investigation through the Bentham manuscripts, nor could I have succeeded in ordering my own thoughts to the extent indicated in this discussion. In so far as insights may be found in it, many of them have resulted directly or indirectly from his guidance. Its errors are, of course, purely my own.

The work of research was made infinitely more pleasant and productive by the generous amounts of time and energy expended in my interest by various members of the Bentham Research Project. My sincere thanks go to Messrs C.F. Bahmueller, M.H. James, M. Woodcock, F. Rosen, J. Phillips, and J. Micklewright for helpful advice and knowledge unstintingly shared.

The staff of the British Museum Library (now the British Library) and the staff of the University College London Library proved invariably kind and helpful, but I must give special thanks to Mrs J. Percival and her colleagues on the staff of the C.K. Ogden Library at University College. Their assistance was especially generous and truly invaluable.

Mr D.D. Carrick read the manuscript in its entirety, provided much appreciated encouragement, and gave generously of his time and wisdom, providing a wealth of perceptive and detailed comments which assisted me greatly in improving the style, structure, and clarity of the work.

Finally I wish to thank my wife for putting up with an eccentric and preoccupied husband through the vicissitudes of research and writing.

This book has been published with the help of a grant from the Social Science Research Council of Canada, using funds provided by the Canada Council, and a grant to University of Toronto Press from the Andrew W. Mellon Foundation.

DL

BENTHAM ON LIBERTY

Introduction

This is a study of the art of thought and the science of social theory as understood and practised by Jeremy Bentham. Bentham thought of himself as a scientist, and saw his works as additions to or codifications of various bodies of scientific knowledge – legal science, moral science, legislative science, the science of political economy, and others. One of the tasks of the present work is to throw light on the roots of his conception of, and passion for, science in general and the 'science of human nature' in particular.

Bentham's analysis of the idea of liberty was an important and integral part of his attempt, as an experimental scientist and a *philosophe*, to perfect a 'science of man' modelled on the Newtonian physical sciences. A second objective of this book, therefore, is to show how Bentham moulded his idea of liberty to fit the requirements, both methodological and conceptual, of his 'system.'

So much for science; but what of art? Bentham was in fact an extraordinarily self-conscious practitioner of what Professor Graham Wallas has described as the 'art of thought.'[1] His success in constructing a coherent and comprehensive system of social sciences was founded, in his own view, upon his mastery of this art. A third function of this discussion, therefore, is to examine the process that Bentham referred to as the 'invention' of ideas. Professor Wallas spoke of the divisibility of a 'single achievement of thought' into four stages: 'Preparation, Incubation, Illumination ... and Verification.'[2] Taking Bentham's definition of liberty as a model of a 'single achievement of thought,' this book attempts to reconstruct as completely as possible the circumstances relevant to its genesis, its distinguishing features, and the course of its development.

The historian cannot actually rethink Bentham's own thoughts. An idea, however, especially one carefully analysed and knowingly prepared to face popular scrutiny, is more than a thought: it is a piece of public property.

Bentham was aware that if his writings attracted attention proportionate to their significance his idea of liberty would be searchingly examined by sceptical and even hostile critics. He was acutely conscious of its novelty and its importance. In the case of such a central and controversial conception there is a great deal that can be done, given adequate historical evidence, to clarify the process of 'invention' as applied to it.

Accordingly, in this book the logical implications, for Bentham's idea of liberty, of his allegiance to the Enlightenment notion of a 'science of man' and to the principle of utility are pointed out. The writings of various authors who appear to have had some influence on his thinking in the all-important period between 1770 and 1784 when he 'invented' so many of his most fundamental ideas are consulted. The issues which drew Bentham into the vortex of public controversy and political debate during the same period are examined. Finally, attention is directed to Bentham's own writings, published and unpublished, including his extensive and largely unpublished correspondence.

This book makes special use of Bentham's hitherto unpublished preparatory manuscripts, in the pages of which he readied himself for the forthcoming promulgation of his system by recording, at moments of 'illumination,' a long succession of insights, definitions, maxims, distinctions, and desiderata: 'achievements of thought' of every description. Each entry in these manuscripts was indeed an intellectual achievement, but at the same time the entire process of defining words was a basic part of Bentham's large-scale preparation. As though to exemplify the preparatory stage of mental effort described by Professor Wallas 150 years later, Bentham readied himself for the task of system-building by 'consciously accumulating knowledge, dividing up by logical rules the field of inquiry, and adopting a definite "problem attitude" '.[3] Such preparation, followed by a period of incubation, laid the foundations for subsequent major illuminations. Indeed, the works on jurisprudence, legislation, and morals, described in the third part of this book as illustrating the 'expansion' of Bentham's system, may be seen as successive illuminations which altered Bentham's view of the dimensions of his system of thought. The pattern formed by this sequence of alterations was one of growth.

Bentham at first thought of his utilitarianism mainly as a basis for a reformed, 'censorial' jurisprudence. His critique of Sir William Blackstone's *Commentaries on the Laws of England*, however, once begun, carried him into the realm of political theory. His theory of sovereignty was expounded as a tangent to his legal theory. He digressed from his *Comment on the Commentaries* to write his *Fragment on Government*. The extremely close relationship between the subjects covered in these two essays was then thoroughly investigated in a series of studies which were in fact but portions of a single magnum opus too large to compress between the covers of a single volume.[4]

This proliferation of works was accompanied by a significant broadening of Bentham's field of vision. His original preoccupation with penal law was superseded by an interest in the whole field of 'morals and legislation.' This involved him in the study of ethics, of civil law, and of what is now called sociology. It also entailed an evolution in his view of the nature of law. Having at first thought of the law as the coercive embodiment of legislative punishments and rewards, he subsequently arrived at the notion of laws as rules or norms. His understanding of political authority underwent a corresponding transformation. His final realization was that the ramifications of his utilitarian insights would extend into the farthest corners of the 'universe of human actions.' Verification of this ultimate illumination could be achieved only in the process of expounding a comprehensive utilitarian social system.

Bentham was particularly anxious that his stock of fundamental definitions and distinctions should be preserved and his method of arriving at them understood. To that end he prepared for publication material for a volume dealing with the 'key terms of universal jurisprudence' and another describing the 'preparatory principles' of his system. In effect, he made every effort to facilitate the historical study of his art of thought at the terminological level. A much more difficult task for the historian of ideas is to explain the relationship between specific concepts and the system into which they are integrated. Bentham's clear determination to achieve such integration and his eventual confidence that he had succeeded in doing so, however, invite the historian to undertake such an explanation in this case.

The picture is, if not beclouded, at least complicated by the fact that it is strictly speaking impossible to isolate for study any one of the preparatory achievements of thought upon which Bentham's system was founded.[5] The more central and significant the concept studied, in fact, the more difficult this problem becomes. The relationship of the given idea to a whole cluster of others is found to constitute an indispensable part of the meaning of the concept itself. Bentham's very definition of the term 'liberty' took the form of a statement of its relationship to the idea of 'coercion.' In his subsequent usages of the idea of liberty, developments in the shape of his over-all system were reflected in significant modifications of the terms in which liberty was described. Bentham's entire system of thought was a fine-spun web of ideas balanced in a state of stable but complex interdependence. Thus the study of Bentham's idea of liberty entails the study of the relevant features of his utilitarianism. The study of any of his most important ideas is perforce a study both of his art of thought and of his science of social theory.

The high degree of methodological self-consciousness here being attributed to Bentham as a theorist arose from his determination to place the art of thought itself on a scientific footing. His philosophical nominalism and materialism were embodiments of his faith in Baconian induction as a basis for the accumulation of knowledge and his Newtonian understanding of the nature of human and non-human actions. His philological perspective on epistemological questions was simply an aspect of his 'scientific' empiricism. What others would call the mental process of conceptualization was for him an exercise in critical philology. The development of this distinctive intellectual outlook can be fully understood only in the light of a knowledge of the influence on Bentham of such figures as Thomas Hobbes, John Locke, James Harris, and John Horne Tooke. Its significance, moreover, can hardly be overestimated.

The complex process of integration involved not only the modification of the idea of liberty to meet the requirements of a scientific utilitarian mode of thought but also a reconciliation between the idea of liberty and Bentham's extraordinarily strong concept of political and social authority. His legal training reinforced the influence of his allegiance to Enlightenment notions of 'science' and 'system' in shaping his strong conceptions of laws, rules, and norms. An additional timely factor was his reading of Sir Robert Filmer's *Patriarcha*. Filmer's patriarchal theory of the origins of social and political authority provided Bentham with the 'domestic' model upon which he was to build his own explanations of those conceptions. Finally, Bentham's disgust at contemporary illustrations of the connection between libertarianism and disruptive political agitation served to intensify his intellectual emphasis on the value of social order.

Bentham's negative definition of liberty was a logical corollary of his positivist view of the nature and importance of social authority. The study of liberty resolved itself, in his eyes, into the study of the legitimate limits of the sphere of justifiable coercion in utilitarian society. Power is essentially, in Bentham's thought, the potentiality for coercion. As such it may be either legitimate or illegitimate, justifiable or unjustifiable. The limits of justifiable social coercion will be the limits of legitimate social power, which is to say the limits of social authority. The impression of authoritarianism which Bentham's writings cumulatively generate arises from his monolithic conception of the structure of social authority. The figure of the sovereign legislator sits at the common centre of the distinctive spheres of legal, political, and moral authority in his system. The study of the array of social controls at the legislator's disposal is the study of the 'system of restraints' to be established in the utilitarian community: by the same token it is the study of liberty in the same community. In this way the analysis of liberty is advanced tacitly, as it were, by every step in the development of Bentham's system of thought.

One recent writer, David Caute, discussing the influence of the Enlightenment on subsequent radical reformers and system-builders such as the Fabians, was moved to observe that 'the rage for order always implies the firing squad for individual liberty. But then ... the freedom to be mistaken is no freedom at all. Is it?'[6] Another commentator has suggested that such thinkers as Sidney and Beatrice Webb, in their interest in social systematization and social planning, and in their illiberal conception of centralized social authority, reflect the influence of earlier utilitarian thinkers.[7] Among the utilitarians, none, we are informed by yet another source, was 'more convinced of the possibility of a science of behaviour or committed to developing it' than Jeremy Bentham.[8] Should Bentham's thought be studied as representing a phase in the development of modern authoritarianism? Did he inherit from the Enlightenment in which he felt so involved a 'rage for order,' which he then bequeathed to succeeding generations of social planners? If so, was he moved by this rage for order to send individual liberty to the wall? If so, in turn, was this the result of an inflexible conviction that the 'freedom to be mistaken' was 'no freedom at all?'

It is all too easy, particularly for those who think of themselves as liberals in some sense of that protean term, to acquire this sort of perspective on Bentham's ideas by juxtaposing the remarks of various commentators. Gertrude Himmelfarb's assertion that 'the principle of the greatest happiness of the greatest number was as inimical to the idea of liberty as to the idea of rights.'[9] seems to indicate that she, for one, might consider Mr Caute's comments concerning the *philosophes'* rage for order applicable to Bentham. In that case, we may ask, what did Bentham mean by declaring that the idea of liberty was a 'cornerstone' of his 'system?' Why did he devote so much attention, in his early preparatory manuscripts, to defining the term liberty?

The answer is simply that Bentham was not, and did not believe his principles to be, opposed either to liberty or to 'rights.' He was thoroughly hostile, however, toward the mischievous misuse of the term liberty by its own most ardent supporters. He attacked with particular force and persistence the employment of an idea of 'natural liberty' based on a theory of 'natural rights.' He considered the 'invention' of a realistic and practicable idea of liberty to represent a necessary and effective response to the contemporary prevalence of fallacious libertarian argument. He viewed the production of a new definition of liberty as one of his most important preliminary tasks as a social and political theorist, and in his mind it formed an integral part of his general reconstruction of the language in which theoretical disputes of all kinds were conducted.

If, then, Bentham was not actually hostile to liberty, he was nonetheless implacably opposed to the idea that the object of politics is simply to maximize liberty in its social aggregate. Utilitarian individualism is not liberal individualism. Halévy emerged from his study of utilitarianism convinced that Bentham and other philosophic radicals had been uncertain about the exact status of liberty as a social and political goal because they had failed to look 'deeply enough into the notion of liberty.' The effect of a deeper analysis, Halévy maintained, would be to show that state intervention in social life is 'necessary not only to make individuals more happy but also to make them more free.'[10] Halévy expanded upon the need for a re-examination of liberty: 'It should not be said that men were born free and founded the State to increase their security at the expense of their liberty. It should be said that men wanted to be free, and that, in so far as they wanted to be free, they constituted the State to increase simultaneously their security and their liberty.'[11]

What Bentham had said was 1/ that men are everywhere and always born into a state of 'subjection, not independence,' 2/ that men desire liberty, not for its own sake, but for the 'power' or the 'ease' which they associate with its possession, 3/ that absolute liberty, accompanied as it must, by definition, be by a prepolitical, anarchic condition of mankind, is intrinsically neither pleasurable nor desirable, and 4/ that men constitute government precisely to increase their security at the expense of their liberty. Bentham believed that, because liberty has no invariable connection with pleasure save through security, the sacrifice of unrestricted but insecure liberties in return for a quantitatively circumscribed field of liberties which are secure and can be enjoyed is a logical and beneficial act. Men thus seek, not to be free, but to possess a maximum of secure pleasure and to be assured of maximum protection against pain. Bentham explicitly denied that, as in Rousseau's theory, the imposition of political and legal restraints on the individual could increase both his freedom and his security. He justified such restraints, without denying the complete incompatibility between liberty and coercion, as restrictions imposed upon liberty in its social aggregate for the sake of security. In short, to 'perfect' liberty was not to maximize it but to secure it.

Nowhere in Bentham's writings is liberty per se described as a source of pleasure or pain, except in so far as the 'uneasiness' characteristic of man in a state of insecurity is considered to stem from the very absence of coercion which leaves the individual in a fearful and disoriented state. The problem of liberty for Bentham was like the philosophical problem of 'substance' in Locke, Berkeley, and Hume. Liberty is a necessary, even what some might wish to call an 'existential,' condition of every pleasure as of every pain. Yet it is a sufficient condition for none. Bentham recognized this, in his own way, by emphasizing that liberty is an incorporeal, 'fictitious' entity—that it is, of itself, not a 'real' (concrete) thing at all. As a species of 'right' and the negative correlative of 'power,' liberty may be desired, but only as a means to an end, and only when the attainment of that end is assured. Similarly, as 'ease,' or relief from pain or exertion, liberty is only desired where its duration is assured. In both cases it is not simply liberty, but *assured* liberty, which is to say security, that is desired.

Liberty in itself is precisely as conducive to painful experience as to pleasure. 'In the doctrine of utility,' Halévy observed, 'liberty is not a good in itself.'[12]

Political humanists from J.S. Mill to C.B. Macpherson have perceived in Bentham a profound hostility toward their concepts of liberty. In response to the Benthamite notion of freedom as an 'absence,' they have found it to be an 'essence.' Where Bentham associated freedom with the absence of certain kinds of activity, they have identified it with a genus of activities which they consider especially important. For Mill, this genus was defined in terms of those 'permanent interests of a man as a progressive being' whose pursuit must be carried on in conditions of freedom. For Macpherson, the 'human essence' is to be located in the 'uniquely human' capacity for certain kinds of experience — religious, emotional, and so on. Both theorists seem to have felt that Bentham was unable to appreciate the uniqueness of the human spirit. Macpherson finally identified the source of the repressive characteristics of 'rationalist notions of freedom' such as Bentham's as 'the Enlightenment belief that men can and should be brought to fuller rationality but cannot do this by themselves.'[13]

Others have concurred in this judgment. Philip Rieff, in his book on Freud, has summarized the position as viewed from the psychological perspective: 'In liberal psychology as it has evolved from Bentham to Dewey, social organisation ... has become the source of and the limitation upon the perfectibility of human nature.'[14]

In the same vein B.R. Barber, in his 'Illiberal defence of liberty,' has argued that 'in the end, not only psychiatry itself but the values reflected in its statistical definition of "normality" serve to condition men to habitual, unthinking, conformist behaviour.'[15] Barber uses Bentham's *Introduction to the Principles of Morals and Legislation* to exemplify what he calls the 'abstract physical-mechanistic' conception of freedom, which, he says, holds that 'as long as men are viewed as reflexive creatures bound to their environment by necessary responses to stimuli which either attract (Hobbesian pleasure) or repel (Hobbesian pain), coercion can be reduced to a problem in the science of human mechanics.'[16] Barber's other model of the relationship between freedom and coercion relies on a view of mankind as, not passive or 'reflexive,' but active, dynamic beings. This is the 'concrete psychological-intentionalist' model, based on the belief that 'when freedom is conceived in active rather than passive terms, and politics is understood as a mode of activity, the traditional liberal dichotomy between freedom and politics can no longer be sustained.'[17]

This brings us, as Barber realizes, into the realm of metaphysics — a species of metaphysics, indeed, far removed from the physical sciences which form the basis of Bentham's type of view.[18] Bentham's conception of liberty epitomizes the sort of enslavement to the 'given,' the 'objective' world, that makes the idea of tolerance and adjustment anathema to neo-Hegelians such as Herbert Marcuse.

It is with this grievance in mind that Marcuse has denounced liberal democracies and social democracies alike, claiming that 'they enjoy a comfortable, smooth, reasonable, democratic unfreedom.'[19] Indeed, when idealist conceptions of freedom prevail, liberalism itself can come to be seen as 'a dangerous sham concealing the most efficient repression ever known.'[20] The instruments, it seems, of liberal repression are 'comfort,' conformity, security, 'adjustment.' The notion of adjustment, it has been asserted, is a crucial concept in the view of the social order supported by 'liberal psychology' (which is said to include Bentham among its advocates) and in the 'physical-mechanistic' view of freedom-vs-coercion.[21] The struggle for existence, as seen by this school of thought, involves two antagonists: 'man' and 'the environment.' The aim is to minimize friction between them. Bentham set out to ensure minimal friction, in spatial terms by exploring and organizing the entire 'universe of human action,' and in temporal terms by the apotheosis of security. In security lay the basis, not only for human happiness, but also for the transformation of politics into a science. Hannah Arendt has found the identification of political liberty with security to be characteristic of eighteenth-century political thought, and has suggested that this identification was an important step toward a complete separation between freedom and the realm of politics: 'The highest purpose of politics was the guaranty of security; security, in turn, made freedom possible [Bentham would have said 'enjoyable'], and the word "freedom" designated a quintessence of activities outside the political realm.'[22]

What others have called 'freedom' – self-fulfilment, individuality, the realization of one's capacity for experience – Bentham called happiness. What Bentham called liberty others would call subjection: enslavement to the dictates of an institutionalized theory of human nature. Bentham did not indulge in Romantic or Idealist paradoxes: he never argued that a state of right subjection actually *became*, by some transvaluation of values, a state of freedom. He simply declared happiness rather than freedom to be the definitive characteristic of the fulfilled human being, and established his priorities vis-à-vis other social values in terms of their relationships to the supreme goal. It is not, then, altogether surprising that he should have doubted the utility of libertarianism, nor that others have denounced the illiberalism of utilitarianism. Liberalism, however, despite its name, has no monopoly of concern for liberty. Enthusiasm and concern are very different things. The libertarians of Bentham's day were certainly enthusiastic – too much so. Their critical faculties were struck dumb in the presence of the political fetish of liberty. Bentham was both concerned and critical. Some two hundred years before B.R. Barber, Bentham produced what can only be called an illiberal defence of liberty. It deserves to be examined in its own terms, in its complete form, and in the context of Bentham's utilitarian thought as a whole. That is what this discussion attempts to do.

PART ONE / INSPIRATION

1

The Enlightenment

The age we live in is a busy age; in which knowledge is rapidly advancing towards perfection.[1]

This was Jeremy Bentham's salutation to the intellectual world of 1776. It was a succinct expression of the character and aspirations of the intelligentsia of the time. Busy they were indeed, and in all their varied enterprises their confidence and enthusiasm were strengthened by a buoyant belief in mental and material progress inherited from their masters, the giants of what we have now come to speak of as the Enlightenment. The words above were far from being the first words written by Bentham, but he was quite aware that they were the words by which he was to introduce himself to the community of thinkers, writers, and reformers whose attention, acquaintance, and, eventually, applause and admiration he hoped to earn.[2] Into this single sentence he compressed a sense of the energy, the aggression, and the confidence of a *philosophe*. Yet more, he injected into it a concise but clear endorsement of the central intellectual tenets of the Enlightenment. He proclaimed his belief in the importance of knowledge to the progress of mankind, and he boldly announced that in his own time he could perceive a 'rapid advance' of knowledge towards its 'perfection.' It was to the perfection of knowledge in all its forms and applications that Bentham dedicated his life's work. From this purpose he never deviated.

To 'perfect' knowledge is not merely to augment it quantitatively but also to refine it in quality. To augment knowledge was in itself, as Bentham saw it, the function of the 'expositor.' Refining knowledge was the special task of the 'censor.' The active process of advancing the cause of Enlightenment began with censure — the criticism of established ideas. In defence of his censorial stance, however, the *philosophe* must surely become his own expositor. The perfection of knowledge was to be achieved by this synthesis of the censorial and expository functions.

The greatest of Enlightenment heroes had embodied this comprehensive synthesis, had themselves been both censors and expositors. Bacon, Newton, and Locke had both demolished and reconstructed. They had shown the rare scope of interest, energy, and intellect required to synthesize. Bentham claimed for himself, in the *Fragment on Government*, only the role of censor. Taking a leaf from Locke's *Essay*, he claimed only to be clearing away obstructions along the path to knowledge: 'with regard to an expositor of the law, our Author [Blackstone] is not he that should come, but we may be still looking for another. "Who then," says my objector, "shall be that other? Yourself?" — No verily. My mission is at an end, where I have prepared the way before him.'[3] This profession of humility, however, seems merely a stylistic flourish when placed alongside Bentham's proclamation of the means by which his essay might disseminate the principles of censorial thinking. He aimed, he said,

to do something to instruct, but more to undeceive, the timid and admiring student: to excite him to place more confidence in his own strength, and less in the infallibility of great names: — to help him to emancipate his judgement from the shackles of authority; to let him see that the not understanding a discourse may as well be the writer's fault as the reader's; — to teach him to distinguish between showy language and sound sense; — to warn him not to pay himself with words; — to show him that what may tickle the ear, or dazzle the imagination, will not always inform the judgement.[4]

The *Fragment on Government* was, in the context of Bentham's intellectual development in the course of his sixty-year career as a writer, only a brief episode. It was, nevertheless, a proclamation of censorial standards by a thinker who aspired ultimately to the supreme role of synthesizer. Bentham's later works exhibit his attempts to systematize his alternatives to established institutions and ideas. What is pre-eminently important is to realize that an unwavering dedication to a single grand design shaped all of Bentham's diverse enterprises.

One further question demands an immediate response: beyond the assertion that critical thinking is the key to the advancement of learning, what more can be said about the means by which Bentham hoped to perfect knowledge? Bentham was self-consciously heir to an entire collection of *philosophe* assumptions about what constitutes valid knowledge and its advancement. The single term which Bentham himself would have insisted must be applicable to all such intellectual principles was 'scientific.' The scientific approach to the perfection of knowledge meant to Bentham an architectural, structural analysis of language, the prime vehicle for the communication of knowledge. It meant what might be called an atomistic analysis of the language in which fundamental principles, propositions, and terms of the various sciences pertinent to or constitutive of the 'Science of Man' were expressed. Words were the atoms of which the world of ideas was constructed. It was especially true in Bentham's early years that he recognized his intellectual friends and foes, those whom he acknowledged as predecessors and others whom he repudiated as disseminators of erroneous ideas, by their use or abuse of certain pivotal terms. Prominent among such terms was 'liberty.' This chapter and the following one attempt to show how Bentham came to be aware of his Enlightenment inheritance, and how he came to focus his censorial sights on the problem of defining that crucial term.

It is sometimes suggested that the young Bentham's reading of Fenelon's *Telemachus* had a significant formative effect on the workings of his mind. The *Times Literary Supplement*, perhaps giving undue weight to this early literary encounter in Bentham's childhood, once observed that 'Fenelon lay behind both Rousseau ... and Bentham,' a statement to which one might wish to reply: very far behind them indeed.[5] Nevertheless, if Telemachus's virtues and adventures did indeed fire the young Bentham's imagination or intellect, it was by implanting in him admiration for such social virtues as those of the 'Tyrians' – industry, competence, and civil or political unity.[6] If young Jeremy had ears to hear, Fenelon could even provide him with an ardent endorsement of the virtuous citizen's love of liberty, for in an ideal state envisaged in *Telemachus*, the people 'had rather part with their lives, than with the Liberty they enjoy under a wise King, who Reigns only by the Dictates of Reason and Justice.'[7]

The intellectual development of the young Bentham making his way through Westminster School and Queen's College, Oxford, to an unhappy rendezvous with legal practice has already been chronicled more than once.[8] But one particular aspect of this development is of special importance to the present investigation, and it is an aspect about which much remains to be discovered: Bentham's flourishing youthful interest in science. It is well known that Bentham went through a phase of keen interest in chemical experiments, that his rooms at Lincoln's Inn were used less as a law office than as a laboratory,[9] and that he read 'Priestley on Airs' as keenly as any book of law.[10] In the opening salvo of the *Fragment on Government* Bentham equates 'discovery' and 'reformation' in the 'moral world' with 'discovery and improvement' in the 'natural.'[11] To illustrate the advance of knowledge towards 'perfection,' he cites, first, feats of geographic exploration and, secondly, 'the all vivifying and subtle element of air so recently analyzed and made known to us.'[12]

Bentham's purpose in these opening paragraphs was to attack the predominant belief that 'in the moral world there no longer remains any matter for discovery.'[13] He was confident that the application to the problems of the moral world of the 'fundamental axiom' that 'it is the greatest happiness of the greatest number that is the measure of right and wrong,' if pursued with 'method and precision,' would yield important new 'discoveries' — 'observations,' as he put it, 'of matters of fact hitherto either incompletely noticed, or not all.'[14] The evidence to be presented here testifies to the energy and the perseverance with which Bentham pursued the discovery of fresh facts and the unmasking of hallowed error throughout his long working life as a reformer. He came eventually to envisage a system of radical, utilitarian reform so comprehensive that the creation and promulgation of an entirely new system of human discourse and knowledge was its essential precondition. Initially, in 1776, he knew only that all must be questioned. He was not yet sure, though as we shall see he must have suspected, that all must be redefined, re-expressed, reconstructed. He was certain, however, of one of the paths his critical thoughts must follow, the critique of law: 'If it be of importance and of use to us to know the principles of the element we breathe, surely it is not of much less importance nor of much less use to comprehend the principles, and endeavour at the improvement of those laws, by which alone we breathe it in security.'[15] The *Fragment* itself was a work dedicated more immediately to the discovery and destruction of error than to the reformation of moral practices. It is typical of many of Bentham's works in being dedicated to the Lockean task of clearing away intellectual rubbish as a prelude to the presentation of new truths and consequent reforming programmes.[16]

Bentham's interest in science was neither evanescent nor shallow. It persisted through time and penetrated beyond the fascination of exciting experimental discoveries to give birth to a real devotion to the perfection of knowledge of man and his world on the basis of experiment and observation — the scientific method of Bacon. Bentham's political motto, 'the duty of a good citizen is ... to obey punctually, to censure freely,'[17] is the sociopolitical equivalent of Bacon's maxim, 'nature, to be commanded, must be obeyed.'[18] Bentham allocated to the 'greatest happiness principle' as applied to the legal and ethical spheres of knowledge a role analogous to that played by Newton's laws of motion in the world of physics. Like Charles Fourier after him, Bentham aspired to be the Newton of the moral sciences.[19] Despite his own disclaimers, he might easily have reckoned himself in some sense its Bacon as well.[20] His love of science was not an infatuation with a particular body of knowledge, although he did retain a special enthusiasm, as his correspondence indicates, for chemical experiments. His was rather an admiration for a scientific methodology, which he believed to be the foundation of real knowledge in every area of intellectual endeavour.

In short, Bentham became a scientist in the sense in which to become a scientist was to become a *philosophe*. He began to explore the whole vast field of human knowledge with the *philosophe*'s critical eye and alert discernment.[21] By the time he was thirty years old he could write to D'Alembert and speak of his beloved Helvétius in glowing terms: 'C'est de lui que je tiens un flambeau, que j'espère porter un jour dans les sentiers les plus étroits de la politique et peut-être de la morale. C'est de vous que je tiens le fil du labyrinthe des connaissances humaines.'[22] He saw admiration for Helvétius as a bond that would render his writings attractive to the representative of Enlightenment ideas par excellence across the Atlantic, Benjamin Franklin. He wrote to brother Samuel: 'Ingenhaus tells Schwede that Franklin has Helvétius constantly on his table. Here you see is a ladder by which my Code, and upon occasion your pretty person or mine might be hoisted up to Franklin.'[23] Indeed, it seems that it was the influence of Helvétius that prevented Bentham from running off to South America some time in the early 1770s in search of 'natural knowledge' in 'Chymistry' and 'Botany:' 'the instruction I gathered from Helvetius ... gradually weaned me from that idea. From him I got a standard to measure the relative importance of the several pursuits a man might be engaged in and the result of it was that the way of all others in which man might be of most service to his fellow creatures was by making improvement in the science which I had been engaged to study by profession.'[24] Bentham returned to the study of law because he had been convinced by his reading of Helvétius − and, no doubt, other like-minded authors − that there was a great need for the reorganization of jurisprudence on a scientific basis, which meant to Bentham a basis of observed physical laws of behaviour. He expected to encounter opposition from entrenched opinion and prejudice. He was aware of the 'Unpopularity of new truths.: 'The Book that recommends itself to a man ... is, not the book that teaches him to take up a right opinion, but that which brings new proof in support/confirmation/of the opinion which he has taken up whether right or wrong' (69.1).

On one early manuscript page we find the heading, more appropriate perhaps than Bentham himself realized as he wrote, 'Beginning.' The first proposition under this head is indeed Bentham's beginning, the first analytical principle of his legal, political, and moral schemes: 'Physical sensibility the ground of law − proposition the most obvious and incontestible' (69.10). In this statement we possess the most concise expression of the logic of the utility principle itself as Bentham saw it, and of the justification for Bentham's belief that the utility principle could and should govern the science of law. For the subject of legal (and of social and political) theory is human action, and particularly the rationale of the motivation and guidance of human action which Bentham described as 'the logic of the will.'[25] For Bentham, it was implicit in this elementary 'proposition the most obvious and incontestible' that the disposition to perform or not to perform an act is based on physical sensibility, that is, on 'apprehended' (present), 'expected' (future), or past pleasure and pain (69.10). He carried this idea through into his definition of 'A Motive': 'an idea of pain or pleasure; pleasure as about to be produced, or pain as about to be repelled by the action to which it is a motive' (69.13). This definition was immediately followed by an observation of inestimable importance to the legislator thinking of the effects of his acts upon his subjects: 'This pain or pleasure is to be supposed to be of the same value in idea as in reality: unless any reason be shown why it should be otherwise (69.13).

These few manuscript excerpts give but one, albeit an important, illustration of the process by which Bentham put forward those 'axioms of mental pathology' upon which he maintained that his whole system of social, political, legal, and ethical theory was founded.[26] If the conceptions of motivation and disposition just examined were expounded primarily with legal applications in mind, they were not without broader social implications, as Bentham's work on 'indirect legislation' and 'deontology' (the ethics of duty) was to show. In a manuscript sheet headed 'Key,' antedating the *Introduction to the Principles of Morals and Legislation*, Bentham applied his physiological definition of 'motive' to the political sphere in a definition of 'Self-government' which also indicates the early direction of his thoughts on liberty: 'It is self-government, when the motive for action is not pain resulting from the will of another person, but pleasure or pain from the powers [?] of inanimate or irrational bodies, or of the parts of one's own body' (69.55). Liberty is here already conceived of, not as an expression of a dynamic self, but as subjection to the hedonistic dictates of the sensory organism in a world of potentially dangerous 'inanimate or irrational bodies.' 'Self-government' means not self-expression or self-development, but self-defence.

A wealth of evidence could be adduced to illustrate the direct and powerful influence of Bentham's enthusiasm for the Enlightenment notion of scientific method on the development of his systematic utilitarianism as a whole and his idea of liberty in particular. In 1777 Bentham wrote to brother Samuel, to tell him that he had read 'the physiological part of my Punishments' (that is, of his work on the Theory of Punishment) to his friend Dr George Fordyce, a medical doctor, 'and got from him some useful corrections.'[27] Medical science and legal science were in his mind related as branches of physical (or physiological) science relevant to the study of man. His love of 'chymistry' did not fade either. In 1779 he prepared to give brother-in-law Charles Abbot instruction in chemistry, remarking that this would require that Abbot be divested of 'QSP-ishness,' that is, of pretentiousness and sententiousness, and (scholastic) 'university prejudices.'[28] In 1783 he wrote to Reginald Pole Carew, a friend with whom he shared an enthusiasm for chemistry, saying 'had I the gift of tongues, I should be as devout a preacher of that science as Dr Tucker has been said to be of trade.'[29] His estimate of the intellectual strengths and weaknesses of brother Samuel, in a letter to the Reverend John Forster, indicates his view of the comparative utility of historical and scientific knowledge in 'metaphysical and political disquisitions': 'Though he has no memory for history and is less acquainted with facts of that class than one could well imagine it possible for a man of his education to be, he is by reflection not ill read in the science of human nature. I find very few so capable as he is of assisting me in my metaphysical and political disquisitions.'[30]

In 1776, as he wrote the *Fragment on Government*, Bentham harboured deep feelings, typical of Enlightenment enthusiasts, about the necessity of replacing the scholastic, cosmetic arts of 'classical erudition' with hard intellectual currency 'drawn from the sterling treasury of the sciences.' Even as he applauded Blackstone in one of the *Fragment*'s best-known passages he revealed his own position as a thinker convinced that a whole new conception of legal ideas, terms, and discourse could take root and grow out of the seed of scientific method fertilized by his own steady devotion to his task:

He [Blackstone] it is, in short, who, first of all institutional writers, has taught jurisprudence to speak the language of the scholar and the gentleman: put a polish upon that rugged science: cleansed her from the dust and cobwebs of the office: and if he has not enriched her with that precision that is drawn only from the sterling treasury of the sciences, has decked her out, however, to advantage, from the toilette of classical erudition.'[31]

Elsewhere, in a more vitriolic mood, Bentham castigated Blackstone for failing to 'teach himself' before 'coming into the awful presence of the public' (96.63). He promised that those versed in the 'physiology' of the human mind would never forgive Blackstone for his influence on young intellects (96.64). In place of Blackstone's 'cosmetic arts,' Bentham himself, during the years when he produced the *Comment on the Commentaries*, the *Fragment on Government*, the *Introduction to the Principles of Morals and Legislation*, and the chapters that would form *Of Laws in General*, strove to complete the edifice of a scientific jurisprudence. Once the want of scientific method is remedied,[32] once the objects of law have been distinguished,[33] once clear ideas have been annexed to the expressions of men whose ideas heretofore were not clear,[34] then,

Bentham foresaw, 'in time the labours of the legislator may make room for the judgment and industry of the Professor: and the fruit of invention be made the subject of Science.'[35]

Ernst Cassirer first expressed the judgment that 'The Enlightenment joined, to a degree scarcely ever achieved before, the critical with the productive function and converted the one directly into the other.'[36] His disciple, Peter Gay, concurred when he wrote his interpretation of the Enlightenment.[37] Gay, the same man who held up Bentham's headnote to the *Fragment on Government* as a suitable motto for students of the Enlightenment,[38] saw Bentham as an 'arch-*philosophe*, who took eighteenth century radical ideas into the nineteenth.'[39] Professor Gay describes 'the *philosophes*' experience' as a 'struggle for autonomy,' to 'secure their independence from the burdensome, stultifying weight of tradition, convention and mythology.'[40] The *philosophes*, he claims, collectively pursued a 'vastly ambitious program': 'a program of secularism, humanity, cosmopolitanism, and freedom, above all, freedom in its many forms – freedom from arbitrary power, freedom of speech, freedom of trade.'[41]

For the *philosophes*, and most certainly for Bentham, the attainment of 'freedom' as intellectual autonomy manifested itself in two phenomena: 'the organized habit of criticism ... solvent of custom, accepted explanations, and traditional institutions ... a potent agent of historical change,'[42] and the dedicated pursuit of pure, 'scientific' knowledge.[43] Confidence in the validity of scientific method and the close connection between scientific investigation and social and political improvement induced the *philosophes* to claim freedom of censure, to run the risks involved, in the faith that the utility of new ideas would ensure their victory in the end. Liberty was a necessary condition of the *philosophes*' endeavours at every stage, but Bentham drew a thoroughly logical and appropriate *philosophe*'s conclusion when he postulated pleasure and the minimization of pain (therefore happiness) as the goal of scientific improvement. In doing so he was certainly in harmony with the vision of Diderot's 'Essai sur les règnes de Claude et de Néron': 'The magistrate deals out justice; the philosopher teaches the magistrate what is just and unjust ... the philosopher teaches the sovereign the origins and limits of his authority. Every man has duties to his family and his society: the philosopher teaches everyone what these duties are. Man is exposed to misfortune and pain; the philosopher teaches man how to suffer.'[44] and, Bentham would add, how to avoid suffering.

Bentham derived inspiration or sustenance for his conception of the science of man and for his idea of liberty from the writings of numerous Enlightenment figures. As soon as he had succeeded in finishing two pamphlets of sufficient substance, the *Fragment on Government* and his *View of the Hard-Labour Bill*, he sent off copies to D'Alembert, Chastellux and the Abbé Morellet in hopes of gaining their attention. The sympathetic D'Alembert applauded, in his reply, the reforming efforts of 'des philosophes tels que vous, Monsieur.'[45] In 1776 Bentham drafted a letter to Voltaire, to whom he hoped to send a copy of the 'Theory of Punishment.' His explanatory remarks are illuminating: 'All that I shall say to recommend it to you is that I have taken counsel of you much oftener than of our own Ld. Coke and Hale and Blackstone. The repose of Grotius and Puffendorf and Barbeyrac and Burlamaqui I would never wish to see disturbed. I have built solely on the foundation of utility, laid as it is by Helvétius. Beccaria has been lucerna pedibus, or if you please manibus, meis.'[46] These *philosophes* were all men whose praises Bentham was moved to sing. If we can believe Bentham's own professions, he would never have done so without critically examining their ideas: 'For my part, if ever I stand forth and sing the song of eulogy to great men, it shall be not because they *occupy* their station, but because they deserve it.'[47]

What had these men to say to Bentham on the all-important subject of liberty? Beccaria had strong feelings about the connection between law and liberty, as he indicated in the same well-known passage in *Of Crimes and Punishments* in which he announced his support for the Greatest Happiness Principle:

If we look into history, we shall find that laws which are or ought to be conventions between men in a state of freedom, have been for the most part the work of the passions of a few or the consequences of fortuitous or temporary necessity; not dictated by a cool examiner of human nature, who knew how to collect in one point the actions of a multitude and had this only end in view, the greatest happiness of the greatest number.[48]

In Helvétius's *De L'Esprit*, Bentham might learn not only that 'the fear of natural pain, or the desire of natural pleasure, may excite all the passions'[49] but also that the possession of liberty was a necessary condition of the attainment of the heights of genius.[50] He might also learn that

Whoever, under pretence of supporting the authority of his sovereign, would stretch it to an arbitrary power, is at the same time a bad father, a bad citizen and a bad subject: a bad father and a bad citizen because he would load his posterity and his country with the chains of slavery; and a bad subject, because by changing a lawful for an arbitrary authority, he is summoning up ambition and despair against the king.[51]

He would, finally, encounter an argument for rule of law, based on the belief that under 'despotic power' the 'abject and submissive subjection in which the people are kept' saps not only their own vigour but that of their rulers as well:

'In the states where the law alone dispenses punishments and rewards, and where obedience is paid to none but the laws, the virtuous, dwelling in safety, contract a boldness and firmness of soul, that cannot subsist in a country which is the seat of despotic power, where property, life and liberty depend on the caprice and arbitrary will of one man.'[52] Helvétius, like some others whose ideas we shall examine, would have implanted in Bentham the conventional notion of the contrast between 'oriental stationariness' and despotism and the proud record of British and European liberty.[53] François Jean de Chastellux, in his *De la Félicité Publique*,[54] must also have impressed Bentham, for, as we have seen, Bentham sought him out with a letter and copies of the *Fragment* and the *View of the Hard-Labour Bill*. Chastellux and Bentham shared the view that a new vocabulary was called for in politics and law to replace the old scholastic traditionalism. Chastellux wrote: 'The time is past, in which the statesman, more the pedant than the citizen, referred to old customs all the principles of government ... The expressions, feudal, fiscal, domanial, must now be driven from our tribunals, whilst the words *property, agriculture, commerce, liberty*, supply the place of the barbarous vocabulary of the schools.'[55]

We have already seen from the evidence provided by his awe-struck draft letter that Bentham viewed Voltaire with a respect bordering on reverence. He shared with Voltaire a deep admiration for the methodology of Locke, the significance of which may become clearer when we look in more detail at Locke's idea of liberty.[56] Their admiration for Locke's cautious method of observation and experimental demonstration went hand in hand with another shared characteristic, admiration for Newton. We can hardly doubt that Bentham would concur in Voltaire's judgment that Newton taught men to 'examine, weigh, calculate, and measure, and never to conjecture.' 'He saw and he made people see;' Voltaire observed, 'but he did not put his fantasies in place of truth.'[57]

The abhorrent but recurrent spectacle of men, ardent lovers of liberty, invariably putting their fantasies in the place of truth whenever the term 'liberty' came under discussion was one of the most important factors in turning Bentham's attention to the task of redefining the concept early in his career as a writer and reformer. The spirit of the *philosophes* endowed him with an additional motive in the form of a strong sense of the necessity of intellectual freedom as a prerequisite of social and political improvement.

Only two further instruments of analysis were required to put Bentham on the high road to radical reform: first a model for a critical investigative methodology (Locke's *Essay* was the outstanding reply to this demand) and, second, a conceptual link between the realms of theory and practice. The latter requirement was to be satisfied in Bentham's system, where such abstract rules as were necessitated by the need for generalization were always based on physiological principles thought to be essential to the very mechanics of human action. Peter Gay has observed that it was an Enlightenment principle that 'the link that made the relation of theory to practice rational rather than fortuitous was ethics.'[58] If this was so, then Bentham's undertaking to write a single volume defining the 'principles of morals and legislation,' and by the same token his comprehensive attempt to unite them in a utilitarian system of ethics, was surely an apotheosis of Enlightenment assumptions and aspirations. On the ominous side, from a libertarian point of view, is the vitiating effect on the idea of liberty consistently exhibited by systems which claim to discover that certain universal, explanatory theoretical principles are invariably and inescapably applicable throughout the practical universe of human actions. It was precisely this conception of the unlimited applicability of science to all facets of human existence that was to end, not in the perfection of freedom, but in what some philosophers have seen as its circumscription.[59] Science may endow man with ever-increasing power, they have observed, but this should not be confused with freedom; for such power may be gained at the cost of the enslavement of man to 'the given' – the material, phenomenal world. Idealism has consistently rejected this subjection and proclaimed the freedom of an Essence or Idea. Bentham's attempts to integrate a significant concept of liberty into his scientific system provide us with detailed study in the fettering of the Idealist 'self' within the boundaries of one materialist's world of objects.

Peter Gay's second volume on the thought of the Enlightenment might have acquired a more appropriate (although a less attractive) subtitle had Gay employed for that purpose the phrase 'The science of power' rather than 'The science of freedom.' Certainly it was power that was the end of Enlightenment science: power for the improvement, the organization, the rationalization of the material world;[60] power, also, to overcome ignorance and uncertainty and the uneasiness derived from them. For Locke 'uneasiness,' for Condillac 'in-quiétude,' for Holbach the uncertainty, of ignorance was the dynamic, the mainspring of life both intellectual and physical.[61] Hume's assertion that 'there is no happiness without occupation' merely put forward another proposal for alleviating the uneasiness of directionless indigence.[62]

In a slightly different way, Condillac, in his *Traité des Systèmes*, reflected perfectly the concerns, principles, and aspirations which so pervasively influenced Bentham. Denouncing fantastic, metaphorical, gratuitous intellectual abstractions, he proposed to replace the method of metaphor with the methods of physical science. The correspondence is rendered even more striking by his dictum that 'the art of reasoning reduces itself to a well-constructed language,'[63] and the key to understanding it is provided by the subtitle of Condillac's *An*

Essay on the Origin of Human Knowledge, published in 1746: 'A Supplement to Mr Locke's Essay on the Human Understanding.'[64] Bentham's kinship with Condillac is a sign of shared descent from Locke. Locke it was whose decision, in his *Essay*,[65] to concentrate on the activities of the mind in thinking rather than to speculate about its 'essence' was echoed by Condillac: 'Our first object, which we should never lose sight of, is the study of the human mind − l'esprit humain − not in order to discover its nature, but to understand its operations, to observe in what manner they are combined and how we should employ them.'[66]

If we accept the argument of Professor Gay, Condillac's belief that *'Inquiétude, tourment*, determines everything'[67] is an expression of his attempt to resolve Locke's duality of sensation and reflection into a unity wherein sensation is the cause even of reflection. He converted, says Gay, the temporal sequence of sensation-reflection into a causal sequence.[68] Surely something like this was the logical consequence of Bentham's own methodological development. From the fundamental position of the 'axioms of mental pathology' in even the ethical and moral spheres of Bentham's system[69] to the much later conception of a 'Table of the springs of action,' Bentham's understanding of the nature of human action, and thence of human liberty, was shaped by this belief that sensation is the cradle of every kind of activity, mental and physical.

A detailed examination of the genealogy of Bentham's ideas will leave us in no doubt that his scientific premises subtly but pervasively influenced, and circumscribed, his approach to the idea of liberty. His thoughts on liberty show the crucial influence on him of two basic Enlightenment attitudes, one epitomized by Hume, the other by Newton and his admirers. In the Introduction to the *Treatise on Human Nature* Hume put forward a principle that became even more fundamental to Bentham's utilitarianism than it was to Hume's own: ' 'Tis evident that all the sciences have a relation, greater or less, to human nature; and that however wide any of them may seem to run from it, they still return back by one passage or another.'[70] With the appearance of 'human nature' at the centre stage of Science,[71] the importance of the concept of human freedom is similarly enhanced. But it is an indication of the significance of the Newtonian influence on Bentham that we break contact with his intellectual frame of reference when we speak of human freedom as though freedom were rendered qualitatively special by the presence of the adjective 'human.' For Bentham, especially in his early analytical efforts, it seemed supremely important to define liberty in scientific terms, which to him meant mechanistic, spatial terms. He might have been taking to heart such expressions of the Newtonian spirit as were exemplified by Roger Cotes's words in his preface to the 2nd edition of Newton's *Principia*. Speaking of the historical progress of natural philosophy, Cotes referred first to the Aristotelians, men who 'attributed to the several species of things specific and occult qualities on which, in a manner unknown, they make the operations of the several bodies to depend.' Secondly, there are 'those who fetch from hypotheses the foundation on which they build their speculations.' These thinkers 'may form, indeed, an ingenious romance, but a romance it will still be.' Separate from either of these deluded categories of thought is the school of Newtonians who 'profess experimental philosophy.'[72] Bentham aspired to be such a thinker. His science of human nature and his conception of liberty were alike founded, not upon a hypothesis about the nature of man, but upon observed phenomena (that is, upon human reactions to external stimuli) that seemed to Bentham to constitute in themselves an adequate explanation of the 'springs of human action.' When Bentham called for, and aspired to, the creation of a 'logic of the will,'[73] he was referring to a scientific study of human action. Bentham's Newtonian perspective becomes clearer when we realize that he had in mind a stimulus-response theory of human motivation, a concept of 'will' as the embodiment of the faculty of response, and a concept of 'liberty' as relating solely to the existence and nature of observable stimuli.

Bentham's tendency, indeed his clear intention, to pursue the study of 'moral science' armed with an intellectual perspective which tended to model the analysis of human motivation on the Newtonian laws of motion had a crucial impact on his conceptualization of liberty. Indeed, it might be said that it prevented his 'conceptualizing' it at all, for it will become clear in later stages of our discussion that Bentham came to define liberty as the idea of vacuity — the notion of the absence of detectable external control, or, as he called it, of coercion. Perhaps, for our purposes, the most pertinent of all the lessons he could learn from the heroes of the physical sciences was that nature abhors a vacuum. There can be no doubt that it is a principle of Bentham's social thought that political society as a whole, in order to exist, must eliminate the sociological vacuum created by unrestricted 'natural' liberty and erect the idols of authority and security within the space thus annexed.

2

The school of example: influential writers on liberty

Conscious of the importance to his own intellectual development of his Enlightenment inheritance, Bentham was nonetheless anxious to acknowledge his indebtedness to his predecessors and instructors, whether *philosophes* or not. Indeed, in the course of a draft 'Prefat' to what was to be published years later as the *Introduction to the Principles of Morals and Legislation*, he paused momentarily in order, as he said, that 'the public' might know 'to whom it is obliged for every article of instruction it receives' (27.148-60).[1] He declared his indebtedness in varying degrees to Helvétius and Beccaria, to Montesquieu (for 'many excellent though ill-digested hints'), and to Voltaire and d'Alembert for 'the distinction between real and fictitious entities, and that strong sense which it were to be wished every man possessed of the unavoidable figurativeness and impropriety of language' (27.148).

He thought of the ideas of such thinkers as 'the *organa* ... as Lord Bacon would call them,' which he had himself employed in the 'construction of my system' (27.160). He was well aware of his intellectual eclecticism. In the realm of social theory he thought of himself as more a systematizer than an innovator. Even the novelty of many of his practical proposals stemmed, in his view, not so much from the originality of his theoretical ideas as from the unprecedented vigour and precision with which he applied principles discovered but insufficiently systematized by others. On the other hand, it is clear that Bentham's chosen vocation was, for better or worse, not quite like that of any other Enlightenment figure. He recorded in his manuscripts, although not for publication, cutting criticisms of 'systems' of thought popularized by Locke and Rousseau. While his own system owed a very great deal to the naturalism of David Hume, it did not embody that philosopher's epistemological scepticism. He felt, and said, that he could have rewritten Locke's *Essay* in a more positive and a more concise manner. During the years when he was beginning to set down

his ideas on liberty and other subjects in a systematic way, Bentham was stirred
to emulation, and to censure, by the writings of a whole spectrum of thinkers.
Not all of them were *philosophes*. But most, whether of an older vintage, such as
Thomas Hobbes, or contemporaries of Bentham, such as Joseph Priestley and
Jean Louis Delolme, could be said to embody much of the Enlightenment spirit.
Bentham was happy to emulate them in spirit and ambition, and was not too
vain to acknowledge his dependence upon their stock of ideas. Never, though,
did he discover a thinker whose system exemplified the attainment of the
heights of comprehensiveness, rigour, and consistency to which he aspired. The
philosophes provided him with a plethora of novel conceptions, however, and we
shall now turn to some of the many sources, within and without the
Enlightenment, from whom he may have received 'hints,' albeit 'ill-digested'
ones, on the subject of liberty.

In *De L'Esprit*, leaving aside the enthusiastic proclamation of the greatest
happiness principle, for which Bentham offered him such effusive thanks,[2]
Helvétius seems to have given little sustained or rigorous attention to the idea of
liberty. His references to it are generally rhetorical, when not conversational. *De
L'Esprit* contains only one substantive argument on a subject related to liberty
which is echoed in Bentham's writings, and that is a hypothesis about the
relationship between liberty and political organization. Just as Bentham was to
assert that all government was restrictive of liberty, Helvétius, despite his own
denunciations of 'despotic' governments,[3] put forward at one point a very crude
philosophy of history in which freedom was said to be the dominant
characteristic of a pregovernmental period in human history, while all
governments were seen as exhibiting a tendency towards the enslavement of the
subject.[4] Helvétius posited a cyclical development in which a phenomenon
referred to as 'depopulation' led to dissolution of government and thence to a
savage, but free, state out of which government might once again arise. We shall
see that Bentham's admiration for Sir Robert Filmer's conception of political
authority was based largely upon their common belief in the inevitability, in any
valid political society, of universal subjection to the will of a single sovereign. His
antiRousseauian belief that 'natural subjection' was more characteristic of man's
real birthright than 'natural liberty' certainly owes much to Filmer's *Patriarcha*,
but it may owe something to Helvétius's account of the historical development
of mankind as well.

The influence on Bentham of Beccaria's *Dei Delitti et Delle Pene*[5] is more
immediately discernible. Although in saying that 'laws are the conditions, under
which men, naturally independent, unite themselves in society'[6] Beccaria clearly
postulates the existence of something like the contractual process and the
natural liberty which Bentham rejected, in the *Dei Delitti* we also find, in the

conception of certain universally applicable laws as the guarantors of liberty, a definite harbinger of Bentham's ideas. Beccaria's justification for the adoption of political organization and his view of the role of laws in preserving the benefits of such organization bear a notable similarity to Bentham's later arguments.[7] The cardinal consideration for Beccaria, as it was to be for Bentham, was the intolerable insecurity and instability of the prepolitical state:

Weary of living in a continual state of war, and of enjoying a liberty, which became of little value, from the uncertainty of its duration, they sacrificed one part of it, to enjoy the rest in peace and security. The sum of all these portions of the liberty of each individual constituted the sovereignty of a nation; and was deposited in the hands of the sovereign, as the lawful administrator. [Each individual] will always endeavour to take away from the mass not only his own portion, but to encroach on that of others.[8]

It is in response to such encroachments that punishments are invoked to create motives for the observance of law and respect for the legal Sovereign. Men are, says Beccaria, reluctant to rely upon legal punishments as the remedy for oppression. Indeed, 'in every human society, there is an effort continually to confer on one part the height of power and happiness, and to reduce the other to the extreme of weakness, and misery. The intent of good laws is to oppose this effort, and to diffuse their influence, universally and equally.'[9] The tendencies of some men to attempt to enslave others and of other men to acquiesce in such enslavement necessitate, in his view, the creation of political sovereignty with powers of punishment:

Every punishment, which does not arise from absolute necessity, says the great *Montesquieu*, is tyrannical. A proposition which may be made more general thus. Every act of authority of one man over another, for which there is not an absolute necessity, is tyrannical. It is upon this, then, that the sovereign's right to punish crimes is founded: that is, upon the necessity of defending the public liberty entrusted to his care, from the usurpation of individuals – and punishments are just in proportion, as the liberty, preserved by the sovereign, is sacred and valuable.[10]

In contrast to his well-known and fulsome praise of Helvétius and Beccaria, Bentham's opinion of Montesquieu was more critical. He held that Montesquieu focused his attention on the idea of liberty as an end to the exclusion of the goals of security and happiness. Beccaria, despite his Bentham-like emphasis on the sociopolitical importance of a sovereign authority possessed of punitive power, had been led by the influence of Montesquieu to emphasize the 'sacred,' or intrinsically important, character of liberty, whereas Bentham's own interpretation of the idea of liberty in terms of his utilitarian principles emphasized the 'valuable' character of liberty as a necessary condition of the enjoyment of pleasures. Bentham certainly did not accept the view that the sovereign's right to punish crimes was founded exclusively upon the necessity of defending liberty. He insisted that the exercise of sovereign power, even through the instrument of law, was always in some sense destructive of liberty. His principle was, in effect, that 'punishments are just in proportion, as the liberty, preserved by the sovereign is ... [*not* sacred, but] valuable.'

Even at this embryonic stage of our examination it is possible to perceive in arguments such as those of Beccaria and Montesquieu a catalytic factor in the development of Bentham's critical approach to the idea of liberty. What Bentham did not accept in these arguments was the assumption of a philosophically 'realist' or 'essentialist' value for liberty. What he did accept was the value of liberty as a prerequisite of pleasure, and thence of happiness. The nucleus of Bentham's nascent critique of liberty can be grasped in the text of two brief manuscript passages in which he attacks Montesquieu's alleged assumption that the object of government is to 'establish the most perfect liberty' and that the function of judicial procedures and laws is to defend liberty. In the first passage Bentham drives home both the basic proposition that security and happiness, rather than liberty, are the legitimate and practicable objects of social and political theory and practice, and the equally basic point that 'government cannot operate but at the expense of liberty': 'Of happiness he [Montesquieu] says nothing: instead of security for the people against their rulers, he talks of liberty, and assumes without directly saying so, that to establish the most perfect liberty is the proper object of all government: whereas government cannot operate but at the expense of liberty, and then and there only is liberty perfect, where no government has place.'[11] In our second manuscript excerpt we find a dismissal of Montesquieu's thesis that 'the judicial forms are the shields of liberty' written by Bentham after 'five and fifty years' of observing their use not as shields of liberty but as a 'screen for corruption': 'The judicial forms are the shields of liberty ... What judicial forms? What liberty? Whose liberty? What in his dictionary means liberty? What? Unless it be liberty in rulers to oppress subjects, and to lawyers to plunder suitors ... The judicial forms are the shields of liberty ... if, instead of liberty, we may read despotism, oppression, degradation, and corruption.'[12] This passage certainly illustrates an important point of contrast between Bentham's utilitarian views and Montesquieu's liberalism. It also serves, as Halévy has noted, to illuminate the foundations of Bentham's hostility to Sir William Blackstone, the disciple of Montesquieu on this point.

Looking back to his jurisprudential forebears as he worked at the *Fragment on Government* in 1776, Bentham gave a brief résumé of the short and hitherto unconsummated development undergone by the censorial school of thought before his own arrival on the scene: 'Before Montesquieu all was unmixed barbarism. Grotius and Pufendorf were to Censorial Jurisprudence what the Schoolmen were to Natural Philosophy.'[13] Montesquieu's work was in Bentham's view an inconsistent and imperfect blend of the censorial and the expository modes of analysis. Beccaria seemed to Bentham a rare, pure jurisprudential censor amid what was still a flood of legal expositors. Bentham even styled him 'the father of censorial jurisprudence.'[14] Yet it is evident from what we have seen of Beccaria's position on liberty and his attitude to Montesquieu that even his contribution to the development of censorial jurisprudence had done little, as Bentham saw it, to clarify the relationship of the idea of liberty to the ideas of law, government, and authority. A more central and fundamental theoretical blind spot could hardly be imagined. The views even of thinkers of the calibre of Montesquieu and Beccaria seemed to Bentham to be altogether too indiscriminately enthusiastic when liberty was the subject at hand. And why? Because the critical, censorial eye had never been turned toward the idea of liberty itself.

Beccaria was not the only thinker who earned Bentham's respect for his censorial position on jurisprudential matters. In the field of constitutional law, Bentham was much taken with the work of the French *philosophe* Jean-Louis Delolme. In his book, *La Constitution de L'Angleterre*,[15] Delolme adopted a number of positions which Bentham was sure to find pleasing, not the least important of which was his observation 'that the word *Liberty* is one of those which have been most misunderstood or misapplied.'[16] This application of the censorial point of view to the ideas of liberty was exactly what was needed. In the *Fragment on Government*, Bentham contrasted the censorial Delolme with the expository Blackstone, saying: 'Our Author has copied, but Mr Delolme has thought.'[17]

It may be useful to recall that *La Constitution de L'Angleterre*, the work on which Bentham bestowed his praise, took the form of an uninterrupted outpouring of admiration for English liberties.[18] Ironically, in view of the approval of Delolme's writings voiced by prominent contemporary Americans deeply involved in the establishment of the independent American republic,[19] Bentham's correspondence contains an endorsement of him as the able translator (into French) of John Lind's *Answer to the American Declaration of Independence*.[20] T.L.S. Sprigge has observed that Delolme's *Constitution de L'Angleterre* 'helped to give the French *philosophes* their high opinion of the English constitution,'[21] and perhaps it was in the light of such factors that

Bentham, in 1780, wished that he could have '£150 to tempt Delolme with' so that a French translation might be made of his *Introduction to the Principles of Morals and Legislation* and *Plan of a Penal Code*.[22] What, one wonders, would have been the effect on the development of Bentham's reputation, and even on our own understanding of his thought, had Jean-Louis Delolme pre-empted the role which later was to fall into the hands of Etienne Dumont? What if Delolme, not Dumont, had been offered the opportunity – and the power – to edit and publish Bentham's writings for the illumination of readers in France, throughout Europe, and beyond?

Several substantial arguments put forward in the course of *La Constitution de L'Angleterre* show an interesting similarity to Bentham's position on the subject of liberty. In the opening chapter, for example, we find a novel argument purporting to show that the secret of English liberty lies in the nature of the English monarchy. Delolme claimed that 'it was the excessive power of the King which made England free, because it was this very excess that gave rise to the spirit of union and of regulated resistance.'[23] His portrait of the invaluable supreme monarch, uniting all of his subjects in defence of their liberties by their very awareness of his uniquely powerful position, shows an unmistakable similarity to the conception of political authority as radiating from a supreme singular will which Bentham was to applaud in the writings of Sir Robert Filmer. It is possible, even likely, that Bentham's strong conceptions of sovereignty and of political authority remained firmly held because they were in fact complementary to, and most certainly did not seem incompatible with, his idea of liberty.

The contrast which Delolme wished to emphasize in this section of his work was to recur persistently in Bentham's writings: that between universal insecurity and oppression under a weak sovereign exposed to the selfish and parasitic plots of 'sinister interests,' and a circumscribed but assured sphere of individual liberties recognized by all in the interests of each under a truly Sovereign Monarch. We have already seen Delolme's description of the latter of these conditions. Of the former state, which we might almost consider his (and Bentham's) historical reply to the abstract contractualist conception of the 'state of nature,' he gave a description having reference, not to a state of non-existent royal authority but to one where it was 'inconsiderable' – the case of mid-eighteenth-century France. He saw there a situation in which the weakness of regal power induced quarrelsome 'Lords' or 'Chiefs' to make war against their King, not for the sake of liberty, but from 'private ambition or caprice.' They fought for no 'cause common to all,' but dragged the people 'blindfold and like slaves' to their standard. The people, mere 'instruments' of 'resistance,' could gain nothing from such struggles, which involved no 'principle of freedom' that would apply to them.[24]

Chapter 8 of Delolme's work, dealing with 'Private liberty, or the liberty of individuals,' opened by drawing a distinction which corresponds precisely to one employed by Bentham in his manuscripts on the subject of a Civil Code in the 1780s: the distinction between 'general liberty,' which Delolme saw as the 'rights of the Nation as a Nation' and which Bentham was to label 'International Liberty' (i.e. national independence), and 'particular' or 'individual liberty.' Delolme's exact dissection of the idea of individual liberty deserves to be quoted in the original French so that his exact meaning can be grasped:

La liberté particulière, suivant la division des Jurisconsultes Anglais, est formée: Premièrement, du droit de propriété, c'est-à-dire, du droit de jouir exclusivement des dons de la fortune ou des fruits quelconques de son industrie: Secondement, du droit de sûreté personnelle: Troisièmement, de la faculté locomotive, soit liberté, prise dans un sens plus particulier.[25]

It is not possible to identify the 'Jurisconsultes Anglais' from whom Delolme derived his analysis. What is clear from manuscript evidence, some of which will be examined below in chapter 4, is that Bentham himself used precisely this tripartite division in his early manuscripts on 'Preparatory Principles.' In several passages the three headings of property, security, and locomotive liberty arise, although they are not presented as constituents of the idea of liberty but rather as classifications of the 'modal objects' of law. At one point they are referred to as 'personal laws,' under the names of the 'Law of Personal Liberty,' that of 'Personal Security,' and that of 'Personal Property' (69.79). At another point the three are distinguished by virtue of their separate modal objects, and the modal objects of the 'general law of liberty' are said to be 'all acts whatsoever on all passive objects whatever whereby the locomotive faculty of any person is obstructed' (69.145). Such a close similarity of terminology suggests either an extraordinary likeness of minds or, what seems more probable, a direct and discernible influence exerted by *La Constitution de L'Angleterre* on Bentham's early writings.

In chapter 5, Delolme takes up another issue revolving around the idea of liberty: 'But, it will be said, whatever may be the wisdom of the English Laws, how great soever their precautions may be, with regard to the safety of the individual, the People, as they do not expressly enact them, cannot be looked upon as a Free People.'[26] As the specific object of his hostility, he confronts Jean-Jacques Rousseau: 'he asserts that 'though the people of England think they are free, they are much mistaken: they are so only during the election of Members of Parliament: as soon as these are elected, the People are slaves — they are nothing(a).'[27] The choice spot-lighted here is between the idea of liberty as related to security and the notion of liberty as power of political participation. Delolme placed Rousseau and his school among those various types of 'writers of the present age' who ignored the crucial question whether or not men were happy under ancient government, to concentrate on the empty ritual of voting: 'the mere giving of votes, under any disadvantage in the manner of giving them, and how much soever the law might be afterwards neglected that was thus pretended to have been made in common, has appeared to them to be liberty.' The argument that 'a Man who contributes by his vote to the passing of a law, has himself made the Law; in obeying it, he obeys himself; he therefore is free' constitutes 'a play on words, and nothing more.' Delolme saw political participation as properly a form of power, leaving 'civil liberty' as the main practical embodiment of the meaning of the term 'liberty' in a precise sense. Thus he accused Rousseau of confusing 'power' and 'liberty,' and emphasized in his own work the distinction between them: 'To express the whole in two words: to concur by one's suffrage in enacting laws, is to enjoy a share, whatever it may be, of power. To live in a state where the laws are equal for all, and sure to be executed, (whatever are the means by which these advantages are attained) is to be free.'[28]

Bentham must have been delighted to read those passages in *La Constitution de L'Angleterre* in which Delolme repudiated Rousseau's idea of liberty and substituted for it the complementary goals of security and happiness. Bentham himself emphatically rejected Rousseau's two most famous sociopolitical constructs: the idea of the social contract and the paradoxical formulation of the relationship between force and freedom. Bentham saw Rousseau as a promulgator of sophisms and himself as the polar opposite: a cold-blooded, empirical social engineer.[29] The object of social engineering in its various forms did not seem to Bentham to be the paradoxical maximization of freedom through its surrender via the mechanism of the social contract, but rather the cultivation of happiness by a policy (quite free of paradoxical sophisms) of maximizing the individual's security in the expectation and enjoyment of pleasures. The 'paradox of forced freedom' appeared to him to consist of a fanciful contractual notion combined with the equally 'fantastic' notion of a general will. Bentham's rejection of the general will idea was just as important to the character of his political and social thinking as was his rejection of the social contract. Both of these ideas are abstractions, derived from an organic view of society and of political authority. This organic view is diametrically opposed to Bentham's aggregative approach as expressed in his assertion that 'the interest of the community is ... the sum of the interests of the several members who compose it.'[30] It was thus quite logical that Bentham should reject Rousseau's contractual theory and seek to construct an alternative explanation of the nature and development of political authority.

The nature of Bentham's approach to the explanation of political authority was made quite clear in the *Fragment on Government*. Rather than postulating, with the contractual school of theorists, a single act of consensus as the basis of political authority and the desire to preserve 'natural,' or pregovernmental, liberty as its justification, Bentham put forward the unlibertarian conception of a 'habit of obedience' as the foundation of political society, setting his readers the task of explaining, not the terms of a theoretical contract, but the historical conditions for the development of a habit.[31]

Perhaps it was his dissatisfaction with libertarian explanations of the nature of political society that induced Bentham to define it in terms of subjection, obedience, and governance – the polar opposites, it would appear, of liberty.[32] Perhaps the cause lay in the influence on Bentham of Delolme's vision of sovereign authority as the foundation, not the enemy, of valuable political liberty. Perhaps his partiality to the sociological side of Sir Robert Filmer's theories of the development of social authority was decisive. Whatever the exact confluence of factors responsible, by the time Bentham had set himself to the task of expounding his 'preparatory principles' in anticipation of political salvos calling, like the *Fragment*, for theoretical foundations, he was already convinced that the efficacy of the State ... 'depends on a previous habit of obedience' (69.203). Bentham was careful to maintain that the habit of obedience itself cannot be explained by reference to any particular law. Habits as such cannot be created by decree. Obedience can be so created, but does not necessarily become habitual thereafter. Bentham's point is clearly that political authority in general (or in its essence) depends on historical and sociological factors extrinsic to law for its stability. The habit of obedience is 'at present firmly rooted in our own and every other civilized nation that we know of. Were it otherwise indeed in any nation, we should not denominate that nation civilized. This is a matter of known indisputable fact' (69.203-4). Bentham did not deem it either practicable or worthwhile to embark on speculation about the exact concatenation of social and historical factors involved in the development of the habit, but he was certain that utilitarianism held the key to its explanation: 'As every habit consists of acts, and every act must have some motive, and every motive is the expectation of some pain or pleasure, for the origin of the habit we must find the expectation of some pain or pleasure, such a capacity subsisting in the superior who first commanded / began to command' (69.204).

It was at least partly in terms of his approval of Filmer's 'system' that Bentham expressed his hostility to the contractual 'system,' whose originator he identified as John Locke. 'The invention,' he said, was a 'most unhappy one,' incapable of 'supporting anything' (100.104). Bentham confronted the essentially metaphorical contractual conception with a stubbornly literal-minded legalism. No such contract had ever existed, he charged, and had one such ever existed it could not in any case have sufficed to establish a right of resistance or to bind a Sovereign.[33] Rousseau appeared to him to be as deluded as Locke in this respect: 'Rousseau born under a commonwealth took up the fiction of Locke and applied it to a commonwealth. Instead of one contract for 25 millions of people, Rousseau takes 25 millions of contracts. In Locke the contracting parties are the King on the one part, and the people on the other. In Rousseau people contract with one another ... one on one part contracting with all the rest together on the other' (100.105). Indeed, in one important respect Rousseau's misguidedness exceeded Locke's, for whereas 'Locke's fiction was applicable only to a monarchy,' Rousseau's 'was equally applicable to every government' (100.106).

While Bentham viewed the contractual theory of the formation of government favoured by Locke and Rousseau as an abstraction, exemplified nowhere in the real world, he found Filmer's patriarchal theory of the origins of governmental authority exemplified everywhere, for it was based upon the structure of authority in that ubiquitous institution the family (100.107). Even more crucial to Bentham's argument was his claim that Locke's theory reversed the proper chronological and conceptual priority as between government and contracts. According to Locke, Bentham said, 'men knew nothing at all of government till they met together and agreed to make one.' To 'agree to make one,' however, would be to make a 'bargain': 'What sort of thing was a bargain? What reason had they for expecting that if made it would be kept? These were questions which it never occurred to him to ask himself. If it had, he would have found no answer till he came to *government*, and thus he would have found [that] ... it was contracts that came from government, not government from contracts.' The habit of obedience to government is thus revealed as the source of popular acceptance of the obligation to keep contracts. The experience of authority in the family context, in turn, is seen to be the mother of the habit of obedience to government. 'It is in the bosom of a family,' Bentham claimed, 'that men serve an apprenticeship to government' (100.108). 'Under the authority of the father, and his assistant and prime minister the mother, every human creature is enured to subjection, is trained up into a habit of obedience / subjection. But the habit once formed, nothing is easier than to transfer it from one object to another' (100.109). The establishment of political authority, if not absolutely impossible without the prior existence of domestic authority, would be incomparably more difficult (100.109).

Bentham unhesitatingly dissociated himself from the theological aspects and implications of Filmer's arguments (100.110-12) but was grateful for his attention to the concept of 'paternal authority,' principally because it afforded 'a complete refutation to the doctrine of universal and perpetual equality.' Indeed, in the phenomenon of ubiquitous paternal authority Bentham found proof, 'beyond possibility of mistake,' of 'the physical impossibility of the system of absolute equality and independence ... by showing that subjection and not independence is the natural state of man' (100.113). That the ideas of natural liberty and natural equality were the principal objects of Filmer's attack is clear from the subtitle of *Patriarcha*: 'A Defence of the Natural Power of Kings against the Unnatural Liberty of the People.'[34] We shall see that the same hostility frequently motivated Bentham. The two thinkers also shared the belief that the notion of the Original Contract was a piece of 'fancy,' not merely 'improbable,' but 'impossible.' Both, moreover, derived their notions of what it is to be governed from the analysis of the individual, not the general, will.[35] The resemblance between their over-all views on the origins and nature of civil and political authority is striking. In addition, however, as we go on to consider Bentham's explanation of the relationship between liberty and law, especially in *Of Laws in General*, we shall be reminded of Filmer's statement: 'every law or command, is in itself an innovation, and a diminution of some part of popular liberty: for it is no law except it restrain liberty: he that by his negative voice doth forbid or hinder the proceeding of a new law, doth preserve himself in that condition of liberty wherein nature hath placed him, and whereof he is in present possession.'[36]

One also discovers in Filmer the exact equivalent of Bentham's distinction, examined below, between 'liberty in perfection' and 'liberty entire.' The essential point for both thinkers is that liberty maximized, that is, 'liberty entire,' is not a practical possibility in any proper society: 'True liberty is for every man to do what he lists, or to live as he please, and not be tied to any laws. But such liberty is not to be found in any commonwealth.'[37] Bentham did not accept Filmer's argument that 'the right of fatherly government was ordained by God, for the preservation of mankind'[38] and was indestructible for that reason. He did, however, agree that, as Filmer put it, for those who acknowledge familial, patriarchal authority 'to dream of an original freedom in mankind, is to contradict themselves.'[39] In fact, in one passage Filmer seems to indicate forebodings about majority tyranny as a threat to liberty such as Bentham seems never to have entertained: 'Men that boast so much of natural freedom, are not willing to consider how contradictory and destructive the power of a major part is to the natural liberty of the whole people; the two grand favourites of the subjects, liberty and property (for which most men pretend to strive) are as contrary as fire to water, and cannot stand together.'[40] Bentham was to take up the question of the relationship between liberty and property, but his early writings show remarkably little sustained interest in the relationship between majority power and a people's liberty.

Bentham adopted the patriarchal perspective as an anthropological insight. The most important implication of this argument for him is the suggestion that such liberties as can exist only in what contract theorists call a 'state of nature,' a pregovernmental state, can equally justly be said to be tenable only before the advent of social family authority; they are therefore effectively rendered irrelevant to the entire course of human history in so far as family authority is considered as having remained stable throughout that course. Valid, practicable liberties do not predate stable authority. The contractualists have got their priorities wrong: liberties, like contractual rights themselves, are founded upon and secured by stable authority. It is not a great leap from this position to a position of legal positivism about liberties, where the very criterion for the validation of liberties is the assessment of their compatibility with the legal order which ensures security for their enjoyment.

Bentham could have found additional support for his position in this respect in the writings of a thinker vastly different from Sir Robert Filmer in both persuasion and reputation, the Scottish *philosophe* David Hume. For Hume, as for Bentham, liberty is made secure, and thence enjoyable, by its very circumscription in a civil society under the rule of law. It is evident, says Hume, that 'passion is much better satisfied by its restraint than by its liberty, and that in preserving society, we make much greater advances in the acquiring possessions than in the solitary and forlorn condition which must follow upon violence and an universal license.'[41] In his own works Bentham postulated a more unqualifiedly anarchic pregovernmental condition of mankind than that which Hume described in the *Treatise of Human Nature*, where he inserted the existence of both a principle of justice and a set of three fundamental laws governing the possession and transfer of property and, especially, the 'performance of promises' antecedent to the establishment of government.[42] The agreement between the two is striking, however, when the status of individual liberty under government is the point to be investigated. Hume's sentiments in his essay *Of the Origin of Government* are clearly reflected in Bentham's early manuscripts. Hume's judgment was this: 'In all governments, there is a perpetual intestine struggle, open or secret, between authority and liberty; and neither of them can ever absolutely prevail in the contest. A great sacrifice of liberty must necessarily be made in every government; yet even the authority which confines liberty can never, and perhaps ought never, in any constitution, to become quite entire and uncontrollable.'[43] On the other hand, however, although 'it must be owned that liberty is the perfection of civil society ... still authority must be acknowledged essential to its very existence; and in those contests which so often take place between the one and the other, the latter may, on that account, challenge the preference.'[44] Clearly Bentham found in Hume a predecessor who was prepared to assess the validity of government in terms of utility, and its utility in terms of stability, authority, and security as well as liberty.

There can be no doubt that John Locke was one of Bentham's principal intellectual heroes.[45] Bentham's admiration for him was mixed, however, with an awareness of important differences. Thinking particularly of epistemological matters, Bentham wrote: 'Without Locke I could have known nothing: but I think I could now take Locke's *Essay* and write it over again, so as to make it much more precise and apprehensible in half the compass.'[46] The use of the expression 'half the compass' was especially appropriate, for Bentham reduced Locke's two classes of ideas, of sensation and of reflection, to a single one. He made sensation the mother of reflection just as he took reason to be the slave of the senses and the understanding to be the negative correlative of the active will. He was convinced, moreover that he could produce a more precise and consistent version of the *Essay* as a result of this modification. What is of the greatest immediate importance for the present discussion is that by eliminating from his epistemology the category of ideas derived from reflection Bentham was removing the foundation for any possible notion of the idea of liberty as an intrinsic good.[47]

In his reminiscences to John Bowring, Bentham was to refer to Locke's destruction of the notion of innate ideas as his special contribution to the progress of moral science.[48] What Bentham found in Locke's *Essay*, however, was not just a critique of innate ideas, but the conceptual basis for a critique of abstractions, or, as Bentham was to call them, 'fictions.' Locke, in Bentham's view, had pointed the way towards a scientific epistemology based on what might be termed philological nominalism. John Horne Tooke's *Diversions of Purley*, a 'philological and nominalist treatise,' greatly impressed Bentham and roused him to emulation.[49] Horne Tooke attacked Locke's notion of the 'composition of ideas,'[50] arguing that only terms, not ideas, can be generalized or rendered abstract.[51] Substantives, he maintained, are 'at the origin of all words' — hence his nominalism. By labelling the process of abstraction a 'purely verbal illusion' productive of 'faulty metaphysics,' he threatened to undermine the conception of 'ideas of reflection,' which in Locke's *Essay* is essential to the processes of generalization and abstraction. Abstraction, Horne Tooke argued, was simply a faulty ellipsis, in which the aggregate meaning of a substantive and an adjective was expressed by the use of a single term. Unfortunately, the adjective was frequently and misleadingly so employed.[52]

Locke had identified and described the process of abstraction in the *Essay* when he considered the operations by which "complex ideas" are formed.[53] Indeed, in his consideration of the particular class of complex ideas described as 'mixed modes,' he anticipated Bentham's objection that such ideas had no 'real' existence:

The mind often exercises an *active* power in making these several combinations. For, it being once furnished with simple ideas, it can put them together in several compositions, and so make variety of complex ideas without examining whether they exist so together in nature ... and to form such ideas, it sufficed that the mind put the parts of them together and that they were consistent in the understanding, without considering whether they had any real being.[54]

However, what were complex ideas to Locke were fictions to the more rigidly materialist Bentham. He did not deny that the operations of the mind seemed to exhibit the 'active power' which Locke described, but, adopting the philological and nominalist perspective, he did argue that complex *terms* could only be defined by decomposition into their component 'real entities,' which is to say 'substantives.' Not unlike James Mill, who was to claim that abstraction meant 'verbal' synthesis without implying 'mental' synthesis,[55] Bentham became a philological nominalist about abstractions such as 'liberty.' Upon this meta-physical and epistemological foundation he built the censorial approach which was to shape his views through decades of political argument and philosophical controversy.

It was greatly to Bentham's advantage to resolve the power of mental synthesis into a power of verbal synthesis, retaining the principle that the springs of action were purely physiological. To this analysis Locke's empiricism could even offer some support, for the notion that the mind, beginning as a *tabula rasa*, is 'furnished' with ideas by 'experience'[56] is precisely the foundation of Bentham's psychology, provided that 'experience' means physiological, sensory, hedonistic experience. So consonant, moreover, are some of Locke's remarks with the *Introduction to the Principles* that one wonders how directly Bentham may have been influenced by them. Consider, for example, Locke's acknowledgement in the *Essay* that 'Nature, I confess, has put into man a desire of happiness and an aversion to misery: These indeed are innate practical principles which ... do continue constantly to operate and influence all our actions without ceasing.'[57] Along with such 'principles of the will and appetite' as these, Locke felt obliged to provide determinate 'principles of knowledge regulating our practice.' A complete analysis of human action must, as he saw it, demonstrate the conjunction of the will and the understanding. The complex operations of the understanding seemed to him to link sensory perception with activity of the will in a reflective rather than reflexive sequence. To be both adequate and innate, practical principles would have to show that both men's 'inclinations' and their 'impressions of truth' are innate phenomena. To identify pain and pleasure as the 'constant springs and motives of all our actions' was to give only half an explanation.[58]

Bentham's account of how men employ the will and the understanding in moving from sensation to action aligns him much more closely with Hobbes than with Locke. Bentham's nominalist and materialist approach to the problems of epistemology, and his philological 'theory of fictions,' whose function it was to resolve abstract ideas such as liberty into verbal conglomerations compounded of simple real entities, tended to undermine the independent status of the logic of the understanding and to reduce even the abstract idea of understanding itself to a concatenation of physiological or sensory stimuli and responses.

Bentham undertook to simplify Locke's *Essay* by radically reconstructing the very object of that study — the understanding itself. It might almost be said that Bentham stood Locke on his head epistemologically. It would be more accurate, however, to see Bentham as negating the whole concept of epistemology, denying the existence of any truly independent logic of cognition by attributing a physiological basis to that very process. Bentham was not interested in 'the understanding,' the 'mind,' or the problems of epistemology except in so far as these conceptions were involved in the analysis of action. Pursuit and escape, enjoyment and suffering are the categories of activity which preoccupy him. He learned much from Locke's dictum that 'the chief, if not only spur to human industry and action is *uneasiness*,'[59] and much also from Locke's identification of the good, as an object of desire, with happiness and the absence of misery. In Bentham's own writings the bogey of insecurity was to become, as we shall see, more and more the chief spur towards the sacrifice of liberty in return for protection, and the good, stripped (as was the idea of freedom) of any intrinsic value, was to become identified with pleasure, the absence of pain, and the secure expectation of the continuation of such a state of affairs.

Locke's explicit comments on the idea of liberty are found in chapter 21 of the *Essay*, entitled 'Of Power.'[60] Here, in so far as Locke attempts to define the idea of liberty by examining the meaning of the term 'liberty' in discourse, he brings to bear on the problem of liberty methodological principles established in his earlier chapters on 'Language in general,' 'The imperfection of words,' and 'The abuse of words.'[61] Thus the background to Locke's definition of liberty has, at least at this general level, much in common with Bentham's analysis of liberty as a fiction.[62] Locke, however, analyses the conditions for human action in terms of freedom and necessity, introducing into the discussion the problem of free will, which interested Bentham not at all,[63] and contradicting, it must have seemed to Bentham, his assertion, cited above, that the innate principles of practical activity could be derived from utilitarian postulates without reference to the categories of freedom and necessity.[64] For Bentham, the definition of liberty involves, first, its application to a particular situation and the discovery of the relationships among real entities which it describes and, second, the examination of the process by which pains and pleasures produce desire or uneasiness, thus 'motivating' (in the sense of mobilizing or activating) the will. The latter operation serves mainly, in Bentham's system, to demonstrate the external and physiological roots of motivation, and thus to render such terms as 'spontaneity' and 'free will' inapplicable to the processes being examined, that is, human actions.

The source of errors in Locke's explanation of liberty, from Bentham's point of view, was his belief that the mind possessed active 'power' – specifically, power to suspend the activities of the will.[65] From Bentham's perspective the mental identification of, and selection among, the objects of desire is evidence, not of a power in the mind to suspend or alter the will, but of the subordinate role of the understanding in expediting the satisfaction of desires in the best possible accordance with the innate principles which govern the operation of the will and of the physical body itself. Such a power, being illusory, could not be the source of liberty unless liberty, too, were to be not an active power but a passive state, important only as a necessary condition of the pursuit of happiness. Here again, Bentham inverts Locke's reasoning to arrive at his own conception of liberty. We shall see that in Bentham 'the liberty a man has' is defined, not in terms of the relationship between his understanding and his will, but in terms of the relationship between his physical self and the objects of desire.

In Bentham's choice of a negative definition of liberty Hume's naturalism to some extent triumphs over Locke's rationalism. By virtue of the same choice, moreover, Thomas Hobbes's negative approach to liberty is preferred to Locke's. Professor Halévy has attributed to Hobbes a moral determinism defined, even in a time before Newton, in terms of a gravitational metaphor.[66] It is not surprising, then, that one should find the elements of a hedonistic calculus present in the section of the *Leviathan* devoted to the study of Man.[67] Nor is it surprising that, sharing their materialism, their nominalism, their scepticism, and their irreverence, Bentham and Hobbes exhibited a common negativity about liberty. Hobbes's treatment of the meaning of 'liberty, or freedome,' in chapter 21 of *Leviathan*, entitled 'Of the *liberty* of subjects,'[68] is strikingly like Bentham's in its negativity and in its unqualified materialism: 'Liberty, or Freedome, signifieth (properly) the absence of Opposition; (by Opposition, I mean externall

Impediments of motion;) and may be applyed no lesse to Irrationall, and Inanimate creatures, than to Rationall. For whatsoever is so tyed, or environed, as it cannot move, but within a certain space, which space is determined by the opposition of some externall body, we say it hath not Liberty to go further.'[69]

Here we see a definition of liberty which fulfils all Bentham's essential requirements; it is scientific, being demonstrable and based on experience and observation; it embodies a linguistic perspective (what do we refer to when we *speak* of 'liberty'?), and it is applicable to both animate and inanimate, rational and irrational entities – hence it can easily be applied to the relationships between men and the objects to which they are related by feelings of desire and aversion. From Hobbes's remarks on the definition of a 'free-man,' his materialism is abundantly clear: 'A *free-man* is he, that in those things, which by his strength and wit he is able to do, is not hindered to do what he has a will to. But when the words *free* and *liberty*, are applied to anything but *bodies*, they are abused; for that which is not subject to Motion is not subject to impediment.'[70]

Liberty pertains to bodies in motion: not a surprising conclusion in view of the ontological premises of *Leviathan*. But what is particularly consonant with Bentham's arguments is Hobbes's caveat that liberty pertains to the motions of various entities or the potentiality of such motions, but not strictly to any condition of the will: 'from the use of the word *free-will*, no Liberty can be inferred of the will, desire or inclination, but the *liberty* of the man: which consisteth in this, that he finds no stop, in doing what he has the will, desire or inclination to doe.'[71]

All of the disdain for the myopic and illogical enthusiasm of ardent libertarians which we shall see exhibited in Bentham's writings is present, too, in Hobbes:

For if we take Liberty in the proper sense, for corporall liberty, that is to say, freedome from chains, and prison, it were very absurd for men to clamour as they do, for the liberty they so manifestly enjoy. Againe, if we take Liberty, for an exemption from Lawes, it is no lesse absurd, for men to demand as they doe, that Liberty, by which all other men may be masters of their lives. And yet as absurd as it is, this is it they demand; not knowing that the Lawes are of no power to protect them, without a Sword in the hands of a man, or men, to cause those laws to be put into execution. The Liberty of a Subject, lyeth therefore only in those things, which in regulating their actions, the Sovereign hath praetermitted.[72]

Bentham was to argue that there was a sense in which a sovereign might enhance the value of subjects' liberties by his acts of regulation, but he was never to lose sight of the fact that every act of regulation emanating from a sovereign was destructive of liberty taken in a purely quantitative sense. If the reader will bear in mind the fact that Hobbes speaks only of what Bentham was to call 'liberty entire,' without distinguishing it from Bentham's important conception of 'liberty in perfection,' then no incompatibility will be found between Bentham's and Hobbes's accounts of the liberty of the *subject*, which is to say the liberty of the individual as against the law, or the possibility of disobedience to sovereigns.

Hobbes awaited the perfection of 'the skill of making, and maintaining Common-wealths,' as the development which would put an end to liberty in lieu of or against sovereignty or law: 'seeing there is no Common-wealth in the world, wherein there be Rules enough set down, for the regulating of all the actions, and words of men (as being a thing impossible:) it followeth necessarily, that in all kinds of actions, by the laws praetermitted, men have the Liberty, of doing what their own reasons shall suggest, for the most profitable to themselves.'[73] Bentham's life-long intention was to construct a body of 'Rules' adequate as far as possible to the task (admittedly impossible, even in Bentham's eyes – or there would have been no need for punishment in his system) of 'regulating all the actions, and words of men.' Hobbes said of the art of 'state-craft' what Bentham was to say later of the 'science of legislation': 'The skill of making, and maintaining Common-wealths, consisteth in certain Rules, as doth Arithmetique and Geometry: not (as Tennis-play) on Practise onely: which Rules, neither poor men have the leisure, nor men that have had the leisure, have hitherto had the curiosity, or the method to find out.'[74]

We have so far observed that the main difference between Hobbes and Bentham on 'the liberty of the subject' seems to be that Hobbes only discussed such unqualified 'liberty entire' as might exist in the interstices of the web of legislation under this heading, while Bentham, as we shall later explain in detail, examined also the circumscribed, reduced, but secure and enjoyable liberties actually guaranteed by the sovereign's regulations. The words 'in the act of our *Submission*, consists both our *Obligation*, and our *Liberty*'[75] are Hobbes's, but the idea expressed was even more important to Bentham than to Hobbes himself. The guarantor of obedience in the subject is, for both thinkers, a formidable punitive sovereign. The guarantee of obedience in the citizen lies in the calibre of the sovereign legislator's punitive statecraft.[76] Bentham undertook to raise to heights of scientific perfection what Hobbes referred to as 'the skill of making, and maintaining Commonwealths.'[77] In his science of statecraft Bentham tried to demonstrate, however, that the completion of an all-encompassing set of rules of social behaviour did not necessarily require the total annihilation of liberty. Hobbes had foreseen the extinction of the individual liberties of subjects if and when regulations should come into force controlling their very words as well as their actions. Bentham's proclamation that the motto of the good citizen is "to obey punctually, to censure freely'[78] was meant to demonstrate his determination to show that strict, certain, and equitable laws could enhance the value of liberty — that they might even become its principal guarantee. Indeed, it was only when Bentham's system grew to extend beyond the province of legal coercion into the murkier region of social control that the extinction of liberty — in the very process prophesied by Thomas Hobbes — became a real possibility. It became, in fact, more than a possibility. Some would say that it became a virtual necessary condition of the perfection of the utilitarian Utopia.

3

The school of experience: some issues and thinkers of the 1760s and 1770s

The famous figures whose influence on Bentham we have thus far examined were important inhabitants of Bentham's intellectual world and of the world of ideas in his day. But they were usually present, for reasons of place or time, only in spirit. What is to be said of Bentham's contemporaries, his fellow citizens of England, and of the events that roused them to vigorous public discussion?

Contemporary men and events conspired to sharpen the young Bentham's awareness of the pre-eminent susceptibility to abuse of the word 'liberty.' The attempts of his fellow Englishmen to theorize about liberty so irritated and disappointed him that he took up his pen to refute and improve upon their works. Their confused and illogical outbursts of libertarianism made him realize what mischief could flow from misunderstandings about liberty. Their attempts at definitions of liberty, proceeding from a basis of passion or partisanship, sparked in him a desire to show that an objective, scientific approach based on utilitarian principles could produce a firm, empirically verifiable definition such as might form one of the pillars of a stable utilitarian social structure.

The critique of liberty, moreover, provided a simpler entrée into the minds of thinking men than did the critique of law. The critic of libertarian enthusiasm might assume the role of the defender of public order: the critic of Blackstone could only appear as the opponent of entrenched order and interests. The critiques of liberty and of existing legal practices and theories, however, were in Bentham's eyes only particular aspects of a unified critique of existing moral, legal, and legislative science. The idea of liberty (properly conceived), the theory and practice of censorial jurisprudence, and the political theories of sovereignty, legislation, and representation, all had their place within the broad context of Bentham's would-be science of Man.

Bentham was not the only English thinker of his day who brought together in one mind a love of scientific method and scientific knowledge and a taste for public controversy and social criticism. Joseph Priestley, too, embodied both the scientific enthusiasm of the *philosophe* and the sociopolitical awareness of the English gentleman of sincere social conscience. It is well known that when Bentham read Priestley's *Essay on the First Principles of Government and the Nature of Political, Civil and Religious Liberty* he was delighted with the passage in which the greatest happiness principle was endorsed.[1]

We should not, however, ignore the fact that this definition was propounded in the context of an investigation into the complementary concepts of government and liberty. The precise meaning of the passage, given its correct context, is that the greatest happiness principle is the 'standard by which everything relating to [a given] state must be determined,' meaning that the optimum definition and distribution of political, civil, and religious liberty within the state, among other things, must be so determined. This was the formulation which Bentham so enthusiastically applauded. The establishment of the principle of utility as the criterion for the definition and distribution of social liberties was an essential step towards the development of a coherent utilitarian sociopolitical theory.

It must have seemed to Bentham, however, that in the remainder of his *Essay* Priestley failed to follow up a promising beginning. Priestley's attempts at a definition of liberty may have stimulated Bentham, but it was a stimulus towards correction and contradiction, not towards imitation. Priestley based his definitions of political and civil liberty on an argument whose validity Bentham could not accept, an argument founded upon two principles whose coexistence was unthinkable to Bentham: utility and natural rights. His endorsement of natural rights was framed in the following terms: 'every man retains, and can never be deprived of his natural right (founded on a regard to the general good) of relieving himself from all oppression.' This, he said, is the only true foundation for the idea of political liberty. He argued that his idea had never been realized, for he found that 'all governments whatever have been, in some measure, compulsory, tyrannical and oppressive in their origins.'[2]

Since political liberty is identified by Priestley with 'the general good,' while 'all governments whatever' are characterized as 'in some measure ... oppressive in their origins,' Priestley quite logically comes to describe perfect political liberty as that social state in which each man's power to resist oppression, and, by the same token, to participate in the process of government, is equal to that of every other man. Thus, if its natural right foundations are ignored for the moment, Priestley's definition of political liberty does bear a prima facie resemblance to Bentham's descriptions of it in the *Fragment on Government*[3] and, later, in his 'Civil Code' manuscripts.

Priestley asserted that 'in countries where every member of the society enjoys an equal power of arriving at the supreme offices, and consequently of directing the strength and the sentiments of the whole community, there is a state of the most perfect political liberty.'[4] Bentham was to qualify and clarify this conception with his distinction between political liberty entire and political liberty in perfection, as we shall observe, but he was to agree that the measure of strictly political liberty was the power of participation in the electoral, representative, and administrative processes.[5] Farther along the path of our present investigation we shall find Bentham describing the distinction between political and civil liberty in terms much like those used by Priestley in the *Essay*'s chapter on 'Political Liberty.' There Priestley argued that 'in countries where a man is, by his birth or fortune, excluded from these offices, or from a power of voting for proper persons to fill them; that man, whatever be the form of the government, or whatever civil liberty, or power over his own actions he may have, has no power over those of another, has no share in the government, and therefore has no political liberty at all.'[6] In the same passage, Priestley went on to observe that when an individual's political liberty is destroyed a threat is posed to his personal and civil liberty as well, because 'his own conduct, as far as society does interfere, is, in all cases, directed by others.'

Priestley's espousal in principle of a universal suffrage as the basis for perfect political liberty, hedged round with modifications designed to favour the propertied classes, disfranchise the class of 'dependents,' and thus 'form an idea of as much political liberty as is consistent with the state of mankind,' is similar to Bentham's position on the franchise.[7] In Priestley, as in Bentham, doubts about the desirability of absolute liberty spring from fears about the tenability of a state of pure equality, and from concern regarding the effects of political turbulence on individual or social security. Indeed, these reservations lie behind Priestley's sceptical observation, 'I by no means assert, that the good of mankind requires a state of the most perfect political liberty.'[8] In view of the similarities we have observed it is not surprising that Priestley defines the political right of resistance, just as does Bentham in the *Fragment on Government*,[9] in terms of a calculation weighing the benefits of resistance against the mischievous consequences or risks involved. It is time to offer resistance, in Priestley's eyes, 'when it is better not to be governed at all than to be governed in such a manner; or, at least when the hazard of a change of govt. would be apparently the less evil of the two.'[10]

In the section of the *Essay* devoted to 'Civil Liberty,' Priestley acknowledges that 'Political and civil liberty, as before explained, though very different, have, however, a very near and manifest connection ... the former is the chief guard of the latter, and on that account, principally is valuable, and worth contending for ... for the more political liberty the people have, the safer is their civil liberty.'[11] The fundamental value of political liberty lies not in its effect upon the form of government, but in its amenability to regulation or restriction in the interests of personal liberty, security, and property: 'The governments now subsisting in Europe differ widely in their forms; but it is certain, that the present happiness of the subjects of them can by no means be estimated by a regard to the form, but that it depends chiefly upon the power, the extent, and the maxims of government, respecting personal security, private property, etc. and on the certainty and uniformity of the administration.'[12] With respect to the relationship between liberty and other social values such as property and security, that is, with respect to most of the distributive problems pertaining to civil liberties, Priestley and Bentham were as much in agreement as one might expect two enthusiastic utilitarian social theorists to be. Priestley's description of the method and purpose of his theoretical attack might equally justly have been used by Bentham to describe his aspirations: 'there is real difficulty in determining what general rules, respecting the extent of the power of government, or of governors, are most conducive to the public good ... experiment only can determine how far this power of the legislature ought to extend.'[13] Again, Priestley described the definition of rights of all kinds, including property rights, by utilitarian general rules in ,a manner strikingly similar to that which Bentham was to employ in his writings on civil law: 'The very idea of property, or right of any kind, is founded upon a regard to the general good of the society, under whose protection it is enjoyed; and nothing is properly *a man's own*, but what general rules, which have for their object the good of the whole, give to him.'[14]

In the eyes of a utilitarian as rigorous and uncomprising in his views as Bentham, however, inconsistencies arising from Priestley's reliance on natural rights theories must have seemed to undermine the latter's understanding of the origins of civil and political liberties, even where such reliance did not impair his grasp of the distributive principles governing their apportionment in society. Priestley professed to be a utilitarian legal positivist about rights, but persisted, perhaps because of the religious thread in his thought, in holding a natural rights position on liberty. On the basis of the postulate that 'no man can be supposed to resign his natural liberty, but on conditions,'[15] he defined liberty as a 'power': 'Political liberty ... consists in the power, which the members of the state reserve to themselves, of arriving at the public offices, or at least of having votes in the nomination of those who fill them ... Civil Liberty [is] that power over their actions, which the members of the state reserve to themselves, and which their officers must not infringe.'[16] But if both political and civil liberties are original, natural liberties which men reserve to themselves in society, how can men be given one in exchange for the other, as in the following passage? 'It is a man's civil liberty, which is originally in its full force, and part of which he sacrifices when he enters into a state of society; and political liberty is that which he may or may not acquire in the compensation he receives for it.'[17]

The abandoning of a purely utilitarian mode of explanation and the adoption of the natural rights perspective on liberty was a source of confusion in Priestley's arguments. Bentham's negative definition of liberty and his analysis of the term 'liberty' as a 'fictitious entity,' the results of an undeviating allegiance to utilitarian principles of explanation, enabled him to escape such contradictions. Bentham was able, in the end, to make sense of the change that comes over individual liberty with the advent of society and government by discarding the notion of pre-existing, 'natural' liberties as 'powers' of the individual and by concentrating instead on the relationship between social organization and governmental coercion and individual happiness, among whose preconditions he numbered liberty defined as the absence of coercion. To Bentham, as we shall have ample opportunity to observe, the justification for the establishment of society and government lay precisely in the fact that individuals were, in the absence of legal rules and sanctions, incapable of 'reserving their liberties to themselves' effectively enough to secure the enjoyment of them. Bentham could not have agreed more completely with Priestley's opinion that the greatest happiness principle 'properly pursued, throws the greatest light upon the whole system of policy, morals, and, one may add, theology too.'[18] He must surely have concurred with Priestley's judgment that

Virtue and right conduct consist in those affections and actions which terminate in the public good; justice and veracity, for instance, having nothing intrinsically excellent in them, separate from their relationship to the happiness of mankind; and the whole system of right to power, property, and everything else in society, must be regulated by the same consideration: the decisive question, when any of these subjects are examined being: what is it that the good of the community requires?[19]

The major flaw in Priestley's attempt at a utilitarian social theory could have been removed had Priestley simply included liberty as part of 'the whole system of right to power, property, and everything else in society' and thus founded it entirely upon utilitarian principles without reference to natural rights.

Part of the explanation for Bentham's partiality to Priestley's writings lies in the fact that, to some extent, Priestley attempted to bring the attitude of the physical scientist to bear on social and political problems. Bentham hoped for more instruction from Priestley than he expected to derive from the rhetorical outbursts of contemporary politicians and journalists. Yet his distaste for 'day-to-day politics'[20] and for partisan political machinations[21] did not extinguish his interest in the political issues of his time. The politics that fascinated Bentham — and provided most of the inspiration for his first writings — were the politics of 'the Constitution.' The idea of the Constitution was a lynch-pin linking the fields of politics and law. It was both an aggregation of legal provisions and a fountainhead of political policies and conventions. In those vital formative years between 1767, when he received his MA from Queen's College, Oxford, and 1776, when he began to make a literary reputation with the *Fragment on Government*, Bentham was moved to put pen to paper mainly in response to political stimuli arising from constitutional controversies, whether in the form of the raucous agitation of the Wilkesites, the literary efforts of John Lind and Richard Hey, the revolutionary theoretical abstractions of Dr Richard Price, or the legal apologetics of Sir William Blackstone.

The activities of John Wilkes and his supporters through the medium of the press provided Bentham with a continuing flow of political controversy on which to feed in the years from 1768 to 1774.[22] Bentham observed the antics of the partisans of 'Wilkes and Liberty'[23] with the derisive scorn born of his admiration for George III.[24] It was the combination of a Wilkesite issue with duplicity (so it seemed to him) among the Wilkesite leadership that first brought the sentiments of the young Bentham into public circulation. It was in 1771 that Wilkes advocated the abolition of impressment. Press warrants were attacked, by Wilkes and others, on the same grounds as general warrants — as violations of the rights and liberties of Englishmen.[25] During the preparatory stages of this campaign, in November 1770, the Wilkesites contrived to bring a query regarding the validity of press warrants before a trio of Lords Commissioners of the Admiralty including Messrs Dunning and Wedderburn and one Sergeant-at-Law John Glynn. The publicly announced decision of the Commissioners was in favour of the validity of impressment. That John Glynn should have concurred in such a decision was astonishing to the Wilkesites, for Glynn was one of Wilkes's most steadfast supporters.[26] The furor over Glynn's duplicity in assenting privately (as some thought) to the passage of a measure towards which he and his fellow Wilkesites were publicly hostile filled many a column in the *Public Advertiser* for November 1770, and among the paper's readers was Jeremy Bentham.[27] Unlike some outraged libertarians, however, he did not deliver a thunderous rhetorical salvo in defence of English liberties.[28] More characteristically, if less heroically, in a letter signed 'Irenius' and printed in the *Gazetteer and New Daily Advertiser* for 3 December, he loosed a bitter attack on John Glynn for his blatant volte-face, not because he had failed in his duty to liberty, but because his inconsistency of action betrayed his ignorance of the true and unequivocal heart of the matter — the utility of pressing:

Law was, at any rate, to be found to disarm government, in this fortunate exigence, of the strength of the able but unwilling. Each vagabond, rescued from the danger of being useful, would be a fresh reinforcement to the squadrons of patriotism: and though every such an one is indeed already her militia-man by birth, yet his important obligation could not but inspire him anew with a tenfold addition of zeal. The Aegis of Liberty was to be held up to cover all, and dazzle the eyes of weak-sighted observers.[29]

In Bentham's eyes English liberties were threatened, not by impressment, but by the Wilkesites' inflammatory and mischievous libertarian enthusiasm.

The next important catalytic agent in Bentham's intellectual development was to be John Lind, a pamphleteer and political opportunist whose family had known Bentham's since the 1750s,[30] who had in fact met the twelve-year-old 'little philosopher' named Jeremy Bentham in 1760,[31] and who returned to London in 1773, after having been a chaplain to the Levant Company in Constantinople and a privy councillor in Warsaw, acknowledged as the minister of King Stanislas of Poland in all but name.[32] In preparation for his return to England, Lind had been armed by King Stanislas with letters to both Lord North and Lord Mansfield. He was 'living in the high world, and in particular in ministerial circles.'[33] He and Bentham now became, as Bentham was later to recall, intimate friends.[34] Bentham emerged as Lind's co-author (although largely unacknowledged as such) in a series of literary undertakings between 1773 and 1778.

Bentham was closely involved in all of Lind's major projects during this period. The *Comment on the Commentaries*, for example, sprang from some attempts by Lind at a critique of Blackstone, which were quickly overshadowed by Bentham's wittier and more incisive efforts. Bentham quickly made the *Comment* his own, but continued, while proceeding with it, to help Lind with his *Remarks on the Principal Acts of the Thirteenth Parliament* and the *Answer to the Declaration of the American Congress*, undertaken largely because Lind had contracted to become a pamphleteer in behalf of Lord North's policies.[35] From Lind's point of view the *Remarks* and the *Answer* served to earn a living for him and a pension for his financially hard-pressed sisters. From Bentham's point of view, as we shall see, these works constituted the earliest public expressions of his political ideas, and opened the way to the pursuit of a lifetime of systematic theorizing.

There can be little doubt that this collaboration did much to establish Bentham's confidence as a theorist. Lind had enterprises constantly in mind, but as a writer he worked too quickly and carelessly to please Bentham: 'Lind's style did not satisfy me. There was a want of accuracy. I used to correct for him, and he assented to all my corrections. Nothing that anybody else wrote ever satisfied me: but I never made an alteration without having a reason for it.'[36] Bentham later asserted, in his reminiscences to John Bowring, that in the *Remarks* Lind had based 'the plan of argument' for his analysis of the acts leading up to the American War on 'two or three pages of private thoughts' Bentham had given him.[37] As for Bentham's own feelings on the war, he later claimed that 'by the badness of the arguments used on behalf of the Americans, on that side of the water as well as on this, my judgment, unwarped by connexion or hope, was ranked on the government side.'[38]

After the publication of the *Remarks* in 1775, Lind (with Bentham as silent partner) went on to publish his *Answer to the Declaration of the American Congress*.[39] Bentham never appears to have claimed authorship of this work, but his interest in 'American affairs' was certainly very keen, and the final shape of the *Answer* is a tribute to the force of Bentham's influence on Lind.[40] It was Bentham who had based his plan for the *Remarks* on the judgment that 'the whole of the [Americans'] case was founded on the assumption of natural rights, claimed without the slightest evidence for their existence, and supported by vague and declamatory generalities.'[41] There is, moreover, ample evidence that Bentham wrote a very important portion of the *Answer*, employing the same theoretical perspective. The true extent of his contribution is reflected by the conclusion, drawn by the editor of that part of Bentham correspondence, that the hints given to Lind by Bentham in a letter dated on or about 2 September 1776 may be supposed to have formed the basis for the argument of the fourteen-page 'Short review of the declaration' which concludes the *Answer*.[42] The examination of points of fact was to be left to Lind.[43] The waging of theoretical warfare, the demolition of the Americans' revolutionary principles, was to be Bentham's task.

From what we have already seen it is certainly indicative of Bentham's influence on the contents that the 'Short review' from its very opening moves relentlessly towards the identification of the theory of natural rights as the fountainhead of American delusions. It is the function of the preamble to the American Declaration, says Bentham, to put forward *A theory of government*: 'a theory as absurd and visionary, as the system of conduct in defence of which it is established, is nefarious.' Not only are the principal maxims of this theory 'repugnant to the British Constitution,' but 'beyond this they are subversive of every actual or imaginable kind of government.' Bentham next turns his attention to the conceptual foundations of this 'absurd and visionary' theory of government. The most important of these is the Americans' reliance on the notion that 'the laws of Nature, and of Nature's God,' support their political claim to 'an equal and separate station' in relation to the British sovereignty and 'among the powers of the earth.' Thus the concepts of natural law and natural rights are quickly brought to centre stage.

The first and most fundamental natural right claimed in the Declaration of Independence is the right of natural equality. The influence of Filmer is evident in Bentham's rejection of the famous claim that 'all men are created equal':

If to what they now demand they were entitled by any law of God, they had only to produce the law, and all controversy was at end.

Instead of this, what do they produce? What they call self-evident truths. 'All Men,' they tell us, 'are created *equal*.' This surely is a new discovery; now, for the first time, we learn, that a child, at the moment of his birth, has the same quantity of natural power as the parent, the same quantity of political power as the magistrate.[44]

Filmer's patriarchal principle, expressed by Bentham in the observation that 'subjection, not independence, is the natural state of man,' provides a link between Bentham's rejection of natural equality under Divine or Natural Law and his subsequent rejection of a natural right to the enjoyment of, among other things, liberty:

The rights of 'life, liberty, and the pursuit of happiness' — by which, if they mean anything, they must mean the right to enjoy life, to enjoy liberty, and to pursue happiness — they hold to be unalienable ...

[At this point, happily, we reach the first words of the extant sheet of Bentham's letter, and can continue the argument by quotation from it.]

This they 'hold to be' a ... 'truth self-evident'. At the same time to secure these rights they are satisfied that Governments should be instituted. They see not or will not seem to see that nothing that ever was called government ever was or ever could be in any instance exercised save at the expence of one or other of those rights, that ... in as many instances as Government is ever exercised, some one or other of these pretended inalienable rights is alienated.[45]

He goes on to illustrate the alienation of such rights at the hands of the Americans themselves. This is not the work of a legal analyst, pure and simple, but the exasperation of a political theorist outraged by what seemed to him the popularity of a pernicious and incoherent form of political discourse in defence of an indefensible theory of government.

Taken together, this reply to the American Declaration of Independence and the critique of Blackstone's apology for accepted theories of sovereignty and of government represent the first flowering of Bentham's political thought. The notion, presented in the *Fragment*,[46] that government is founded, not on a natural right to liberty, but on a 'habit of obedience,' and the demonstrations of the alienation of the 'unalienable right to the enjoyment of liberty' in the *Answer* to the American Declaration rest on the same premise: that the value of such entities as liberty and equality cannot be assessed or defended by an ultimately senseless or tautological reference to other abstractions such as 'natural law' or 'natural right,' but can only be established by reference to the principle of utility, whose dictates are derived from the empirical calculation of the concrete consequences of particular policies for assignable groups of people and things.

In the *Gazetteer* for March and early April of 1776, John Lind published a series of eight letters signed 'Attilius.'[47] In the third and fourth letters he gave a definition of liberty. In later ones he promised to define also the word 'right.' Bentham wrote to him to demand a public acknowledgment of his title to the authorship of both ideas. 'Right,' he said, he had defined in the *Fragment on Government*. Lind had 'meant' to quote it, but had in fact published his letters (by a change of plan) too early to be able to do so. As to 'liberty,' Bentham reminded him,

It may have been half a year or a year or more, I do not precisely recollect the time, since I communicated to you a kind of discovery I thought I had made, that the idea of *liberty*, imported nothing in it that was positive: that it was merely a negative one: and that accordingly I defined it 'the absence of restraint': I do not believe I then added 'and constraint': that has been an addition of your own. You mentioned it to me t'other day with this addition. In the meantime I had discovered the defect: and had changed in my papers, the word *restraint* into *coercion*, as that which would include both *restraint* and *constraint*. This new term I then communicated to you, and you have adopted it in preference to the other two.[48]

Bentham demanded that Lind 'exculpate' him from any suspicion of plagiarism regarding his idea of liberty. This notion was too distinctive and too important to his system to be allowed to escape into other hands: 'The Definition of Liberty is one of the cornerstones of my system: and one that I know not how to do without.'[49] He received the acknowledgement he had demanded when, shortly afterward, Lind published his *Three Letters to Dr Price*, a prominent and substantial pamphlet. For good measure, he received also a touch of advance promotion from Lind, who informed his readers that 'this notion of liberty will make a leading principle in a work which this gentleman means, and I hope soon, to give the world. In that work, whenever it appears, Dr Price may learn, what he already professes to teach, without having learned – to give "correct ideas," "distinct and accurate views".'[50]

The immediate cause of this outburst of polemics on the subject of liberty was, of course, the work of 'the Doctor,' Dr Richard Price, non-conformist minister and author of *Observations on the Nature of Civil Liberty, the Principles of Government, and the Justice and Policy of the War with America* (1776). It was quite natural that Lind should focus his attention on Dr Price's *Observations*, for it was a work of the greatest popularity, reckoning by its sales in 1776, and can be 'regarded as one of the inspirers of the Declaration of Independence.'[51] As Lind was Lord North's pamphleteering defender, Dr Price was naturally his enemy, just as the authors of the Declaration of Independence were to become objects of his wrath later in the year. Bentham, for his part, was to recall many years later in his memoirs that 'Dr Price and his "self-Government" made me an anti-American' (170.175). Price was a zealot – a libertarian enthusiast who, by the admission of the man who eulogized him at his funeral (Joseph Preistley), added little or nothing to 'the clearness of the principles' governing liberty, but inspired his readers with 'love of it, and zeal for it.'[52] Zeal was no substitute for clarity in Bentham's opinion. In manuscript passage listing a number of illustrious thinkers (Locke, Blackstone, and others), together with brief summaries of his complaints against them, he inscribed two objections beside Price's name: 'Liberty not the child of law. Security not destroyed by unlimited Supremacy' (69.43).

Dr Price posited liberty as an end in itself, a condition comprehending and containing within itself the essence of happiness. His deeply held religious convictions may account for his vision of happiness as beatitude or as knowledge of virtue. We have seen, however, that Bentham, for his part, rejected the notion of any invariable connection between liberty and happiness or liberty and virtue. His conception of happiness as an aggregate of pleasure in a physiological sense was incompatible with Price's vision. It was spiritual freedom which constituted, for Price, an opening of the gateway to man's predestined path to happiness and virtue. It was his faith in the existence of an innate will to rectitude and virtue that separated him from Bentham by an unbridgeable abyss: 'every man's will, if perfectly free from restraint, would carry him invariably to rectitude and virtue; and ... no one who acts wickedly acts as he likes, but is conscious of a tyranny within him overpowering his judgment, and carrying him into a conduct for which he condemns and hates himself. The things that he would he does not; and the things that he would not, those he does. He is, therefore, a slave in the properest sense.'[53]

Freedom for Dr Price meant the absence of certain wicked impulses, and complete subservience instead to others – a conception, one would think, not unlike Bentham's notion of total subservience to our 'sovereign masters,' pleasure and pain.[54] To Bentham, of course, the two theoretical constructs were as different as night and day – or as theology and physiology. Bentham's subservience would lead, demonstrably, to happiness. Price's ideas would serve as 'a cloak, and pretence, and aliment, to despotism.'[55]

It was Price who initiated debate, attacking in his *Observations*[56] Lind's proposition, stated in his *Remarks*, that 'a people has no rights other than those allowed by its civil governors.'[57] 'In every free state,' Price argued, 'every man is his own Legislator. – All taxes are free gifts for public services. All laws are particular provisions or regulations established by *common consent* for gaining protection and safety. – And all *magistrates* are trustees or Deputies for carrying these regulations into execution.'[58] As a complement to this definition of personal liberty within a free state, Price also put forward a definition of civil liberty as the liberty characterizing the actions of the state itself: 'a power of a *civil society* or *state* to govern itself by its own discretion; or by laws of its own making, without being subject to any foreign discretion, or to the impositions of any extraneous will or power.'[59] Lind's response to these hypotheses was, as we know, to expound and advocate Bentham's negative ideas of liberty and of right in his *Three Letters*. Dr Price acknowledged the *Three Letters* in his *Additional Observations of the Nature and Value of Civil Liberty*, published in 1777. He took explicit exception to Bentham-cum-Lind's notion of liberty, and lashed out with some venom at 'Attilius': 'Civil liberty, he insists, is nothing positive. It is, an *absence*. The absence of coercion, of constraint and restraint. Not from civil governors, (they are *omnipotent* and there can be no liberty against them). But from such little despots and plunderers as common pick-pockets, thieves, house-breakers etc.'[60]

Bentham had tried to emphasize the distinction between declaring the sovereignty of governors to be unlimited and declaring it to be difficult to circumscribe: 'the field, if one may say so, of the supreme governor's authority, though not *infinite*, must unavoidably, I think, *unless* where limited by express convention, be allowed to be *indefinite*.'[61] This point he had carefully worked out in the *Fragment*, which Dr Price might well have read by 1777. For Price the problem was how to reduce the power of governors and increase the quantum of 'liberty against them.' For Bentham it was to define, and thus limit by 'express convention,' the powers of governors so as to minimize the effective need or demand for 'liberty against them' as contrasted with liberty secured by them.

John Lind was by no means the only person to publish a response to Dr Price's *Observations*. Among Price's 'critics without number' there was, in fact, one other with whom Bentham almost went so far as to establish contact. This was Richard Hey, a young member of the Middle Temple and, in his own particularly hesitant fashion, a utilitarian. In his *Observations Concerning the Nature of Civil Liberty*,[62] Hey diffidently and tentatively examined the possibility of analysing liberty as the product of a utilitarian system of morals and legislation. He made so bold as to say that he felt Locke's theory of the role of the majority of validating laws and governments was based on utilitarian premises: 'It is, then, upon the principle of utility that he builds his reasoning – the foundation of all laws Civil and (perhaps) Moral.'[63] Hey argued that Price's proposition, that a state governed by its own will was free, was a tautology. In a statement reminiscent of Bentham in the *Fragment*, he asserted: 'A *state* is neither more nor less free, according to his definition, on account of its power being lodged in proper or improper hands.'[64]

Somehow, perhaps by pure coincidence or perhaps because of its espousal of utilitarianism, Richard Hey's work caught Bentham's eye as well. After reading Hey's *Observations*, Bentham drafted a letter to Lind in which he pronounced himself pleased with the work as a whole: 'I have just been perusing with no small pleasure and satisfaction a pamphlet just published on the subject of Liberty and Government by Mr Hey of the Middle Temple: which I think cannot fail of throwing considerable light on those important and much-debated topics' (69.57).

A multitude of possible applications of utilitarian principles to the problems of liberty and government were suggested in Hey's *Observations*. In a section dealing with the 'General idea of the perfection of civil liberty,' Hey described the 'principle of legislation' which 'leads to the point of Perfection in Civil Liberty.' It is 'to avoid, as much as possible, multiplying restraints upon the subject.'[65] On the other hand, as a utilitarian, he was able to defend those civil restraints which actually contribute to the public's capacity to enjoy its liberties, as Bentham would wish:

'Where they are the necessary means to such an end, the best part that human wisdom and human benevolence can act, is to impose them. And, when imposed, they may possibly increase the Liberty of the peaceable citizen. Not indeed his *civil liberty*, understood as the *absence of civil restraints*; for that must certainly be diminished by every additional civil restraint. But a law may, by tying up the hands of the violent and unprincipled, contribute more to the liberty of the peaceable citizen than it takes away from his liberty by the new restraint which it does itself impose.'[66]

Hey grasped the idea, which was to be an important principle for Bentham, of the essential evil of all restraint.[67] He also brought forth a utopian vision to which Bentham must surely have responded sympathetically, for it was the embodiment of principles that either already were, or were to become, central to his own writings. If the understandings of men, Hey said, were adequate to the complexities of society, and their discipline great enough to make that understanding always direct the will, 'we should be in a condition superior to the necessity of civil restraints.' We should then enjoy a liberty 'as much superior to that Perfection of civil liberty which the present Ignorance and Perverseness of men will (under the best legislation) admit, as this is to the civil liberty enjoyed in states oppressed by tyranny, or disturbed by licentiousness.'[68] The crucial difference between Hey and Bentham lies in the fact that Hey, good Christian and obedient Lockean that he was, aimed only to augment the powers of understanding, while Bentham, religious cynic and skeptic and critic of Locke's *Essay*, intended to condition the will itself by a system of socially engineered motivational stimuli – a behavioural psychologist's maze of pleasures and pains. This approach, too, might render restraints invisible and painless and thus transport men to a condition beyond sensitivity to them, but only by the annihilation of such sensitivity, not by the elimination of restraints.

Hey's *Observations* began with 'the common Acceptation of the word, Liberty,' and it was Hey's attitude to 'disputes about mere words'[69] that excited most of Bentham's direct comments. Hey argued, with special reference to liberty, that care, clarity, and consistency in the definition of key terms was fundamental to constructive debate.[70] After providing several examples of common usages, Hey drew the conclusion that 'the idea of liberty is merely negative, and is only the *absence of restraint*.'[71] Having reached this position, he read 'with pleasure and attention' Attilius's letter in the *Gazetteer* of 27 March 1776. He took issue with Bentham and Lind on the question whether or not constraint should be brought into the definition, concluding that he remained inclined towards retaining his own definition.[72]

Bentham responded with some relish to this implicit invitation to a dialogue. He drafted, at one point, a statement, to be inserted by Lind in a future edition of the *Three Letters*, which reveals his own plan to write a paper for publication, defending his definition of liberty against Hey's arguments. Lind's announcement was to read as follows:

Since the above sheets were printed off I have received from the friend from whom I have already acknowledged myself to have taken the first hint of the

Definition of Liberty given in ... the following paper. The purpose of it is [to] justify that definition against an objection contained in a pamphlet just published ... by Richard Hey F.R.A. and Barrister at Law. As it may serve to throw some further light upon one of the subjects that have been handled in the foregoing paper, I thought it might be of use to subjoin it here. (69.57)

Bentham penned eleven folio pages of notes for this paper, and a large part of this body of material was devoted to clarifying the distinction between Hey's opinion that 'the common notion of Liberty is *merely* absence of *restraint*'[73] and Bentham's assertion that to be complete the definition ought to include the absence of constraint as well, and thence the absence of coercion, which could be understood to include both restraint and constraint. It was, in itself, a mild and minor dispute. Bentham was using the point partly as a pretext on which to start a dialogue with Hey. He admired Hey's 'candour and discernment' as a writer, and hoped to convert him to his own way of thinking – or even to be converted by him (69.57). He claimed to sense a certain fellowship with both Hey and Lind because they were as aware as he of the practical importance of questions of definition and terminology.

Men of reflection, who, like you and Mr Hey, are in the habit of carrying your views into the depths of Jurisprudence, know that the import of words, and particularly of thus-frequent and fundamental words, is the hinge on which the main body of the science turns. They see that it is not uncommon for questions of the first practical importance to depend for their decision upon questions concerning the import of these words ... Tis from a particular construction put upon the word liberty and a few others that the popular divine [i.e. Dr Price] whom you combat with so much force has inferred the impropriety of waging the war against America. (69.60)

Bentham turned next to the overemphasis on restraint as the enemy of liberty, and the resulting underemphasis on constraint, which had, as he saw it, led Richard Hey astray (69.59). In explanation he commented that 'in a survey of human life points of negative duty offer themselves to our view in rather greater number than points of positive duty.' From the personal point of view, 'we have more frequent occasion to consider what we are *not* to do, than what we *are* to do' (ibid.). As for governments, they have more occasion to use the rein than the spur. Enlarging upon this point, Bentham expounded his conception of the idea of property and its relationship to liberty. In practical life, he said, the notion of property is always before our eyes, for almost every object we observe is someone's legal property, 'and what constitutes legal property as we have so often said to one another is nothing but restraint; the imposing ... of negative duty, the making it the duty of every man but the proprietor to abstain from ... [meddling with] the thing in question' (69.59).[74] Also fundamental to daily living, he continued, is the 'faculty of locomotion' by which we are enabled to pursue and procure all manner of benefits and to avoid or avert evils. It is solely by restraint that we are deprived of this faculty. Instances of positive duty, or constraint, were admittedly 'copious' in England, but in the aggregate the sum of positive duties paled into insignificance, quantitatively and qualitatively, by comparison with the negative duties which 'establish property' and 'confer personal security.' 'In that state of regular / singular / polity in which we live in Britain,' Bentham concluded, Britons felt the pains of restraint more frequently and prominently than those of constraint.

This does not mean that polities do not exist where constraint is much the more predominant evil. Examples were close to hand: 'in the West Indies or the Southern Provinces of North America, where the spectacle of slavery is continually before men's eyes, the latter seems to be that which would be most forward to occur' (69.59). Bentham's basic point is that when we think of a slave regaining his liberty we think of him as ceasing to be constrained to work. Where simple punishment is deprivation of liberty by restraint, enslavement is deprivation of liberty by constraint. Bentham did not wish to deny that the term 'liberty' was used to denote the absence of constraint on account of the element of restraint which constraint 'necessarily includes.'[75] He merely proposed to add that liberty can also be used to denote the absence of the greater evil of constraint in cases where that evil is 'more forward to occur' than is the fortunate case in England's 'happy island.'[76]

It is not surprising that when the abuse of terms and the importance of clear language and rigorous terminology were uppermost in Bentham's mind some of the elements of his 'theory of fictions' seem to be present in embryo.[77] To begin with, it is clear, Bentham's distrust and dislike of 'fictions' stemmed largely from a belief (reinforced, as we have seen, by Dr Price's activities) that they were symptoms – indeed causes – of the infectious disease of 'political enthusiasm': 'A sober and accurate apprehension of the import of these fundamental words is a true key to Jurisprudence and the only effectual antidote against the fascinations of political enthusiasm' (69.62). The fundamental conceptual error about liberty is to forget that it is a 'fiction' and to treat it as though it were itself a real entity, a concrete object: 'We speak of it as being abridged, that is made shorter, of its being invaded, broken in upon, as if it had a piece cut out of it, of its being violated ... It is manifest that it is only by means of fiction that Liberty is anything that can be the subject of these or any other operations' (69.61). Bentham shows concisely how the fictional manner of speaking about liberty can be translated into language referring to 'nothing but realities':

To say that the cost that is on your back is what you have a property in and that in virtue of the restraint imposed on me by the Law, i.e. the body of Governors for the time being, I am not at liberty to meddle with it, is but a loose and figurative though familiar way of intimating what is the real state of the case; viz: that by the mode of conduct habitual in those Governors, a certain kind [?] of punishment, i.e. of pain, is made [the] probable consequence of any act whereby against your consent I could be said to meddle with it. In this latter mode of phraseology we have nothing but realities — substances, motions or perceptions ... The former serves to convey the truth no otherwise than by the chances it has of suggesting indirectly, as it were derivatively, those ideas which are suggested directly and originally by the latter. (69.61-2)

Where others had referred to liberty as an abstraction, Bentham came to call it a 'fictitious entity.' It was not, he decided, a substance, a motion or a perception; hence, not a 'real entity.' Hey, he observed, had correctly concluded that liberty was a word incapable of definition, but for the wrong reason — because he believed it to stand for a simple idea (69.62). Examples of simple ideas would be 'You' or 'I' (substances), 'meddling' (any *specific* instance of such), or 'Pain' (a perception). Liberty is not a simple idea because it is not the idea of a real entity; it is a fiction, and the truth is that there is no idea 'belonging to it.'

Liberty, in a word, can not be defined: but it may be made up with other words into a sentence: and the import of that sentence may be rendered determinate and clear according to the method of the Author of the Fragment, by being paraphrased, that is by being turned altogether into another sentence. Property, Restraint, Liberty are not any of them either substances, Motions or Perceptions ... If then these words can any of them serve to represent things that can be discoursed of as existing, it is only in the way of metaphor and by a fiction. (69.62-3)

By his reasonings Jeremy Bentham hoped to persuade Richard Hey ('this intelligent and candid writer') that he might 'upon further consideration see reason to depart from / relinquish [his position]' (69.67-8). Bentham's notes on Hey's *Observations*, however, give us far more than the record of an abortive attempt to win over the mind of an obscure writer on a narrowly semantic question. In Bentham's own eyes the implications of this dispute were anything but narrow. In the course of it he became fully aware that a radical reconstruction of legal and political discourse would be a necessary precondition of the advancement of the cause of practical legal and political reform in England as elsewhere. He had no doubt that this order of priorities was correct.

The entire course of his writing and reform activities testifies to the fact that once awakened to the importance of the definition of fundamental words even in the most practical disputes, and to the mischievous consequences of the abuse of 'fictitious' terms, his critical faculties never slept thereafter.

PART TWO / INVENTION

4

Fundamental words

The first methodological principle of Bentham's censorial reforming system was: Define your words.

Define your words says Locke: Define your words says Helvetius. Define your words says Voltaire: Define your words says every man who knows the value of them, who knows the use of them, who understands the things they are wanted to express: Define them for the rules of Physics: define them for the sake of Ethics; but above all define them for the sake of law. Philosophers, I have obeyed you. I *have* defined my words: and with more especial care, where with venturous / presumptuous / grasp I have taken in hand the sceptre of legislation. (27.45)[1]

To the force of example was added the force of utility. Bentham summed up the utility of clear and conclusive definitions in another early manuscript fragment: 'The words defined are all so many given quantities and possessing them, the Jurist finds himself rich in means for the solution of any problem in his science' (69.161).[2] Definitions must be the tools of the law reformer, as, indeed, they ought to be those of the legislator himself. In the early 1770s Bentham set out to sharpen his own analytical tools by radically reconstructing the meanings of those fundamental words on whose definitions the value and validity of his scientific endeavours was to hinge.

Under the influence of the infuriating natural rights arguments advanced by the American revolutionaries in 1776,[3] and especially disturbed by the contractual theory of the origins of government propounded by the Americans' oracle, John Locke,[4] Bentham embarked on a critique of common usages of the term 'liberty,' which was to provide the terminological basis for his rejection of 'natural liberty' as well. His first step was to reject the 'common notion concerning rights': 'that they subsist, at least many of them some how or other of themselves: and that then human laws come in and enforce them. That they do not in themselves originate from human Laws; consequently that it is not from the notion of human Laws that the notion of these rights is to be derived' (69.213).[5] The common notion of rights, and the sort of discourse so frequently derived from it as a premise, seemed to Bentham to epitomize the substitution of empty rhetoric for thought: 'Talk of *right*: — say a man has a *right* to such a thing in such a case, and we have no matter of fact to encumber ourselves with — When you have said he has a right — insist upon it: ... all proof is needless. The business is thus settled in a trice by the help of a convenient word or two, and without the pains of thinking' (69.6-7).[6]

The next step was to denounce the theory that natural right forms the foundation of civil right: 'True, say they, it is by punishment that the civil right is constituted: but antecedent to the establishment of Government, antecedent to the introduction of punishment, there was a certain natural right on which this civil right was grounded. Yes on *utility*, if that will serve the turn, there was; or otherwise the establishment of the civil right is not to be justified' (ibid.). Bentham's contention is in fact that only utility will serve the turn. To ground one species of right upon another species of right is tautological. If the primary or validating species is an abstract, metaphysical species, validation by reference to it is worse than tautological: it is delusive. Unless natural right is understood to be a redundant and confusing code word for utility, it has no meaning at all. To an adherent of the common notion of right, however, it is the word 'right' as a sort of fetish that matters, not the meaning conveyed by it nor the facts of the specific case: 'No — at all events we must have the word *right*. Talk of utility, and of pains and pleasures, this is grounding your doctrine on matters of fact: and to enquire into and duly to collect the matters of fact takes more *trouble* than they are *willing*, and perhaps more sagacity than they are *able*, to bestow' (ibid.). The connection between the discussion of the term 'right' and the idea of liberty is made quite clear when Bentham asserts that 'of Rights some are synonymous to Powers others to Liberties — limitations to Public Constitutional Powers and created by the absence of coercion' (69.213).

Bentham proposed to ground his doctrine on matters of fact, instead of on mere words, by making words and matters of fact always interchangeable, that is, by constructing a vocabulary reducible to simple ideas. His attack was thus directed towards the enemies of such progress: complex ideas, and especially 'abstractions' and 'fictions.'

In terms of the analysis in Locke's *Essay Concerning Human Understanding*, liberty falls into the category of general ideas or abstractions, whose genesis is described in the chapter on 'Complex ideas.'[7] There Locke explains that 'all *complex ideas*' are made by an 'act of the mind ... combining several simple ideas into one compound one,' that *'ideas of relation*' are formed by a mental act juxtaposing two ideas, simple or complex, 'without uniting them into one,' and that *'general ideas*' are formed by a process called 'abstraction,' by which ideas are separated 'from all other ideas that accompany them in their real existence.'[8] In a later chapter Locke goes on to distinguish between 'real ideas,' which is to say 'such as have a conformity with the real being and existence of things, or with their archetypes,' and 'fantastical or chimerical' ideas, 'such as have no foundation in nature, nor have any conformity with that reality of being to which they are tacitly referred, as to their archetypes.' Strictly speaking, Locke finds that complex ideas fall into the latter category, for 'being combinations of simple ideas put together, and united under one general name, it is plain that the mind of man uses some kind of liberty in forming [them].' He is even more emphatic about 'Mixed modes and relations' (liberty belonging in some instances to the mixed mode category): 'there is nothing more required to this kind of ideas to make them real, but that they be so framed, that there be a possibility of existing conformable to them.'[9] Locke's theory is that the mind, the passive receptor of simple ideas, exercises 'an *active* power' in combining simple ideas to make complex ones. Thus all complex ideas are ultimately 'resolvable into simple ideas, of which they are compounded and originally made up.' To enumerate all the mixed modes 'which have been settled, with names to them' seemed to Locke to be a task outside the scope of his *Essay*: 'That would be to make a dictionary of the greatest part of the words made use of in divinity, ethics, law, and politics, and several other sciences. All that is requisite to my present design, is to show what sort of ideas those are which I call mixed modes; how the mind comes by them; and that they are compositions made up of simple ideas got from sensation and reflection; which I suppose I have done.'[10]

Bentham shared Locke's view that 'the mind is wholly passive in the reception of all its simple ideas.' He also held, with Locke, that simple ideas are 'the materials and foundations of the rest.'[11] But on the question of mixed modes such as liberty, and 'how the mind comes by them,' Bentham took a position fundamentally different from Locke's. Of the three 'acts of the mind, wherein it exerts its power over its simple ideas' mentioned in the *Essay*, that is, combination, juxtaposition, and abstraction,[12] only juxtaposition could, in the view of Bentham, the philological nominalist, be said to occur without recourse to fiction. The mind might compare, but it could not truly compound nor abstract. Bentham did not attempt to deny the existence of compound or complex ideas, but he did insist that, once formed, they were only truly meaningful when the user and the hearer were aware of their fictitious nature. He argued that 'correspondent to each species of Material real Entities is a fictitious one' and that 'Fictitious Entities are feigned in imitation of real ones.' He gave examples: 'Instances of Fictitious substances are Qualities, Powers, dispositions, anything which not being a substance is said to Act or which a man is said to hear' (106.2).

As another, perhaps less sinister, way of describing incorporeal entities or the ideas which stand for them, Bentham used the term 'abstract.' In a manuscript page headed simply 'Entities,' he divided entities in general into 'real entities,' 'abstract entities' of the first, second, and third orders, and 'Anomalous abstract entities,' including 'the passions, the appetites, conditions, circumstances etc.' – and thus, we may add, including 'liberty' (106.2-3). According to his draft outline of the preparatory principles of his system, he planned to devote at least three analytical subsections of his argument to the task of showing that abstract ideas have, in themselves, no reality. The headings involved were to be 'No Ideas purely abstract / No abstract ideas / Imaginary existences no proof of abstract ideas.'

Bentham's intention was not to deny that abstract terms were formed in discourse by generalization and combination of simple terms, and hence composed of simple ideas. It was all too clear to him that this happened constantly. As an admirer of the philological perspectives of James Harris and John Horne Tooke, however, he attacked these ingrained linguistic habits as the fountainheads of fiction and the ultimate sources of the kind of word fetishism exemplified by the Americans' political rhetoric. For purposes of discourse, of communication, fictions were constantly necessary. This did not alter the fact that they embodied illusions and were frequently the source of errors of immense practical significance.

With these views in mind, Bentham turned to the task, which Locke had refused, of enumerating all the mixed modes 'which have been settled, with names to them.' This was indeed, as Locke had said, 'to make a diction-ary ... [of] the greatest part of the words made use of in divinity, ethics, law and politics, and several other sciences.'[13] At one point, in 1779, temporarily hampered by eye troubles, Bentham discovered an 'excellent job' for a 'man without eyes.' This was 'to get a boy and set him to read Johnson's Dicty, for me to class the words by bidding him mark one with M. for Metaphysics, another E. for Ethics (etc.) ... I shall also number them M_1, M_2 etc.' By this means, Bentham believed, one could arrive at 'a compleat vocabulary for each science.'[14]

Nor was his enthusiasm restricted to the study of vocabulary. In the fields of grammar, syntax, and etymology, taken together, he hoped to find the linguistic foundations for the transformation of legal, ethical, and political argument. The Science of Man would have its roots in philology. He showed great interest in such works as James Harris's *Hermes, or a Philosophical Enquiry Concerning*

Universal Grammar and John Horne Tooke's *Diversions of Purley*.[15] On the subject of Harris's *Hermes* he told his brother Samuel of his enthusiasm for the
enterprise and his awareness of the shortcomings of Harris's way of pursuing it:
'The whole business of [Harris's *Hermes*] is to explain the relations, the
differences and resemblances of the several "parts" (as they are called), of
speech ... Being simple in the expression, he takes for granted that they are so in
the idea. But several of them are not so.' As a guide to 'the mechanical
disposition of the words' in discourse, Bentham drew up 'a rough *tree*' which he
looked forward to showing to his brother when next they met.[16] Nine months
after the letter in which *Hermes* and Bentham's 'tree' were discussed, Bentham
thanked Samuel for his 'grammatical communications' and congratulated him on
his adoption of Bentham's 'systematical strain.' 'I hope,' Bentham counselled,
'you will not want courage to persevere.'[17] Bentham himself did not lack the
necessary courage. The systematic definition of key terms in important spheres
of discourse became a major preoccupation in the years preceding the
completion and, in some cases, the publication of his main works. Moreover,
when those works appeared they reflected faithfully his devotion to the
development of a vocabulary for each and every science, adapted to its
perspective and purpose, minimizing ambiguity and maximizing the scientific
characteristics of precision, universality, and invariability. In Bentham's view,
the provision of such a vocabulary was the prime function of 'Metaphysics, the
most sublime and useful of all human sciences, according as it is applied, or the
most futile' (69.155). We shall now examine Bentham's 'Metaphysics' from the
perspective afforded by his analysis of the idea of liberty.

Throughout the 1770s and the early 1780s Bentham strove to bring forth a
magnum opus, a capital work of censorial jurisprudence, yet in the course of all
those years of unremitting effort only the *Fragment on Government* in 1776 and
the *Defense of Usury* in 1787 were published, and the *Fragment* circulated as an
anonymous work. The works now known to us as the *Introduction to the
Principles of Morals and Legislation* and *Of Laws in General*, the essays on 'The
influence of place and time in matters of legislation' and on 'Indirect legislation,'
and indeed the *Comment on the Commentaries*, had all been brought to
completion in some sense by 1782, yet none of them entirely satisfied Bentham.
He wanted to present a system to the world — not a succession of isolated
pieces, but the whole intricate intellectual mosaic taking shape in his mind.
Determined that his specific works and his comprehensive system should be
properly understood and appreciated, he was unwilling to publish individual
works unless both he and the public could achieve a clear understanding of their
relationship to his system as a whole. Potential readers would have to wait
patiently as the long and arduous process of honing ideas and framing a more

and more comprehensive system proceeded. His waiting over, the reader would have to be prepared to abandon any or all of his comforting and conventional beliefs to be initiated into a new realm of knowledge. In a spirit reminiscent of Locke's 'Epistle to the reader' at the outset of his *Essay*,[18] Bentham stressed, in a letter to his father, the inevitable difficulties of his work and his determination to go forward with it in search of such rewards as might be attained by one engaged in this sort of endeavour. To a query regarding the 'abstruseness' of his reasoning he replied: 'excuse the liberty I take in supposing that with regard to some parts that abstruseness may possibly appear greater to you in common with others of your former profession [i.e. lawyer], than to men at large as, besides having a new language to acquire, you have the old one to unlearn.'

Bentham tried to convince his father that he was immersed in a sincere, indeed compulsive, search for 'deep truths' such as might win him the attention and respect both of the public at large and of the masters of his chosen science. Nor did he fail to emphasize the importance of his services to human understanding: 'any tolerable share of success in such an undertaking as mine, you are sensible, must needs work a considerable revolution.'[19] In late 1776, referring to the 'Theory of punishment,' on which he had probably been working when he wrote to his father in 1772, he showed the same Lockean spirit in a draft letter (unsent) to Voltaire: 'Perhaps what I have done may be found but cobweb-work. Such as it is however it is spun out of my own brain. As such I send it you. It is neither borrow'd nor pilfer'd. I have spent upon it in the whole already about 7 years. I mean to bestow upon it the rest of my days.'[20] Bentham's 'cobweb-work,' the process by which ideas were 'spun out of his own brain,' deserves close attention.

In a letter of July 1784, Bentham's spirits apparently sagged under the weight of a sense that he had completed the task of inventing his ideas without as yet having made much progress in putting them in order: 'I have no relish for anything that is commonly called pleasure ... all conversation in short which does not bear a reference to my own or my brother's pursuits, is become insipid to me. My own ideas are become no less so: for the task of invention has for some time been accomplished, and all that remains is to put in order ideas ready formed.' Moreover, he added, 'to put them in order according to my notions of order, I must have them all before me at once ... in black and white.'[21] From the organized manuscripts extant it should have been quite possible by the late 1770s for Bentham to order his key ideas on a number of important subjects then before his eyes 'in black and white.'[22] These manuscripts, some of them dating from the early 1770s, are largely devoted to concise, aphoristic expositions of the meanings of fundamental terms. 'Liberty' is prominent among them; so are 'security,' 'law,' and 'property' — all concepts whose relationships to liberty were of great interest to Bentham. Successive passages do not blend into a narrative flow, and sometimes the sequence of ideas dealt with on a page is not logical. On the whole, the manuscripts have the appearance of the first draft of a glossary of political terms. They comprise, not drafts of works, but 'Keys,' collections of concepts and specific analytic insights such as would provide a ready reservoir of arguments (and of the building blocks of argument) for the purposes embodied in larger works both systematic and polemic. It should not surprise us to find that as Bentham turned his mind more and more intensively toward the task of presenting his system in print, he increasingly concentrated, as a first step towards political argument, on the work of clarifying the meaning of the fundamental terms and propositions, that is, the basic ideas, on which his system was to be built. One might well wonder why, if their importance was so great, Bentham's preparatory manuscripts were never published. Apparently, as these manuscripts grew in complexity and volume, while the field of terminological analysis continued to stretch endlessly on before him, Bentham became convinced that such lengthy deliberations over terminology should not in fact be made public. On a manuscript page headed PPI he inserted the following note: 'It is of importance that decisions concerning the construction of words be not preserved: of such [as] these there is no end. 'Tis they that more than anything else contribute to the voluminousness of a system of jurisprudence' (69.36).

Further light is thrown on the nature of these manuscript sheets by another comment, this time alongside the marginal note 'Prefat. Chain of Definition a Ladder to Science': 'An orderly, unbroken, well compacted chain of definitions is the only sure ladder whereby a man can climb / make his way / up to / place himself on / the heights of science' (69.158). Considerations such as these weighed heavily in Bentham's mind as he added more and more sheets to the Key and Inserenda manuscripts. The relationship of these seminal fragments of analysis to the arguments finally presented in the *Fragment on Government*, the *Comment on the Commentaries*, the *Introduction to the Principles of Morals and Legislation, Of Laws in General*, and so on, would, if it proved possible to determine, require a volume of its own for a full exposition. What is important here is that the idea of liberty receives frequent consideration in these manuscripts and that the ways in which Bentham defined his words there exerted a fundamental influence on his later attempts to expound the essential principles and propositions of a new legal and legislative science.

Passages from the preparatory manuscripts can be used to throw light on widely scattered applications of the idea of liberty to various problem situations as they arose in Bentham's writings. For example, two pages under the heading 'Pugna Sanctionum' (i.e. the battle of the sanctions) are devoted to a consideration of the relative weights and characteristics of the political and moral 'sanctions,' Benthamic concepts later analysed in the *Introduction to the Principles of Morals and Legislation*.[23] The threat posed to personal and political liberty by the political sanction is recognized when Bentham observes that, should the political overpower the moral, 'the nation would groan under the most cruel tyranny.' This comment should be borne in mind by those, such as Gertrude Himmelfarb, who feel that the Bentham who designed the circular 'inspection-house' for the control and supervision of prisoners, patients, or employees, known as the 'Panopticon' could not have valued liberty.[24] Neither the practices employed in the Panopticon nor the theory of punishment it embodied threatened the extinction of liberty by sheer force of political power. Elsewhere in his discussion of the 'pugna Sanctionum' Bentham maintains that the political sanction is 'one of the grand supports of society' and that if it were overpowered by the moral sanction that support would be 'enfeebled and trampled down' (69.158). Nevertheless, when one becomes aware of the roles of punishment, reward, 'indirect legislation,' and education in Bentham's system, one realizes that the basic threat to liberty posed by it arises, not from the possibility of rampant political oppression, but from the possibility of all-pervasive and inescapable conditioning of individual behaviour by the manipulation of the moral sanction itself. To find the seed from which oppression grows within Bentham's thought it is necessary to look to such passages as the following, in which he deals with 'Offences against morality':

The State takes upon it to controul those acts of a man the consequences of which are in the first instance interesting only to himself, and that for two reasons. 1st that his happiness is the happiness of the community: 2ndly that his strength is the strength of the community.

If there be any difference it is the latter consideration that gives the state the best and most incontestible title it has thus to interfere. It may be a matter of doubt / question / whether there is reason to expect that the state will do / in general be apt to manage / better for a man than he will manage / do / for himself: but it is a matter that does not admitt of being questioned that the state will be apt to manage better for others than he will be apt to do / manage / for those others. (69.29)

In relation to the effect on liberty of the political and moral sanctions, this is clearly a rougher and less qualified statement of the ideas later dealt with in chapter 17 of the *Introduction*, section 1, 'Limits between private ethics and the art of legislation.' In our later discussion of that section, we shall bear in mind this justification of state interference with 'those acts of a man the consequences of which are in the first instance interesting only to himself' in the form of control imposed primarily through the instrument of the moral sanction. The justification of the use of the straightforward political sanction is that it is 'one of the grand supports of society.' The justification for 'controul' is much more expansive: the above manuscript passage seems to justify a total effort to 'manage' individual acts of initially private consequence in the service of a public 'strength' and a public 'happiness' with which, in this case, individual strength and happiness are 'artificially identified' in a truly authoritarian way. We shall not be surprised to find that Bentham later modified this position.

If part of Bentham's attention was focused on defining the nature and limits of sanctions and of state control generally, another large portion of his thought was devoted to the definition of that liberty which social control seemed so ominously to jeopardize. Liberty, however, is most frequently defined in Bentham's early manuscripts by its opposition to the coercive force of law (i.e. of the political sanction), not to control. In the manuscripts headed 'Crit. Jur. Crim.,' we find a clear expression of the necessarily coercive, and thus in a sense necessarily 'evil,' force of all law and all government:

'Woe be it to him who doeth evil that good may come. It is necessary that evil come, but woe be to him by whom it cometh.'
It is manifest that this text literally interpreted plucks up political society by the roots. To do evil that good may come is the universal role, and constant employ of Legislation / Government /. A Law when efficacious is either obeyed or executed. Where it is obeyed it displays itself in restraint: where not obey'd but executed, in punishment. (69.18)

In a sheet headed 'Key,' Bentham reinforces this picture of the nature of the force of law: 'an act of law is but an expression of will: and if a man wills anything in relation to any act it can but be one of two things; that it *shall* be done, or that it shall *not* be done. There is no medium: nor any other possible variety' (69.44).

Although on the next manuscript page Bentham unveiled the two important additional categories of 'Permission' and 'Counter-mandment,' he proceeded directly to define 'coercion' and thence 'liberty' solely with reference to command and prohibition:

In either of the two cases of command or prohibition, the person whose act it is that is in question, may be said (on account of such act) to be coerced: to be under coercion.
In the case of command he may be said to be constrained: to be under constraint.

In the case of prohibition he may be said to be restrained: to be under restraint.

Coercion then is distinguishable into constraint and restraint.

[And, under the marginal heading 'Free-Liberty':]

When a person is neither constrained nor restrained with respect to an act, neither constrained to do it nor restrained from doing it, he is said with respect to that act to be free, to be at *liberty*'. (69.44)

On the following manuscript sheet, in a passage quoted in part by Halévy in *The Growth of Philosophic Radicalism*,[25] Bentham repeats his assertion that the direct product of legal coercion is security, not simply liberty, and adds that permissive or countermanding laws only *appear* to create liberty. This they do by acting to remove pre-existing coercive laws. The crucial significance for him of the distinction between the 'genuine, original and proper sense of the word liberty,' which is the 'negative' sense of the term, and the idea of liberty as produced by law, which is to say as integrated into the concept of security, is once again emphasized as he discusses the relationship between the law and liberty:

Liberty then is neither more nor less than the absence of coercion. This is the genuine, original and proper sense of the word liberty. The idea of it is an idea purely negative. It is not anything that is produced by law. It exists without law and not by means of law. It is not producible at all by law, but in the case where its opposite *coercion* has been produced [by law] before. That which under the name of Liberty is so much magnified, as the invaluable, the unrivalled work of Law, is not *liberty*, but *security*. (69.44)[26]

On the next manuscript sheet he adds an emphatic postscript to this argument: 'It is of pernicious, most singularly exemplarily pernicious consequence to confound under one and the same name things in themselves so different from one another, and which have such frequent and such important occasion to be distinguished / and contrasted' (69.45).

Seven sheets below in the UCL manuscripts, we find Bentham reopening his discussion of the relationship between liberty and security as objects or products of law. His basic hypothesis is still that coercive law can never produce liberty directly – only indirectly, by implicitly or explicitly countermanding or replacing by a permission some previously existing coercive law or laws. When the law thus enlarges the areas in which liberty can be enjoyed, it does so, in effect, by means of its very inaction; by any other means legal coercion can produce only security. Bentham tells us that 'Political Liberty and Political

Security are things of a totally different nature. They are created by different operations: if operations these may still be called whereof the one consists in doing nothing. Liberty subsists by the restraints not being imposed upon ourselves. Security is produced by restraints being imposed on others.'[27] Later, however, in a passage also quoted (in part) by Halévy, Bentham in effect defines security as 'that Liberty that is produced by Law':

The Law to produce Liberty in any body must act on somebody. To act on somebody it must coerce. To coerce it must either restrain or constrain. From him whom it either constrains or restrains, it takes away liberty ... Law therefore cannot produce liberty but it must produce coercion at the same time: and it is by means of that very coercion and of nothing else that liberty is produced by it. Where there is no coercion, there is no security: there is none of that Liberty that is produced by Law. (69.56)

When we meet Bentham's doctrine that liberty is merely a branch of security we shall remember this passage, which captures better than any of Bentham's published pronouncements the exact implications of that doctrine. Considering the consistency with which analysts have concluded from his published pronouncements that Bentham was simply hostile to the idea of liberty, such clarification is of no small value. It is made quite evident in the preparatory manuscripts that Bentham saw a contrast amounting to antithesis between the man who imposes and accepts no restraints whatever upon his own actions, thus claiming absolute liberty at whatever social cost, and the man who lays claim to that security which is provided for him by restraints imposed upon other men as the essence of his social liberties. Bentham had no intention of endorsing an unrestricted authoritarianism identifying all liberty paradoxically with all coercion. He did, however, feel that restraints issuing from government could well have the effect of protecting some men from the restraints which might otherwise be imposed upon them by others: 'Is it by all coercion, then, that liberty is produced? By no means ... Is it then by all restraint? ... By no means. But of those acts alone [by] which were he to do them, he would restrain the liberty of another man: and thus it is plain it is not in that man whose acts it restrains that it produces liberty, but in the other. It is not in that man on whom it operates, but in that man whom it lets alone' (69.56).[28] Bentham here demonstrates his completely unambiguous opposition to unrestricted authoritarianism. The legislator, he says, can only claim to use the law to enhance or produce liberty when it is clear that the effect of the law is to restrain attempts by one man (or group) to invade the sphere of liberty of another. All other legal restraints (and presumably *all con*straints) can only be justified by the utilitarian consequences flowing from them – they cannot be justified on libertarian principles alone. The abiding, inherent evil of the law is that even in cases where it acts to secure liberties it 'produces liberty exactly in proportion as it produces coercion' (69.56), because under a system of law liberty is always related to security and is always secured by the employment of coercion. A general, unrestricted liberty is, for Bentham, by definition a state of anarchy: 'The Liberty of all persons with respect to all acts, subsists without Law, and cannot subsist with Law, (ibid.).

Liberty may be good or evil, laudable or licentious. It may subsist in opposition to law, to security, and to happiness or by virtue of law in intimate partnership with security in the service of happiness. Thus, 'according to the side he has occasion to take, it is the idea of liberty or that of coercion that a man dwells on with the most complacency / gives the greatest extent to. If it be to defend a measure of the ruling powers, then liberty in general is in great danger to pay for it. If it be to attack, then as the assailants are generally more violent than the defenders, coercion, that is government, is almost elbow'd off the stage' (ibid.). Throughout all of this, however, 'the idea of liberty is not for anything that has been said the less a negative one. That Law which is the cause of Liberty is something positive. But the liberty itself which that Law produces is but a negative. It is but the absence of coercion' (ibid.).

On a manuscript sheet from the 'Crit. Jur. Crim.' group (69.209), Bentham establishes a clear and highly significant distinction between two contrasting usages of the word 'liberty.' Beside the marginal heading 'Liberty political in perfection' he writes: 'A man might be said to possess political power in perfection if the Laws and Institutions of the society he lived in were such as subjected him to no other coercion than the good of the society required him to be subjected to.' Next follows the marginal heading 'Liberty personal,' with no corresponding text – a fact which may indicate that at this stage in his thinking Bentham was not prepared to hazard a definition of so broad a concept, preferring to restrict his observations to the political sphere. The next marginal heading, however, is 'Liberty political entire,' and Bentham's remarks under this head are clearly related to those given under 'Liberty political in perfection': 'A man might be said to possess political liberty entire if he were not subjected to any coercion whatever by the laws and institutions of any society whatever.' 'Liberty political in perfection' is an Aristotelian 'mean' – it lies between the two extremes of oppression on the one hand and 'liberty political entire' on the other. This illustrates another important characteristic of Bentham's thoughts on liberty: what he was most vehemently opposed to at every turn was what we would call, using a term of Bentham's own coining, the 'maximizing' argument: 'the more liberty the better.' Bentham's argument in the passages just cited, and again where he asserts that the quantum of liberty in a society is 'not in proportion to the bulk of law' (69.148), is that as liberty is not the *direct* product of law in any case, and as the enlargement of the liberty of one party by law generally involves infringements of the liberties of other parties, to say 'the more liberty the better' is not simply wrong, but also so confused and unrealistic a proposition as to be almost meaningless. One might as well say 'the more law the better.' Just as the value and effectiveness of law is not in proportion to its pure bulk, so the value of liberty is not related to the aggregate quantity of it in a society as a whole.

In some manuscript passages we find evidence of the alternative with which Bentham replaced the 'maximization' argument that he encountered in so much of the libertarian rhetoric of his day. Having reached the conclusion that liberty was neither the direct work of law nor proportional in its quantum to the bulk of law, Bentham turned to reconstructing his own view of its exact relationship to law. One important postulate, established in a passage headed 'Key,' is that to be accurate we must remember that what the law takes into direct consideration in all its operations is action and its consequences. The law does not act to maximize liberty, but to extend it, annihilate it, or restore it with regard to a certain act or class of acts in accordance with the law's calculation of the social consequences. In the following passage, for example, the advisability of an increase or decrease in the degree of liberty permitted depends entirely on the apparent consequences of the act itself:

If what is understood concerning [a man] be that he never has been coerced at all with respect to the act in question: that he neither has been constrained to do it, nor restrained from doing it, he is said to have been left free, to have been left at liberty: If what is understood concerning him be that he has been coerced in either way, and that afterwards the coercion has been taken off, he is said to have been *made free again*, or to have been restored to liberty. (69.44)[29]

In Bentham's mind the law could do more for the man who was and always had been at liberty to perform a given act than simply to leave him to it. The law could act positively (indeed coercively) to 'secure' him that liberty: thus the confusion, a truly crucial one in Bentham's estimation, between 'security' and 'liberty,' arose from the popular but fallacious opinion that liberty was the gift of law, when in fact the law could only restore liberties once previously held and now lost, or secure liberties presently held but not enjoyed because insecure:

The way in which Liberty came to be confounded with Security seems to be this. – You are the person, suppose, who in this sense owe your liberty to the

Law. That is, you are the person who are secured by it. I am the person *against* whom this liberty of yours is preserved by it. That is, I am the person *against* whom you are secured. I am restrained by the Law (with respect to the acts whatever they are that are in question) from either constraining or restraining you. (69.55).

He goes on in the same passage to distinguish between liberty as the indirect result of law, or, in other words, as the result of the absence of legal coercion, and security as the result of legal coercion aimed at preserving a given liberty or set of liberties:

Now in this case [the case above discussed] true it is that the liberty which you possess you are indebted for to the Law. That, in other words, this Liberty of yours is the work of Law. But then who are you in whom this Liberty is produced by it? The person on whom it acts? No, but the person on whom it forbears to act, and on whom it prevents me from acting. Liberty then is not the direct work of Law, but only the indirect. The effect of the Law is not in any way to produce liberty in him on whom it acts. For the only possible direct way in which it can act is either to produce coercion that is either constraint or restraint: or else to remove it after having laid it on. (69.55)

The Law, then, serves not to produce liberty but to endorse and secure certain specific liberties by the production or redistribution of sanctions, that is, of coercion. It would be within the spectrum of theoretical possibilities that liberty, at one extreme, might exist without security, which is to say without law. Bentham was to give his attention to this case once more in *Of Laws in General*; but, in a passage from the 'Key' manuscripts, he indicated that the value of liberty is much reduced by the absence of that security which law supplies: 'Liberty without security is that which is possessed by Hottentots and Patagonians. Liberty by security is that, the possession of which is the pride of Englishmen. The former are they who possess in perfection what has been called self-government: that is no government at all. Each man in particular governs himself: that is has nobody else to govern him: has nobody else to coerce him, for government is coercion' (69.55).

At the opposite end of the spectrum of theoretical possibilities, liberty may cease to exist in a case where government neglects it totally for the sake of a maximum of stability and order. Bentham argues, under the heading 'Security may exist without liberty,' that the individual needs protection against the law-making power as much as against other individuals:

It is not enough for me that I am at liberty as against you. It is not enough that I am secured from being constrained or restrained by you. My happiness may be as effectually destroy'd by my being constrained or restrained by the Law, as by you or any one ... To be restrained or to be constrained is Pain. It is pointless Pain, if the act I am restrained from doing be not an act the doing which would produce more pain than the not doing it would, that is to say, pain either to myself, or to some other person whom the Law is equally concerned to take care of. (69.55)

On another sheet, headed 'PPI,' Bentham focused attention on the characteristics of various law-making bodies, and attempted to distinguish between a 'popular government' and a 'free government' (69.158). 'The Government is popular,' he said, in proportion as the number of persons in the Government is great with respect to the number of persons in the State, and the powers that are lodged in great bodies of the Government [are] great in proportion to the powers lodged in small bodies.' The 'popularity' of a government in Bentham's sense of that word is thus measured by a calculation of the degree of popular participation in it, together with the degree of power actually wielded by bodies in which a broad spectrum of political participants are represented. The passage relating to 'Government free' is, sadly, partly illegible. Yet even what can be gleaned from the fragmentary remains is interesting: 'In a Government to some degree popular In proportion as the subjects know before hand the extent of the several powers executed over them [in margin: 'as the extent of the several powers of persons in the Government is fixed, so that ...'] ... condition of the people is free, or rather secure: and thence improperly by a Metonymy, the Government is said to be free.'

A government may be tyrannical or 'popular,' but it cannot truly be said to be 'free.' It is the essential function of government to organize, to coerce, to secure. Government cannot truly, directly make its subjects free, but it may make them secure, and thus maximize their access to those freedoms which serve the cause of happiness in compatibility with security. Freedom in the subject is not a power. Specifically, it is not the power to participate in government or to coerce others. Such freedom is essentially antisocial; it is against law, against society, and against security. Freedom in the subject is security of expectation: it is awareness that 'the extent of the several powers of persons in the Government' is fixed, and that the rules of social conduct he is bound to observe are 'known before hand.' Only in such circumstances is the citizen-subject free: free of anxiety, of insecurity, of the gnawing pain of uncertainty. Those pleasures allotted to him by law and social convention are guaranteed. Not for him the pain of isolation, of ostracism, of non-conformity. The burden of moral self-determination is gently lifted from his shoulders by the same hands (those of reason and of law) whose task it is to 'rear the fabric of felicity' in utilitarian society.

Only if one is not a utilitarian can one make the charge that Bentham's utilitarianism ultimately deprives the individual of his power of moral self-determination. Utilitarianism defines both the nature of the self and the canons of morals. If these definitions are accepted, utilitarianism becomes the very embodiment of moral self-determination, of the 'logic of the will.' If it is in fact true that 'every effort we can make to throw off our subjection' to the dictates of utility 'will serve but to demonstrate and confirm it,'[30] then there is no unjustifiable sacrifice of liberty in such subjection. The motto of the 'good citizen under a government of Laws,' is first of all 'To obey punctually.'[31]

Bentham in fact saw liberty and security as complementary products (directly or indirectly) of legal activity. It is clear, too, that he wished to forewarn and defend the citizen against the extinction or sanctification of either of them. The crucial task of clarifying the relationship between liberty and security he was to wrestle with throughout the 1770s and 1780s. He was confident, however, that liberty, if closely related to security, was less intimately involved with certain kinds of political state and with the 'multiplicity of laws' within a state than was commonly thought. He wrote:

Nothing can be more false than the notion that liberty is in general favoured by the multiplicity of the Laws: when spoken of thus [?] in the lump.

Political liberty, that is more properly speaking, political security is indeed in some degree in proportion to the multiplicity of the Laws.

Of Laws of the constitutional class indeed to a certain length it is true / on these depends the power of the governors and the security of the governed. On the one hand they confer ... public fiduciary powers: on the other hand they prescribe limits to those powers / narrowing the description of the modes of acting authorized.

Now the regulations that serve to prescribe these limits must occupy a certain space: as far as the space necessary for that purpose extends, so far is the bulk and multiplicity of Law favourable to Liberty ...

But under every other title the more Laws the less Liberty ... Let us consider the Laws of Property ... A great number utterly unnecessary burthensome to the proprietor in a much greater proportion than they are profitable to any one else, / detestable offspring of the Feudal Anarchy / actually infest the Laws of almost every nation in Europe. Of these the number is capable of being yet further augmented in infinitum. (69.148)[32]

Bentham's argument in this passage is specifically related to, and perfectly consistent with, his definition of 'liberty political in perfection.' There is a point, he is saying, at which the law provides a maximum of protection for the individual against his governors. The laws which contribute most prominently to this protection are constitutional laws, but any variety of law having to do with the securing of social 'conditions in life,' such as the ownership of property, has by definition the function of legalizing, and thus securing, the liberties and powers implicit in such ideas as 'title'[33] or 'possession.'[34] In this analysis we see the harbinger of the classification of liberty into 'personal,' 'political,' and 'constitutional' species which Bentham employed in the 1780s in manuscripts headed 'civil code.' We can also see why this trisection was important to Bentham: in the case of constitutional law, the proportion of the bulk of the law likely to be favourable to the relevant kinds of liberties ('constitutional' liberties) is high. In the political, but not expressly 'constitutional,' branch the proportion will be lower, for the primary function of such laws is as much a matter of the coercion of citizens as of the protection of citizens against coercion by their governors. Within the personal sphere, it is questionable whether any legal intervention whatsoever can be justified in logic. The law, as Bentham had already argued earlier in the preparatory manuscripts, was essentially and unalterably coercive. When personal, as distinct from political, liberties are at issue the only possible effect of the invocation of legal sanctions is to restrict or annihilate liberty. The consideration of the personal sphere of liberties exposes us to the area of private ethics and self-regarding acts — an area Bentham was as anxious to protect from legal or legislative invasion as was J.S. Mill. Bentham was putting into the terms of his own discussion the characteristic sense of superiority felt by many of his British contemporaries vis-à-vis France with regard to personal liberty when he wrote: 'In France where they have so much less liberty than we have, they have much more Law. It is the characteristic of law to produce restraint. Liberty is the absence of restraint. How should Law then produce Liberty? (69.148).

In the 1770s, therefore, Bentham confronted a number of the analytical difficulties surrounding the idea of liberty and produced what may, despite the prefatory and fragmentary nature of these manuscripts, be called a theoretical analysis of the role of the idea of liberty in political thought and of the term 'liberty' in political discourse. The exact sequence in which his ideas occurred to him is virtually impossible to reconstruct because the numerous sheets of manuscript are largely undated, and because the nature of such projects as 'Key,' 'PPI,' and 'Crit. Jur. Crim.' did not require that one be finished before another be started. Indeed, it is not difficult to imagine Bentham altering the heading of his manuscript sheets from 'Key' to 'Crit. Jur. Crim.' to 'PPI' as his conception of the work to which these ideas were to contribute changed from that of an opus on punishment to a criticism of the Blackstonian hymn to existing English law, then to a code of penal law, and finally to the full-scale multivolume project described in his Preface to the *Introduction to the Principles*, written in 1789.[35] The pattern formed by the larger works produced by Bentham, together with internal evidence, indicates that these manuscripts were written mainly during the 1770s. They document Bentham's persistent attempts to analyse certain fundamental terms of jurisprudence as the opening phase in his campaign to construct a complete and universal system of laws and legal discourse. The process of definition and clarification of concepts, however, was thought of, not as 'preliminary,' but as 'preparatory.' This first phase was to be the foundation of all later phases. One can hardly overemphasize the extent to which the arguments of Bentham's later publications are founded upon insights brought to light in the preparatory manuscripts of the 1770s.

For the purposes of the present discussion we have chosen for examination a number of manuscript passages addressed to a single issue viewed from varying perspectives. That issue was the nature of liberty (or rather liberties) as an object of, or an element in the operation of, law. Bentham was confronted with the relationship between law and liberty as expressed in the confusing and unrealistic political rhetoric of his contemporaries. He broke the simplistic bond between law and liberty consistently postulated by them by asserting the essentially coercive nature of law and defining liberty as the absence of coercion. It might have suited his taste for iconoclasm and paradox to leave the argument in that shape had he been a less serious, less constructive, less perceptive, or less systematic thinker. Instead, he undertook a theoretical reconstruction of the relationship between liberty and law. He did not necessarily disagree with Price's and Priestley's claim that liberty meant 'self-government.' He was willing to equate the two, however, only if his views were accepted as to the exact character of the 'self' and as to how it is 'governed' by its own nature. His negative notion of liberty was logically implied by his negative notion of the self as receptor of pleasures and pains. His preoccupation with security was a function of his preoccupation with individual adjustment to a hostile and uncertain environment. His whole analysis of the function of law, of government, of sanctions vis-à-vis liberty, was predicated upon the belief that it is the presence or absence of security, which may be defined as the assurance of duration with regard to either the experiencing of pleasures or the avoiding of pains, that determines when liberty is enjoyed.

With some appreciation of the unattractiveness of his thoughts on law and liberty Bentham nevertheless put forward a definition which equated the state with the coercive force of law: 'A State is a number of persons in succession

agreed or accustomed to / obey the commands concerning any matter whatsoever or to conduct themselves in all things according as a person or persons of a
certain [account] have commanded / submit to punishment for any matter
whatsoever at the hands of a certain person or certain persons' (69.89).[36] This
was in substance the same definition of a state in terms of the 'habit of
obedience' which was to achieve some fame by its embodiment in the *Fragment
on Government*. But as a footnote to the definition as presented in his
manuscripts Bentham added an expression of his fear that he would be thought
to be an 'advocate of slavery' on account of his definition. He denied any such
advocacy:

Note (*a*) This definition will not easily go down at first with men whose
affections are warm on the side of liberty. To such it will be apt to give at least a
momentary shock. To these all I can say is to request them to suspend their
censure till they have proceeded a little further. They will be apt to tell me that
this is a definition of a slavish state, and of no other.

But my notion is that what is called Liberty in a state does not depend upon
any circumstance that will take it out of this definition. For the present, let
them be assured that slavery will find no advocate in me. But this is a definition
framed to include every state well-governed or ill-governed, and whether by
Laws or without them. It is my care throughout to keep distinct by every
attention possible those two ideas so apt to be confounded, the idea of what *is*,
from the idea of what *ought to be*. (69.89)

Bentham hoped to make his readers understand that the state, like the law
(indeed because its essence *was* law), was essentially a force for the *control* of
behaviour and thus essentially a destroyer and reducer of liberty regarded as a
quantum. He also sought, however, to show that we must be philosophical
nominalists, not realists, about liberty: that we must look, not to its quantum or
its aggregate, but to the significance of the existence or denial of liberty in
connection with specified acts or sets of acts in a given context of social
relationships. In this view what is assumed is that the value of law and of the
security it gives to pleasures and against pain is greater than the value of an
unlimited and anarchy-inducing liberty for the pursuit of pleasures.

5

A 'Comment' and a 'Fragment'

In one sense the *Comment on the Commentaries* and the *Fragment on Government* may be seen as interruptions of, or digressions from, the course of development of Bentham's magnum opus on critical jurisprudence. As one might expect, however, a close examination of the text and context of these two works reveals that they have a clear, if tangential, connection with the evolution of the central project which shaped Bentham's intellectual development in the 1770s and the early 1780s. The logical relationship between the 'Elements of Critical Jurisprudence' or 'the Principles of Legal Policy' and the *Comment on the Commentaries* is not difficult to appreciate. What is particularly relevant to the present phase of our discussion, however, is that there is evidence which connects the intellectual frame of reference of the *Comment* explicitly to the development of Bentham's idea of censorial jurisprudence and, more specifically, to the view of liberty conveyed in the manuscripts of the 1770s whose place in that development was discussed in the previous chapter.

We begin by examining some of Bentham's comments on Blackstone's idea of natural law. It will be recalled that Bentham's hostility to the notion of natural law was expressed in the PPI manuscripts. In the course of some vitriolic remarks in the chapter of the *Comment* devoted to the 'Law of Nature,'[1] Bentham observed sarcastically that in one place[2] Blackstone had come near 'advancing a proposition that would not only have been intelligible, but fundamentally important and unquestionably true.'[3] Bentham reprinted the passage from the *Commentaries* with extensive alterations and additions of his own, which here appear in small capitals:

This is the foundation of what may be called CRITICAL LAW OR CRITICAL JURISPRUDENCE. The several articles into which it MIGHT BE branched in our systems amount to no more than demonstrating that this or that MODE OF

CONDUCT tends to man's real happiness, and therefore very justly concluding that the OBSERVANCE of it ought to be either COMMANDED OR ALLOWED OF By the Law of the country where it has that tendency: or, on the other hand, that this or that MODE OF CONDUCT is destructive of man's real happiness, and therefore that (providing the mischief of enforcing the prohibition do not exceed the mischief of the mode of conduct meant to be prohibited) the LAW of the country ought to forbid it.[4]

This passage makes it evident that Bentham approached the task of writing a critique of Blackstone in part as an opportunity to publicize some of the features of a censorial system of jurisprudence. There was no need to put his labours on his magnum opus to one side; he could consider the attack on Blackstone as the opening of a second front in the campaign to organize and disseminate his ideas. The letter which signaled to John Lind Bentham's willingness to take over from him the task of writing the critique of Blackstone included an indication that Bentham had spent 'two or three years' before October 1774 in becoming 'master of the subject' of critical jurisprudence.[5] Moreover, on a manuscript page headed 'Comment' in the UCL collection, Bentham professed to be 'heartily sick of the Logical and Metaphysical researches into which he [Bentham] has been driven to seek lights in order to dissipate the confusion in which our Author has involved the subject [of Law]' but promised to maintain his efforts to 'pave the way to a somewhat less inaccurate conception of it than he has given us' (96.69).[6]

Bentham had the continuing saga of the 'Elements of Critical Jurisprudence' firmly in focus as he wrote the *Comment*. Blackstone was to be his foil: to emphasize, by the very depth of his confusion and the very vacuity of his arguments, the novelty and importance of Bentham's censorial approach to the law. The immense bulk (260 pages) of the PPI manuscripts may well explain why Bentham was 'heartily sick' of his 'Logical and Metaphysical researches' by the time he came to apply the fruits of those researches to the problem of unravelling Blackstone's arguments. With his return to the execution of his 'capital work' in late 1776, however, Bentham left Blackstone's labyrinthine prose behind and made a fresh start at giving his own account of the *is* and the *ought* of the law. The result was the completion of a cluster of works whose contents we shall examine. In this chapter we focus our attention on the *Comment* and the *Fragment* themselves, and ask to what extent the principles of censorial jurisprudence, as worked out in the manuscripts, are reflected in their pages.

Two problems concerning liberty dominate Bentham's thinking in the manuscripts on the 1770s, the *Comment*, the *Fragment*, the *Introduction*, and

Of Laws in General: the problem of liberty as a fundamental term in legal and political discourse, and the problem of liberty as the object of legislative policy. A synthesis of these two issues was taken for granted in *Of Laws in General*, where Bentham concluded that the term 'liberty,' as a 'fictitious legal entity,' could be given meaning only by reference to a particular, real situation exemplifying the operations of the laws upon real objects (that is, upon persons and things). The argument of the *Comment* can be seen to move in the direction of this synthesis: setting out to attack Blackstone's abuses of the term 'liberty' in legal discourse, it resolves the process of definition into an analysis of the operation of a hypothetical legal polity.

Referring to a paragraph in Blackstone's *Commentaries* comparing the force of 'counsel' with the force of 'law,'[7] Bentham located the root of the rhetorical vacuity of Blackstone's arguments in his failure to give clear and accurate meanings to words such as 'liberty ... reasonable ... unreasonable ... etc.': 'had he [Blackstone] settled with himself the meaning of all these words before he had sat down to write the paragraph they stand in, men's ears would have lost some entertainment; but their conceptions would have been spared the vexation of seeking for instruction where no instruction is.'[8] The Bentham of this passage is clearly the disciple of Locke, the painstaking lexicographer of fundamental words, the grammarian of politics. However, as soon as Bentham began to put forward his own definitions it became clear that they took the form of outlines of varieties of concrete situations. In the case of the term 'right', for example: 'A right then to a thing is, as I understand it, the relation a man is in with respect to a thing which that man is left free to convert to the purposes of his own pleasure, punishment being denounced against any other man who shall impede him from so doing, or does the like as the first man with respect to that thing, without his consent.'[9] Nothing could illustrate better than this passage the character of Bentham's legal positivism concerning rights and liberties in political society. No alternative to punishment as a basis for civil rights is considered. Of more particular interest to us in the present phase of our discussion is the fact that this definition transforms a linguistic problem into a practical political problem. In *Of Laws in General* Bentham was to envisage as the primary function of law the securing of such liberties and rights as could not be made and kept secure in a pre-political (and pre-legal) condition where their only support had been the physical sanction – the physical ability of their possessors to defend them by brute force against invasion by others. An investigation of some additional passages from the *Comment*, however, shows that a complete basis for these views as expressed in *Of Laws in General* was established in the *Comment*.

Bentham's argument that the law was (or rather ought to be) the foundation of rights and liberties was tempered by his awareness, articulated elsewhere in the *Comment*, that the law could not actually do anything to enlarge the aggregate quantum of liberty in political society unless that quantum as it stood were artificially restricted by a pre-existing (and presumably disutilitarian) coercive law. All that was in most cases possible was a redistribution of existing liberties.

A Law that enlarges the liberty of acting, restrains the powers and by that means the Law that before restrained it: a Law that restrains the liberty of acting makes the system of power established in restraint of it larger than it was before.
    The truth is, till this matter be settled, there is no statute whatever that ought to be called an enlarging one, but ought for as good a reason to be called a restraining one: for to enlarge the power of one man, there is but one way, and that is, to restrain the conduct of another.[10]

To define liberty was to describe the operations of the 'system of power established in restraint of it.' The task of reforming language and the task of constructing a new legal and political system had, in this case, become one and the same thing. Blackstone's failure to define his words had been inextricably connected with his failure to visualize a legal or political system capable of sustaining 'political liberty in perfection': 'One thing therefore we find that [according to Blackstone] is necessary to the good of society is, to forbid actions ('a great number' of them) that do no harm in it [I *Comm.*, 43].

This (if he had any) would be our Author's notion of the chief good that is to be done by human laws ... What it does no harm to do he would make us not do: what it does no harm *not* to do he would make us *do*.'[11] The two failures were in fact aspects of the same phenomenon: Blackstone's inability to achieve a censorial, utilitarian perspective on the interaction of liberty and authority in political society.
    Bentham confronts Blackstone's declaration that written laws are not always necessary to enshrine those natural rights that are already sanctified by 'God and Nature'[12] with the reply of one who is clearly a legal positivist about liberty: 'I am heartily glad of the aid of human laws to invest in me my life and liberty ... and ... were it not for the said laws, I should be much puzzled to say what right I had to them at all.'[13] Bentham attacked Blackstone's notion of constitutional liberty in much the same way: he found it, like Blackstone's idea of personal liberty, to be based on abstract and rhetorical premises never subjected to a proper critical scrutiny. In a passage echoing Delolme's

Constitution de L'Angleterre,[14] Bentham attacked Blackstone as representative of an all-too-large number of legal theorists, lawyers, and politicians, who spoke in glowing terms of a 'free constitution' validated by the consent of its subjects freely given, yet who were willing to accept as adequate evidence of such free consent, not the actual consultation of the people in the course of the legislative process (let alone active participation in it by them), but mere passive obedience to the law once promulgated. Bentham's hostility to both the mythological historical basis of such judgments and the emptiness of their claims to a consensual foundation was vehement: ' "Where," says this lawyer, "is the difference whether the poeple give their assent to a law by suffrage, or by a uniform course of acting accordingly." "Where," he might just as well have said, "is the difference between acting by coercion and acting spontaneously?" '[15]

Bentham objected to such reasonings, not becuase he was a democrat, but because he was a utilitarian and a critical legal theorist. He could find no support for Blackstone's notion of constitutional liberty in either analytical or historical evidence. Historically, he attacked any suggestion that the British Common Law had ever been validated by popular consultation or consent:

[Section heading: 'Common Law: How far consented to by the People?']
Under our own government the finest and most excellent for all its imper-fections of any the world ever yet saw, I should be glad to see anything like such a doctrine [i.e. of popular consent] avowed by the Legislature. I should be glad to find any passage in any act of Parliament where the good liking of the people, I mean the body of the people at large is openly alleged as a consideration wanting to be attended to. No, the productions of our popular legislature are still tainted with the breath of ancient despotism.[16]

Bentham went on to say that to his ears even the more general claim to found 'the authority of the Laws' upon 'the will of the people' did not ring true. Legislators, he felt, did not in fact 'consult' the people.[17]

Turning from historical evidence to analytical examination, Bentham referred to Blackstone's judgment that 'it is one of the characteristic marks of English liberty, that our common law depends upon custom; which carries this internal evidence of freedom along with it, that it probably was introduced by the voluntary consent of the people.'[18] This was in fact another expression of Blackstone's notion that obedience implies free consent. Bentham would have none of it. He could only excuse Blackstone's misguidedness in this case by recalling that Blackstone, as a lawyer, was simply exemplifying the self-inter-ested species of prejudice typical of members of the legal profession of the time: 'Let us deal fairly by our Author, and confess that in this notion of his he is by no means singular. It is indeed a vulgar and popular error among lawyers; dear to their prejudices, and by no means unfavourable to their passions.'[19] Bentham's view was that much, perhaps most, of what passes for 'customary law' is in fact 'judge-made' law. By judge-made law the power of judges and of the legal profession from which they are drawn is enhanced. But judge-made law, said Bentham, is neither made nor consented to by the people: it is even less so than law made by their representatives in a legislative body. At their roots arguments such as Blackstone's were invalidated by a fallacy: 'The fallacy lies in the abusive application of the term "assent": in the giving to a uniform course of action according to a Law, after that law is passed, and punishment threatened for the breach of it that same name "assent," as is given to an express declaration of the party's will with the Law before its passage.'[20]

The object of Bentham's critique was to clarify the distinction between obedience and consent as foundations for the justification of government. Blind, passive obedience could not constitute assent, while, on the other hand, assent given on a single occasion could not irrevocably bind the subject to obedience in situations then unforeseen. The question naturally arises: precisely what alternative to Blackstone's prescription for indiscriminate obedience did Bentham offer? The most succinct and aphoristic expression of Bentham's answer was to be given in the *Fragment on Government*: 'Under a government of Laws, what is the motto of a good citizen? *To obey punctually; to censure freely.*'[21] The analysis upon which this conclusion was grounded, however, was largely carried out in the *Comment*. There Bentham explained in the clearest possible terms what was to be expected of the subject, what must be understood as the legitimate role of the legislature, and what characteristics might be exhibited by a stable political condition resting on a correct inter-relationship between governors and governed. Of the subject, it must be grasped that 'what the subject sees, he may perhaps obey: what he does not see he cannot obey. What he must see is the Will of the Legislator when it is intelligibly expressed. What he may or may not see in general without being told of it, is the mischief to be averted or good to be attained that became the motive to that will.'[22]

This is reminiscent of the definition of 'government free' in the UCL manuscripts.[23] What Bentham is dismissing is, quite literally, blind obedience. The subject must see, and must be enabled to see and to understand, those regulations which are the expression of the will of the legislator – the laws. Subjects must 'know before hand the extent of the several powers executed over them.' 'The extent of the several powers of persons in the Government is fixed,' so that the condition of the citizen and subject is secure and thence 'free.' If, however, the fullest and most 'punctual' obedience is desired, the will of the legislator – the law – must be 'intelligible' to each and every subject who is expected to obey. This requirement was manifestly unfulfilled even by most English Statutes, not to speak of invisible judge-made law in Bentham's time. Moreover, there was a further requirement: the subject should, where necessary, be enabled to understand the legislator's motives. In other words, the utilitarian justification of every law must be, or be made, visible and coherent to every subject and citizen. Knowing the balance between 'mischief to be averted' and 'good to be attained' in each case, the subject could, as was made clearest in the *Fragment*, determine whether obedience or resistance to government would be the correct course in the circumstances.

The equilibrium thus established between liberty and authority would be as stable as the concept of utility itself – and as unsteady as the commitment of governors to the principle of the greatest happiness of the greatest number. Common sense, Bentham maintained, is a sufficient instrument for the adjustment of the equally voracious claims of authority on one hand and liberty on the other:

Nothing is unlawful that is the clear intent of the Legislature. Nothing can be void: neither on account of opposition to a pretended Law of Nature, nor on any other. To say it is a contradiction. Nothing is gained to Liberty by such language, and much is lost to common sense. Yet it is much used by the advocates for Liberty. We hear it every day. I am always sorry when I hear it.

The Legislature cannot do that which is unlawful (as it is not unlawful if they do it). But it may do that which shall render it inexpedient to obey it.

We have a Constitution. We have our liberties, our rights. Our kings have boundaries to their authority. This constitution is found by experience to possess a greater degree of expedience, to be more highly conducive to the happiness of those who live under it, than any other yet exemplified. Of this there is scarce a doubt. (28.30-1)[24]

Immediately applying these principles, Bentham went on to describe the specific circumstances under which he himself could be prompted to resistance:

To be deprived at once by any act of the Legislature of everything that distinguishes this constitution to its advantage would be to see a measure taken in the highest degree inexpedient. To such a degree inexpedient that at no time [the] mischiefs resulting from forcible opposition to it could be equal I suppose to the mischiefs of a compliance ... I will take up arms whensoever the Legislature shall pass an Act, giving the force of Statutes in all cases and for this country I write in, England, to the Sovereign's Proclamations ... that is if I can get what I think enough to join with me: else I will fly the country. (28.30-1)[25]

The *Comment* was much more than a pure polemic. The fury and flamboyance of Bentham's attack on the emptiness of Blackstone's arguments should not blind us to the important passages in which Bentham showed that the meaninglessness of Blackstone's language reflected the inadequacy of his comprehensive view of jurisprudence and politics. Bentham did not merely wish to make Blackstone look ridiculous. He had far more substantial aims than that:

Would to God the state of things painted by our Author in another place were as realised as possible, and 'that every man might know what to look upon as his own, what is another's; what absolute and what relative duties are required at his hands; what is to be esteemed honest, dishonest or indifferent; what degree every man retains of his natural liberty; what he has given up as the price of the benefits of society; and after what manner each person is to moderate the use and exercise of those rights which the state assigns him, in order to promote and secure the public tranquility. (Ibid.)[26]

The *Comment* has far more to tell us than is commonly acknowledged about the exact nature of Bentham's aspirations as a censorial jurist and about the precise means by which he proposed to realize them.

The *Comment* gave birth to the *Fragment*. In the first eleven paragraphs of his Preface to the *Fragment*, Bentham explained that he had originally set out to investigate 'the most conspicuous, the most characteristic part of our Author's work, and that which was most his own,' Blackstone's Introduction.[27] 'The rest,' Bentham wrote, 'was little more than compilation.'[28] In the middle of Blackstone's definition of the 'Law municipal' Bentham found 'the digression which makes the subject' of the *Fragment*.[29] This fact emphasizes the intimacy of the connection between the *Comment* and the *Fragment* in so far as they both deal with the idea of liberty, for it was in the section of the *Comment* dealing with 'Municipal Law' (that is, with Blackstone's account of it) that the most important of the remarks on liberty and government referred to so far in this chapter were made. The substantial size of the text which Bentham quickly produced on the subject of Blackstone's 'digression,' together with the fact that this subject appeared to him to be susceptible of treatment in relative isolation from the remainder of the *Comment*'s contents, convinced Bentham that his reflections on this portion of the *Comment* should be published separately. He proceeded to publish it as the *Fragment on Government*. He looked forward to publishing the remainder of his remarks on Blackstone's legal apologetics 'under some such title as that of *A Comment on the Commentaries*.'[30]

Bentham thus made no conceptual distinction between the approaches or purposes of the *Comment* and the *Fragment*. Fundamental principles, such as those embodied in Bentham's 'motto of a good citizen' or his criteria for the correct 'juncture for resistance' to government, are shared by the two works and given similar expression in each.[31] Indeed, the UCL manuscripts, the *Comment*, and the *Fragment* all exhibit a basically consistent approach to the two principal problems pertaining to liberty: its definition and its realization. If there is a particular aspect of this approach which takes centre stage in the *Fragment*, it is the consideration of the relationship between the contrasting (but, for Bentham, complementary) concepts of liberty and sovereignty. Bentham devoted two chapters of the *Fragment* to the concept of sovereignty, that is, the right or duty of the supreme power to make laws. In the first of these, he referred to a passage in which Blackstone spoke 'of the several forms of government now in being': ' "However they began," says he, "or by what right soever they subsist, there is and *must be* in all of them a *supreme, irresistible, absolute, uncontrolled* authority, in which the *jura summi imperii*, or the rights of sovereignty, reside.' "[32] Bentham observed that at this point Blackstone's arguments 'dribble away in a string of obscure sophisms':[33] not a surprising development, for 'a courage much stauncher than our Author's might have wavered here': 'A task of no less intricacy was here to be travelled through, than that of adjusting the claims of those two jealous antagonists, Liberty and Government. A more invidious ground is scarcely to be found any where within the field of politics.'[34] Nevertheless, Bentham proceeded to 'travel through' this task in the *Fragment*, using the same signposts he had chosen in the *Comment*.

In a passage defending the censorial approach to jurisprudence in the Preface to the *Fragment* Bentham coined the aphorism which expresses best of all his position on the question of the proper extent of political (or 'constitutional') and civil liberty: 'For my part, I know not for what good reason it is that the merit of justifying a law when right should have been thought greater, than that of censuring it when wrong. Under a government of Laws, what is the motto of a good citizen? *To obey punctually; to censure freely*.'[35] We have seen that the extensive groundwork which must necessarily precede the employment of such an important leading principle was laid in the *Comment*. In a sense the entire mass of evidence surveyed in the present investigation could be considered an elaboration on the contents of this single dictum. In juxtaposing punctual obedience and freedom of censure not simply as separate goals but also as complementary constituents of political life, Bentham synthesized two contrasting aspects of his view of liberty; but he did more than that: he made it clear that in a comprehensive system of ideas such as his own no single political concept such as liberty, sovereignty, or even political society could be adequately understood in isolation from the web of reciprocal relationships of command and obedience binding men together in any social group.

An important attempt to integrate the antagonistic concepts of freedom and authority within a coherent and cohesive political view occurs in chapter 4 of the *Fragment*, the 'Right of the supreme power to make laws.'[36] Here Bentham directs a frontal attack on the problem Blackstone had evaded: that of 'adjusting the claims of those two jealous antagonists, Liberty and Government.'[37] His argument is that 'freedom in a government depends not upon any limitation to the Supreme Power.'[38] Referring to the problem of resistance to the 'supreme governor's authority,' he maintains that it can not be founded on the idea of a right of resistance unless the notion of right is understood to mean a utilitarian calculus of the 'probable mischiefs of resistance (speaking with respect to the community in general)' as weighed against 'the probable mischiefs of submission.'[39] His is essentially an attack on the concept of a fixed, immutable, 'natural right' of resistance. As another way of exposing the same fallacy, he denies that any commonly acknowledged sign can be discovered by which the point at which resistance is justified may be recognized: '*Common* sign for such a purpose, I, for my part, know of none: he must be more than a prophet, I think, that can shew us one. For that which shall serve a particular person, I have already given one — his own internal persuasion of a balance of *utility* on the side of resistance.'[40]

Given, then, that no such sign can be produced, liberty, in so far as it is taken to involve the right of resistance, does not depend upon any factor which distinguishes a free from a despotic government:[41] 'the field, if one may say so, of the supreme governor's authority, though not *infinite*, must unavoidably, I think, *unless* where limited by express convention, be allowed to be *indefinite*. Nor can I see any narrower, or other bounds to it, under this constitution, or under any other yet freer constitution, if there be one, than under the most despotic.'[42]

Such views should not surprise us when we are aware of Bentham's belief, expressed in his preparatory manuscripts, that the degree of liberty enjoyed within a state, whether high or low, has no necessary connection with or correlation to the essential habit of obedience upon which sovereignty and the state are founded. There *is* a distinction to be made between free and despotic states according to Bentham's view, but it has to do neither with the nature nor with the limits of power. Resuming a theme first expounded in the *Comment*, he denies that the basing of laws upon custom modifies the *nature* of sovereign power in the direction of liberty: 'Is it that those persons in whose hands that power is lodged which is acknowledged to be supreme, have less power in the one [a 'free government'] than in the other [a 'despotic' one], when it is from custom that they derive it? By no means.'[43] Nor do the *limits* of power vary from free to despotic states: 'It is not that the power of one any more than of the other has any certain bounds to it.' A free state is, in fact, characterized for Bentham firstly by its possession of a government thoroughly accountable to the citizen populace for its acts and therefore, presumably, *worthy* of punctual obedience, and secondly by the existence of a free press and freedom of association, the necessary conditions of continuing freedom of censure. 'The distinction,' he says, meaning that between a free and a despotic government,

turns upon circumstances of a very different complexion: − [i.e. different from those supposed to limit supreme power] − on the *manner* in which that whole mass of power, which, taken together, is supreme, is, in a free state, distributed among the several ranks of persons that are sharers in it: − on the source from whence their titles to it are successively derived: − on the frequent and easy *changes* of condition between govern*ors* and govern*ed*; whereby the interests of the one class are more or less indistinguishably blended with those of the others: − on the *responsibility* of the governors; or the right which a subject has of having the reasons publicly assigned and canvassed of every act that is exerted over him: − on the liberty of the press; or the security with which every man, be he of the one class or the other, may make known his complaints and remonstrances to the whole community: − on the liberty of public *association*; or the security with which malcontents may communicate their sentiments, concert their plans, and practise every mode of opposition short of actual revolt, before the executive power can be justified in disturbing them.[44]

In the following paragraph (no. 25), Bentham admits that the conditions of a free state may *facilitate* the organization and mobilization of resistance to the supreme power. This will alter the point at which such resistance is justified. 'Grant, then, that by reason of these facilitating circumstances, the juncture itself may arrive sooner, and upon less provocation, under what is called a free government, than under what is called an *absolute* one: grant this; − yet till it *be* arrived, resistance is as much too soon under one of them as under the other.'[45]

All government, however, free or despotic, must, to be *called* government in a meaningful legal sense, demand unqualified and punctual obedience until such point as the individual calculation of the comparative mischiefs of submission and resistance turns so many individuals into the path of resistance as to undermine its authority by eroding the habit of obedience. Liberty is achieved neither by a restriction of the quantity nor by an alteration in the quality of supreme power, but by the embodiment of that power, in all its plenitude, in a government which is representative, responsible, equitable, and responsive to free public censure registered by the press and by 'associations' of 'malcontents,' which in Bentham's description look much like political lobbies or pressure groups.

Bentham's aim on all of these points is clearly to show how a free government is open to criticism and change in every conceivable way, barring actual disobedience of its commands. Free government in a stable social condition is characterized by a balance of punctual obedience and free censure, which leads to a steady and secure form of social change and progress. As an enlightenment partisan of the 'science of man' and as a social philosopher in the context of the industrial revolution and the socioeconomic upheaval it caused,[46] Bentham was here propounding a solution to what must surely have seemed a fundamental problem of contemporary civil society – the problem of social change. The polity Bentham envisaged was meant to be not totalitarian but liberal, not static but dynamic, not the oppressor but the champion of the individual. Unfortunately, the same cannot always be said of the institutions Bentham conceived as embodiments of these thoroughly admirable political intentions. When, in his Preface to the *Fragment*, he expressed his antagonism towards 'that spirit in our Author which seems so hostile to Reformation, and to that liberty which is Reformation's harbinger,'[47] he was not calling for political revolution but defending his own critical posture, his desire to shake his fellow jurists out of the awed silence that afflicted them in the presence of the aura of Blackstone's authority. He was defending 'the right of private judgment, that basis of everything that an Englishman holds dear.'[48] He was seeking, as he himself said in the final paragraph of chapter 5, 'to help ['the timid and admiring student'] to emancipate his judgment from the shackles of authority.'[49]

Bentham doubted that what he described for polemical purposes as a free government in the *Fragment* could or should be referred to as being free in the popular sense of the term. In one manuscript passage he argued as follows: 'The expression a Free government, a Free constitution originates from the improper sense of the word liberty, where it is used for [domestic] security against those in authority. The proper expression would be a popular government, a popular constitution. Every / A / government being necessarily all powerful can be no otherwise than free, that is unrestrained by any restraint that can be called legal' (69.153).[50] Moreover, the same passage informs us that a government may be said to be free in another sense, that is, 'as providing for the freedom ... of the governed.' Bentham felt the need to correct this manuscript text by inserting 'i.e. security' after the word 'liberty,' and continued thus: 'A Government may be said to be more or less free, as more or less care is taken in it / by it / of the / political liberty / security of the people.' In the text of the latter sentence 'security' is the primary manuscript reading, with 'political liberty' the alternative. In a passage quoted earlier, Bentham concluded that 'in proportion as the subjects are able to know before hand the / extent of the several powers exercised over them / rules of conduct they will [be] bound to observe / as the several powers of persons in the Government is fixed, so / the ... condition of the people is free, or rather secure: and thence improperly ... the Government is said to be free' (69.158). These statements illustrate the extent to which, by the time of the publication of the *Fragment* in late April 1776, Bentham's investigation of liberty had led him to conclude that neither government nor citizenry ought to be described as free under a system of laws.

To refer to a certain government as free in a laudatory tone is misguided: all governments are free in the sense that their powers of action are unrestricted. Freedom is characteristic of all sovereigns in such a sense that it ceases to be employable as a term of approbation referring to any particular one of them. This leaves the question: when is the condition of the people free? The answer to this question, in terms of legal and legislative theory, is that they are left free to the extent permitted by the 'system of restraints' which is the web of positive law. Positive law, however, does not literally create negative liberty. What law creates is security. By making clear the lines of restriction circumscribing the sphere of permissible liberties, however, the law endows the pursuit and enjoyment of those liberties with a security it had not possessed before the advent of the legal system. Only thus can men's frequently misguided desire for liberty be reconciled with their overwhelming desire and need for happiness. This reconciliation must inevitably come about, given the existence of a society in which the governance of the dictates of utility is effectively, if not universally, acknowledged. From experience men will learn, their minds primed by a utilitarian education, that the pursuit of certain kinds or quantities of liberty yields an undesirable balance of pain over pleasure on the whole.

The idea of the subordination of liberty to the goals of security and happiness, which becomes a recurrent theme in Bentham's later writings, has its roots in the distinction, made in the early manuscripts, between liberty, as an indirect product of certain kinds of legislative and legal activities, and security and happiness as the two pre-eminent direct products of those activities. Later references by Bentham to liberty as a 'branch' of security represent a sort of faulty ellipsis: an abbreviated reference to the chain of thought processes established in the years so far surveyed in this discussion. Anyone advancing the charge that Bentham wished to subordinate or even annihilate liberty for the sake of happiness might well claim that he did so in his very definition of the idea, that his negative, materialist notion rendered an essentially spiritual concept barren of intrinsic or philosophical value. One cannot, however, argue that he meant to devalue it by granting it only a peripheral position within his system. For it was at the beginning of April 1776, just one month before the publication of the *Fragment*, when the *Comment* and many of the manuscripts we have examined had been written, that Bentham loosed his wrath on John

Lind for publishing his (Bentham's) definitions of 'right' and 'liberty' without acknowledgement. Bentham claimed: 'The Definition of Liberty is one of the corner stones of my system: and one that I know not how to do without. I must make use of it; and perhaps at no long time hence.'[51]

Bentham anticipated further modifications in his views on political liberty and on government when, at the conclusion of chapter 3 of the *Fragment*, entitled 'British Constitution,' he wrote:

21. Thus much for the British Constitution; and for the grounds of that pre-eminence which it boasts, I trust, indeed, not without reason, above all others which are known. Such is the idea our Author gives us of those grounds. – 'You are not satisfied with it then,' says some one. – Not perfectly. – 'What is then your own?' – In truth this is more than I have yet quite settled. I may have settled it with myself, and not think it worth the giving: but if ever I do think it worth the giving, it will hardly be in the form of a comment on a digression stuffed into the belly of a definition.[52]

A few clues can be extracted from this passage about Bentham's own views on the British constitution. These views do not, of course, accord with Blackstone's, but they do acknowledge that there is some justification for the constitution's claim to a 'pre-eminence ... above all others which are known.' Bentham's hint that he may have 'settled' his views 'with himself' could possibly refer to the existence of some of the preparatory manuscripts by the time this passage was written, or it could simply refer to his mental preparedness to write them upon his return to the task of producing the *Elements of Critical Jurisprudence* after setting aside the *Comment* and completing the *Fragment*. One additional clue to Bentham's views on the constitution, and especially to his views on its relationship to political liberty, is his statement that there will be no desire to have his views made public 'by those, who have read what has been given us on this subject by an ingenious foreigner.' To this foreigner, Englishmen are indebted for 'the best idea that has yet been given of a subject so much our own.' It was to J.L. Delolme's *Constitution De L'Angleterre* that Bentham referred, asserting that 'our Author has copied: but Mr De Lolme has thought.'[53] It is more than a mere coincidence that Bentham showed such high respect for an author whose intention in studying the British constitution was to show by what means it secured English liberties and by what means it might be enabled to do so more effectively. In so far as that objective was compatible with his allegiance to utilitarian principles, it was Bentham's as well. In late 1776 he returned to the task, his analytical and polemical tools sharpened, and the constituent segments of the 'Elements of Critical Jurisprudence' began to materialize.

6

Fundamental propositions

The *Fragment on Government* was published on or close to 18 April 1776.[1] On 1 October 1776 Bentham wrote to tell his father that 'I am now at work upon my capital work: I mean the Critical Elements of Jurisprudence.' This long-standing project was now entering a new phase: 'I am not now as heretofore barely collecting materials but putting it into the form in which I propose that it should stand.'[2] Bentham was beginning to realize that his 'Critical Elements of Jurisprudence' was an enterprise too large and complex to be encompassed in a single volume. He was planning to detach a part and publish it separately from the rest. Taking for his province the whole of the criminal law, he divided it into laws relative to public wrongs and those relative to private wrongs. Within the sphere of private wrongs he singled out three categories of injuries: to person, to property, and to reputation. Upon this framework he hoped to build a 'natural' classification of offences which would supersede Blackstone's 'technical' mode of division. The long chapter on the 'division of offences' in the *Introduction to the Principles of Morals and Legislation* had its origins in this project.[3] The earlier, more purely 'metaphysical' chapters of the *Introduction* grew out of the early portion of Bentham's work as projected in 1776 — the portion containing the general principles governing his detailed, practical proposals. In October 1776 the plan of this part of his work was 'pretty well settled,' and the materials were 'in good measure collected.'[4] From the autumn of 1776 until April 1780, when the *Introduction* was about to go to print,[5] only one other project made major claims on Bentham's attention: his theory of punishment.

From late 1776 until mid-1778, when he decided to concentrate on producing a 'Plan of legislation on criminal matters' as a candidate for a prize offered by the Berne Oeconomical Society, Bentham gave first priority to his work on punishments, perhaps hoping to complete it quickly and gain a reputation. This may explain his draft letter, unsent, to Voltaire, intended to accompany a copy of the 'Theory of Punishments.'[6] Having devoted so much effort in the years before 1777 to defining liberty as the absence of coercion, he turned with some confidence to the study of punishment, that is, a study of the principles governing the social distribution of coercion.

Bentham's view of the intrinsic qualities of punishment can be stated quite simply: punishment is evil, but necessary. Further, it is necessary that it be evil, and that it be seen to be so. Only by comparison with the ultimate perniciousness of crime itself can punishment be viewed with approval.[7] Given that 'punishment, whatever shape it may assume, is an evil,'[8] the distributive principle governing the application of punishment is clear: the dosage must be sufficient to ensure that it is publicly apparent that crime does not pay. Yet punishment must never be excessive; it must never be invoked for its own sake, in view of its intrinsically evil qualities.

Despite its manifest service to the cause of utility, and thence to felicity, punishment must inevitably remain unpopular. The people *ought* to like it, but 'whether they *will* like it or no after all, is another question.' In so far as the populace allow their judgments to be guided uniformly and exclusively by the principle of utility, they will indeed endorse judicious punishment, and thus show themselves, in Bentham's view, to be 'humanised and enlightened.' Taking, as is only right, 'the great mass of the people ... into the account,' rather than, as is too commonly the case, 'confining [our] views ... to men of rank and education,' deference to the utility principle will be seen to be more 'uniform' in England than in less intelligent and favoured countries.[9]

Even Englishmen, however, do not render unto the utility principle the undeviating acquiescence in its dictates which is to be desired. This failure manifests itself in the variety of 'capricious objections' to which each particular mode of punishment is exposed. This variety is limited only by 'the fecundity of the imagination,' but, with some slight exceptions, four headings cover the field: liberty, decency, religion, and humanity.[10] Objections grounded on considerations of decency and humanity are misguided; they denounce that very intrinsic and evident odiousness which, as we have seen, is essential to the utility of any and all punishment. Religious objections are rooted in the world of doctrine and dogma, and in the principle of asceticism. The libertarian objection is the most straightforward and realistic of the four types, but Bentham sees no difficulty in refuting it. Those 'enthusiasts,' he says, who condemn certain modes of punishment as a violation of the 'natural rights of man' ignore the basic truth that all punishment is an infringement on liberty and that no one willingly submits to it: 'In a free country like this, say they, it ought not to be tolerated, that even malefactors should be reduced to a state of slavery. The precedent is dangerous and pernicious ... Examine this senseless clamour, it will resolve itself into a declaration that liberty ought to be left to those who abuse it, and that the liberty of malefactors is an essential part of the liberty of honest men.'[11]

The evil of coercion ought to be measured by its destructiveness, not of liberty, but of pleasure. The incompatibility of certain forms of coercion with the existence of some species of liberty must not prevent the institutionalization of such forms of coercion if they are demonstrably conducive to the maximization of happiness in its social aggregate.

The study of punishment entailed an investigation of a limited variety of actual or potential legislative principles and policies. The study of offences, as Bentham was to construe it, involved the cataloguing of all possible forms of human social behaviour and the circumstances in which they might constitute offences. These two studies provided Bentham with complementary perspectives on the system of restraints that is the legal fabric of society. It had taken most of 1777 and part of 1778 for the theory of punishments to take shape. The difficulties involved in framing a theory of offences dwarfed those which had beset the theory of punishments. Bentham's return to work on his research into offences in mid-1778 marked the beginning of a search for a theoretical framework for a full theory of offences that was to end only with Bentham's recognition, in *Of Laws in General*, that the subject of these researches was nothing less than the entire 'universe of human actions.' The enlargement of Bentham's theoretical field of vision required by this broadening conception of the theory of offences as an aspect of the study of penal or criminal law resulted in a corresponding enlargement of the dimensions of Bentham's system as a whole. A critique of criminal jurisprudence or a plan for a penal code would soon cease to suffice as an embodiment of Bentham's intellectual ambitions. Nothing less than a complete social science – a system of morals as well as legislation – would do.

The first tangible result of Bentham's interest in constructing a theory of offences as the basis for a plan of a penal code was the printing, in 1780, of his 'natural classification of offences,' together with the preliminary part containing general principles as conceived of in 1776. These two parts, taken together, were to form the introduction to a detailed plan of a penal code.[12] The plan itself never saw the light of day. The introductory portion was finally published in 1789, despite Bentham's deep dissatisfaction with it, as the *Introduction to the Principles of Morals and Legislation*, Bentham's 'driest of all dry metaphysics,'[13] the harbinger of an important new period of growth for Bentham's censorial reform program and his utilitarian social theory in general.

The principles stated in the opening paragraph of the *Introduction* are not calculated to warm libertarian hearts. The utilitarian system of morals and legislation is founded, we are told, not on liberty, but on subjection: universal and inescapable subjection to mankind's 'sovereign masters' pain and pleasure. They govern both the *is* and the *ought* of every aspect of life. Most important of all, 'every effort we can make to throw off our subjection, will serve but to demonstrate and confirm it ... The principle of utility recognizes this subjection, and assumes it for the foundation of that system, the object of which is to rear the fabric of felicity by the hands of reason and law.'[14] Farther on in the argument we are acquainted with the warp and woof, as it were, of the fabric of felicity. The happiness of the members of a community is their pleasures and their security together. The maximization of this happiness is the sole end pursued by the legislator, and 'the sole standard, in conformity to which each individual ought, as far as depends upon the legislator, to be *made* to fashion his behaviour.'[15] Thus Bentham welded security and pleasure firmly together as constituents of happiness. In his system a modicum of liberty would be a necessary, but not sufficient, condition of happiness (i.e. the *enjoyment* of pleasures) and thence an aspect or branch of security. An indirect relationship is thus postulated between liberty and happiness: one wherein liberty contributes constantly to happiness, but solely in its role as a constituent of security. What is never sympathetically considered in his system is the possibility of a direct link between liberty and pleasure or happiness without reference to considerations of security. Liberty holds no intrinsic charms for Bentham. The realm of liberty is for him not a subjective, boundless world of potentiality, but a circumscribed space reserved for the use of some particular agent as a means to the omnipresent end of happiness. Circumscription of the sphere of liberty is the key to security for the pursuit of pleasures, but it is also the principal symptom of the emasculation of the idea of liberty as an intrinsic good in Bentham's system.

The first three chapters of the *Introduction* initiate Bentham's attempt to define the broad social framework within which the various 'sanctions' can act to regulate individuals' liberty to pursue pleasures and avoid pains in conformity with the dictates of utility. It is not solely the force of sanctions, however, that ensures that individuals will in fact take advantage of every possible opportunity to enjoy pleasures and escape from pains. Much of the motivating force within Bentham's system — in a sense, all of it — is provided by human nature itself. The principle of utility, indeed, simply recognizes man's subjection to the requirements of his own nature. It does not abandon him mercilessly to a total subservience to the coercive forces embodied in the four sanctions (i.e. the physical, the political, the moral, and the religious). Far from it: other principles, says Bentham, may introduce a 'despotism' of one man's opinion over another's, but the principle of utility does not.[16] What devaluation of individual liberty there is in Bentham's system stems not from an excessive indulgence in frontal assaults on individual liberty in the form of unjustified legal restraints, but from Bentham's strong and distinctive views on the characteristics of human nature itself. Ironically, Bentham's feeling that he could be certain that human nature, left to itself, would propel the individual along a path of activities governed by considerations of pleasure and pain and lending to the maximization of the utility of his actions was not at all unlike Dr Price's confidence that he could predict that men left to themselves would follow the path to virtue. The essential difference between the two views lies in the fact that Bentham's was founded upon personal observation and generalization from experience – the scientific method of his time – while Price's was based on an amalgam of faith, hope, and piety.

The *Introduction* was to be a reservoir of general principles, not a catalogue of particular practices. Like the later *Deontology* and *Constitutional Code*, both of which are clearly attempts to complete themes of argument it initiated, the *Introduction* was framed in the most general terms possible.[17] In it, Bentham began to sketch out once and for all the lines of restraint which were to circumscribe the sphere of liberty. Is it at all surprising, considering the complexity and importance of this task, that in his eyes the *Introduction* always remained incomplete?

We shall have many opportunities to ask what the limits of legal or social coercion in Bentham's system are. But what of the other side of the coin? What space does Bentham leave for liberty? One way of showing the boundaries of liberty is illustrated in chapter 13 of the *Introduction*, which deals with 'Cases unmeet for punishment.' There, employing the basic principle, already enunciated in his work on punishments, that punishment 'ought only to be admitted in as far as it promises to exclude some greater evil,'[18] Bentham introduces some significant limitations to the field of actions to which legal coercion in the form of punishment is applicable.[19] The immediate principal end of punishment, he says, is 'to control action.' This control may take the form of either the 'reformation of the will' or the 'disablement of the physical power' of those upon whom the law acts. By example, moreover, even the behaviour of those who are not direct objects of legal coercion may be influenced, although only through the will, not through disablement.[20] Whenever the evil of the act in view is less than the evil of the smallest quantum of punishment which can practicably be applied, we read, the case is unmeet for punishment. It should be borne in mind, however, that indirect coercion, for example through 'indirect legislation' or the moral sanction, is not ruled out where direct legal coercion is unjustified.

There are, Bentham tells us, four classes of situations in which punishment cannot, need not, or should not be applied: where punishment is groundless, inefficacious, unprofitable, or needless.[21] The first and fourth classes deal with cases where either there is no real mischief, or what mischief there is may 'cease of itself' – or at least upon the employment of some less painful or coercive means of prevention. Where, for example, a patently mischievous act has received the consent, 'free, and fairly obtained,' of the party adversely affected by it, Bentham considers such consent to be sufficient indication that no harm of punishable dimensions has been done. Again, the mischief of an act may be outweighed by its beneficial consequences, or complete and certain compensation for mischief caused may be obtained outside the law.[22] In all such cases punishment is groundless. 'Instruction,' as an example of a 'cheaper' means of prevention of mischief, is applied to a situation where it renders punishment needless: 'the disseminating pernicious principles in matters of duty ... whether political or moral or religious.' Where the disseminator misguidedly believes that his principles are beneficial, the answer is to instruct him. Should his intentions themselves be pernicious, the populace will soon recognize the mischief thus caused. Even if the sovereign must become involved actively, 'the pen is the proper weapon to combat error with, not the sword.'[23]

In the second and third of Bentham's four classes the punishment cannot be made to fit the crime and therefore remains inefficacious or unprofitable.[24] An important cause of inefficaciousness is the frequent failure to promulgate laws properly. In defiance of the old adage he asserts, in effect, that ignorance of the law is a sufficient excuse, for promulgation is clearly the legislator's responsibility.[25] The other main source of inefficaciousness relates not to the actions of the authors of law, but to those of its objects. Bentham here[26] gives us virtually a full discussion of the legal problem of intention, the *mens rea* problem. Infancy, insanity, intoxication (a species of temporary insanity), unintentionality, unconsciousness, and 'mis-supposal' are all circumstances which render punishment inefficacious by removing from the calculation of the mischief of the offence (and that of the corrective effect of punishment) the crucial factor of criminal intent. It is clear that punishment is inefficacious where the offence is not freely and deliberately perpetrated. Direct physical coercion or coercion in prospect in the form of physical danger or 'threatened mischief' may constrain an individual to commit an offence in order to avoid the greater evil with which he is confronted by an extra-legal agent.

Perhaps the most interesting of the four heads of cases unmeet is the third, under which punishment is *'unprofitable, or too expensive'* because the mischief it would produce would be greater than what it prevented.[27] The evil of punishment, we are told, may be greater than that of the act punished.[28] Of the four aspects of the evil of punishment distinguished in this paragraph, one is the evil constituted by a man's apprehension that he is to be punished, another is the pain directly inflicted by the act of punishment, and a third is the 'pain of sympathy' suffered by those connected with the actual sufferers of punishment. These three evils are determined almost entirely by the nature of the punishment applied. The fourth, however, varies in its intensity with the nature of the act from which the individual is to be deterred by punishment. It is constituted by the denial of the liberty of performing the prohibited act. It is 'The evil of coercion or *restraint*: or the pain which it gives a man not to be able to do the act, whatever it be, which by the apprehension of the punishment he is deterred from doing. This is felt by those by whom the law is *observed*.'[29]

Bentham here recognizes that the law imposes restraints not only on those who break it, but also on those who observe it. His point in this passage is that the liberty to engage in a given type of behaviour should not be annihilated unless it can be shown that the evil of the punishment invoked as preventive sanction is no greater than the evil caused by free indulgence in the behaviour in question. Elsewhere Bentham allows that even a punishment that, strictly speaking, confers more benefit than evil on the affected populace may be withdrawn in the face of the pressure of public (or even foreign) opinion.[30]

Bentham's account of 'cases unmeet for punishment' gives a useful indication of the stages by which an 'introduction to a plan of a Penal Code' became the *Introduction to the Principles of Morals and Legislation*. Presumably the original plan of a Penal Code, an extension of the idea of a classification of 'private and public wrongs,' involved a systematic explanation of the ways in which subjects could cause harm to each other and the ways in which they could be effectively coerced into desisting from such behaviour. What complicated this task was indubitably Bentham's insatiable desire to 'get to the bottom' of things, his inability to go on with what lay before him while anything behind lay 'unexplor'd.'[31] Commencing a study of the interaction between the law and the subject, he could not refrain from making the attempt to define his words even with reference to such basic terms as those two. Unable to carry on, he turned back and began to explore. To establish the essential coerciveness of punitive law was not enough: from what source did such law emanate? By what means was it communicated to the subject? What were the possible modes of coercion? Having exhausted these modes, he could not avert his glance from the wider and more complex study of the sanctions in general, their interaction, and their effect on the subject. How could the subject's reaction to punishment be gauged without a previous awareness of his condition in life, his rights and expectations as a master or servant, sovereign or subject, citizen or slave? Behind these endless ramifications, this infinite regression towards a social *primum mobile*, lay simply the old belief that words are fundamental, that they are the hinges on which a science of legislation turns.

Bentham never satisfactorily solved the problem of the relationship between the real and fictitious entities of the social world, but the intensity of his efforts to do so and his awareness of the importance of the task is reflected in one very clearly observable phenomenon: his growing preoccupation with civil law. He felt that the definition of the elements of the social status quo must precede and shape the analysis of the operations of the law in altering or maintaining that status. Thus he ultimately concluded that the civil law was the foundation of the penal law and logically prior to it. He attributed to the civil law the defining and distributing functions with regard to 'corporeal' and 'incorporeal' objects of law. This was in effect to endow civil law with the power to identify and to alter the status quo, leaving to the penal law only the task of defending it as given. The chapter in the *Introduction* dealing with cases unmeet for punishment marks only the beginning of Bentham's attempts to integrate the operations of the legal sanction into a social system in which moral, physical, and religious sanctions also operate. With his growing awareness of the complex interaction of social forces in which the subject is caught up (the 'pugna sanctionum' briefly referred to in his early manuscripts) comes a new sensitivity to the importance of a broad range of social controls of which coercion is merely one particular variety. Bentham's confidence that all forms of social control could be employed in the service of a single hierarchy of utilitarian ends makes an interesting contrast with John Stuart Mill's fear of a 'tyranny of the majority' in a society tending to treat individuals as homogeneous units. It was only in the works written *after* the *Introduction*, i.e. *Of Laws in General* and the essay 'Indirect legislation,' that the analysis of social control was undertaken in detail, and even when those works were completed Bentham did not consider his study of the subject to be finished.

The first important effect of Bentham's broadening vision in the *Introduction* is his conclusion that a considerable variety of activities should be left free of interference by the legal sanction. In this and in his argument that free public opinion and free public discussion are essential to the welfare of society and not lightly to be restricted by the use of legal authority one might well see only the logical application of the maxim that punctual obedience and freedom of censure go hand in hand.[32] Frequently, however, Bentham abstains from applying the legal sanction simply because one of the others offers a more effective means of securing the desired effect. His concentration on the legal sanction in *Of Laws in General* may tend to obscure the real interest in the preservation of political liberties from extinction at the hands of law which is more evident in the *Introduction*. The difference in perspective between these two works on the other hand should not blind us to their unity of intention towards liberty. The *Introduction* examines liberty in the context of a theory of morals and legislation. *Of Laws in General* views it solely in its relationship to a system of laws.

The emphasis in chapter 13 of the *Introduction* on limitations of the use of the legal sanction is maintained in chapter 16, 'The division of offences,'[33] and chapter 17, 'Of the limits of the penal branch of jurisprudence.'[34] Chapter 16 begins with a reiteration of the basic thesis of chapter 13, expressed this time in terms of offences rather than punishments. It is within the power of government, Bentham asserts, to name any act as an offence, but the 'ought' of the matter is that an act should only be labelled an offence when 'the good of the community' requires it. He repeats the point, expressed first in the first chapter of the *Introduction*,[35] that the interest of the state and the interest of the individuals within it are identical in so far as acts detrimental to parties within the state are in the same measure to be considered detrimental to the state itself. A 'community or political state' is simply a fiction, an imaginary compound body constituted by the whole assemblage of any number of individuals.[36] No special category of political crime or political mischief exists as distinct from simple public or semi-public offences. Bentham's justifying criterion for the use of coercion and control is clearly the same one employed by J.S. Mill in *On Liberty* – 'self-protection' by the community.

Bentham divides offences into four basic classes, distinguished from one another by the scope of the field of interests affected by the offence: private (extra-regarding) offences, semi-public offences, self-regarding offences, and public offences.[37] The measurement of the detriment caused to the individuals who constitute the community or political state by extra-regarding, semi-public, or public acts involves an application, in each case, of the principles we have thus far extracted from the thirteenth and sixteenth chapters of the *Introduction*. In theoretical terms this process· is relatively straightforward, although its mechanics can be complex and formidably difficult.[38] The most substantial conceptual problems are attached mainly to the definition of self-regarding offences, the mischief caused by them, and the appropriate remedies.

Self-regarding offences, Bentham says, are such as 'in the first instance are detrimental to the offender himself, and to no one else, unless it be by their being detrimental to himself.'[39] By calling such acts offences Bentham is not necessarily condoning coercion or control of the individual for his own good in contravention of the 'simple principle' of governmental intervention which J.S. Mill was to put forward. For one thing, self-regarding cases may remain largely unmeet for punishment. For another, even Mill did not deny that acts which are initially detrimental only to the actor can nevertheless have extensive second- or third-order consequences for the community.[40] All that is 'missing' from Bentham's account of self-regarding acts by comparison with J.S. Mill's is the misleading assertion that the whole analysis is governed both theoretically and practically by one 'very simple principle'.

Bentham does not assume that all acts productive in the first instance of only self-regarding mischief ought to or will be made offences. He merely asserts that if in any case it should be 'thought fit to constitute them offences' they will form such a class. As to the questions what acts produce self-regarding mischief and which of them should be made offences, 'these are points, the latter of which at least is too unsettled, and too open to controversy, to be laid down with that degree of confidence which is implied in the exhibition of properties which are 'made use of as the ground work of an arrangement.'[41]

In a series of footnotes to chapter 16, Bentham does, nevertheless, give some examples of possible self-regarding offences.[42] Like J.S. Mill's description in *On Liberty* of the acts which a man may legitimately be induced to perform or abstain from performing, Bentham's list includes acts either enforced or prohibited by either the moral or the legal sanction. Self-regarding offences against the person include 'self-denying and self-tormenting practices' such as 'fasting, abstinence from venery,' self-flagellation, and self-mutilation, species of intemperance such as gluttony, drunkenness, and 'excessive venery,' and, in a class by itself, suicide.[43] Self-regarding offences against reputation are illustrated by 'incontinence in females' and incest.[44] One's own property is offended against by idleness, gaming, and 'other species of prodigality.'[45] The 'sacrifice of virginity' and certain 'indecencies not public' exemplify a class of self-regarding offences against person and reputation.[46] Under the heading of self-regarding offences against person and property, however, we find, simply 'none.'[47]

Later in the same chapter Bentham expresses doubts about whether self-regarding offences really produce any primary mischief at all. 'Secondary,' he asserts flatly, 'they produce none.' The only individuals with any natural interest in prosecution will be the few parties connected with the offender by bonds of sympathy or interest upon whom 'a mischief of the *derivative* kind may happen to devolve.' The mischief produced by self-regarding offences is apt to be 'unobvious' and in general more questionable than that of any of the other classes. Indeed, 'the best plea for punishing them is found in a faint possibility ... of their being productive of a mischief which, if real, will place them in the class of public ones: chiefly in those divisions of it which are composed of offences against population, and offences against the national wealth.'[48]

Like government, popular opinion may consider any act to be, at least offensive, if not strictly a legal offence, and such feelings of antipathy can mobilize the considerable force of the moral sanction against an act. The application of legal sanctions, however, is to be governed, as we have seen, purely by utilitarian considerations. On these grounds self-regarding offences are largely unmeet for punishment. They are, however, exceedingly meet for public censure. In fact 'they are ... apt, many of them, to be more obnoxious to the censure of the world than public offences; owing to the influence of the two false principles; the principle of asceticism, and the principle of antipathy. Some of them more even than private offences.' Moreover, 'among the inducements to punish them, antipathy against the offender is apt to have a greater share than sympathy of the public.'[49]

The extent to which Bentham, in his treatment of self-regarding offences, laid the groundwork for J.S. Mill's arguments in *On Liberty* is striking. Indeed, Bentham's account of self-regarding acts and the appropriate social attitude towards them is, as has been observed,[50] less confused and confusing than Mill's. In his remarks on the reaction of public opinion to self-regarding offences Bentham even seems to glimpse the shadow of majority tyranny falling across the field of individual liberty, a shadow that caused much concern to J.S. Mill. Yet, in the final analysis, Mill saw the moral sanction as an irreparably tyrannical conformist force, while Bentham entertained the highest hopes that this malleable mass of opinion could be pried loose from the principles of asceticism and antipathy and shaped to the standards of utility.

To the three categories of injuries originally outlined in 1776 (i.e. injuries to person, property, and reputation) he later added a fourth: injuries to one's 'condition.' The use of this category arose from Bentham's recognition that a man may derive his happiness from both the things and the persons with which he has contact. He may enjoy the use of or an interest in a thing or the services of a person. When one person owes another his services in some respect by virtue of a specific, identifiable connection (aside from general coexistence) between the two, the receiver of those services is said by Bentham to possess a 'kind of fictitious or incorporal object of property,' which is called his condition (e.g. as husband, master, servant, citizen). A man's condition has its connections with the idea of his reputation, and of course his property.[51] The welter of complexities surrounding these fictitious legal entities, and other terms of the same sort such as power, right, and liberty,[52] made Bentham feel obliged, as he put it, 'to lay the foundations of another work by drawing up (without inserting) an analysis of the possible modifications of peoperty.'[53] In the next chapter we shall look in some detail at this analysis, now published as appendix B to *Of Laws in General*. A foretaste of that full analysis is given in paragraph 27 of chapter 16 of the *Introduction*, where liberty is used as a specimen of the class of fictitious entities which are persistently viewed as concrete objects of property: 'Even *liberty* has been considered in the same point of view: and though on so many occasions it is contrasted with property, yet on other occasions, being reckoned into the catalogue of possessions, it seems to have been considered as a branch of property.'[54]

The theme of liberty as an incorporeal object of property is again touched on when Bentham discusses modes of servitude and the category of 'domestic relations which are purely of legal institution' (an example being the reciprocal relations of master and servant) in the course of his analysis of offences against condition: 'As to the power by which the condition of a master is constituted, this may be either *limited* or *unlimited*. When it is altogether unlimited, the condition of the servant is styled pure slavery ... Whenever any such limitation is prescribed, a kind of fictitious entity is thereby created, and, in quality of an incorporeal object of possession, is bestowed upon the servant.'[55]

Thus is the species of right known as liberty (or, sometimes, privilege, immunity, or exemption) born. The variations in the terms upon which relations between master and servant are based are as diverse as the forms of service which can be demanded. The unsteadiness of the rules of language governing the use of the term 'slavery' has left the definition of slavery at the mercy of self-interest and of the principles of sympathy and antipathy. The need for a solution to this problem brings to Bentham's mind a sense of the importance of the realm, relatively uncharted in the *Introduction*, of civil laws: 'as to the question, whether any, and what, modes of servitude ought to be established or kept on foot? This is a question, the solution of which belongs to the civil branch of the art of legislation.'

Bentham goes on to argue that a condition of servitude, even when absolute, may yet confer valuable benefits when compared with absolute servitude worse circumstanced. Indeed, he insists, 'the condition of the servant may be so eligible, that his entrance into it, and his continuance in it, may have been altogether the result of his own choice.'[56] No matter how dismal his condition, it is clear that, given Bentham's criteria for cases unmeet, such freely given consent to servitude could exempt any master from punishment.

Bentham left the very important task of defining the rights and duties attached to various social conditions, whether of natural institution or of legal institution, largely to the civil branch of law. In the 1780s, as we shall see, he concentrated his attentions more and more exclusively on that legal sphere. At one point in chapter 16 of the *Introduction*, however, discussing the notion of guardianship, he raised the question of when and why one man should legally be endowed with power over another. His answer was that such power was permissible only where it resulted in a clear augmentation of the happiness of the subordinated individual. Any given person, he asserted, requires three things in order to pursue and augment his own happiness successfully: knowledge, inclination, and physical power. In general this argument supports personal independence and self-determination, for while other individuals may hold an advantage in power, this can never outweigh a man's own pre-eminence in knowledge of himself and inclination toward the satisfaction of his desires: 'who should know so well as you do what it is that gives you pain and pleasure?' Further, there is no man who is so sure of being *inclined*, on all occasions, to promote your happiness as you yourself are.'[57] In sum, 'If ... there be a case where it can be for the advantage of one man to be under the power of another, it must be on account of some palpable and very considerable deficiency, on the part of the former, in point of intellects, or (which is the same thing in other words) in point of knowledge or understanding.'[58] There is, however, a form of guidance to which a man may, and indeed ought to, submit in all his actions: the guidance of the art and science of private ethics. In chapter 17 of the *Introduction* the distinction between private ethics and legislation as forms of social control comes to centre stage.[59]

The argument of section i of chapter 17, 'limits between private ethics and the art of legislation,' is summarized in paragraph 20: 'Private ethics teaches how each man may dispose himself to pursue the course most conducive to his own happiness, by means of such motives as offer of themselves; the art of legislation (which may be considered as one branch of the science of jurisprudence) teaches how a multitude of men, composing a community, may be disposed to pursue that course which upon the whole is the most conducive to the happiness of the whole community by means of motives to be applied by the legislator.'[60] The distinction here made between the operations of legal coercion (externally applied motives emanating from the legislator) and those of ethical guidance (based upon such motives as 'offer of themselves') is, in effect, a restatement of the distinction between political obedience and moral duty in the *Fragment*: 'Moral duty is created by a kind of motive which, from the uncertainty of the persons to apply it, and of the species and degree in which it will be applied, has hardly yet got the name of punishment: by various mortifications resulting from the ill-will of persons uncertain and variable, – the community in general; that is, such individuals of that community as he, whose duty is in question, shall happen to be connected with.'[61] Clearly, then, the strength of the guidance provided by private ethics is derived from the moral sanction. 'Ethics in general' includes both private ethics and an additional, more public, sphere. Where private ethics is considered the art of *self*-government, 'as to other human beings, the art of directing their actions to the above end [happiness] is what ... upon the principle of utility, we ought to mean, by the art of government.'[62]

The role of the moral sanction thus encompasses both private and public spheres. It is from the unhesitating endorsement of the all-pervasive social control exerted by the moral sanction as the operative embodiment of 'ethics in general' that the most profound threat to liberty in Bentham's system arises. The moral sanction is to be moulded by the legislator and the educator, but there is no provision for direct resistance to it by the private person. Bentham does not conceive of the universal rule of utilitarian ethics as involving coercion, for he believes that its principles are immanent in the nature of every individual. Yet the endorsement of such a universally applicable ethical system implies that deviation from its norms is always suspect. Even an act which is in the end judged unmeet for punishment has nonetheless, in a sense, been presumed guilty until proved innocent. Nor does abstention from legal punishment of the act imply any alleviation of the pressure of the moral sanction. Indeed, the suspension of punishment is predicated upon the power of the moral sanction to reform behaviour. When Bentham defines the art of education as a branch of the art of government,[63] it becomes clear that he sees a utilitarian system of education as a powerful social conditioning agent, inculcating in 'persons in a non-adult state' the complete encyclopedia of utilitarian ethical dictates, whether those of 'state-regarding' or 'non-state-regarding' ethics, as *Chrestomathia* puts it.[64]

The subject of ethics, Bentham asserts, is duty. Ethics teaches a man to show prudence in the discharge of his duties to himself and probity and beneficence in discharging his duties to others, probity in abstaining from acting so as to impair their happiness and beneficence in acting where possible so as to augment it.[65] Bentham's picture of civil society is not simply a portrait of selfish hedonists requiring constant restraints and restrictions in order merely to coexist. Physiological hedonism does not necessarily imply ethical egoism in his view. Selfish motives are always 'adequate' (i.e. if unopposed) to determine behaviour, but they are not irresistible: 'it cannot but be admitted, that the only interests which a man at all times and upon all occasions is sure to find adequate motives for consulting, are his own. Notwithstanding this, there are no occasions in which a man has not some motives for consulting the happiness of other men. In the first place, he has, on all occasions, the purely social motive of sympathy or benevolence: in the next place, he has on most occasions, the semi-social motives of love of amity and love of reputation.' Social (or, at least, not anti-social) motives are always present in some degree. They are a natural resource ripe for exploitation by a scientific ethic which seeks to manipulate both subjective 'sensibility' and objective circumstances. Is such control not truly coercive? The qualitative distinction between conditioning (the manipulation of motives which naturally 'offer of themselves') and coercion (the application of external motives, usually the legislator's) is implicit in Bentham's examination of the distinction between private ethics and legislation, but is never comprehensively stated. At one point is seems that its explication is imminent, but in the end the distinction between ethics and law is stated in quantitative terms only: there are cases in which ethics ought, and legislation ought not (in a direct manner at least), to interfere.[66] To determine the factors (if any) which might exempt some individual behaviour from the dictates of ethics, we must revert to the criteria of chapter 13, 'Cases unmeet for punishment,' and this is what Bentham proceeds to do.[67]

Turning first to cases where punishment would be groundless, he finds that 'it is because, upon the whole, there is no evil in the act, that legislation ought not to endeavour to prevent it. No more, for the same reason, ought private ethics.'[68] He divides acts with reference to which punishment would be inefficacious into two classes. In the first class the inefficaciousness results from a problem of timing (e.g. ex post facto law): 'The acts here in question then might, for anything that appears, come properly under the department even of coercive legislation: of course do they under that of private ethics.'[69] The second class contains those acts having to do with problems of intentionality. 'These, however, are of such a nature as not only to exclude the application of legal punishment, but in general to leave little room for the influence of private ethics.' In cases of infancy, insanity, unintentionality, unconsciousness, mis-supposal, and so on, 'if the thunders of the law prove impotent, the whispers of simple morality can have but little influence.' Cases where punishment would be unprofitable are 'the cases which constitute the great field for the exclusive interference of private ethics.'[70] In these cases two principal factors require that ethics supplement the efficacy of law. Both arise from the difficulty of proportioning punishment exactly to the evil of a given offence. The punishment may amount to an intolerable expense, even supposing the application of it to be 'confined altogether to delinquency.' On the other hand, it may involve the innocent in the fate designed only for the guilty.[71] Clearly the idea here is that these difficulties in applying legal sanctions require that moral sanctions be invoked instead.

The discussion breaks off at this point, omitting all consideration of cases where punishment is needless, and Bentham turns to an analysis of the relationship between private ethics and the art of legislation from a new perspective. He reiterates the three ethical virtues of prudence, probity, and beneficence, asserting that 'the degree in which private ethics stands in need of the assistance of legislation, is different in the three branches of duty above distinguished.' So far as a man's duty to himself depends on the quality of prudence, Bentham's argument, as we might expect, seems most favourable to individual liberty: 'Of the rules of moral duty, those which seem to stand least in need of the assistance of legislation, are the rules of prudence. It can only be through some defect on the part of the understanding, if a man be ever deficient in point of duty to himself.' Bentham here gives his clearcut account of the limitations on the use of legal sanctions to induce a man to exercise prudently his duty to himself:

It is a standing topic of complaint, that a man knows too little of himself. Be it so: but is it so certain that the legislator must know more? It is plain, that of individuals the legislator can know nothing concerning those points of conduct which depend upon the particular circumstances of each individual, it is plain, therefore that he can determine nothing to advantage. It is only with respect to those broad lines of conduct in which all persons, or very large and permanent descriptions of persons, may be in a way to engage, that he can have any pretence for interfering, and even here the propriety of his interference will, in most instances, lie very open to dispute.[72]

Moreover, the legal sanction cannot hope to 'produce a perfect compliance' unless it is founded upon the thrust of the moral sanction: '[the legislator] must never expect to produce a perfect compliance by the mere force of the sanction of which he is himself the author. All he can hope to do, is to increase the efficacy of private ethics, by giving strength and direction to the influence of the moral sanction.' Finally, Bentham explicitly defends individual liberty with reference to the moral duty of prudence: 'It may be observed, that with regard to this branch of duty, legislators have, in general, been disposed to carry their interference full as far as is expedient. The great difficulty here is, to persuade them to confine themselves within bounds. A thousand little passions and prejudices have led them to narrow the liberty of the subject in this line, in cases in which the punishment is either attended with no profit at all, or with none that will make up for the expence.'[73]

While prudence is the quality most requisite in the fulfilling of self-regarding duties, probity and beneficence are involved in the ethics of other-regarding behaviour. What has Bentham to say on these two heads? As to the rules of beneficence, 'these, as far as concerns matters of detail, must necessarily be abandoned in great measure to the jurisdiction of private ethics,' for it is characteristic of acts of benevolence that they are 'free and voluntary, according to one of the many senses given to those ambiguous expressions.' Like J.S. Mill, however, Bentham can see no reason why the law should not be extended beyond its present limits to endorse and, in fact, require, *some* acts of sympathy for and assistance to one's fellow man on pain of punishment: 'why should it not be made the duty of every man to save another from mischief, when it can be done without prejudicing himself, as well as to abstain from bringing it on him?'[74] The duty of not bringing mischief upon one's fellows is that of probity, and 'the rules of probity are those, which in point of expediency stand most in need of assistance on the part of the legislator.' The case of the duty of probity is the antithesis of that of prudence, for 'there are few cases in which it would be expedient to punish a man for hurting himself; but there are few cases, if any, in which it would *not* be expedient to punish a man for injuring his neighbour.'[75] Indeed, in the case of what, using a category provided in chapter 16 of the *Introduction*, we may call offences against 'social conditions of legal institution,'[76] legislation defines the very conditions whose infringement is deemed an offence. Bentham's later study of civil law was to result in a great broadening of this category. The two classes of such offences named by Bentham at this point, however, were offences against property and offences against the state.[77] Their discussion provides us with a logical bridge between the *Introduction* and *Of Laws in General*, as far as their relevance to the problem of liberty is concerned.

The idea of liberty most deeply probed in *Of Laws in General* is liberty as in some sense the creation of law. In the *Introduction*, however, the explanation of this matter is at least begun: Bentham informs us that 'with regard to that branch of probity which is opposed to offences against property, private ethics depends in a manner for its very existence upon legislation. Legislation must first determine what things are to be regarded as each man's property, before the general rules of ethics, on this head, can have any particular application.' In *Of Laws in General* as well Bentham argues that the law must determine the nature and distribution of property on utilitarian principles before the liberties pertinent to the holding and use of property can become known. In the *Introduction* he maintains that 'the case is the same with regard to offences against the state. Without legislation there would be no such thing as a state: no particular persons invested with powers to be exercised for the benefit of the rest. It is plain, therefore, that in this branch the interference of the legislator cannot anywhere be dispensed with. We must first know what are the dictates of legislation, before we can know what are the dictates of private ethics.' 'Without legislation there would be no such thing as a state.' Nothing could express more clearly than this Bentham's understanding of the relationship between 'censorial jurisprudence' and the study of a 'legal polity.'

What had originally been conceived of as an introduction to a plan of a penal code, and an unsatisfactory one at that, was finally published in the guise of a full statement of the principles governing a series of treatises covering the various branches of the subject of morals and legislation.[78] A segment of a work of censorial jurisprudence was pressed into service as the theoretical foundation for a vast and complex edifice of social thought. The *Introduction* bears the structural burdens of an exploratory work. Nothing in the early manuscript examinations of words and phrases, nothing in the sprightly sarcasms of the

Comment or the *Fragment*, could adequately prepare the way for a work as intricately systematic, comprehensive, and novel as the *Introduction*. The earlier pithy aphorisms about liberty and the system of restraints imposed upon it by government had to be qualified in the light of Bentham's candid recognition of the diversity of conceivable forms of social control on one side and social behaviour on the other. Circumstances alter cases, and the *Introduction* was an exhaustive catalogue of both. It was not so much the problem of adjusting the claims of liberty to the necessities of a system of legislation that troubled Bentham so deeply as the task of integrating the notion of liberty into a system of morals. After the pages of the *Introduction* had been printed, he began to view them with coolness, then with disgust. The work seemed shot through with flaws. It was only the absolute indispensability of the principles put forward, however unsatisfactorily, in the *Introduction* to the understanding of his subsequent works that induced him eventually to publish it. It had all along been his wish to work his principles up into a better form, but 'cogent considerations' and 'the irksomeness of the task' combined to render that impracticable.[79]

Bentham attempted to repair the deficiencies of the *Introduction* in some of his subsequent works. *Of Laws in General* was intended to cut through at least part of the 'metaphysical maze' laid open to view in the *Introduction*.[80] His essays 'The influence of place and time in matters of legislation' and 'Indirect legislation' dealt with additional aspects of the problem of constructing a system of social controls complete in every aspect. His continuing concern with the relationship between penal and civil law, his work on a civil code, and his later interest in a deontology, or system of ethics, all point to the source of Bentham's 'disgust.' He had, in the *Introduction*, brought to centre stage the question of the relationship between government and society, between legislation and ethics, between the legal sanction and the moral sanction: these are but different names for the same problem. He confronted it again in *Of Laws in General* as the relationship between penal law and civil law. His scope of vision by now dwarfed his previous narrow concept of law as essentially penal. The *Introduction* had confronted Bentham with the infinitely subtler but equally important civil function of law. It was to take far longer for him to reach a conclusive position on the nature of a system of civil law than it had taken him to produce a theory of punishments.

APPENDIX: BENTHAM AND J.S. MILL ON LIBERTY

The arguments advanced by Bentham in his attempts to outline the respective provinces of liberty and authority in political society anticipate, as one commentator has observed, a good deal of J.S. Mill's essay *On Liberty*.[81] In that essay Mill set out to define 'Civil, or Social Liberty: the nature and limits of the power which can be legitimately exercised by society over the individual.'[82] A dichotomy persisted throughout Mill's attempt to characterize the 'dealings of society with the individual.' These dealings involved compulsion, physical force, and legal penalties on one hand and control, moral coercion, and public opinion on the other (pp. 72-3). In chapters 16 and 17 of the *Introduction* (especially the latter), Bentham confronted the same dichotomy and attempted to analyse it in terms of the distinction between legislation and the wider field of ethics. Bentham's analysis lacked Mill's rhetorical flair. He put forward no claims to clarify the whole complex problem of social control and individual liberty by the use of 'one very simple principle.' Mill himself may have found his principle simple to state, but it was not at all simple to apply. Only 'self-protection,' he said, could be a sufficient warrant for interference with the liberty of action of individuals by others singly or collectively: 'the only purpose for which power can be rightfully exercised over any member of a civilised community, against his will, is to prevent harm to others. His own good, either physical or moral, is not a sufficient warrant' (pp. 72-3). When Mill proclaimed this principle Bentham had long since dissected it. Mill claimed to base his defence of liberty solely on his notion of utility (p. 74), and he rested his notion of utility upon his conception of certain 'permanent interests' which he found to be inherent in the character of 'man as a progressive being' (p. 74). Although he rejected any support offered to his argument by 'the idea of abstract right, as a thing independent of utility' (p. 74), it is difficult to find anything of utility as distinct from abstract right in the permanent interests of man as a progressive being. This spiritual view of the human essence, whatever its merits, was not based on Benthamite promises. Mill was grafting idealist concepts on to a utilitarian stem.

It was by reference to this special class of permanent interests that Mill defined the sphere of actions wherein spontaneity must reign free of control: 'These interests, I contend, authorise the subjection of individual spontaneity to external control, only in respect to those actions of each, which concern the interest of other people' (p. 74). Thus he introduced his own version of the crucial distinction between self-regarding and other-regarding actions expounded many years before, as we have seen, by Bentham. When Mill turned to his practical proposals for adjudicating in cases of conflict between the interests of each and the interests of the rest, however, the relevance of his conception of man's special 'permanent interests' was sometimes difficult to discern, and the applicability of his very simple principle was on some occasions questionable. He sanctioned, for example, punishment of private acts hurtful to others by 'legal penalties' or 'general disapprobation,' and, just as Bentham had done almost 80 years before, went further, to propose that individuals might 'rightfully be compelled to perform ... many positive acts for the benefit of others.' He reasoned that 'things which whenever it is obviously a man's duty to do, he may rightfully be made responsible to society for not doing' (p. 74). J.C. Rees, in his 'Re-reading of Mill on liberty,' has justifiably remarked that in view of Mill's awareness of the myriad forms of social interaction, 'one wonders how it ever came to be thought ... that he wished to declare a whole area of human behaviour "self-regarding" because the actions so named had "no effects" on others.'[83]

The difference between Mill and Bentham has less to do with the extent of the sphere of inviolate personal liberty within civil society than with the objects against which liberty must be protected. Bentham's interest in the protection of liberty against the potential tyranny of political rulers seems at first glance to place him among the theorists of a period which Mill claimed to have left behind, a time when the struggle between Liberty and Authority was essentially one between subjects and Government (p. 65), when the aim of patriots was to limit the power of the ruler over the community, and this limitation was what was meant by liberty (p. 66). But we have seen that in the *Fragment* Bentham denied that liberty in a polity depended upon the limitation of sovereign power.[84] He argued that the limits of such power were the same for all states, free and despotic, and were established in every case by the principle of utility. His arguments characterized a later phase in the struggle between Liberty and Authority, in which the object was to reconcile the dispute by identifying the interest and will of the rulers with the interest and will of the people (p. 67). Bentham helped put forward a new demand for elective and temporary rulers which 'superseded, to a considerable extent, the previous efforts to limit the power of rulers' (p. 66).[85]

Mill felt that such faith in the power of elective, responsible government to preserve liberty could only have been maintained before the actual establishment of popular government had revealed its liabilities. Pre-eminent among these was an inherent tendency towards a 'tyranny of the majority' (p. 68). We have said that Bentham and Mill were concerned with the same dichotomy in the forms of social control. But Mill placed a much heavier emphasis than Bentham on the threat posed to liberty by the 'moral coercion of public opinion' (p. 72): 'Protection ... against the tyranny of the magistrate is not enough: there needs protection also against the tyranny of the prevailing opinion and feeling; against the tendency of society to impose, by means other than civil penalties, its own ideas and practices as rules of conduct on those who dissent from them' (p. 68). Bentham's psychology and — to transplant a term — his sociology did not induce him to fear, or even to comprehend, the notion of the 'tyranny of the majority.'

He defended dissent and public discussion, not because they were a protection against a stultifying conformity or an asphyxiating blanket of consensus, but because in his view discussion tended always to breed consensus by reducing disagreements in attitude to calculations couched in the common terms of utility. Mill's dynamic conception of the human spirit could never be completely reconciled with Bentham's comparatively passive and literally 'reactionary' picture of man. Thus Mill was preoccupied with a form of tyranny against which Bentham felt no need to guard. It was in this way that Bentham and Mill developed disparate approaches to the problem of liberty. Mill made a new and distinctive contribution to the analysis of what Bentham had called the 'pugna sanctionum.' His contribution took the form of a study of the possibility of a tyranny of the moral sanction over the others, a case, as he put it, 'when society itself is the tyrant ... and the result is a tyranny penetrating ... deeply into the details of life, and enslaving the soul itself' (p. 63).

Bentham's system emphasized heavily, almost exclusively, the security-oriented aspects of the human personality. His vision of utilitarian society embodied the idea of a near-unanimity of wills founded upon a near-homo-geneity of individual personalities. A community rendering undeviating obedi-ence to the dictates of utility would represent at one and the same time the apotheosis of majority tyranny in J.S. Mill's terms and the maximization of the Benthamite values of security, predictability, stability, and physical comfort. Bentham aimed to reconcile the demands of liberty with the requirements of a basically static social framework. Mill sought to devise ways of escaping from a stultifying, stagnant social conformity in order than an open-ended, creative, and dynamic liberty might be enjoyed both as an end in itself and as an indirect source, through free social innovation, of great benefits to political society in general.

Both Mill and Bentham set out to construct a science of society based on a science of man. Bentham's system aimed to shape individual behaviour to the requirements of society in the belief that society was the necessary condition of human happiness. Mill aimed to rescue the individual from the clutches of social conformity, believing that personal freedom was a necessary condition of a fully human (as opposed to animal) existence at both personal and social levels. The roots of the inadequacies which Mill detected in Bentham's view of human nature[86] lay in what Bentham recognized as the 'dryness' of his metaphysics. Yet in Bentham's mind this dryness was unavoidable, the price of scientific objectivity. In Mill's opinion it was the aridity of a mind whose conception of human nature was simplistic and incomplete, and whose idea of individuality had been eroded by the search for universal principles of behaviour.

PART THREE / EXPANSION AND APPLICATION

7

Of Laws in General

Having set out to write an introduction to a plan of a penal code, Bentham had been led deeper and deeper into the labyrinthine maze of legal metaphysics by the insatiable hunger of his own intellect for firm and full first principles. As he struggled to mould his theoretical premises into a printable form he was almost overwhelmed by the complexities and the sheer bulk of the manuscripts thus generated. Yet their organization and presentation to the public still seemed to him to be an essential stage in the construction and promotion of a new and comprehensive system of law. Nor could he isolate and publish the particular theoretical principles relevant to a specific branch (the penal branch) of legislation. The experience of writing the *Introduction to the Principles of Morals and Legislation* convinced Bentham that the plan of his magnum opus must be 'enlarged, so as to take in the whole body of the law as well as the penal branch.'

The pages of the *Introduction* were printed in 1780 but remained unpublished until 1789. The process of enlarging the introductory portion of his magnum opus, however, began almost immediately after the completion of the text of *Introduction*. Within a little over two years its appearance was substantially altered. Bentham outlined a new, expanded conception of the theoretical foundations of his work in a letter to Lord Ashburton dated 3 June 1782.[1] Bentham's great friend and patron, Lord Shelburne, had frequently urged him to show Lord Ashburton the printed pages of the *Introduction*.[2] Bentham claimed in his letter to be reluctant to allow his hopes for the approval of so distinguished a reader to rest upon the merits of a work in 'so imperfect a condition,' 'a book which is not only without beginning or end but which must undergo several alterations before it faces the public eye,'[3] But he implied that Lord Shelburne had insisted that he come forward. Presumably it was in an effort to acquaint Lord Ashburton with the true extent and nature of his projected work that Bentham appended to his comments on the shortcomings of the *Introduction*, the pages of which were enclosed with his letter, a description of 'the chapters ... which contain the remaining part of the matter designed for the introduction' as he then envisaged them.[4] Only by examining the contents of this expanded introduction can we reach a full understanding of the theoretical foundations Bentham considered adequate to the task of building a system of morals and legislation.

The introduction described in the letter to Lord Ashburton was to be a work of fully forty chapters.[5] The contents of the first eighteen of these chapters are effectively embodied in the seventeen chapters of the *Introduction* as printed in the new edition which forms a volume in the *Collected Works* series.[6] Chapters 19 to 37 inclusive constitute the text of the work recently published in the *Collected Works* series and described by its editor, Prof. H.L.A. Hart, as a continuation of the *Introduction*.[7] To that work, *Of Laws in General*, we turn in the present chapter. The remainder of Bentham's enlarged introduction consisted of chapter 38, explaining the 'Idea of a compleat *corpus juris*' and its various branches, chapter 39, 'Of indirect or preventive legislation,' and chapter 40, the 'Influence of *time* and *place* on the expediency of a law.'[8] I now propose to examine first *Of Laws in General*, then the manuscripts in the UCL collection which will form the text of the forthcoming edition of the *Essay on Indirect Legislation* (still another addition to the *Collected Works* series), and finally the manuscripts which will form the substance of the projected *Collected Works* edition of Bentham's inquiry into the 'Influence of place and time in matters of legislation.' Each of these works or works-to-be had a distinctive relationship to the printed *Introduction*, and each made its characteristic contribution to Bentham's idea of liberty. The 'compleat *corpus juris*' will receive attention later, as will the work on the subject of 'reward,' which Bentham described in his letter to Lord Ashburton as approaching completion.[9]

Chapter 16 in *Of Laws in General*, which is chapter 32 of the larger, forty-chapter 'introduction,' is devoted to the subject of the '*completeness* of a law – or – what it is that goes to the making of a complete law.'[10] In the letter to Lord Ashburton, printed in appendix E to *Of Laws in General*, chapter 32 is given as 'What it is that constitutes a compleat law.'[11] In one of the draft versions of Bentham's letter to Lord Ashburton, as presented in Bentham's published *Correspondence*, however, we find a significantly different version: 'Ch. 32. What is it that constitutes a compleat law? The general laws of liberty form a sort of expanse in which the several coercive laws have a / their respective locality / place as islands in the ocean, or stars in the immensity of space.'[12] We have previously seen that in 1776 Bentham had entertained the notion of publishing an essay on the idea of liberty as an appendix to John Lind's 'Three letters to Dr Price,' but that the essay was never written. The chapter on the 'General laws of liberty' hinted at in the draft letter just quoted suffered the same fate. The 'Idea of a complete law' has maintained its claim to a place in *Of Laws in General*,[13] but Bentham's discussion of the idea of a 'universal law of liberty' now forms only a part of paragraph 16 ('Use of non-commanding and originally-permissive provisions') of section iv (dealing with 'Alterative' laws) in chapter 10 of *Of Laws in General*, which is entitled 'Aspects of a law.'[14]

In logical, conceptual terms the discussion of the nature of the 'pre-existing universal law of liberty,' as given in *Of Laws in General*, is the very starting point of Bentham's explanation of how the legislatorial will begins to make a cosmos out of the chaos of pre-legal social relationships and conditions. Cumulatively, the arguments in *Of Laws in General*, with regard to liberty purport to provide us with a detailed explanation of the process alluded to in a passage we have quoted from chapter 17 of the *Introduction*: the process by which legislation defines the terms in which ethical rules are framed with regard to legal creations such as property and the state. Another way of viewing the same cluster of conceptions, of course, is as setting out the conditions required for the theoretical definition of political and proprietary liberties.

One manuscript passage (69.145) indicates that very early in his career Bentham made at least a tentative effort to formulate a general law of property and a general law of liberty on the basis of the 'modal objects' upon which these divisions of law in general were to act. Another passage (69.101) shows that Bentham characterized the laws of property as 'so many exceptions,' along with 'the Laws constitutive of constitutional powers,' to the 'Law of security' and the 'Law of liberty.' In the latter passage he put forward two definitions as follows:

The general law concerning / on behalf of / Personal Security is that no man shall do anything to / that is, exert any act on the person of / any other man against that other's will: [marginal insert: 'that is make the person of any other man the object of any action of his'].

The General Law in behalf of Personal Liberty is that no man shall do any act whereby the motion of any other man's person may be prevented or impeded.[15]

The general law of liberty is related to its modal objects as follows: 'The modal objects of the general Law of Liberty are all acts whatsoever on all passive objects whatever whereby the locomotive faculty of any person is obstructed' (69.145).[16]

In retrospect, these characterizations of the idea of a general law of liberty form the conceptual background to a more complex and careful examination of it in *Of Laws in General*. There the idea of a general law finds its equivalent in the abstract or fictitious concept of the 'will of the legislator,' while the modal objects which give shape and character to various types of general laws have their analogues in the several modes of conduct upon which the attention of the legislator may be focused: 'The will of the legislator, like that of any other person is a uniform unvaried surface: susceptible indeed of as many different colours as it may have aspects; but in other respects deriving its distinctive character no otherwise than from the various images, which are reflected upon it as it were from the several modes of conduct towards which it turns itself.'[17] The abstract fictitious entity known as a general law of liberty thus makes its appearance in concrete form, embodied in the attitude of the legislator toward certain modes of conduct. Specifically, it is embodied in either 'non-commanding' or 'originally-permissive' legislative provisions, provisions which Bentham described as 'unobligative.'[18] In his lengthy description of how any man may discover the general characteristics of the most basic varieties of law by observing the operations of concrete particular laws in specific cases, Bentham provides us with yet another manifestation, very similar to those we have seen in the *Comment*, the *Fragment*, and the *Introduction*, of his determination to construct a legal and political mode of discourse in which all general or abstract terms can be translated into propositions involving relationships among real entities.

The employment in *Of Laws in General* of the concrete image of the will of the legislator, where previously only the existence of an abstraction had been postulated, constitutes a characteristic and significant application of Bentham's metaphysical principles of explanation. By his own admission, the particular objective Bentham had in mind in writing *Of Laws in General* was a metaphysical one – to answer two essential questions about law: 'Wherein consisted the identity and completeness of a law? What the distinction, and where the separation, between a penal and a civil law?'[19] To the latter question we shall turn our attention in a subsequent chapter. The former question reflects Bentham's self-conscious attempt to reinforce the metaphysical arguments of the *Introduction* at one of their weakest points. The correctness and completeness of his utilitarian system as a whole depended, in his eyes, on his ability to define on one hand the operations of law, and on the other hand the conduct of the individual, in terms which would clearly show the necessity (indeed, inevitability) of the control of society by minds acquainted with the dictates of utility. The *Introduction* provided its readers with an account of the hedonistic, utilitarian theory of human nature which was at first sight more complete and more persuasive than its account of the numerous coercive and conditioning forces to which human nature stood exposed in community life. So it must have seemed to Bentham at least, for the works in which he sought to shore up the metaphysical weaknesses of the *Introduction* all have to do with the definition and the mechanics of the social forces to which he attributed the greatest impact on the subject or citizen, that is, the four sanctions. His essay on 'Indirect legislation,' dealt with in the next chapter, concentrated mainly on the moral sanction but made reference to the others as well. The essay on the 'Influence of place and time in matters of legislation' was not restricted exclusively to the study of any one of the sanctions. In *Of Laws in General* the legal sanction came under the microscope. The *pugna sanctionum* began afresh. A lasting settlement of their conflicting claims was sought.

The search for such a settlement was to last throughout Bentham's long career. He was to become convinced, by 1789, that to give a complete and correct answer to the questions which had prompted him to write *Of Laws in General*, to find a way out of the metaphysical maze,[20] and to erect a comprehensive legislative system, 'it is but too evident that the relations and dependencies of every part of the legislative system, with respect to every other, must have been comprehended and ascertained.' This points towards the problem of the relationship between penal and civil law as one of the central issues. Yet at least one problem must be solved before the examination of relationships among branches or parts of the system of laws as a whole can begin: 'it is only upon a view of these parts themselves, that such an operation could have been performed. To the accuracy of such a survey one necessary condition would therefore be, the complete existence of the fabric to be surveyed. Of the performance of this condition no example is as yet to be met with any where.' One could not embark upon a study of the relationships linking the subdivisions within a complete body of law when no adequate specimen of such a *corpus juris* could be found. One must begin with making one.[21] The shape of the whole could not be known by observation; therefore the features of the parts could not be ascertained. One could only begin with the particular, with the questions Bentham asked in the 'intimation of the nature of the task,' given in the Concluding Note appended to the *Introduction* in 1789: 'What is a law? What are the parts of a law?' More precisely still, he specified that 'the subject of these questions, it is to be observed, is the *logical*, the *ideal*, the *intellectual* whole, not the *physical* one: the *law* and not the *statute*.[22]

It is quite evident from the very chapter-titles in *Of Laws in General* that Bentham kept the above remarks firmly in mind as he pressed on with that work.[23] He focused attention in part on the relationship between the coercive and permissive aspects of individual laws. To understand the relationship between liberty and coercion under a system of laws is to understand the 'states of the mind' which may be embodied in a legal mandate.[24] Just as the 'aspect of the will' expressed by a law may be decided or undecided, so the particular law itself may be 'imperative' (obligative, coercive) or 'unimperative' (unobligative, uncoercive).[25] The balance between liberty and authority in political society reflects the interaction between unobligative laws, that is, non-commanding or originally-permissive provisions, on one hand, and more active and efficient laws on the other. This conflict, in turn, may be witnessed on each and every occasion when an 'efficient' law takes the place of a pre-existing, originally-permissive one:

The only use of a provision of either of the unobligative kinds is to introduce some provision of a more active and efficient nature: the former serving as a basis to which the latter in the shape of a limitation or an exception may adhere. When regarded in this point of view every efficient law whatever may be considered as a limitation or exception, grafted on a pre-established universal law of liberty: and thus a kind of medium of connection may be established in the mind, whereby the idea of every law that can be conceived may be confronted with, and rendered as it were commensurable to that of every other.[26]

This portrait has both benevolent and malevolent aspects: everything depends on which aspect one chooses to emphasize. A universal law of liberty is postulated, in terms of which coercive laws are merely limitations or exceptions. Could Bentham be a libertarian after all? Certainly not. We must not forget that Bentham never abandoned his definition of all law as essentially coercive in nature. We are reminded in the manuscript passage just quoted that the only use of unobligative laws is to introduce other, patently coercive ones. The universal law of liberty is both a crucial and a paradox-laden concept. It is at the same time an expression of the boundlessness of the theoretical realm of individual freedom and a declaration of the legislator's power to regulate or restrict liberties whenever there is a utilitarian case for doing so. It is not by the proclamation of liberties, but by a declaration of the intention of the legislator to subordinate them to the requirements of security and of law, that cosmos is brought out of chaos: 'The non-commanding and permissive phases of the law placed side by side and turned towards the universal system of human actions are expressed by the before-mentioned universal law of liberty: a boundless expanse in which the several efficient laws appear as so many spots; like islands and continents projecting out of the ocean: or like material bodies scattered over the immensity of space.'[27] Thus the general law of liberty is defined in concrete terms by its modal objects. It is given its particular set of dimensions. In space, it is coextensive with the universe of human actions. In time, it is prior to those efficient laws by which 'islands and continents' of ordered, controlled behaviour are carved out of it. Law and order go hand in hand; they are, in fact, identical. If Bentham's imagery is to be accepted with all its implications, however, we must acknowledge that it identifies liberty, even liberty in the form of a general unobligative law, with the forces of chaos.

From the prohibitions which are based on efficient, coercive laws, specific and circumscribed exemptions are made. These are the foundations of such rights in general, and particularly of such liberties and proprietary rights, as are legally instituted. The practice of legislation consists largely of determining the exact nature and extent of the prohibitions which are to be embodied in efficient laws, and of defining the exemptions which are to be made 'in favour of the general interests of the community' or 'of the liberty and property of other persons whose interests may interfere with those you have.'[28] Only to a very limited extent can it be asserted that it is the purpose of political policies to preserve such liberties as are derived, not from exemptions articulated in efficient laws, but directly from the 'pre-existing universal law of liberty.' Bentham did not intend to allow such a concept to be interpreted as a fountainhead of natural liberties.

The universal law of liberty, in Bentham's view, pre-exists those efficient laws grafted on to it, yet it remains not a natural but a positive law. The idea of a universal, non-commanding, originally-permissive law sounds very much like a description of what some would call a natural law, or an immanent, categorical, ethical norm. Yet in his opposition to the ideas of natural law and natural rights Bentham clings to the argument that the universal law of liberty remains a creation of the system of laws as a whole. It is a fictitious entity, a conception which serves to describe that vast and indeterminate vacuum in which the law stays its hand but maintains its presence. The law refrains from acting coercively by the grace, as it were, of the legislator. As in the case of the creation of an inexclusive property in a piece of land, so in the present case, to say that the law does not act is at the same time to leave undisturbed the tacit assumption that it *could* act but refrains from doing so.[29] Whence this tacit assumption? From the nature of sovereignty itself and of 'law in general.' In fact, in Bentham's view, the basis of that assumption is itself an act of law, but an unobligative one.[30] Here we see the full depth of Bentham's legal positivism. The will of the legislator pervades the whole universe of human actions, and must be understood by every subject as doing so.

In the rule of law Bentham found the guarantor of government and sovereignty. These two things could remain secure only as long as the citizens of a polity regarded all liberty of every kind as liberty under the law, never liberty against the law, existing by grace of the legislator's permissive attitude toward many of the shadowy, little-known recesses of the universe of human actions.

Hence Bentham found the ideas of natural liberty and natural rights pernicious. In fact, he found them subversive of every kind of government based on law. In place of the Lockean state of nature, Bentham posited a hypothetical anarchy of lawless liberty and total insecurity, ended by the acknowledgment of a single power, no matter how discovered, how justified, or how constituted, great enough to extend the powers of permission and prohibition throughout the universe of human action from which a community arises. In fact the limits of the extent of the sovereign's will constitute the only definition of the community. Only a sovereign who, within those limits, could claim to administer a universal power of permission and prohibition extending to all acts could bring the cosmos of society out of the chaos of lawless liberty.

In all of this, liberty was clearly enough a 'cornerstone' of Bentham's system. It was, in Bentham's thought, essential to all government that the citizen should acknowledge in this fashion that his rights – his powers and liberties – were his by permission of government where not by means of the more efficient force of command or prohibition. Even those actions which, as Bentham argued in chapter 17 of the *Introduction*, were fit objects of the moral but not the legal sanction[31] must be felt to be potential objects of legislative coercion in the event that circumstances should render them of a hedonistic social significance great enough to be of discernible political weight. Thus what might appear to be liberties against law in Bentham's political society are in fact something very different – liberties *under* law.

We turn next to the problems encountered by Bentham in analysing the 'division of offences' in chapter 16 of the *Introduction*,[32] and pursued in a substantial manuscript now published as appendix B to *Of Laws in General*. The argument begins as an analysis of the terms 'power' and 'right,' but broadens into a typical Benthamic treatment of legal and political abstractions:

[Marginal heading: 'Rights, powers and other fictitious legal entities to be explained by their real entities']

Power, right, prohibition, duty, obligation, burthen, immunity, exemption, privilege, property, security, liberty – all these with a multitude of others that might be named are so many fictitious entities which the law upon one occasion or another is considered in common speech as creating or disposing of.[33]

How literally should the implications of common speech be interpreted? Does the law simply and straightforwardly create and dispose of liberty? Initially he refers to this notion as 'the mere work of the fancy.' He does not, however, mean to say that all fictions, as works of the fancy, are irrelevant to reality. The use of a fictitious entity in discourse is 'a kind of allegory.' The explanation of the meaning of fictitious entities, of fictions in legal discourse, consists in unravelling the meaning of the allegory. It is 'a riddle of which the solution is not otherwise to be given than by giving the history of the operations which the law performs in that case with regard to certain real entities.' These real entities include the parties involved, the acts in view and the 'aspect' of the law turned toward them, and the circumstances relevant to every facet of the case in view. We have returned, in effect, to the analysis of language, the theme of the 'meaning of fundamental words' which, we have seen, so centrally occupied Bentham's attention in his early manuscripts. Only by tracing the meanings of fictitious expressions back to their foundation in real entities can we attach 'ideas to our words.' Otherwise, our rhetoric remains at best empty and at worst pernicious. 'The ingenuity of the first authors of language which if not compelled by necessity was at least invited by convenience, has thrown a kind of veil of mystery over the face of every science, and over none a thicker than over that of jurisprudence.' What is perhaps surprising, although it is entirely consistent with Bentham's understanding of the role of fictions in discourse, is that he offers, in this instance, a defence of this opacity of language: 'This barrier it will not be practicable perhaps not even expedient altogether to remove,' provided always that we 'have learned upon every occasion how to pierce through it at pleasure before we can obtain a clear perception of the real state of things.' In the concluding words of the paragraph, Bentham contrives to acknowledge the occasional expediency of fictions while still finishing with a warning of their potential mischievousness: 'These fantastic denominations are a sort of paper currency: if we know how at any time to change them and get sterling in their room, it is well: if not, we are deceived, and instead of being masters of so much real knowledge as by the help of them we mean to supply ourselves with, we possess nothing but sophistry and nonsense.'

The fictitious entity called liberty can either by a basis for sophistry and nonsense or a guide to real knowledge. To determine which of these is the case for a given usage of the term we must revert to the concrete situation to which it is applied – to the persons, the acts, and the circumstances described in the given instance of liberty. Moreover, just as the ideas of fictitious entities themselves may be cleansed of ambiguity by such a method, so, too, can the nature of the law be clarified, for 'it is to this abstract way of speaking, these fictitious entities alone that the law owes all its obscurity. Avoid them or explain them by the relation they bear to real ones and the law is clear.'[34]

In *Of Laws in General*, paragraph 2, appendix B, Bentham proposes to embark on an 'explanation of the several fictitious legal entities.' His method, he says, will be to demonstrate how fictitious entities are by-products of the operations by which the law creates offences. Turning to liberty first of all, however, he affixes a marginal heading implying that his explanatory method has already been overthrown: 'Before the law acts liberty is universal.' At first, we read, liberty is unconfined:

As yet there is no law in the land. The legislator hath not yet entered upon his office. As yet he hath neither commanded nor prohibited any act. As yet all acts therefore are free: all persons as against the law are at liberty. Restraint, constraint, compulsion, coercion, duty, obligation, those species I mean of each which issue from the law are things unknown. As against the law all persons possess as great a measure of this great blessing of liberty as it is possible for persons to possess: and in a greater measure than it is possible for men to possess it in any other state of things. This is the first day of the political creation: the state is without form and void.[35]

Bentham presents this image of a pre-legal, pre-political state of unbounded liberty in a way which bears some resemblance to his treatment of the idea of equality in political economy. The distinction Bentham was to make there between 'practicable' and 'perfect' equality was remarkably similar, in turn, to the distinction postulated in his early manuscripts between 'liberty political in perfection' and 'liberty political entire.' Unrestricted liberty and unqualified equality alike were seen as leading to anarchy – and, beyond the tortures of anarchic chaos, to their own limitation. Universal and unconfined liberty is, in the passage quoted, a state of perfectly equal possession by everyone of a good – the good of liberty of action *against* law because in lieu of law. In the case of liberty, as in the case of equality, however, this state of things 'cannot endure for a day,' for human nature itself revolts against it. In both cases the craving of man for power over man induces men to accept limitations on their liberty as against the law:

As yet then you and I and everyone are at liberty. Understand always, as against the law: for as against one another this may be far from being the case. Legal restraint, legal constraint and so forth are indeed unknown: but legal protection is unknown also. You and your neighbour, suppose, are at variance: he has bound you hand and foot, or has fastened you to a tree: in this case you are certainly not at liberty as against him: on the contrary he has deprived you of your liberty: and it is on account of what you have been made suffer by the operation which deprives you of it that the legislator steps in and takes an active part in your behalf. Since the legislator then takes an active part, how is it that he must demean himself? He must either command or prohibit: for there is nothing else that he can do: he therefore cuts off on the one side or the other a portion of the subject's liberty.[36]

In all of this, Bentham has not lost sight of his original hypothesis that liberty, as a fictitious legal entity, is a by-product of the operations of law. He is not here arguing, in contradiction of the manuscript evidence we have examined, that all liberty is produced by law. He is showing how the idea of liberty arises in specifically legal discourse. In this context Bentham's first aim is to show that liberty is normally *viewed* as a by-product of the operation of law, that this is the conventional meaning of that term in legal discourse. His second point, however, clearly maintained by his choice of allegorical explanation, is that this 'creation' of liberty, as the manuscripts suggest, is in fact no more than a redistribution or transformation of a pre-existing quantum of liberty. This becomes clearer in a later passage from *Of Laws in General*, but is quite evidently an echo of his judgment, found in UCL Box 69, that the law can only 'produce' liberty by the removal of some coercive restriction previously in force. 'Liberty then is of two or even more sorts, according to the number of quarters from whence coercion, which it is the absence of, may come: liberty as against the law, and liberty as against those who first in consideration of the effect of their conduct upon the happiness of society, and afterwards in consideration of the course taken against them by the law, may be styled wrong-doers.'[37]

It is in this passage that we find a more objectively analytical expression of the striking and well-known rhetorical question published in Dumont's edition of Bentham's *Theory of Legislation*: 'Is not the liberty to do evil liberty?.'[38] Liberty against the law and liberty against wrong-doers are equally properly referred to as liberty, even though 'these two sorts of liberty are directly opposed to one another: and in as far as it is in favour of an individual, that the law exercises its authority over another, the generation of the one sort is, as far as it extends, the destruction of the other. In the same proportion and by the same cause by which the one is increased, the other is diminished.'[39] The universal and unconfined liberty of the pre-political world, in Bentham's view, is entirely (by definition) liberty against law, *because* it is liberty in lieu of law. But such freedom from legal coercion simply means greater exposure to coercion by individual agents who are in fact wrongdoers, but who live without fear of punishment because there exists no superior punitive force. A Hobbesian condition exists where only distinctions in guile or physical power disturb the equality of men engaged in a war 'of every man, against every man,'[40] a 'perpetuall and restless' struggle for 'power after power,' that 'ceaseth onely in Death.'[41] Bentham's chosen task is to explain the impact of the establishment of a legal system upon this anarchic condition. His explanation is that the law, acting directly on real entities (persons and things), creates an intricate web of powers and restraints, rights and duties, striking a balance between the oppressiveness of a total liberty of action against wrongdoers and the chaos of a state of unbounded liberty against law: neither of these liberties is thus possessed in entirety, but each is possessed in that perfection which marks an Aristotelian mean between oppression and anarchy. The action of the law directly on persons and things initially takes the form of the creation of offences against specified individuals and objects or against specified classes of them. The result is, for 'the rest of the community, restraint,' while for the specified individuals or objects it is 'personal security and protection.'[42] It is at this point that Bentham first speaks explicitly of 'rights.' We know very well, of course, that he wished to refute theories of natural rights, and propounded the theory that rights are created, in the sense in which liberties are created, that is, are *secured*, by the law: 'it gives you, when corroborated by the requisite apparatus of subsidiary laws, a right of being protected by the hands of its ministers against the endeavours of any who would inflict on you such injuries.'[43]

We have seen that Bentham's early manuscripts yield the following brief summary of his idea of rights: 'Of rights — some are synonymous to Powers others to Liberties — limitations to Public Constitutional Powers — created by the absence of coercion' (69.213). The rights guaranteed by the laws giving rise to personal security and protection are thus liberties. It may be that such laws create rights in the form of powers as well: these will be powers bestowed upon officers of the law to *preserve* such personal security and protection as the laws establish. Paragraph 4 of appendix B to *Of Laws in General* explains how the individual, conceived of as the vulnerable and passive object of aggressive wrongdoers, is protected by law against what Lockeans might call invasion of his person. Invasion of his property is dealt with in paragraph 7. Paragraph 5 deals with the protection of such modes of action as ought to be secured from the restraining or constraining influence of other individuals. This species of legal action gives rise to two modes of liberty: liberty of 'locomotion' which consists in the 'absence of confinement or the absence of banishment,' and the broader liberty of 'behaviour in general,' which is the 'absence of restraint or the absence of constraint.' Paragraph 6 deals with the same legal operation, this time with the protection of the individual's reputation as its object. Paragraphs 7 to 11 deal with what Bentham refers to as the creation of property by law and the subsequent creation of offences against property, resulting in further species of liberty.[44] This was a theme to which Bentham returned in his 'Civil Code' manuscripts, where, as we shall see, he made it clear that 'there is no arrangement more contrary to the principle of utility, than community of goods, especially that kind of indeterminate community in which the whole belongs to every one.'[45] It would be totally self-defeating for Bentham to posit the law as acting to bring about a state both indeterminate and contrary to the principle of utility. It is *private* property that the law is observed to create in these paragraphs. In paragraph 7, however, we are asked to consider the situation when the law takes no action whatever with regard to some object, 'a piece of land, for instance.' 'The result [is] on all sides liberty as before.' Bentham was clearly struck by the similarity between the process by which the law gives rise to personal liberty and that by which it creates private property. As he portrays it, the pre-legal state of community of property is by the same token a condition of anarchic, unconfined liberty. In fact, Bentham's views of these two states are complementary. In his support for the institution of private property and the liberties that accompany it, he echoes, faintly but appropriately, Locke's dictum that 'a man hath a propriety in his own person.'[46] Person and property are in Bentham's view to be secured for the same reason – because, and in so far as, they are sources of pleasure. Where, however, the state of pre-legal, unconfined liberty of all against all is incompatible with the existence of law and government, community of goods is merely indeterminate, counterproductive, and highly inexpedient. 'With respect to by far the greatest part of the land under its dominion,' the law does in fact command all but a specified 'one or a few' not to 'exercise any act upon that land.'[47] Bentham seems to feel that a given individual, in relation to a piece of land about which the law is silent, is said to possess a power over the land or a property in the land only because the law has not explicitly forbidden any acts by any individuals upon that piece of land:

As this same sort of property is given not to you only, but to me and everybody else, no restraint with respect to the use of the land being laid on anybody, that which is given to you may on that account be styled *inexclusive*: an inexclusive power over the land: an inexclusive property in the land. The land in this case is said to be the common property of us all: and each of us is said to have a property in it in common with the rest: and each man may even be said to have the property of it, so as this phrase be added 'in *common* with the rest.'[48]

Paragraph 8 deals with a property in land granted to a limited group of assignable individuals. Such a property, from the point of view of an individual member of the group, is exclusive of all other individuals except the other members of the group, with regard to whom it is 'inexclusive.' In paragraph 9 the concept of totally exclusive (or private) property is introduced, but in paragraph 11 we are reminded that in fact an exclusive title to land can never completely exclude the claims of, say, *raison d'état*. In paragraph 11 it is also pointed out that the law may go beyond the securing of the mere title to a piece of land:

In this case the law not only permits you to exercise such power over the land as without its interference you were enabled to enjoy, but interferes itself in your favour, and takes an active part in your favour in securing to you the exercise of that power by taking measures for averting such obstacles as might be opposed to the exercise of it by the enterprises of other men. The power or liberty you had before as against the law may now be said to be corroborated or assisted by law.

Thus private property is based upon the transformation of 'liberties against law,' by which private property is accumulated, into liberties *under* the law *against* wrongdoers, by virtue of which property is enjoyed and exploited. The sense in which the existence of property is considered by Bentham to be a liberty against law created by law is clarified in a passage of the 'Key' manuscripts in which he discusses the creation of 'Public property appropriated' (or 'Public property in common') by law: 'What the Law does therefore when it constitutes Public Property *appropriated* is in the 1st place as in the case of private property to restrain persons in general / at large / from meddling with the thing in question, then to repeal that restriction in favour of a certain person or persons of a particular description' (69.55).

The granting of a property, even in the inexclusive form, that is, property in common, is according to this account a specific exemption from a general prohibition, which was itself preceeded by a chaos of conflicting powers and claims. It would appear that, in theory at least, and, what is of more practical importance, in law, a condition of the creation of law, sovereignty, and government is the surrender of all liberty and all property, whereupon specific and determinate liberties and properties are sanctioned and protected by law and government. The justification for all of this lies in the insecurity of all pleasure and the constant vulnerability to pain arising from the condition of liberty and property before government. The best of governments can, however, secure individual liberty and property only subject to 'various exceptions, as well in favour of the general interests of the community as in favour of the liberty and property of other persons whose interests may interfere with those which you have.'[49]

The exact determination of the nature and extent of such exemptions was the task to which Bentham, stimulated by the questions raised by his investigations in the *Introduction* and *Of Laws in General* into the relationships between penal and civil law and between ethics and jurisprudence, turned in his manuscripts on civil law and his notes toward a 'Civil Code' in the 1780s. We shall take up that story in a subsequent chapter. In the interim, we return to the remaining components of the expanded introduction to the theory of morals and legislation envisaged by Bentham in 1782: the essays on 'Indirect legislation' and on the 'Influence of place and time in matters of legislation.'

8

'Indirect legislation' and 'Matters of place and time'

Like the *Fragment on Government, Of Laws in General* was in a sense a digression, a tangential voyage through the maze of legal metaphysics.[1] Assessing his achievements to date in the final chapter to *Of Laws in General*, Bentham was confident that in its pages he had made progress toward the elevation of the 'art of legislation' to the level of 'science,'[2] and that he had emerged from his labyrinthine journey clutching in hand a set of theoretical principles upon which a complete *corpus juris* could be built.[3] He was anxious, however, to 'resume the regular thread of the discourse,' and to turn to what, in a succession of vivid military metaphors, he described as the study of the strategy and tactics of the legislator's 'attack' on mischief.[4] This was no longer metaphysics. This was war. Battle was to be joined: the *pugna sanctionum* was to be concluded, or at least controlled. The diverse social forces at the legislator's disposal must be reduced to a state of co-operation in, or at the very least compatibility with, his grand design. The legislator as commander, in alliance with the moral and religious sanctions, must send into battle against the enemy (political mischief) an army of punishments (his shock troops) and rewards ('an occasional subsidiary force too weak to act alone'). The art of tactics had already been discussed. Strategically, the commander could choose between direct legislation (frontal attack) or indirect legislation, 'a secret plan of connected and long-concerted operations to be executed in the way of stratagem or petite guerre.'[5] Of all the aspects of the legislative war on mischief, only indirect legislation, the irregular system of warfare, remained to be analysed.

Men in general, Bentham felt, would prefer the ingenuity and economy involved in indirect legislation to the 'inevitably odious programmes of open force.'[6] He had given a guide to economy in the use of punishments in the *Introduction.*[7] He now began his exposition of the art of indirect legislation by giving it the status of a branch of the science of 'political œconomy.' He asserted that the task of political economy was to guard the community against calamity, hostility, delinquency, and misrule. Calamity and hostility he 'laid aside as foreign to the purpose' of an essay on indirect legislation, leaving as his proper field of study the making of provisions against misrule (i.e. by governors) and delinquency (of subjects): in other words, the preservation of a stable political condition somewhere between tyranny and anarchy (87.2-4).[8] There would be (as he had intimated in his letter to Lord Ashburton) no 'analytical exhaustion,' no dryness or metaphysics in this work.[9] He would simply 'bring to view' practical means toward realistic ends (87.7a and 54).

The object of indirect legislation was to be nothing less than the conditioning and even mutation of human behaviour: the remoulding of human nature, as manifested in the social activities of Bentham's contemporaries, into conformity with the shape of human nature as it ought to be. The task of direct legislation in all its branches had been simply to achieve, and then to maintain, a reasonable distribution of various species of rights (99.188). Indirect legislation involved, contrastingly, cultivation and management: 1/ culture of the moral sanction, 2/ culture of the religious sanction, 3/ culture of the principle of benevolence, 4/ improving the management of the political sanction, 5/ application of the physical sanction (87.5). Direct legislation confronted crime. Indirect legislation would combat 'criminal propensities in general.' Direct legislation could oppose 'pernicious desires' only by penalizing the 'pernicious practices which those desires give vent to.' Indirect legislation could undermine the influence of such desires by cultivating 'the less dangerous desires which are their rivals' (87.62).[10]

It was by thus 'Devoting [i.e. diverting] the current of the desires' that men's very wishes were to be directed away from objects whose pursuit could lead them into delinquency (ibid.). Bentham listed three 'occupations or pursuits or modes of living ... from which it would be of use that the current of the desires should be devoted' [diverted]: 1/ the love of Vengeance, the gratification of the malevolent affections, 2/ the love of intoxication, 3/ the love of indolence or idleness (ibid). In view of the fact that Bentham later identified the love of 'ease' as an important ingredient in the emotion commonly described as the love of liberty,[11] it is interesting to note that the love of idleness, although not evil in itself, is described by him as conducive to indulgence in the evils of malevolence and intoxication, to the accessory offences of gaming and prodigality, and to the crimes to which, 'when coupled with poverty,' they are accessory: 'offences of indigence' (87.174): 'men who know not what else to do with their money and their time, buy liquor and get drunk: their drunkenness makes them quarrel-some, destroys their health, and makes them unfit for labour, for every other enjoyment, and for every kind of duty' (87.61). The implicit condemnation of liberty here is, of course, restricted to that liberty which is undeniably a precondition of idleness — the liberty of doing nothing at all. There is certainly nothing inconsistent with Bentham's comments on liberty, as so far examined, in such a condemnation. However, one is struck by his describing the widespread and recurrent crimes related to drunkenness in the England of his day as offences of indigence. What is noteworthy is the firmness and vehemence of his faith in the value of disciplined industry as one central foundation of a stable, well-ordered, and happy community. There is in his approach more than a hint of a work ethic very literally interpreted. The influence of such views on the development of his Poor Law schemes and his Panopticon plan should not be overlooked.

Bentham's general view of preventive legislation was that it aimed to prohibit acts by depriving men of the inclination, the knowledge, or the power requisite to their performance (99.110). He ranked the 'cultivation of the moral sanction' as the first of five possible expedients for taking away inclination (ibid). The aggregate force of the moral sanction he considered to be a function of its 'intensity' and its 'extent' (ibid). He seems to have been confident that the intensity of the moral sanction as embodied by each citizen would increase as popular awareness of the dictates of utility grew. Therefore all that was required was freedom of the press and of public discussion (under, presumably, a government of laws informed by the dictates of utility) and movement in the right direction, enhanced perhaps by the strategic use of public media such as drama and literature (87.18-19), would soon be underway. The same means were to be employed when the increase of the *extent* of the moral sanction was the object in view: 'Extent is given to it by leaving the people at liberty to form and communicate their judgement of approbation or disapprobation. 1. On the conduct of men at large. 2. Of courts of justice — in real and recent instances' (99.110). He went on to list the 'expedients which belong to this head':

1/ Establishing the publicity of judicial proceedings.
2/ Permitting the freedom of the press with regard to
    1/ strictness on the conduct of individuals in recent instances
    2/ Political history
    3/ biography
    4/ moral tales
    5/ dramatic entertainments.
3/ Subjecting theatrical exhibitions to censure.
4/ Encouraging the publication of moral writings upon concerted plans.
5/ Establishing the use of such writings in houses of education.
6/ Providing for the cure of popular prejudices in matters of morality.
7/ Commanding the force of the moral sanction by attaching to the principal offence an offence obnoxious to the moral sanction. (99.110)[12]

In spite of Bentham's apparent endorsement of some important liberties, his plan offers noteworthy opportunities for subtle forms of repressive conditioning. His concept of 'the freedom of the press' sees it primarily as an instrument for imposing various 'strictures on the conduct of individuals.' The 'cure of popular prejudices' could serve as a 'eulogistic' (flattering) description of any form of manipulation of public discussion. The potential for propagandizing in his scheme for 'the publication of moral writings upon concerted plans' and the 'use of such writings in houses of education' is undeniable. Truly, the 'force of the moral sanction' was to be placed under the legislator's command, and against whom was it to be used if not against the eccentric individual, the deviant − the persistent adherent to principles of action incompatible with the dictates of utility, and especially such as might be inclined to resist the appropriate forms of conditioning?

At every point in Bentham's argument his case came to rest ultimately upon his conception of freedom of the press and of public discussion.[13] The 'cultivation of the moral sanction' was to be based largely upon the legislator's distribution of these freedoms. They were also to play a crucial part in the control, if not preceisely the cultivation, of the religious sanction, the second of the five expedients for encompassing the ends of indirect legislation listed by Bentham. Bentham's opposition to the use of coercion to induce formal adoption of religious beliefs did not override his continuing awareness that the evil of such coercion might be compensated for by some resulting good (87.20). He knew very well, however, that freedom of religious inquiry and discussion tended to undermine the strength of the religious sanction. The secret of that strength lay in the command, as he put it, to 'cherish ignorance' and 'stifle inquiry': 'The attachment of the people to their religion is in proportion to its absurdity. Why? because the more absurd their religion the sooner they are obliged to come to the principle of non-examination and explicit faith.' 'But if once they examine,' he cautioned, 'all is over' (99.121). Bentham asserted that in his time even Anglicans who claimed to be friends to religion were convinced that the very freedom which had nourished the early church and fueled the reformation 'would now infallibly prove mortal to it in its maturity' (87.25 and 58). This merely reflected for Bentham the fact that, while the strength of the moral sanction was in direct proportion to its degree of conformity to the dictates of utility, the strength of the religious sanction showed, in the same situation, an inverse proportion. Only by legislatorial manipulation could it become a force for worldly happiness (87.20-4).

Third in the list of expedients for confining men's propensities within the pale of utility came the 'culture of the principle of benevolence' (87.27). It will be recalled that in chapter 17 of the *Introduction* Bentham had argued that it was the province of ethics to 'exhibit the rules' of prudence, probity, and beneficence.[14] Prudence being a self-regarding attribute and a characteristic deeply imprinted upon the personalities of us all, as Bentham suggested in the same section of the *Introduction*,[15] it should not surprise us that he says little about it in his manuscripts on 'Indirect legislation.' Equally logically, however, he has some comments to make in relation to the subject of the other-regarding virtues of probity and beneficence. His position on the subject of probity is expressed with admirable clarity and brevity: 'in proportion to the sensibility of men to the force of the moral sanction is the general sum of the probity in a community: in proportion then as that sensibility is diminished, the stock of national virtue is diminished' (87.20-4). Benevolence, says Bentham, is partly 'the effusion of instinct and the gift of nature' (87.27); it has its very origins in the 'remaining principles which are to be found in human nature,' and which are all either 'self-regarding or at best semi-social.' It is because 'this best element of our nature' is 'so delicate, so fastidious,' that 'blushing for its origin it pretends to be self-born' (ibid). Bentham has here devised a very gentle way of making the point that even benevolence, when viewed realistically and without sentiment, is largely the product of, and perfectly compatible with, enlarged self-interest. Hence his opinion that it is a proper and possible function of a utilitarian educational system to cultivate it: 'in a great degree at least, if not altogether, it is the produce of industry, the cultivated fruit of education' (ibid).[16]

So much for 'inclination,' or 'criminal propensities.' What of the control of knowledge and power through legislative policy? In dealing with the manipulation of the moral and religious sanctions, the exploitation of a free press and public discussion, and the control of education, we have already implicitly covered 'knowledge.' 'Power' remains unexplored, and with it the two as yet unanalysed tasks of indirect legislation: 'improving the management of the political sanction' and 'application of the physical sanction.' It is difficult to conceive of an indirect application of the physical sanction, unless Bentham was thinking of the use of punishments as examples to prospective criminals; the paucity of his remarks on the subject suggests that he took this view. There can be no doubt, however, as to the means by which the management of the political sanction was to be improved. 'Knowledge of the conduct of the rulers and of the ground for it,' as 'an expedient against misrule,' was to be 'promoted by circulation of newspapers' (99.112). Thus while the legislator would be busy attempting to eliminate delinquency, the citizens would be equally preoccupied with protecting themselves against misrule. With a view to the prevention of misrule by advice rather than by resistance, Bentham cautioned the legislator in three ways: first, he must accept the inherently evil character of that coercion which is the almost exclusive medium of government action (87.44, 75); second, he must realize that by direct coercion subjects can be reduced to obedience, but never moved to real support and allegiance (87.20-4); third, he must recognize the extent of his own inability to provide for the satisfaction of men's desires (87.86).

Bentham held coercive persuasion to be unjustified even when exerted upon the minds of the undecided (87.20-4). A man frightened into a state of belief is never secure there. The price of what 'precarious repose' he does enjoy is 'an enfeebled understanding ... a state of obsequious imbecility': 'in a word he must have made himself a weak man in order to avoid being an unhappy one' (ibid). In one special case only, 'coercion has not only utility to defend it, but necessity' — the case of the armed forces: 'The state could not exist without an army: nor an army, with the members who compose it at liberty to withdraw themselves at pleasure' (87.52). Indeed, the 'Indirect' manuscripts contain a defence of a policy of constraining any unemployed individual to take up a job (his choice of several menial ones). Bentham's feelings on impressment had not changed since the 'Irenius' letter of 1770 (87.14-15).

The legislator, Bentham argued, must realize that there are 'scarce any desires but what are insatiable ... by any means whatsoever, much less by such limited means as the funds which are capable of being at the disposal of the legislator will afford.' He should allow individuals to seek to satisfy their own desires 'by their own industry.' What government owes to the people can be divided into three categories: 'liberty, protection, sustenance': 'Protection as much as is wanted: liberty as much as consistently can be granted: sustenance for such and such only as are unable to procure it for themselves' (87.86). It would seem from this evidence that the dispensation of 'protection' by government was to be prior to the distribution of liberties in both importance and chronology. Yet elsewhere in the 'Indirect' manuscripts Bentham seems to give unqualified first priority to the establishment of liberties: 'The first law then with which every body of laws should open should be an all comprehensive law of liberty: a law restraining the hand of delegated authority from exhalting itself but on such or such specific causes, the specification of which constitutes the several *powers* that are thought fit to be established in a state' (87.117). He refers, in fact, to a 'famous clause in Magna Charta' which was at least intended to be such a law. For the resolution of the evident conflict of these two judgments on the respective positions of protection and liberty on the legislator's priorities we must have recourse to the more fully elaborated arguments in *Of Laws in General*, where the solution is found to lie, as we have seen, in the exact nature of the 'universal law of liberty.' Only brief glimpses of an explanation can be gleaned from the 'Indirect' manuscripts: from the passage, for example, where Bentham asserts that 'as the permission granted to men in office constitutes their power, so the indemnity of the people is constituted by the restraints imposed upon them' (99.130-1), or when he claims that perfection in legislative policy would be reached when 'security would be the companion of innocence: affliction would dwell only with guilt: and there would be no mischief but what fell upon the heads of the contrivers that plotted it' (87.194) — a formula which has much to do with protection but little with liberty.

The proposals which are the practical correlatives of the theoretical formula of security for innocence and punishment for guilt seem to involve Bentham in a frontal attack on important individual liberties. He suggests the employment of paid informers to give court-room evidence (87.181), and the regular reception of 'secret informations' (87.123). He attacks five of 'the most striking maxims of the English law,' maxims embodying such fundamental principles as that of the protection of the individual against self-incrimination (87.185).[17] Yet he emphatically proclaims that his opposition to them is based on a plea for 'humanity' in the face of a threat (unfortunately unexplained in the manuscripts) to 'vest an arbitrary power in the crown.' Their utility lies, he claims, in 'the inefficacy they have given to certain inexpedient laws.' From the resulting 'debility of the powers of justice ... the multitudinousness of crimes and the insecurity / of life liberty and property / of whatever is dear to men in a civilized society takes its rise' (ibid).

More expedient laws, together with the removal of the ban on self-incrimination, could, he felt, help to ensure punishment for the guilty and security for the innocent, but one problem would remain untouched by such measures: the problem of identification. 'Against a man who is not to be found,' Bentham asserted, 'power itself is impotent' (87.55). And again: 'To punish a man in almost any way whatever you must know whom he is' (87.182). Bentham considered the possibility of identification by clothing (ibid). He considered the suggestion of the use of silhouettes of eighteenth-century 'mug-shots.'[18] But he gave most attention to the idea of 'marking' — using indelible tattoos to facilitate the identification of criminals (and corpses) and to prevent crimes (87.179, 189). Names, he found, are not an adequate mark, because 'when a man's name is grown dirty he throws it off as he would his shirt, and takes another' (87.193).

How did Bentham defend what seems to be a grotesque and potentially brutal invasion of individuals' persons? In fact, he listed the objections to his proposals on grounds that free men should not be subjected to such an indignity as among the species of argument most totally irrelevant to the point at issue. He claimed that, in effect, marking would 'be highly favourable to personal liberty,' as it would end false or unjustified arrest due to mistaken identity (62.190). Further, every criminal would, whether legally punished or not, remain quite literally a marked man exposed to 'perpetual punishment' at the hands of the moral sanction in proportion to the mischievousness of his crime. Actual arrest and imprisonment would be required 'in those cases only in which the evil of punishment is so great that the evil of perpetual punishment may fall short of it' (ibid). Thus a measure which, viewed out of context, smacks of the most unmitigated authoritarianism is defended, in the context of Bentham's utilitarian system, as a boon to liberty.

Bentham's justifying criteria in this case are clearly analogous to those he employed, as we have seen, to defend the utility of punishment: 'Under a regular government, the necessity of vengeance is superseded by legal redress, and the irregularities of it are repressed by punishment' (87.62).[19] A 'civilized state of society' owes its superiority over a state of nature, not to the augmentation of the quantum of liberty permitted within it, but to the use of systematic legal redress to transform a breed of idle 'savages' into a race of industrious 'husbandmen' and 'manufacturers' (87.63). Perhaps the paradoxical relationship between punishment and happiness (if not liberty) in Bentham's mind is best summed up by his conclusion that, in view of the efficacy of 'apparent' as opposed to 'real' punishment, 'the business is therefore out of a given quantity of the former to make as much as possible of the latter. Humanity consists in seeming to be cruel' (87.137). In view of the manifest utility of punishment, and indeed of all the various social controls employed by the enlightened legislator, Bentham found it appalling that 'in London of all places ... you will find people trying to persuade themselves that if their lives and their properties were guarded to any purpose their liberties would be in danger / at an end / destroyed. I wonder what liberty it is they are so much afraid for? The liberty of robbing or their liberty of being robbed?' (87.134).

Just as he had argued previously[20] that the distinction between good (we should not say 'free') and despotic government lay not in the extent but in the manner of exercise of its coercive powers, so in the 'Indirect' manuscripts he urged legislators, as 'Sovereigns,' to 'stand forth in the character of instructors' more than they had hitherto done – to prefer the 'milder ... and not less honourable function' of enlightenment to the use of brute power (87.135, 167). In fact he put forward a whole array of 'Recommendations for government' intended to counteract the tendency of government to become 'despotical.' They included

1.   Dividing power into diverse branches,
[2.] Distributing particular branches of power each among diverse sharers,
[3.] Vesting the power of displacing in different hands from the power of appropriating,

4. Not suffering governors to remain long in the same district,
5. Discarding the members of a governing body by rotation,
6. Establishing the liberty of the press. (87.102-7)

These measures were to assist in the effort to 'break down subordinate irresponsible despotisms,' such as 'hereditary jurisdictions' and the clergy — enclaves of influence having 'power to prevent good without the motive to prevent evil' — and in 'excluding the possessors of one branch of power from the despotical influence of those of another' (87.133).[21] The legislator's goal should be firm but fair government: he must avoid both despotisms within government and despotism by government as a whole, but he must not allow his social control in general to slacken. The sovereign preoccupied with popularity will too frequently tend to substitute the attractions of reward for the evils of punishment. He must remember that where reward is used to mould opinion and behaviour in lieu of punishment, 'the shape of the mischief is alter'd indeed, but the mischief itself is not removed' (87.20-4). Moreover, reward to Paul requires the deprivation of Peter (ibid); it has its concealed punitive aspect. The humanity of the legislator who cannot bear to combat terrible crimes with terrible and remorseless punishments is 'the humanity of the surgeon who will not bear to amputate a limb' (87.194).

Bentham was aware that the degree of harmony exhibited by the moral and political sanctions is directly proportional to the degree to which government is 'popular' (meaning the opposite of 'despotic') (87.20-4). He realized that a people held in a condition of 'abject slavery,' weighed down by 'vain terrors, useless obligations, and tormenting self-denials' might be 'quiet and submissive,' but not by any means happy (87.98). In fact he argued, with Helvétius and Beccaria, that 'in managing the affairs of society, political policy and morality ought to go hand in hand,' and denounced 'the vulgar notion, which pronounces them incompatible' (87.55). The harmonization of the sanctions, the solution to the problem of the conflicting demands of expediency and popularity, and the stabilization of 'popular' (in his terms, responsible, representative, and effective) government — all of these things would be facilitated by the legislator's consulting the populace: 'When experiment can be made, neither in this case nor in any other is there any prudence in trusting to vague conjecture. Are you apprehensive the people will be as adverse to your measure? propose it to them and see. If they should not, the objection is at an end: if they should, you are but where you were' (87.135).

The replacement of conjecture and presumption with experiment would go hand in hand with an active press and vigorous public discussion to ensure an immensely beneficial increase in the spread of knowledge. That benefits would come was not to be doubted, for 'it is from the monopoly of knowledge and not by the abundance of it that mischief has ensued: break down the monopoly, and the mischief is at an end' (87.95-7). He recommended 'an universal and unreserved publication of proceedings and accounts' by governments, designed to make such varieties of information 'as public as a large court-room, open doors, and the operations of the press can make them' (87.170). The responsibilities of the press should be enlarged to include 'giving publicity to the reasons in which acts of state have been grounded. As also to the data referred to by those reasons' (87.110), and reporting more extensively the debates in the House of Commons (87.115).[22] In sum, a free press should, in a society of utilitarians with a utilitarian legislator, be a guide to the sovereign at every step: 'The chance of a King's doing right on any particular point who excludes the liberty of the press is inversely as the number of people in the state capable of giving advice upon the point to the number of persons within whose department it happens to fall' (99.130).

By failing to support or permit a free press, the sovereign would cut himself off from the vast reservoir of informed comment and criticism that is the interested public. It struck Bentham as being immensely ironic that it was only as a result of 'the perjury of jurers and the anarchy that was the consequence' that the common law judgment to the effect that 'individuals have no right to pass censure in print upon the proceedings of the government' had been rendered 'a dead letter.' Thus 'the liberty of the press such as we enjoy it now is one of the long catalogue of blessings for which we stand indebted not to the wisdom, the consistency, the power of the law, but to its folly, inconsistency or impotence. *De facto* we have enough of it and more than enough: but *de jure* we have no such thing' (87.108). 'Detesting the cause,' concluded Bentham, 'let us rejoice in the effects.'

Among the numerous pieces of political advice embodied in the 'Indirect' manuscripts there remains one final, striking suggestion which has so far gone unexamined: Bentham's proposal for 'Establishing the right of arming and association' (87.119-20). We have previously investigated Bentham's theoretical conception of a 'pre-existing universal law of liberty' as one of the foundations of a system of laws. The present more practical proposal, free of the theoretical preoccupation with sovereignty and the nature of law which coloured the account given in *Of Laws in General*, gives an impression more favourable to the partisans of liberty. Bentham begins with the categorical assertion that 'among the rights which should be reserved at the institution of a government, this may be looked upon as the principle as being the basis of the rest' (87.119). After digesting the arguments presented in *Of Laws in General*, the reader may well have reached the conclusion that Bentham did not acknowledge the existence of any rights or liberties 'which should be reserved at the institution of a government.' Yet here we are informed that the right of association, in particular, 'is the best and perhaps the only effectual security they [i.e. subjects] can have for any other: that it is not so dangerous as it may appear to be: and they may be warned that on no pretence [should] they suffer themselves to be bereft of it' (87.119). Bentham denies that such a reserved right is incompatible with government, though he admits it may 'seem for want of a little attention' to be so. Assuming, as Bentham does, that government stands established and that it possesses 'an army of regulars,' a real threat to the government by force of arms can only arise 'as a conclusive sign that the cool and deliberate sense of the nation is against the government.' In such a case Bentham confesses himself unable to conceive of any reason why the government should continue unchanged: 'Nations being composed of men are fallible like men: a nation may chance not to understand its own true interests so well as its rulers. All this is very true: but I must own when I see a whole nation or a great majority of it on one side, and its rulers on the other, the former is the side I should always choose to bet on.'

Next Bentham turns to the relationship between freedom of association and the threat of insurrection. Denying that associations are 'efficient causes' of insurrection, he proclaims that they are rather 'very powerful preservatives, against such mischiefs.' Insurrections, he maintains, are the products of desperate minorities, 'the convulsions of weakness deriving a momentary strength from despair': 'They are the efforts of men who are not suffer'd to speak their sense or who if their design were known would not have force to back it' (87.119). Free of frustration and the erratic irrationality born of desperation, 'those who are left free to associate unquestioned, unmolested, in the face of day under the protection of the law will never have recourse to insurrection, until that rare and never enough to be regretted period at which rebellion shall have become necessary' (87.120). Until that period has been reached, he argues, insurrection is less likely where associations are permitted than where they are forbidden. Bentham is at pains to emphasize that he recommends associations 'as physic, not as food,' that he applauds their establishment as a countervailing force where government already exists. Given such conditions, associations become the vehicles for that essential process, the spread of knowledge. Freedom of public discussion, of the press, and of association all serve the same end: 'in proportion as associations are formed, being formed in security, the grounds of them will be communicated and discussed. Liberty and knowledge will go hand in hand: liberty will smooth the way for knowledge, while knowledge checks the wanderings of liberty' (87.120).

The proposition that an intelligent and benevolent prince might bind his successors to a wise course of government if he were to 'settle their understanding (and fix them on his side)' by, first, 'giving reasons of his laws,' second, 'encouraging the liberty of the press,' and, third, 'increasing the stock of knowledge' (100.25) could be taken as a summary of the arguments we have presented from the 'Indirect' manuscripts, but it was in fact put forward in the course of Bentham's 'Essay on the influence of place and time in matters of legislation.'[23] That essay was, along with the work on 'Indirect legislation,' an integral part of the expanded, forty-chapter introduction described in Bentham's letter to Lord Ashburton.[24] It is accordingly quite logical that it should reinforce many of the observations given in the 'Indirect' manuscripts.[25]

On one particular subject pertinent to the present discussion, however, Bentham had more to say in the manuscripts for his essay on 'Place and time' than almost anywhere else — the subject of constitutional law, 'that branch of the laws, of which the office is to set bounds to the power of the prince' (142.212). In the task of perfecting constitutional law, England had surpassed all other nations. Thus, 'the constitutional branch of the law of England, taking it in its leading principles, would probably be found by far the best beyond comparison that has hitherto made its appearance in the world: resting at no very great distance, perhaps, from the summit of perfection' (87.29). On what did the maintenance of the standard of constitutional law, as Bentham saw it, depend? On the strength and steadiness of the habit of censure on the part of the populace, and on the sense of moral responsibility (or 'shame,' as Bentham put it) of the legislator (142.212). At least one of the basic guidelines of legislative policy, he believed, was fixed in favour of liberty: 'Take what nation you will, give them what character you please, where could have been the advantage that injuries should have been left without redress; that the liberty of men should be teazed and perplexed by a chain of minute and frivolous obligations' (87a.40). The easiest innovation a legislator could conceivably undertake, and in Bentham's eyes a most commendable one, would be simply to 'refuse to a coercive custom the sanction of the law' (100.6).[26]

Some of Bentham's remarks in the course of his 'Place and time' writings might easily be construed as pertaining to his interpretation of Rousseau's famous paradox of forced freedom.[27] As a specimen of the sort of prejudice which frequently deludes both governors and governed, Bentham at one point refers to the widespread belief that law reform is mischievous and generally undesirable, a view resting on the unreasoning assumption that 'the lawgiver is wise, [and therefore] the law itself may perhaps be a wise one too, how foolish soever it may appear to you' (87a.44). He then points to a number of legislatorial acts overthrowing old or creating new religions and redistributing political powers, acts in which the people at large have concurred when, as

Bentham would have it, they might have expected to object. At times, he concludes, the people have been seen (misguidedly) to approve pointless or useless restraints while on other occasions resisting the imposition of necessary ones by the legislator. What is unimaginable to him, however, is that the people should ever themselves have demanded the imposition upon them of restraints both irksome and unnecessary: 'It is natural enough they should oppose any wishes he might express or might be suspected to entertain, of subjecting them to new and irksome restraints or obligations, although among the most necessary restraints and obligations, we shall find some of the most irksome. But a supposition that is not by any means a natural one is that by dint of menaces and clamour they should have forced him to fetter their own freedom by a heap of idle, trifling, and ridiculous obligations and restraints' (87a.44).

Bentham is here attacking the notion, given its most dramatic expression by Rousseau, that the formation of political society, characterized as it is by the submission of the citizenry to the fetters of government, actually leaves unimpaired the quantum of freedom per capita possessed by those involved. It is ridiculous, Bentham responds, to conceive of the people as seeking the imposition of restraints because they do not restrain. In Bentham's own analysis of the formation of political society, as we have seen, what is given up is 'liberty entire,' unbounded but insecure and hence largely unproductive of pleasure. What is received in return is a set of secured liberties circumscribed but at the same time guaranteed by the imposition of restraints. What is quantitatively augmented is not liberty, but the pleasure derived from the innumerable activities of which liberty is a necessary precondition.

It is, from Bentham's point of view, a deluded but sadly prevalent belief that men can be forced to be free. There can be no doubt, however, that they can in some sense be forced to be happy. Whether or not Bentham was self-consciously jousting with Rousseau on this issue is difficult to say, but he did pronounce judgment in no uncertain terms upon such minds as could be persuaded by the views he had described: ' "My people will not endure even the most necessary restraints: I have therefore heaped upon them a vast multitude of restraints that are of no use." Such logic may pass upon some minds: but they must first of all have been prepared by a pretty ample dose of prejudices' (87a.43). Whether the paradox Bentham had in view was or was not specifically Rousseau's, it remains a paradox inherent in the logic of the maximizing arguments of libertarian liberals. It must be admitted, moreover, that when placed alongside Bentham's hard-headed utilitarian practicality this particular specimen of liberal argument seems a romantic wish-fulfilment fantasy.

As he drew near the completion of 'Place and time' and the rounding-off of his major statement of theoretical principles, Bentham was prompted to look both backward and forward; backward to the roots of his own enterprise in the faith in human and social perfectibility of his Enlightenment colleagues, and forward to his own acceptance of new challenges. He expressly associated himself with his old friends and *philosophes* Priestley and Chastellux in the belief that the maximization of human felicity, thanks to progress in the Science of Man, was now in sight, largely because the constituents of human happiness had now been exhaustively catalogued (142.211-13). Then, in a long passage filled with extraordinary insight and bursting with confidence, he declared, in effect, that the object of his life's works was to be nothing less than the perfection of the condition of mankind. Utopian vision and plan of attack were merged into one proclamation:

The perfection of the law will be at its *acme* and the condition of mankind as far as depends upon the law will be at its *optimum* when the following signs are visible: when palpable injuries are unknown except by means of the laws by which they stand prohibited; when no acts to which man's nature is prone are included in the catalogue of offenses that do not deserve to be so; when the rights and duties of the various classes of subjects are so well defined by the civil code that there are no longer any controversies in which the question turns upon the point of law; when the code of procedure is so formed that the few controversies which arise purely out of the matter of fact are terminated without any unnecessary expense or delay; when the courts of justice are seldom filled, though always open without intermission; where the military forces of nations being broken down by mutual stipulations not by mutual impotence, the burthen of taxes is render'd imperceptible; when trade is so far free that no branch which might be carried on by many is confined to few, nor any branch pinched by pressure of taxes into a smaller compass than it would otherwise assume; when for the encouragement of such branches of industry as require positive encouragement, positive encouragement is given; and liberty, perfect liberty to such as require nothing more. When the constitutional law is settled on such a footing and the rights, powers and duties of the servants of the public are so distributed and circumscribed, and the dispositions of the people to submission and to resistance so temper'd and adjusted, that the prosperity resulting from the preceding circumstances is fix'd; lastly, when the law, which is the rule of men's actions, is concise, intelligible, unambiguous, and in the hands of every man.

In other words, when men are in possession of the works of Jeremy Bentham on the subjects of penal law, civil law, procedure, international law, political economy, and constitutional law the way to Utopia will be clear, if they have but the inclination, the knowledge, and the power to follow it.

Even such a utopian state would retain the inevitable blemishes which mar the complexion of present life: 'Fire will burn, frost pinch, thirst parch, hunger gripe as heretofore: toil even as now must be the prelude to subsistence: that the few may be wealthy, the many must be poor: all must be tantalized more or less with the prospect of joys or supposed joys, which they are out of hopes of tasting, and how much lighter soever coercion may sit than it does now, coercion must be felt, that all may be secure.' Such a state, warts and all, is perfection within the range of vision of the utilitarian world-view, and to Bentham no other view was imaginable 'so long as man remains man' (142.200).[28]

9

Two branches of the law

The peroration from 'Time and place' characteristically linked the optimization of 'the condition of mankind' with 'the perfection of the law.' The key to the perfection of the law, in turn, was in Bentham's view the construction of a complete *corpus juris*. In his review of his achievements to date at the end of *Of Laws in General*, Bentham laid special stress on the fact that, as he saw it, he had shown in that work and in the *Introduction* that his 'natural and universal principles' for the division and classification of laws constituted a 'foundation for the plan of the complete body of laws ... constructed *ab origine.* '[1] By 1782, moreover, the classification of laws meant more to him than the distinction between, say, private and public acts or offences. By then Bentham had gained, as Professor Hart has pointed out, 'a deepened appreciation ... of the great difficulties and profound importance for the understanding of the nature of a legal system of the issues raised by the apparently simple question: what is the nature of the distinction between civil and penal law.'[2] Bentham's examination of this distinction was to provide the foundation for a significant clarification of his ideas regarding the characteristics of a complete *corpus juris*; moreover, it was to usher in a new phase in his analysis of liberty.

The penal-civil distinction emerged in the course of the *Introduction* and *Of Laws in General* as the key to the definition both of the necessary constituents of any particular law and of the complementary aspects of a comprehensive legal system. This emergence took some time, and the several chapters in the *Introduction* and *Of Laws in General* devoted to various facets of and perspectives on the penal-civil distinction illustrate the depth and persistence of Bentham's interest in the problems involved.[3] The analysis in those pages was sometimes pedantic and occasionally repetitive, but from it several fundamental conclusions emerged. Bentham became convinced that in the fabric of every individual law, and of every law code, penal and civil threads were inextricably interwoven. This by itself was enough to make him conclude that he must raise his analysis of the idea of civil law to a level of clarity and completeness comparable to that achieved in his investigations of penal or criminal law. In addition he adopted the view that the penal and civil aspects of a law could not in practice be isolated from each other without rendering the law either incomprehensible or impotent, but that a clear and fundamental distinction could nevertheless be made between their complementary legal functions. He proceeded to expound that distinction. To the penal aspect of law he allocated the simple but carefully calculated coercive function without which the law would embody no effective sanction. To the civil aspect he allotted the defining and distributing functions, the task of the exposition and, as he put it, 'liquidation' of rights, powers, duties, liberties, and so on. No law could be complete were it lacking either civil, 'circumstantiative matter'[4] to define the context within which its sanctions were to operate, or a penal, coercive aspect describing those sanctions and the mechanics of their operation. Without a civil aspect the law would be incomprehensible; without a penal aspect it would be impotent.

Bentham stressed the necessity and inevitability of the combination of penal and civil matter in the content of every individual law. Modern juristic theory and practice has not explicitly repudiated Bentham's views on this point, but it has certainly established as its standard a view of the relationship between the penal and civil sectors of a legal system which is clearly not based upon the penal-civil distinction as defined by Bentham. Penal laws are now understood to be those which impose penalties for the commission of certain acts. They are not thought of as containing a civil part or as requiring any admixture of civil matter (in the present-day meaning of that term) in order to be complete as individual laws. Civil law is defined as law pertaining to the private rights and remedies of the citizen, and as such is considered to be a self-sufficient body of law, separable from the penal. Bentham's description of the practical distinction between penal and civil suits, which we are soon to examine, shows some points of applicability to present-day legal practices. His theoretical statement of the penal-civil distinction, however, does not.

In his letter to Lord Ashburton of June 1782, Bentham claimed to have shown in chapter 34 of his projected forty-chapter magnun opus that the penal branch of law ought naturally to 'take the lead' of the civil and constitutional branches, that it served best to 'exhibit the lineaments of the whole' of a *corpus juris*, and, indeed, that the civil branch was 'only a development of certain parts' of the penal.[5] Yet, without directly contradicting any of the points in the Ashburton letter, certain passages from the UCL manuscripts clearly dating from the period when *Of Laws in General* was being written indicate that in spite of the expository and conceptual priority he granted to penal law, Bentham was well aware of the immense importance of the civil branch of a code of laws. In those manuscript pages he argues that each and every law both possesses a declaratory part and imposes a sanction. In penal laws the sanction is expressed and the declaratory part 'supposed.' In civil laws the reverse applies, 'but a Law to be a law, must include both either tacitly or expressly, or for want of the appropriating [i.e. civil] part it will be nonsense and unintelligible: of the sanction, intelligible but nugatory and inefficacious' (96.102-3).[6] He notes at one point that the penal class of laws is in fact 'formed out of the subjects of the two ... other classes' (i.e. the civil and the constitutional as defined by him) and goes on to acknowledge explicitly that civil provisions must in some cases constitute the foundation for penal ones (ibid.). For example, 'the Criminal Jurisprudence concerning possessions supposes a distribution already made of them by the Civil Jurisprudence' (ibid).

Arguments presented in chapters 16 ('Separation of the civil branch from the penal'), 17 ('Division of the laws into civil and criminal'), 18 ('Distinction between penal and civil procedure'), and 19 ('Uses of the eighteen preceding chapters') of *Of Laws in General* trace out a line of intellectual development much like that suggested in the manuscript excerpts quoted. Chapter 17, which bears the closest relationship of any of those chapters to the manuscript excerpts examined, reiterates Bentham's point in terms, once again, of the criminal-civil distinction, which is really, as he sees it, the penal-civil distinction described in alternative terms: 'The business ... of establishing and limiting rights as well over persons as over things belongs not to the criminal branch of the law: all such business it supposes to be performed already by the civil branch.'[7] Chapter 19 comes closest of any to giving a balanced account of Bentham's position regarding the relative importance of the two branches of law under study. There he claims, on one hand, that the civil branch is 'but the complement of the penal,' while 'it is on the penal that every proposition ... in a book of law depends for its obligative force.' Yet, on the other hand, in the same passage he asserts that although the penal branch comes first 'in the order of intellection and enunciation,' yet 'in point of importance the civil branch ... might possibly be found to precede the penal.'[8] Chapter 16 establishes the pre-eminent role of civil or 'expository' law in enunciating and endorsing individuals' rights to both corporeal and incorporeal objects of property[9] as well as to 'person' itself,[10] to 'reputation,'[11] and to 'condition in life.'[12] It recognizes the possibility, not often given due emphasis by Bentham, that the dictates of the moral sanction may 'by reason of some prejudice ... be at variance with the dictates of utility.'[13]

The discussion in chapter 18 of the difference between a civil and a penal suit brings to light Bentham's interesting conception of the 'liquidity' of rights: 'In a penal suit as such the plaintiff's complaint is that some right of his which is already liquid and needs not the intervention of anyone to liquidate it, has been violated; ... In a civil suit as such he does not allege that any liquid right of his has been violated; but says, that he has a right not yet liquid which he prays the Judge to liquidate.'[14] This distinction between the objects and mechanics of civil and penal (or criminal) suits was applicable to the system of justice as administered in Bentham's day (i.e. in what he considered an unreformed condition). It was meant by Bentham to be applicable as well to a reformed, utilitarian legal system, given only that judges in civil suits in a utilitarian (Benthamite) polity would base their liquidating decisions on the provisions contained in a civil code, not on their interpretation of a body of customary, common law in the form of legal precedents. The same distinction might, with some qualifications, even be thought applicable to present-day legal practices. The judge is, at the outset of any given case, confronted with a claim. If it is asserted in that claim that a liquidated right (one that is already recognized and defined by law) has been violated, judgment consists of a decision either to impose or to withold punishment. The right involved being a liquidated one, the circumstantiative basis for the invocation of penal sanctions, in whatever measure, is supposed (i.e. understood). A penal judgment is rendered, based on penal law. The sanction thereby imposed is made explicit. In civil suits, the situation is reversed. The right claimed is unliquidated (or undefined legal status), and the judge's function is to liquidate it: to define it explicitly. What is supposed is the power of the judge to resort to penal sanctions to enforce acceptance of his definition of the legal status of the right at issue.

In Bentham's time the word 'liquid,' referring to proofs or expositions, was understood to mean that such demonstrations were clear and manifest: that they succeeded in 'liquidating,' in making plain or rendering unambiguous, some particular point or points. It was in this sense that Bentham referred to civil judgments as liquidating the claims evaluated in them. This exact sense of 'liquid' or 'liquidate' is now obsolete. The term 'liquidation' has since Bentham's day come to be applied mainly to the calculation by agreement or litigation of material or monetary indebtedness. The fiscal world, too, has adopted and refined the term 'liquid.' In finance the liquidity of an asset is the measure of its convertibility into negotiable currency. Economists speak of a 'liquidity preference,' meaning a general preference for highly liquid as against less liquid assets, face values being equal. In all of its uses, liquidity has stood for a desirable characteristic possessed by something of value. For material goods this characteristic has been convertibility into cash. For abstract goods, such as rights, it has been what Bentham would have thought of as the faculty of convertibility into the hard currency of pleasure or protection against pain.

Liquidated rights were in Bentham's view preferable to the unliquidated variety because their status was legally defined and recognized. Any individual entitled to enjoy the benefits of a liquidated right could feel secure in that enjoyment: he could know that penal sanctions would be invoked to restrain others from disturbing his pleasure. The redeeming feature, we may conclude, of the limited liberties enjoyed in political society by comparison with the unbounded field of liberties which predates government, is that they are liquidated liberties, enjoyable because they are secure, and secure because they are recognized and defined by the civil law and protected by the penal. The notion of liquidation provides Bentham with an answer to the question Does the law create or produce liberty? The answer, as he sees it, is that it clearly does not. The law liquidates and secures liberties: it does not actually create them. Bentham described this process, as he understood it, without naming it, in appendix B to *Of Laws in General.*

Appendices A and C in that work also deal with the penal-civil distinction. In appendix A, Bentham locates the source of many of his analytical difficulties in the extraordinary 'inexpressiveness' of the very term 'civil.'[15] There and in appendix C he touches tantalizingly, if not conclusively, upon the process by which the civil law endows individuals with liquidated powers over other persons and over things.[16] In appendix A, moreover, he gives the briefest imaginable answer to the question Where lies the distinction between the penal and civil branches of law?: 'Nowhere. They are inextricably interwoven. What individual law is civil and not penal? There is no such thing. What law is penal and not civil? There is no such thing. In every law must be comprised two things: 1/ a specification of the cases in which the punishment is to attach; 2/ a specification of the punishment itself.'[17]

In terms of the development of Bentham's system, the analysis of the interdependent, complementary, but distinctive functions of the civil and penal aspects of law was the key to the description and construction both of complete and coherent individual laws and of the *corpus juris* that was, by simple 'arithmetic,' to be constructed out of them. The essential constituents of each and every particular law were now known to be constant in character in certain respects. In some degree, then, all laws constructed according to the principles derived from this knowledge would be commensurable: 'They may be placed contiguous, they may be connected together: and one book will hold them. On that one book any man may lay his hand and say, "Within this cover is the sole basis of my rights, the sole standard of my duties ... here I shall be sure to find them: elsewhere I have no need to look for them." '[18] This was the apotheosis of certainty, of security; this was the optimization of the condition of mankind in so far as that meant nothing more or less than the perfection of the law.

Between the covers of the complete *corpus juris* a man might discover 'what acts it is his duty to perform for the sake of himself, his neighbour or the public: what acts he has a right to do, what other acts he has a right to have others perform for his advantage: whatever he has either to fear or to hope from the law.'[19]

Must a man define his duties *to himself* only and always by reference to the *corpus juris*? If so, does this constitute irrefutable evidence of Bentham's ultimate infidelity to J.S. Mill's 'simple principle?' What it does demonstrate is the formal, stylistic contrast between Mill's liberal rhetoric and Bentham's systematic authoritarianism. The individual who looks into the *corpus juris* will there find confirmation that even offensive self-regarding acts are largely unmeet for punishment, but it must be admitted that he will also find a blueprint for social control so comprehensive as to make the process of conditioning of behaviour look irresistible — or rather, through the eyes of a utilitarian born and bred, so 'natural' as to be in a sense invisible, just as the music of the spheres was once thought inaudible. Bentham's awareness of the inevitability and necessity of limitations on direct legislative interference with individual behaviour is here overshadowed by his belief that, to be effective, political and legal authority must pervade the community, existing even where no overt coercion testifies to its presence. The influence of 'laws' in all their diversity upon the behaviour of citizens in a utilitarian polity will be as subtle, pervasive, and inexorable as that of the Newtonian laws which govern their purely physical motions. They will channel and shape human endeavours not only by opposing or prohibiting certain forms of activity but also by defining the very limits of the range of conceivable human actions. After all, in Bentham's view man is by nature just as unable to throw off his subjection to his 'sovereign masters,' pleasure and pain, as he is to throw off his subjection to the force of gravity. There can be no escape: 'In a map of the law executed upon such a plan there are no *terrae incognitae*, no blank spaces: nothing is at least omitted, nothing unprovided for.'[20]

Not only was the scope of legislatorial control as provided for in the complete *corpus juris* to be universal, but its strictness was to be in direct proportion to the social significance of the actions considered. In a manuscript page intended to form part of the 'Prefat' to his projected view of a complete body of laws (99.4), he proposed that the law should be 'tender of liberty,' and that 'it should never abridge any man's liberty in any the slightest article without a reason.' Yet in the same passage he illustrated the preoccupation with social control which was the source of his most authoritarian proposals. The same law which he had said must be 'tender of liberty,' he also said must be 'jealous of power': 'It should never give any more power to any man than just what is sufficient to enable him to perform the service that is expected of him: Jealousy, not confidence, is the characteristic of wise laws' (ibid). If the relations between the law and those subject to it are to be characterized by suspicion and jealousy, however the ensuing tension may be relieved by the provision that the law is to be tender in its regard for liberty, how can such a social system claim to maximize individuals' happiness within its boundaries? When Bentham's thought is seen from this perspective the viewer is made particularly aware of the subordinate position of liberty on the scale of social values which characterizes his utilitarianism. However tenderly the law was to treat liberties, it was nonetheless expected to deal with them, and to Bentham that meant with every liberty which was of any conceivable social significance. The greater the social hedonistic significance of a given liberty, the more it begins to resemble a power. The more it resembles a power, the more jealousy replaces tenderness as the law's predominant motive. This phenomenon is made additionally important by Bentham's legal positivism about civil liberties. In Bentham's system the law's jealousy of power can always find opportunities for expression, for all liberties – indeed, all rights – in political society are thought to be held by virtue of some legal validation, whether given explicit expression in civil laws or judgments, or grounded implicitly upon the universal law of liberty. Indeed, one is inclined to ask in what sense the specific efficient laws grafted on to this general law by the legislator may be said to liquidate the liberties held under it: in Bentham's sense, where liquidation means endorsement and clarification, or in another, more contemporary and colloquial, sense of the term, where it means extinction?

As of 1782, Bentham's systematic works on the penal branch of law comprised a substantially complete if unpublished theoretical introduction and an incomplete and unpublished plan of a code. His work on the constitutional and civil branches consisted of practical proposals and theoretical insights scattered through a number of works, and a relatively sustained investigation of the relationship between the penal and civil branches of law. His most urgent need, given his aspirations to the completion of a comprehensive *corpus juris*, the 'perfection of the law,' and the optimization of the condition of mankind, was for an extensive study of the nature of civil law and a plan for a civil code. He turned immediately to the task of meeting that need.

10
Civil law

It is possible at this stage of our inquiry to detect the existence of two distinct phases in the development of Bentham's idea of liberty. The dividing line between them and the catalytic agent in the movement from the earlier to the later, which is to say from the simpler to the more subtle and complex phase, is the discussion, conducted mainly but not exclusively in *Of Laws in General*, of the distinction between civil and penal law.

Bentham's simple definition of liberty as the absence of coercion was arrived at in the earlier phase of legal and political analysis. It was an adequate definition only in so far as it was applied to the relationship between liberty and legal coercion pure and simple. By itself it could suffice to deal only with cases where the legislator must either act, and thereby annihilate liberty, or stay his hand and permit its continued existence. But Bentham also wished, as we have seen, to show that in a political community the law could act so as to liquidate, rather than to annihilate, at least certain species of liberty. This function would presuppose a less simplistic relationship between liberty and law than that postulated in Bentham's analysis of punishments or penal law. One of the most important themes in *Of Laws in General* is the development of Bentham's awareness that this additional function of law, which defines the civil law as distinct from the penal, also renders that distinction fundamental to the structure of a complete code of laws and hence to the nature of a viable plan for the achievement of a polity founded upon such a code.

In the second phase in the development of Bentham's idea of liberty he realized that the simple hypothesis employed to explain the relationship between law and liberty in the first phase afforded only a partial view of liberty, one adequate only in the context of a study of the coercive (i.e. penal) aspect of the law. He became convinced that a coherent and complete analysis of liberty must include what we, borrowing a Benthamic term, may call a liquidated conception of liberty as an object of the operations of civil law — as a 'fictitious, incorporeal object of property.' Accordingly, in contrast to the first phase, the second emphasized, not the coercive and destructive functions of law, but its definitive and distributive functions. Liberty was therein examined, not simply as a negation or an absence, but as an abstraction, a fictitious entity. A full understanding of Bentham's idea of liberty and of its place within the context of his utilitarian system can only be achieved when each of these phases has been examined and comprehended, and when the inquirer has grasped the fact that the relationship between them exhibits the same characteristics as that between the penal and civil branches of law. Clearly distinguishable one from the other, civil and penal aspects are nonetheless intimately, indeed inextricably, woven into the fabric of every law, and hence, we may add, into the 'fabric of felicity' itself.[1]

It should not surprise us, then, that Bentham's idea of liberty exhibits both a penal and a civil aspect. Throughout the second phase of the development of his idea of liberty, Bentham's postulate, established in what we have called the first phase, that the law can never act but at the expense of *some* liberty, receives, and indeed requires, no modification. The examination of Bentham's thought on civil law, however, elucidates the criteria by which the coercive character of legal action can in his view be defended as a necessary condition of the preservation of liberties essential to the maximization of happiness in its social aggregate. As we turn, in the civil branch of law, to the problem of how to expedite individuals' efforts to increase their happiness, we find that the accumulation of happiness depends for Bentham primarily on the economic appropriation of material possessions or pleasures and the psychological security which gives the individual's pleasures the valuable dimension of assured duration. The individual seeks to achieve subsistence and, if possible, abundance. But he also seeks to maximize the sense of security which he derives from the assurance that the pleasures of the moment will last, and thus to minimize the likelihood of experiencing the pains of disappointment.

In the manuscripts which now form appendix B to *Of Laws in General,* the definition of liberty (along with those of power, right, etc.) as an incorporeal object of property[2] exerted a crucial influence on the development of Bentham's perspective on the civil and constitutional branches of the legal system. Seizing on the idea of distribution as his new conceptual leitmotif, he set himself the task of analysing the operations of 'private distributive' law (meaning the civil law and the laws of the science of political economy) and 'public distributive' (or constitutional) law.[3] How were personal, civil, and constitutional liberties to be distributed so as to maximize individual security and thence human happiness? That was the new and important question to which he turned.

Within the intricate pattern traced out by the 'hands of reason and of law,' a thread of liberty was to remain an essential and discernible part of the 'fabric of felicity.' In its guise as an incorporeal object of distributive law, liberty refers to a social situation: a set of relationships which, by virtue of the law's definition and assignment of duties and obligations on one hand, and its creation of correlative rights and powers on the other, creates for the individual a path of no resistance, a space for certain activities in whose performance he is not to be impeded by the law or by any other agent. Of all the constituent conditions making up a given social situation, liberty alone is not, for it can never be, the direct work of law. What the law is directly responsible for is the creation of duties and obligations. These by their nature define their correlatives – rights, powers, and liberties. The personal, civil, or constitutional liberties of an individual or a group are given their dimensions implicitly by the law's imposition upon others of the duty of refraining from meddling with the person, property, condition in life, or reputation of that individual or group.

In chapter 16 of *Of Laws in General*, where Bentham describes the 'Circumstantiative matter' belonging to the several titles of a penal code, he provides us, in effect, with a categorization of individual liberties in so far as they can be defined by the process to which we have just alluded.[4] The basic rule about an individual's person is that no man has the right to meddle with the person of another. A complete collection of the laws relevant to persons would have to incorporate this rule and support it with a provision for punishment of its violation, but to be truly complete it must further specify those cases in which exceptions to the rule must be made. The making of such exceptions constitutes the legal endowment of certain persons with powers over the persons of others, for instance as husband, parent, guardian, master, judge, or sovereign. The conferring of such powers must always be justified by demonstration that its beneficial consequences will exceed its mischievous ones. Beyond this set of exemptions, the principle stands that 'with regard to a man's person, it may be laid down as a general proposition that in most cases it is unpleasant to him to have another meddle with it. Every act therefore by which the person of another man is affected ought prima facie to be treated as an offence.'[5] Bentham clearly recalls, however, that the criteria defining 'cases unmeet for punishment' in the *Introduction* apply here also, with the effect of modifying this general principle.

He next considers offences against property. The objects of property, he asserts, are 'either things or persons.' These are the two types of corporeal entities, he adds, 'into which may be resolved those other fictitious objects [including liberty] which are styled *incorporeal*.'[6] This implies that property can always be resolved into a right to the use of a thing or the services of a person. The rule previously applied to the liberties of persons applies here again, but 'with regard to things no such general rule obtains as the above mentioned one concerning persons. On the contrary concerning every object of the class of things (concerning every such object at least with which a man's meddling or not can be material) the general rule is that there is always some one person at least who has a right to meddle with it.'[7] One or more persons will always, according to this general rule, have a title to the thing in question. A large portion of the corpus of civil law, the portion relating to 'titles,' has the function of defining and distributing the legal right to meddle with property and thereby eliminating any significant extralegal right to such meddling.

When Bentham turns to the category of offences against reputation, we find an echo of his frequently reiterated belief in the value of free public discussion and the tutelary influence of public opinion (i.e. the moral sanction) on individual behaviour: 'For the sort of behaviour to which the world in general is wont to annex its ill-will is for the most part that sort of behaviour which in some way or other is pernicious to society. To annex this ill-will to any sort of behaviour is in other words to punish that sort of behaviour with the punishment of the moral sanction.'[8] Knowingly to aid and abet the dissemination of libellous opinions tending to injure a man's reputation is a punishable offence, for 'to contribute to the spreading abroad such notion is at the same time to prosecute the delinquent as it were before the tribunal of the public and to bear a hand in the infliction of that punishment.' Bentham's opinion of the nature and strength of the 'love of reputation' is a guide to his conception of the purpose and strength of the moral sanction. He describes the love of reputation as a 'tutelary motive,' indeed, 'the very best in point of general tendency, of all the tutelary motives after that of benevolence: and in point of force it is superior even to that.' The 'regular and ordinary tendency' of such tutelary motives is 'to restrain men from every sort of behaviour which is pernicious to society: not to mention the tendency which it has to prompt men to actions which are of a beneficial tendency.'

Bentham is cautious enough to realize, however, that the force of the moral sanction may be derived from prejudices which render it 'at variance with the dictates of utility.' In such cases, as in cases where the pain given to individuals by the disclosure of some act or fact would outweigh the benefit resulting to the public from the punishment of it, an attack on a man's reputation may constitute an offence, albeit perhaps an offence itself unmeet for punishment. The general rule gives first priority to the protection of the individual's reputation: 'If the notion, being prejudicial to a man's reputation is at the same time a false one, the general rule is that no man has a right to propagate it: and to this there can scarcely be any exception.'[9]

The heading 'offences against reputation' thus brings to light considerable material illustrating Bentham's view of the tutelary role of the moral sanction in subtly but inexorably shaping private life to public standards. The case, finally, with regard to offences against condition in life[10] is that such offences can generally be resolved into offences against person or property, for these two, when accurately ascertained, are the essential constituents of an individual's social condition. Bentham assigned the task of recognizing, defining, and distributing the various distinguishable social conditions, naturally enough, to the civil branch of law.

Having dealt with the four categories of private offences, Bentham continued his review of the types of offences by turning to 'semi-public' ones. These, he observed, 'are determined in a great measure by the relation they bear to private ones.' They are, in fact, 'but so many ways of producing the same mischiefs as are apt to result from private offences, only with less certainty and upon a larger scale.'[11] On the subject of 'Self-regarding offences,' Bentham made few remarks, commenting that few, if any, acts of this class would require treatment as offences.[12] This is for Bentham primarily the domain of the moral sanction, though only because the public consequences of self-regarding acts tend to be insignificant while the private pains of punishment cannot fail to be substantial. Finally, Bentham's examination of public offences is coloured by the clear (and consistent) assumption that the absolute security and authority of all public institutions sanctioned by the sovereign must be maintained.[13] The bulk of the law relevant to such offences is constitutional, occupied with the definition of the exact nature and extent of public programmes, institutions, and powers. The distinction between constitutional and civil law, as we shall see, is in Bentham's view simply that between 'public distributive' and 'private distributive' law. For our present purposes, however, the most noteworthy effect of Bentham's comments on self-regarding, semi-public, and public offences is to confirm that the kernel of Bentham's notion of civil liberty lies in his treatment of private offences, and, within that treatment, in his definitions of the individual's rights to person and property, definitions whose liberal tone belies their derivation from Bentham's legal positivist notions of political sovereignty and political society. Nowhere, however, could Bentham be expected to come any closer to defining concisely and explicitly the limits of individual liberty within the utilitarian polis than in chapter 16 of *Of Laws in General*.

In chapter 17, principally concerned with the distinction between civil and criminal law, Bentham opens another line of argument which emphasizes and clarifies the link between individual liberty and the civil law. In paragraph 4, whose marginal note reads 'To mark out rights belongs not to penal law,' Bentham says: 'The business ... of establishing and limiting rights as well over persons as over things belongs not to the criminal branch of the law: all such business it supposes to be performed already by the civil branch.'[14]

That this civil function has an essential place in the operation of all laws is clear from a passage near the beginning of chapter 18 in which Bentham asserts:

On what occasion soever the law does any thing in favour of any person, it thereby confers on that person a right. [fn. *a*: It follows that a power is a species of right.] But there is no law whatsoever that does not operate in favour of some person or other: consequently there is no law whatsoever that does not confer on some person or other a right. Now the violation of a right is an offence: nor is there any thing else but the violation of a right that is an offence.[15]

This passage, however, states only half Bentham's argument. The other half can be found in appendix A to *Of Laws in General*: 'Whatever business the law may be conversant about, may be reduced to one sort of operation, viz: that of creating duties. To make duties, in the first place it must define them: in the next place it must mark out the punishments to be inflicted for the breach of them.'[16] The distinction here between the task of definition and that of enforcement clearly corresponds to the distinction between the functions of civil and penal law. In a footnote Bentham adds an important point: by one and the same characteristic legal process the law creates a balanced, reciprocally related set of rights and duties, for 'it is by creating duties and by nothing else that the law can create rights. When the law gives you a right, what does it do? it makes me liable to punishment in case of my doing any of those acts which would have the effect of disturbing you in the exercise of that right.'[17]

It is as species or modes of duty and right that Bentham defines the ideas of obligation and power. In chapter 18 of *Of Laws in General*, Bentham asserts that there are two ways for a judge to enforce a duty imposed by a judgment at law. He may resort to 'physical influence,' direct coercion by his agents, or he may use 'moral influence.' Moral influence, we are told, operates by the force of 'certain *motives*' either of the coercive or of the alluring kind. The idea of obligation refers to the use of coercive motives: 'to give birth to action of any kind on the part of any person by the force of coercive motives, is in other words to lay him under an obligation.'[18] Bentham does not here deny the existence or efficacy of moral as distinct from legal obligation, but he does seem to be saying that the force of legal obligation springs not from moral 'principles,' but from the coercive and alluring force of punishments and rewards in prospect. In the reference we have quoted Bentham takes but a first glance at a problem which was to occupy his attention throughout his efforts to organize a systematic 'deontology.' The difference between an obligation and a duty, however, appeared inconsiderable to him when he wrote *Of Laws in General*. We may compare with the above explanation of obligation the statement of how the law creates duties given in appendix C of *Of Laws in General*: 'In as far as by coercive methods it [the law] causes or endeavours to cause an action to be abstained from or performed it thereby creates a duty. Duties accordingly are either duties of *abstinence*, i.e. negative duties, or duties of *performance*, i.e. positive duties.'[19]

The concept of power refers essentially to the capacity to enforce the performance of a duty. At various points Bentham equates the notion of a power with that of a property, an interest, a trust – and with a particular sort of liberty: 'When the acts you are left free to perform are such whereby the interests of other individuals are liable to be affected, you are thereby said to have a power over those individuals. In this case in as far as you possess the power in question you possess an exemption from the duty of *abstinence* as far as concerns the acts to the performance of which your power extends.'[20] A liberty is not a kind of power; power, rather, is a particular kind of liberty. But clearly it will be precisely those liberties which are of social significance, those which involve the interests of numbers of individuals, which will be viewed as powers in Bentham's system. This explains the infrequency of actual references to liberty in the main body of Bentham's writings, and illustrates Bentham's criteria for determining the significance and validity of particular liberties under specified social circumstances.

A concise summary of Bentham's conclusions on the legal significance of the group of incorporeal legal fictions which we have examined can be gleaned from paragraphs 15 and 16 of appendix C of *Of Laws in General*:

What is it that every article of law has in common with the rest? It issues commands and by so doing it creates duties, or, what is another word for the same thing, obligations. The notion of duty is a common measure for every article of law.

The notion of command leads to that of duty: that of duty to that of right: and that of right to that of power ... A right is another fictitious entity, a kind of secondary fictitious entity, resulting out of a duty ... Right is either naked or armed with power ... [the notion] of exemption [leads] to that of privilege: power and duty together to that of trust.[21]

The function of civil law is to define and distribute rights, duties, powers, obligations, privileges, trusts, and all the other members of that troublesome collection of abstractions which Bentham calls incorporeal legal fictions; the function of penal law is to enforce the given distribution. The whole body of the law thus has a great deal to do with the idea of liberty, although the word itself does not occur often in Bentham's writings. The definition and distribution of rights, duties, and so on defines also the social boundaries of the spheres of liberty and coercion. Bentham rightly viewed liberty as a cornerstone of his system because it was implicit in the logic of his utilitarianism that the possession of liberty in some degree is a necessary condition of the enjoyment of every right, power, or privilege in civil society. Yet by its very nature the idea of liberty more than any other concept posed a continual threat to the completeness and stability which Bentham sought in his 'science of human nature.' The indeterminate, open-ended quality of the libertarian view of man was alien to Bentham. He sought rather the perfection of a neo-Newtonian social physics. His complete code of civil law was to be founded upon a comprehensive knowledge of the statics and dynamics of man and society. The felicitarian calculus systematized the dynamics of the individual's pursuit of a maximum net excess of pleasures over pains. Civil law was to apply Newton's third law of motion to problem of social equilibrium. For every grant of a liberty in a specified instance there must occur an equal and opposite denial of liberty to some correlative agent. Taking Bentham's social thought as a whole it is clear that the values of statics – security and equilibrium – are ascendant over those of dynamics – principally freedom. J.S. Mill tried to reorder these social priorities, emphasizing in *On Liberty* the importance of the innovative and 'progressive' role of the social non-conformist. His synthesis of the values of social statics and dynamics was to many more pleasing than Bentham's, but also more precarious and less determinate.

Bentham addressed himself to the problem of analysing the civil law in the manner of a man convinced that he was applying reason to a field hitherto dominated by a scholastic obscurantism: 'What the language of the schoolmen is to the reasoning of the Newtonian philosophy, the mode of reasoning employ'd in many a branch of legislation, and in particular to that which has got the name of *civil*, is to the only mode of reasoning which deserves the name' (157.32). Indeed, the Newtonian philosophy and the only mode of reasoning which deserves the name are one and the same. Drafting a preface to his projected 'civil' opus, Bentham included a dramatic proclamation of that fact: 'The present work as well as every other work of mine that has been or will be published on the subject of legislation or any other branch of moral science is an attempt to extend the experimental method of reasoning from the physical branch / department / world / to the moral. What Bacon was to the physical world, Helvétius was to the moral. The moral world has therefore had its Bacon, but its Newton is yet to come' (ibid).

As the Newton of the moral world, Bentham's intention was, as we have seen, to endow that world with its own special laws of motion in the guise, ultimately, of the 'axioms of mental pathology.' Most immediately, however, he set out to define the goals of the civil branch of legislative policy. In manuscript sheets headed 'Civil – beginning' and 'Droit Privé Contents' he listed the same four ends: Subsistence, Abundance, Security, and Equality (32.160).[22] On another manuscript sheet, this time headed 'Civil – Four ends – Beginning,' he started a study of the relationships linking these four ends. The tendency of his observations was to underline the pre-eminence of the goal of security. He noted that subsistence depends on and is indeed a branch of security, and that in certain circumstances one branch of security, such as liberty, might have to be sacrificed in the interest of another branch, such as subsistence or abundance (32.1-2). Security, subsistence, and abundance, he observed, 'coincide and run into one another' (32.160). On a manuscript sheet headed 'Civil – Proj. Matière – Beg. May 1786,' he wrote that 'Le gouvernement tout entier n'est ... qu'un système de sacrifices' (32.14).[23] This may have been referring either to the sacrifices necessitated by particular circumstances of one or more of the four ends of distributive law in favour of one or more of the others, or to the consistent and logical sacrifice of other less essential goals for the sake of the four chief ones.

In a manuscript sheet of an unusually late date (1795) considering its contents, he made particularly clear, perhaps with the advantage of hindsight, the formal framework of his civil investigations as it had emerged in the course of his researches in the 1780s. Listing the envisaged chapters of a projected 'civil' work, he devoted the first chapter to the subject of the chief end of civil legislation – happiness. Chapter 2 was to deal with the four 'ends subordinate.' The object of chapter 3 was to show that there were 'no others' to rival the selected four (99.47).[24] 'Ends Subord. – no others,' sometimes accompanied by a reference to 'chapter three,' was the heading under which Bentham had most comprehensively discussed relations and priorities among the four ends 'immediately subordinate'[25] to happiness, and among other ends of less central significance, in his 'civil' manuscripts of the 1780s. On one page he listed the subjects to be examined in chapter 3: 'Subordinate ends whether any others on a level with the foregoing 1. Sense of Security 2. Tranquillity 3. Peace 4. Liberty 5. Good Order 6. Power 6. [sic] Virtue 7. Religion 8. Knowledge 9. Good education.' He acknowledged that many other desirable social objects could be named 'whose title to the appellation of blessings is indisputable ... but which are either not within the sphere of the activity of the law, or which however much they may contribute to the mass of happiness, do so no otherwise than in virtue ... of the relation they bear to one or more of the blessings enumerated in the first line i.e. in virtue of the tendency which these blessings of the 2nd order as they may be termed have to operate as efficient causes of the blessings of the first order already enumerated and analyzed' (100.150).

It is evident that two of the four ends subordinate consistently named as such by Bentham, subsistence and abundance (also termed 'opulence' on occasion), have to do principally with purely economic pursuits, while the other two, security and equality, carry a broader social connotation. The question of the relationship of liberty to the goals of subsistence and abundance is an economic one in Bentham's eyes. The relationship of liberty to security and equality is more properly, and more broadly, a civil matter. We shall have occasion to refer again to Bentham's judgment that liberty is a branch of security. At present, we simply note Bentham's acknowledgement in the Civil manuscripts of the 'impossibility of doing anything in the way of law but at the expense of liberty as against coercion by individuals, which may be regarded as one branch of security.' (99.47) Liberty against the law, Bentham is saying, is a branch of security against law. The fact that these two are equally misguided and mischievous conceptions does not alter the fact that they are as intimately related as are liberty under law and security under law. As if to emphasize the intimacy of this relationship, Bentham put forward in a manuscript sheet headed 'Civil Introd. 2. Ends Subord.' a negative definition of security significantly similar to his idea of liberty. The security of the individual, he asserted, is constituted by the absence of certain kinds of coercion. He listed six: '1/ Simple corporal damage, 2/ Simple mental sufferance, 3/ Irreparable corporal damage, 4/ Coercion in general, 5/ Coercion with reference to the faculty of locomotion, 6/ Death.' These he described as 'modifications of personal security,' and he added that 'under the head of personal security as security for or in relation to person, is included personal liberty, security for or in relation to personal liberty' (100.173). Finally, he emphasized the point that constitutional (i.e. political) and international liberty involve 'other political advantages of a very different nature' from those implied by the existence of personal liberty, although these three varieties of liberty 'are in use to be confounded with one another under the cover of the same name' (100.174). In fact the element of power was a far more important constituent of political liberty than of personal liberty for Bentham, as we shall see when we turn to his comments on constitutional and international liberty.

When listing the four ends of distributive law Bentham observed that three of them, subsistence, abundance or opulence, and security, 'coincide and run into one another.' But the fourth goal, equality, was set off from the rest. Although a certain amount of equalization of social conditions was implied by the terms of the Greatest Happiness Principle itself and by the phenomenon, visible to Bentham as Dr Stark has noted,[26] of the diminishing marginal utility of pleasure, Bentham's firm basic conviction was that 'Inequality is the natural condition of mankind': 'Subjection is the natural state of man. It is the state into which he is born: it is the state in which he always has been born and always will be so long as man is man. It is the state in which he must continue for some years of his life, on pain of perishing. Absolute equality is absolutely impossible. Absolute liberty is directly repugnant to the existence of every kind of government' (87a.69).

From the claim that the subjection of wife to husband and of children to parents is essential to the continuation of the species, he drew the conclusion that 'subjection then is the natural and unavoidable state of at least two-thirds of the species, and if it were possible that any thing like independence could subsist among any part of it, it could only be among the remaining third' (87a.70). The only equality capable of approaching universality in extent and totality in degree while retaining a modicum of stability would be the servile equality of the victims of a total and universal oppression:

As the doctrine of universal independence is repugnant to possibility and the nature of things, so is the doctrine of universal equality absolutely repugnant to the existence of general independence, in as far as independence is possible ... Universal equality by independence you cannot possibly have. Equality as universal as you please, by subjection, as universal as you please, you may have, if you desire to have it, with one exception only, that of the Monarch. (ibid.)

That modicum of liberty which might be enjoyed in a stable and enlightened polity must, in spite of its attractiveness to the eye of the individualist and the libertarian, always be recognized for what it is − a luxury. What is basic and essential is precisely what is incompatible with unbounded liberty − government: 'The great point is, to get any government at all. It is the most useful point and the most difficult. When once you have got your government, and got it tolerably fixed, then is the time to temper it' (ibid). On the other hand, however, a degree of equality in respect of constitutional or political liberty is permissible where such a degree of equality, if extended to the more general and fundamental civil institution of property, would be fatal to society. Referring to the franchise and to the Parliamentary arena of government, Bentham granted that 'equality in respect of this branch of government is free from the objection which is so fatal to equality in matters of property. Equality in property is destructive of the very principle of subsistence: it cuts up society by the roots. Nobody would labour if no one were sure of the fruits of his labour. Equality in respect of the right of voting, is attended with no such inconvenience. Push it to the utmost, the motives for labour remain untouched' (129.19).

Not only is liberty of political participation via the franchise free from the disadvantages which plague the idea of equality of property, but it is also demonstrably connected with the essential social goals of security of expectation and prevention of disappointment. If the extent of the individual's political liberty (his power of political participation) is the measure of his ability to exert an influence on the actual law-making process, then political liberty is very important indeed to the individual's security of expectation, for 'the case is that in a society in any degree civilized, all the rights a man can have, all the expectation he can entertain of enjoying any thing that is said to be his, is derived solely from the law' (37.157).

In addition, of course, it should not be forgotten that personal liberty, as a 'branch' or necessary condition of personal security, in its simple and fundamental guise as the absence of coercion, is essential both to security of expectations and to prevention of disappointment. In the 'civil' manuscripts Bentham was already well on the way to the formation of his disappointment-prevention principle: 'The want of the regard due to the existing interests of individuals is one of the most powerful causes as well as in many instances the sufficient warrant of the opposition made to plans of reformation: and so serious is the objection, so considerable the sum of evil which thus comes to be set against the sum of good expected from the measure, as in many instances to leave no balance in point of utility in favour of it' (100.177). In a 'brouillon' headed 'Civil reforms' he argued that 'expectation is the basis of every proprietary right: it is this affords whatever occasion there can be for giving / adjudging / a thing to one man rather than another' (29.6). And in another manuscript sheet headed 'Civil' he termed 'the principle of expectation' 'the ground of civil rights,' or, alternatively, the 'only true principle of civil justice' (32.4).

Bentham was, of course, concerned with objectives other than security. In a letter to his father in December 1785 he expounded the importance of 'subsistence' as a sociopolitical goal: 'in a political view, amongst the most important of the features by which the condition of a people can be depicted are those which relate to their subsistence and the arts by which it is supplied.'[27] But 'subsistence' was itself clearly founded on security. So, indeed, were 'abundance' and 'equality,' the remaining two of the four ends which Bentham postulated as the embodiments of the dictates of utility in the field of legislation. 'Security, Subsistence, Abundance and Equality — to one or other of these four heads may be referred the reasons of whatever dispositions of law the principle of utility will be found to suggest within the pale of civil and penal legislation' (32.2). This judgment expressly excludes from consideration the field of ethics, and thus of the moral sanction. Bentham is here thinking essentially of the economic basis of political society, and he sees the cohesiveness of that basis as embodied in the notion of security (which, lest we forget, harbours within it as its own precondition the notion of liberty). 'The multifarious provisions necessary to the establishment of security in all its various [forms] is accordingly what occupies the great mass, and constitutes the great business of the civil and penal codes' (ibid). The goal of subsistence, Bentham observed, could be largely, if not absolutely, subsumed under that of security:

The consideration of subsistence might appear to be comprised under that of security, as there can be no subsistence where there is no security, nor any security without subsistence: were it not that political security has other branches besides that which regards subsistence [e.g. the branch concerned with liberty], and that the providing of the means of subsistence is an object that may be pursued by dispositions of law different from those which contribute to the same end by taking security for *viz*: that branch which respects [?] property the means of subsistence for the immediate object of their care. (ibid)

By the same token, abundance clearly exhibits a close relationship of interdependence with security. What, then, of the fourth end, equality? We are told that 'without security, equality may not outlive the day / has no duration' (ibid). To place security so firmly at centre stage, however, is to spotlight not merely the subordination of other ends to it, but also the inevitability of conflict between contrasting facets of security itself: 'It is not only Abundance and Equality must give way to security, but security in one shape must give way to security in another: nay what is more as security for liberty is one branch of general security, and nothing can be done in the way of law but at the expense of liberty, those inferior / subordinate / ends if prosecuted at all can not be prosecuted without some sacrifice made, how slight soever in the way of security' (ibid).

    In the conflict of values envisaged here the inferior ends of subsistence, abundance, and equality are grouped on one side and the goal of security for liberty (of person, of property, etc.) is placed on the other. The connection between liberty and security is seen as being so strong that to sacrifice one is to sacrifice the other. Bentham clearly judges that sacrifices of liberty are essential to the functioning of law and the attainment of the rival ends of subsistence, abundance, and equality. This is nothing new; the antagonism between liberty and legal coercion is one of the elementary principles of Bentham's system. But it is important to realize that the ascendancy of security as a value in the utilitarian system is, throughout Bentham's works, at the same time the ascendancy of a form of liberty. There is no neglect of liberty, no antagonism towards it. Those who have pointed to passages from the 'civil' manuscripts where Bentham defines liberty as a branch of security, arguing that Bentham was deserting the cause of liberty, have been misled. What damage was done to the idea of liberty in Bentham's writings was done, as we have seen, long before 1785. Bentham's vitiation of the concept of liberty originated in the psychological postulates which influenced his original formulations of the term liberty. What we see in the civil code is, rather, an attempt to underline the role of the negative conception of liberty in the field of political policy and legislation by emphasizing that the assured absence of coercion, which is to say security, is the *sine qua non* of social cohesion and social welfare in the utilitarian polis. The Benthamite replacement for the contractual and organic theories of social cohesion he so vitriolically ridiculed was the notion of a tradeoff: a bargain whose terms were so universally recognizable and so unmistakably advantageous that all men could be presumed to understand and accept them. The individual would always trade an unlimited, but lawless, and thence insecure, field of liberties for a reduced, circumscribed scenario of activities shaped by the inducements and prohibitions provided by legal fiat, given that the satisfactions offered within the scenario were certain and secure. The triumph of security, certainty, and expectation over potentiality, creativity, and spontaneity is the triumph of the given over the ideal, of the negative over the positive concept of self, and of happiness over liberty. All of this follows logically from Bentham's beginnings – his faith in and conception of laws and rules, and his psychological postulates.

The widening of Bentham's intellectual field of vision and the accompanying evolution in his conception of the character of systematic utilitarianism from the original idea of a censorial jurisprudence to a more broadly conceived social system of morals and legislation are reflected in the growth of Bentham's interest in civil law in the early 1780s. Once he had arrived at an understanding of the importance of the distributive function in a system of laws, however, it was not long before he turned his gaze towards what was in his day the newest and most dazzling of distributive systems, the science of political economy. The incorporation of this new science into Bentham's system is, indeed, complete in all but title in the 'civil' manuscripts we have examined. The four ends of civil law are all to some degree economic in nature. They are viewed in the 'civil' manuscripts as ends of legislative policy and thus as properly part of a civil code, but no repudiation of this perspective is required by the attempt to define them also as objects of the science of political economy. Indeed, political economy is thus more clearly exposed (by juxtaposition with 'private distributive' law) as a branch of legislative science – the branch dealing with the corporeal objects whose distribution has such a profound effect on human happiness: money and the various other forms of material wealth.

The 'civil' manuscripts, however, are far more than mere forerunners of Bentham's economic writings. The incorporeal objects of law – rights, liberties, powers, duties, and obligations – are as essential to happiness (although not necessarily to subsistence) as are its corporeal objects. Moreover, the definition and distribution of rights, liberties, and the like can be far more difficult than the distribution of the purely material prerequisites for subsistence, opulence or security. In a series of long manuscript passages expected to form part of an introduction to a civil code, Bentham focused attention on the difficult task of defining the various modifications of one of the incorporeal objects of civil law – liberty. In so doing, he was induced to explain the ideas of 'constitutional' and 'international' liberty and to clarify to some extent the distinction between the personal and civil modes of liberty on one hand, and the constitutional and international modes on the other.

In the pages of the 'civil' manuscripts headed 'Civil – Introd. 3. Ends Subord. no others,'[28] Bentham set out to show that the four 'ends subordinate' of civil law – security, subsistence, abundance, and equality – exhaust the field of distributive legislation, and that there are thus no others of comparable status. Among the candidates listed as possible additional ends (all, presumably, to be later rejected) such goals as tranquillity, peace, power, and virtue appeared together with the idea of liberty. Bentham's intention was to show why these ideas either do not deserve or do not require separate status. In the case of liberty, for reasons with which we are now familiar, his tone was firm and rhetorically assured: 'All this while, what is become of Liberty – A catalogue of political blessings given, given as a compleat one, and Liberty not comprised in it? ... Liberty, the only branch of liberty here in question, is comprised in it; it is a branch of security – of personal security' (100.167). Turning, however, from personal liberty, the branch of liberty in question in political economy, to political liberty, Bentham moved, quite logically, from the field of distributive law in its private (i.e. personal) aspect, to public distributive, or constitutional, law, and to its codicil, international law: 'Liberty in a political sense is sometimes used (1) with a view to constitutional law, and sometimes (2) with a view to international law' (100.168). The long subsequent discussion of political liberty reveals Bentham's continuing dissatisfaction with the term liberty because it was susceptible of rhetorical abuse, and his determination to abjure it in favour of some other term (principally 'security') for that reason. It also shows the degree of separation Bentham envisaged between the personal and political spheres of liberty. Lastly (although the text quoted begins with this point), it demonstrates Bentham's political identification of libertarianism with democracy, and perhaps suggests that he entertained the same scepticism and suspicion about both notions:

In the first [i.e. constitutional] sense it is the absence of all government other than democratical according to the purest that is the most thorough sense of democratical government conceivable ...

I am deprived of constitutional liberty in as far as the government of the state under which I live deviates from one / the sort of government / in which every act of government is exercised by an assembly into which every member of the community / individual in the country / without exception, male, and female, adults and minors, sane and insane, convicts and convicted has a vote. (100.168).

Evidently, for Bentham, just as the freedom to do evil is as much a liberty as the freedom to do good, so the state of general constitutional liberty under democracy means constitutional liberty for statesmen and lunatics, philanthropists and malefactors. One will not, therefore, expect to find that Bentham views such a maximization of liberty in the constitutional sphere with any more favour than he has shown towards it in the personal and civil spheres.

Bentham was anxious to emphasize the distinction between personal and civil liberty on one hand and constitutional liberty on the other. Just as he was willing to endorse a degree of equality of political power such as would be unacceptable if applied to the more strictly civil sphere of property rights, so he was prepared to espouse a notion of constitutional liberty reminiscent, to our ears, of Priestley and even of Rousseau. Yet he doubted that the evidence of experience would demonstrate a close correlation between personal / civil liberty and constitutional / political liberty:

Which is best off? — a man who is flung in a jail at Paris, a man who is sitting in the House of Lords at Dublin, or a man who is sitting on the Senate at Petersburg or Copenhagen. The first man comes off but short in the larger branch of personal liberty and still shorter in the narrower branch; but then he enjoys political liberty in perfection in both branches, constitutional as well as international, in as good perfection at least as the progress hitherto made in national illumination will admit of.

Which after all is best off upon the whole? Cicero, had the question been put to him in his Tusculan villa would have been clearly on the Frenchman's side.

The name of liberty having been transferred / passed / from the personal sense to the political, political liberty seems to have been regarded as a security [synonym?] for personal, it having been taken for granted it seems that in proportion to the share a man had of political liberty was the share he would be likely to maintain of personal liberty. Is the connection between the two senses of liberty / a necessary one / so close an one? This is a question of probability to be calculated from experience. Look to ancient Athens and modern France on one hand — look to China ancient or modern or to Denmark / or to ci-devant France / on the other. (100.169)

The degree of personal and civil liberty possessed by an individual vis-à-vis society might conceivably vary independently of the degree of political liberty possessed by him in relation to government. The status of 'government' lies at the heart of the matter, being clearly involved in both the political and the civil spheres of activity in Bentham's system. Given Bentham's strong conception of sovereignty, his broad definition of law, and his extensions of the idea of legislation into the field of 'indirect' social control, government for Bentham is far more than a strictly political term, just as utilitarianism is far more than a political system. The task of the utilitarian theorist (and the utilitarian legislator) will be to snuff out the flame of libertarian enthusiasm which is fed by the abuse of liberty in its political sense – to deprive 'liberty' of its position as a political fetish, and possibly even to eradicate the term if it cannot be successfully divorced from its unfortunate political connotations:

At the mention of liberty every man conceives it to be his right, and many a man conceives it to be his duty to fall into a passion.

Liberty therefore not being more fit than other words in some of the instances in which it has been used, and not so fit as others, the less the use that is made of it, the better. I would no more use the word liberty in my conversation when I could get another that would answer the purpose, than I would brandy in my diet, if any physician did not order me: both cloud the understanding and inflame the passions. (100.170)

In one group of manuscript sheets headed 'Civil – Introd. 3. Ends Subord. no others' (100.153-5),[29] Bentham has provided us with a detailed description of the modes and features of constitutional liberty, prefaced by a brief restatement of the division of liberty into its personal, constitutional, and international branches and a reiteration of the definition of personal liberty as 'a branch of personal security, the absence of coercion' (100.153). One of the two 'very distinct and disparate senses' of constitutional liberty, we are told, is the sense in which 'it is synonymous to constitutional security'. In this sense it appears to be a particular branch of civil liberty. It means 'security in all its branches in as far as the security of the individual depends upon the texture of the constitution or form of government: or more particularly security from damage of all sorts considered as liable to accrue to individuals by reason of abuse of power on the part of persons exercising the powers of government. In this sense it is the absence of danger to individuals from abuses of power on the part of persons exercising the powers of government' (ibid). There is, however, another sense of the term constitutional liberty, which Bentham describes as 'the party sense.' In this usage it announces not only the effects of the form of government in question whatever it be in this point of view, but it involves in its import the consideration of a particular form of government. It involves in the considera- tion of the degree of security as against damages resulting from abuses of power on the part of persons exercising the power of government the assertion that the measure of that branch of security existing in every community is exactly in the proportion as the share which the whole body of the people to be governed possess in the exercise of the powers of government. (ibid).

Re-expressing this same point somewhat more clearly, he goes on to say that

In this sense the quantity of constitutional liberty in a country is in exact proportion to the share which the whole body of the people possess in the exercise of the powers of government: and as the perfection of security, or security spoken of without limitation means the absence of all damage, so the perfection of constitutional liberty in this sense mentioned without limitation consists not in the absence of defalcations of security resulting from abuse of power in the hands of the persons exercising the powers of government, but in the exercise of the powers of government on every occasion by every member of the community, by every one of the persons to be governed, by every member of the community men and women, adults and minors, sane and insane, convicts and unconvicted, without exception made of a single individual. In this sense liberty is the absence of all government other than democratical government constituted and conducted in the way just mentioned. In this sense, liberty, as referred to the individual seems to be synonymous to power or a chance of power: the power of coercing other individuals — the power of controuling the liberty of other individuals. (100.153-4)

Did Bentham intend his readers to accept a hypothetical situation in which the powers of government would be exercised on every occasion by every member of the community as a possible and practicable social state? It is more likely that, by conjuring up such an unlikely image of political liberty in a direct democracy, and by pointing out that in such an egalitarian direct democracy political liberty becomes a coercive power of one individual over others, he meant to show that, as he had argued elsewhere, such degrees of equality and independence could not last a day, and would ultimately be self-defeating.[30] The curious question brought to mind by these passages on constitutional liberty is this: could political liberty, in the guise of political power of participation, ever be at loggerheads with personal and civil liberty as branches of security? The answer, provided by the arguments in *Of Laws in General*, is yes. If we ask which mode of liberty would then be forced to give way, the answer is equally clear: liberty as power against law must give way to liberty as a branch of security. The power of an individual to coerce other individuals is not as fundamental, unless such coercion be sanctioned by law, as the right of individuals to security against extralegal coercion. Politics, and political liberty, must accept its place as a mere aspect of the utilitarian social system: 'In whichever of the three last senses [see preceding quotations] *liberty* be understood, it is either a branch of security, it is either comprised under the head of security, or it is of no value. Supposing security in every branch of it as above distinguished as entire under/in a pure monarchy as in a pure democracy, the most zealous partizan of democracy would hardly find a reason for numbering the establishment or preservation of democratic government among the ends of law' (100.155).

The third of the senses referred to by Bentham was, of course, the international sense. International liberty was in Bentham's view 'the same thing with national independence': 'It is the absence on the part of one nation of dependence in relation to the government of another nation ... I stand deprived of a greater or less share of liberty in an international sense by belonging to Guernsey, to Jamaica, to Canada, to Bengal, instead of belonging directly to Great Britain' (100.155). Even national independence, however, will properly and willingly be sacrificed, it seems, if the price of independence is loss of security. The case parallels that of constitutional liberty:

Supposing security in every branch of it as above distinguished as entire in a dependent nation as in an independent nation, the most zealous stickler for national independence would hardly find a reason for numbering the establishment or preservation of national independence among the objects worth contending for. As to the numbering it among the ends of law, this would in general be to little purpose: for as nation and nation do not recognize the authority of the same law, if a nation that has been accustomed to dependence on another nation happens to conceive that independence is become necessary to its security, it is not by law (alone) that such an object can be accomplished. (ibid)

In the 'civil' manuscripts the intimate interdependence of liberty and security and the expendability of political liberty for the sake of civil security are established as firm theoretical principles in Bentham's utilitarian social system. We are shown that, in Bentham's view, society is much more than a polity and 'government' involves much more than pure politics. In sum, we are taught that in a society dedicated to the pursuit of happiness the value of liberty, when considered without reference to its role as a necessary condition of security in certain circumstances, is marginal indeed.

With his views on civil law established, Bentham became far more than the proponent of a system of critical jurisprudence. He was now the architect and advocate of a new sociology (and before the discovery of the term at that!). His speculations on civil questions had led him to erect a complete theoretical framework for the utilitarian analysis of the tangible and intangible constituents of human happiness. Just as his uniquely elastic definition of a 'law' in *Of Laws in General* had signified the broadening scope of his legal interests at that stage of his work, so now his study of the 'ends' of civil law carried profound implications for his views on ethics and political economy, the sciences dealing with the pursuit, respectively, of the 'fictitious' and the 'real' constituents of happiness.

11

The fruits of invention

In the summer of 1784, depressed by an eye ailment which prevented him from reading, Bentham felt he was passing from a period of invention of ideas into one of ordering and applying them: 'all conversation ... which does not bear a reference to my own or my Brother's pursuits, is become insipid to me. My own ideas are come no less so: for the task of invention has for some time been accomplished and all that remains is to put in order ideas ready formed: to put them in order according to my notions of order, I must have them all before me at once ... in black and white.'[1] It may have been on the basis of evidence such as this that Professor C.W. Everett concluded that the education of Jeremy Bentham was 'in a very real sense' complete before 1789. Everett in fact made no reference to the Bentham correspondence to corroborate his claim, but he did observe that Bentham's later writings were 'either completions of plans sketched in his early years or works published then which it would have been dangerous to avow earlier, or applications to contemporary political or legal situations of views arrived at in youth or early manhood.'[2]

In the present chapter we put Everett's judgment to a test: were some of the most substantial projects of Bentham's later years (in this case the years after the end of the period of invention in 1784) either applications of previously invented principles or completions of undertakings begun earlier? More specifically, did Bentham make any fundamental alterations in his idea of liberty in the context of new and different enterprises?

Early in 1784, Samuel Bentham, for several years involved as a marine architect and engineer in various grandiose projects put forward by the exasperating Prince Potemkin, had suggested that Jeremy spend six months with him: 'you would enable me to turn to account any ideas of improvement which at present lay perfectly useless.'[3] Bentham was still at work on his investigations into civil law and was busily amassing the voluminous 'projet' manuscripts from

which Étienne Dumont was to extract the *Traités de Législation*.[4] He actually
undertook a journey to Russia, lasting from mid-1785 to 1787, to examine the
concrete problems encountered by Samuel in his efforts to bring improvement
to Russia. He was quick to find projects to pursue. Having already deepened his
appreciation of the distributive problems of social life in his civil researches, by
the end of 1785 he was beginning to show signs of interest in the integration of
economic considerations into his social theories: 'in a political view, amongst the
most important of the features by which the condition of a people can be
depicted are those which relate to their subsistence and the arts by which it is
supplied.'[5] By July 1786, however, he was expressing boredom with Russia in a
letter to Prince Dashkov. He could, he complained, get no access to a printing
press, and he had 'nothing else at heart but the finishing a Scribbling Job I want
to dispatch out of hand.'[6]

His voyage to Russia seems to have marked a watershed in the development
of his career. Undertaken, at least in the eyes of the rich uncle who financed it,
to enable Bentham to present to Catherine the Great an 'all-comprehensive code'
to govern Russia, it ended with the code incomplete, untranslated as yet into the
appropriate language, and hence unpresented, and with Bentham's attention
focused on projects of a new type, which were to usher in a long and important
phase in his career.[7] His 'scribbling job' was the *Defence of Usury*. It was to
initiate a twenty-year period of intense interest in the new and fashionable
science of political economy. His other new interest was the ill-fated
'Panopticon,' a plan for an all-purpose 'inspection house' intended for the
accommodation and control of criminals, the poor, the idle, the sick, and others
in need either of subsistence or of supervision. His fascination with Panopticon
was to reshape his career, his mind, and his condition in life through the course
of an extraordinarily long period of involvement – and frustration.

In the autumn of 1786 Bentham's old friends George Wilson and James Trail
began to urge him to return to England, to nip the Rev. William Paley's
plagiarisms in the bud and make a name for himself with the *Introduction to the
Principles of Morals and Legislation*.[8] Bentham replied by sending off the
Defence of Usury in the hopes of making a name for himself *before* coming
home.[9] In the Defence he simply applied to the case, hitherto unjustly neglected,
of the 'liberty of making one's own terms in money bargains' a conception of
liberty derived from two sources: the principle of freedom of contract,
implicitly endorsed, as we have seen, in the *Introduction*, and the principle of
free competition for rewards, established in the 'Essay on reward,' which had
been almost complete as early as 1782.[10] His basic proposition was that 'no man
of ripe years and of sound mind, acting freely, and with his eyes open, ought to
be hindered ... from making such bargain, in the way of obtaining money, as he

thinks fit. And again, more explicitly resting his case on freedom of contract (which, it should be recalled, is a species of freedom of competition): 'You, who fetter contracts; you, who lay restraints on the liberty of man, it is for you ... to assign a reason for your doing so.'[11]

When Bentham's 'Essay on reward' was eventually published as the *Rationale of Reward*, chapters in it were devoted to the principles of free competition and freedom of contract. In the chapter on 'Competition as to rewards,' Bentham enumerated enthusiastically the 'advantages resulting from the most unlimited freedom of competition,' and defended competition against monopolistic arrangements, which, he said, injured the national wealth by limiting competition. It was upon the basis of the principle of free competition, he maintained, that 'the father of political economy' had 'created a new science.'[12]

In the chapter on 'Trust and contract management,' he pointed effectively to the contrast between the contractor, whose role unites duty and interest, and the commissioner, who labours in the service of another.[13] When his attention turned from punishments to rewards, and from the necessary evils of legal restraint to the gentle inducements provided by systems of reward, Bentham was capable of exhibiting an apparent distaste for unnecessarily harsh legislative interference in individuals' lives. Of married couples he could say 'do not constrain them even in their domestic arrangements, and above all, in that which can please only under the auspices of liberty. In a word, leave them to live as they like, under the single condition of not injuring one another.'[14] Viewed in context, however, these liberal-toned remarks indicate only that Bentham did not support systematic inducements to marriage and, indeed, to procreation, in the interest of 'population.'[15] Are we to praise his liberal scruples or to be troubled by the evident fact that he would have been prepared to support even such interference as this had its effects proved beneficial in their social aggregate? We would be no more justified in concluding, with W.H. Alexander,[16] that Bentham's support for freedom of contract made him a 'legislative libertarian' than in assuming that he opposed every restrictive activity of the moral sanction (and we have seen that he did not) because he opposed controls on the breeding of the human species.

The *Defence of Usury*, then, drew upon the stock of principles accumulated during Bentham's years of invention, but it applied them in a new area: the fiscal sphere. Bentham was to return to fiscal affairs and to broaden his interest in political economy considerably a few years later. For the moment, the other project seized his attention. He immersed himself in the writing of a series of letters on the subject of the construction and operation of a Panopticon, letters addressed to 'a friend in England' from 'Crecheff in White Russia.' The lengthy unabridged title of the printed volume in which those letters were eventually collected and published indicates the extraordinary breadth of the social role which Bentham hoped would be allocated to institutions embodying the architectural and managerial principles of the Panopticon. The keeping of 'persons of any description ... under inspection' was a function that institutions from hospitals to prisons to schools were thought to perform. The idea of schools operating upon principles of constant inspection and supervision like those incorporated into Panopticon's design must trouble the mind of anyone with the slightest partiality to liberal ideas of education. Educational and other applications of the Panopticon idea, however, gripped Bentham's imagination and intellect. The prospects for shaping utilitarian behavioural propensities in an environment where the activities of a group of inmates (the word suggests itself irresistibly) could be inescapably and incessantly scrutinized by a supervisor located at the centre of a circular structure and where at the same time were dispensed punishment, poor relief, or education obviously appealed to him. The Panopticon project was to retain its, at times painful, hold on Bentham's mind for fully twenty years. Perhaps the idea evolved quickly during his stay in Russia because Panopticon management, which was Bentham's main concern, involved yet another application, as has been noted, of the 'Contract principle'[17] which figured so prominently in his theories of reward and of political economy. The principles of the Panopticon from the ethical and political points of view, as distinct from the economics of its administration, will be considered later. By mid-1788 Bentham had been distracted, once again, from his principal enterprise. The culprit this time was France.

At the beginning of March 1789, Bentham declared that his 'head and heart' had been 'altogether in France' for 'five or six months past.'[18] Perhaps his period of distraction had begun when Louis XVI had called the Estates-General some nine months before. Shortly before 1 March 1789, Bentham had taken the *Introduction* from the printer's, 'put a patch at the end, and another at the beginning,' and, despairing of ever being able to make enough alterations for an acceptable revised version, published it.[19] Both the *Introduction* and the *Defence of Usury* did well.[20] But Bentham's passionate interest was in his 'Essay on political tactics,' by which he hoped to gain leverage for his influence in France as the French proceeded with their new experiment (so it seemed to Bentham) in parliamentary government.[21]

The fact is that Bentham's interest in French affairs (as distinct from French *philosophes*) was aroused, not by the prospect of a revolutionary war of liberation waged by oppressed citizens, but by the prospect of a parliament meeting as if for the first time with the intention of creating its own conventions and rules of behaviour. A revolution along the lines of 1688 would have suited Bentham's purposes perfectly. His motives were, as always, utilitarian rather than libertarian. Samuel Bentham knew that his brother would be tempted to meddle in the violent ferment of French disputes for two reasons: to press his utilitarian schemes of government on legislators anxious to be shown their way, and to nip natural rights libertarianism in the bud. By 1791, Samuel told Jeremy, he had already read 'some hundreds of pages of verbiage on Liberté and droits d'homme which a few lines of your principles would show as clear as the sun at noon.'[22]

Bentham's emphatic rejection of the French Revolution was an event of the 1790s. It was foreshadowed by the additions made at the beginning and end of his *Introduction* before its publication in 1789. These additions, however, also reflect Bentham's increasing interest in the problems of political economy.

The Preface prepared in late 1788 or very early 1789 is principally remarkable for its emphasis on the importance of civil, or distributive, problems within the sphere of 'legislation in general.' A remarkable inversion of priorities showing an important change of perspective is found in Bentham's assertion that as an introduction to the principles of legislation in general his work should have been devoted 'exclusively to the *civil* branch,' rather than to the penal, 'the latter being but a means of compassing the ends proposed by the former.'[23] In yet another important revelation, he added that the heart of an adequate analysis of civil law would be an exhibition of the 'axioms of mental pathology,' which, by showing the connection between individuals' 'feelings' and 'the operations performed by government, in the creation and distribution of proprietary and other civil rights,' provide the sole standard for evaluation of the utility of such operations.[24] These 'axioms of mental (and later moral) pathology' constituted the *primum mobile* of Bentham's system of morals and legislation. He was to return to the task of expounding them in the course of his economic writings. In the Preface to the *Introduction*, Bentham claimed that they were as difficult to discover as the axioms of mathematics but also as indisputable, 'since, referring to universal experience as their immediate basis, they are incapable of demonstration, and require only to be developed and illustrated, in order to be recognized as incontestable.'[25] The axioms of mental pathology were seen as defining the boundaries within which even the field of individual liberty would be confined. The death-warrant of an open-ended existentialist or idealist conception of liberty was signed at this point in the development of Bentham's thought. Enslavement to the given, if enslavement it be, was assured.

The Preface was not merely retrospective. Bentham was also looking forward in 1789 to what he now conceived of as a ten-volume series of works which would apply the principles and 'complete the designs' described in his published and (more often) unpublished past works.[26] Bentham's description of these ten volumes concisely indicates how much of his later life was devoted to completing his early designs.[27] Pride of place, appropriately, was given to civil law, 'more distinctively termed private distributive, or for shortness, distributive, law,' the alternative title being a clear indication of Bentham's awareness of the close connection between civil law and economics. The second part was to deal with penal law, the complement, as we have seen, of the civil branch. The third part, on 'procedure,' was evidently conceived as growing out of what is now *Of Laws in General*, chapter 18, 'Distinction between penal and civil procedure,'[28] to whose arguments we have already referred. Part 4 would be built around the 'Essay on reward' of 1782. The subject of part 5 was to be constitutional, or more precisely 'public distributive' law. Part 6, suggesting that Bentham published the *Introduction* with one eye on the Rev. Paley and the other on France, was to cover political tactics; Bentham described it, in effect, as a constitutional procedure code. Part 7 would deal with international law, part 8 with finance, part 9 with 'principles of legislation in matters of political economy,' and part 10 with the ideas of a complete body of law and a universal jurisprudence.

The centrality of civil or distributive law in Bentham's system as here described is truly remarkable. The idea of distributive law is of fundamental importance to every work on the list. Penal law is described in the Preface as the complement to civil law. Constitutional law is the public branch of distributive law. Procedural law is thought of as dealing largely with the distinction between penal and civil suits and judgments. Finance, political economy, reward – all deal with distributive problems.

If the distributive function of law was spotlighted in Bentham's preface, his concluding note restated a theme of ominous significance, given the trend of French events: the denunciation of theories of natural rights. Bentham's way of dealing with the Declaration of Rights enacted by North Carolina in September 1788 sounded an indirect but unmistakable warning to French revolutionaries who would attempt to limit the law-making powers of supreme assemblies by enacting declarations of inalienable rights. Such 'unhappy attempts' were most numerous in the United States, but other examples could be found among many nations. Would one be found in France? Bentham attacked the first and fundamental article of the North Carolina declaration, which proclaimed 'that there are certain natural rights, of which men, when they form a social compact, cannot deprive or divest their posterity, among which are life and liberty, with the means of acquiring, possessing, and protecting property, and pursuing and obtaining happiness and safety.'[29] He interpreted this article as claiming that 'every law, or other order, *divesting* a man of *the enjoyment of life or liberty*, is void.' This, he concluded, would imply the negation of every coercive law, including all laws imposing punishment, especially imprisonment, and even the laws requiring the payment of taxes.[30] No doubt Bentham's interest in American declarations of rights, and, indeed, in American affairs altogether, was genuine. Nonetheless, January 1789 was not a time when American affairs called pre-eminently for this kind of comment. Bentham, via Lind's *Answer* in 1776, had already contributed his comments at the real moment of crisis in America. It was in France that he hoped his arguments might be heard now.

The French revolutionaries were not long in dashing his hopes. They did not merely ignore him; they misunderstood him. He gave them a set of plans for a judicial establishment and a manual of parliamentary tactics.[31] They gave him honorary citizenship and proclaimed their admiration for him in the name of that very *liberté* whose utility he so doubted.[32] Although Bentham was made an honorary French citizen as of 26 August 1792, he was not notified of this honour until some time after 16 October 1792.[33] Meanwhile, on 9-12 August he had written to Lord Lansdowne comparing France to a 'Bedlam,' and claiming that he (Bentham) was tempted to 'take a peep into one of the cells.'[34] Further letters to Lord Lansdowne of 2, 5, and 10 September 1792, indicate Bentham's increasing estrangement from the movement which had already, without his knowledge, honoured him. He expressed emphatic distaste for the 'mob' and rule by force. He regretted the total disruption of parliamentary processes.[35] He mourned the passing of le Duc de la Rochefoucauld[36] and the return to France 'to face Marat' and 'perhaps to hang' of other virtuous French aristocrats.[37] 'By and by,' he lamented, 'there will not be a single honest man left in that accursed country.'[38]

His response to the news of his honorary citizenship was a proclamation that, although he was a republican in Paris, he remained a royalist in London and a plea for amnesty for the émigré aristocracy among whom he had found so many friends.[39] No one could have entered less enthusiastically into the revolutionary spirit. In May 1793, writing to Henry Dundas, he dissociated himself from Republicanism, claiming that 'without any change of sentiment' he was now 'writing against even Parliamentary Reform.'[40] By October he was prepared to hold 'no price too dear' for the extermination of Jacobinism in France.[41] In September 1795 he applauded a pamphlet by 'D'Ivernois' showing that, as a result of 'the discredit of the Assignats,' the 'French Panadomonium [*sic*] must soon fall to pieces.'[42] The French revolutionaries became, in Bentham's vocabulary, the Pandemonians.[43] He poked sarcastic fun at his honorary citizenship and those with whom he shared the honour.[44] By 1796 he was prepared to go with Lord St Helen's to France, but only for the 'business' purpose of mastering 'the freshest discoveries in French chemistry.' Politics would be nothing more than an amusement.[45] By 1797, Bentham was referring to French Republicanism as 'the raging pestilence of the times,' and was seeking to disseminate an 'antidote.'[46]

His best antidote was ready by 1796. He contemplated the irony of his situation in a letter to William Wilberforce: 'were they to see an *Analysis* I have by me of their *favourite Declaration of Rights*, there is not perhaps that being upon earth that would be less welcome to them than I could ever hope to be: – but there it lies, with so many other papers that would be equally obnoxious to them, very quietly upon my shelf.'[47] This analysis he entitled 'Anarchical fallacies,' showing thus his opinion of the French declarations of rights. Bentham was to offer this work in 1801 to the editors of the *Anti-Jacobin* magazine as 'Pestilential nonsense unmasked' (146.239).[48] Its purpose was to portray France as a 'monster in politics,' a 'country without a government,' a specimen of anarchy and tyranny erected side by side, not by accident or negligence, but by deliberate policy (146.18). The heritage left to Frenchmen by the Revolution would be 'the legislation of a country enslaved for ever to an Assembly of dead Barbarians without a possibility of emancipation' (108.114). The rights proclaimed by the *Declaration of the Rights of Man*, Bentham asserted, are 'in point blank contradiction to one another': 'Perfect liberty, perfect property and perfect security is to be the lot of every man. Not that one item of property can be given to any one but at the expense of the property as well as the liberty of all the rest, not an item of security but at the expense of the liberty of all the rest' (ibid). In his comments on 'Parts of the Declaration of Rights' as proposed by Citizen Siéyès, hatred of loose and delusive language and disgust at the political folly of natural rights theories were welded together in a ferocious hostility:

A man turned crazy by self-conceit, takes a word in universal use, and determines ... that he will use it in such a sense as a man never used it in before. With a word thus poisoned, he makes up a proposition, – any one that comes uppermost; and this he calls ingenuity: – this proposition he endeavours to cram down the throats of all those over whom he has ... power or influence – more especially of all legislators ... of the present and all future times; – and this he calls *liberty*: and this he call[s] *government*.[49]

Bentham was to retain his interest in 'fallacies' throughout his life. The notions of fallacy and fiction were to serve as focal points for his linguistic critique, the basis of his continued 'censorial' attitude. From time to time between 1806 and 1821 he returned to specific work on fallacies, work which laid the foundations for his 'Book of Fallacies.'[50] In it Bentham set out to defend 'the legitimately persuasive force of professional [i.e. 'scientific'] authority' against the prevalence in political theory and practice of authority derived from such inferior sources as power, opulence, and reputation.[51] His basic objective was to vindicate the 'right of private inquiry' by making authority the offspring, rather than the oppressor, of reason.[52] Given progress in the realms of legislative science[53] and education,[54] Bentham believed that the human race could be rescued from a ubiquitous and absolute slavery rooted in the constant recurrence of fraud and abuse by power-holders and perpetuated by the absence of 'either public press or public opinion.'[55] Exposing the element of involvement of 'sinister interests,' such as lawyers, sinecurists, contractors, and country gentlemen in the conspiracy to halt political innovation,[56] he then applied this political model to the common arguments of 'official malefactors' against all criticism of established governments, maintaining that criticism of government agents implies not hostility to political authority but respect and concern for government as it can be and ought to be.[57] The 'Book of Fallacies' was essentially a crystallization of Bentham's opinions regarding the immense importance of freedom of the press and public discussion to the well-being of any political society. Compared to it, the earlier 'Anarchical Fallacies' appears narrower in scope and more episodic, having been precipitated by and preoccupied with one particular species of political fallacy: the natural rights argument.

The French Revolution, when in its earliest stages it still retained the appearance of a parliamentary revolution, had excited high hopes in Bentham. It ended by arousing his most profound hostility. Improbable as it may seem, however, even such dramatic events as these constitute but a subplot in the story of Bentham's activities in the late 1780s and early 1790s. The development during this period which Bentham himself expected would shape his entire future life was the progress of his Panopticon scheme.

When George Wilson and James Trail decided they must persuade Bentham to return to England and resume his literary labours, they tempted him with the promise that his *Introduction* would earn him great renown, cautioned him that the Rev. Paley might steal his thunder, advised him that Paley had failed to understand political economy, and finally appealed to his interest in penal reform. For the latter purpose they referred to the work of the great prison reformer John Howard, to the employment of transportation as a punishment, and to the grotesque shortcomings of the old naval hulks being used to house prisoners in lieu of proper penitentiaries.[58] Bentham was eventually to attack both the hulks and transportation as patently inferior rivals to the Panopticon.[59] What is equally important but less commonly acknowledged is the strong influence of John Howard's example on Bentham's approach to penal law and penal reform. In a draft preface in 1780 to what was to become the

Introduction, Bentham had included a paragraph of earnest praise for Howard's character and work, headed 'To Howard' and crowned by the highest compliment: a promise of emulation: 'your name and mine will be handed down to posterity on the same page' (27.126). How is it that Panopticon, a project at least partly inspired by sincere admiration for a humanitarian prison reformer, has come to symbolize more than anything else the irresistible and pervasive repressiveness of Bentham's system of social conditioning and control? Is any contradiction or misrepresentation involved? Not necessarily.

Gertrude Himmelfarb has pointed out in her study of the idea that while the Panopticon sprang from an 'amalgam of Toryism and Enlightened Despotism,' it survived Bentham's conversion to 'radicalism and democracy.'[60] Noting, moreover, that J.S. Mill never criticized Panopticon, 'even when he was most critical of Bentham,' and that Alexander Bain, Henry Brougham, and James Mill all held the idea in the highest esteem, she has concluded that it represented 'nothing less than the existential realization of Philosophical Radicalism.' So impressed is she by the consistency of the Panopticon with Bentham's utilitarian principles and those of the Philosophical Radicals collectively that she questions the accuracy of 'Bentham's image as the father of democracy' and of the image of Philosophical Radicalism as 'the genesis and prototype of our own democracy': 'Benthamism may turn out to have as little in common with our democracy or democratic ideas as the Panopticon has with our actual, let alone model, prisons.'[61]

Leaving aside the separate question of the nature of Philosophical Radicalism, Professor Himmelfarb's conclusion that the Panopticon epitomizes some of the characteristics of Bentham's systematic thought is quite justified. She intends that this conclusion should constitute a damning criticism of the Panopticon and Bentham's thought alike by present democratic standards. The pivotal element in these standards, in the present context, is their conformity to what Himmelfarb calls, without further elaboration, the 'idea of liberty.'[62] Bentham would have found it difficult to understand how the operating principles of a penal institution could be anything but illiberal by definition. Are even those of the model prisons referred to by Professor Himmelfarb anything less than hostile to liberty? Such differences as do exist are neither more nor less than matters of degree.

Panopticon is consistent with Bentham's utilitarianism as a whole, and incompatible with any penitentiary plan which attempts to reconcile efficacy of punishment with the quantitative maximization of freedom. In society as a whole, in Bentham's view, liberty is constantly sacrificed for the sake of security. In Panopticon, the liberty of evil-doers is annihilated totally and invariably in order that the security of the law-abiding may be total and uninterrupted. Punishment for guilt and security for innocence are both 'perfected.' Within the context of his severe and inflexible distinction between the liberty of evil-doers and the liberty of honest and law-abiding men, however, Bentham's most fundamental desire was to achieve an amelioration of prison conditions and to defend it on utilitarian grounds: 'to any one who should be apprehensive of seeing the condition / of convicts / made too desirable, I have only this answer – Art lies in meliorating men's lot: any bungler may make it worse.'[63] Bentham's description of the Panopticon as 'a mill for grinding rogues honest and idle men industrious'[64] has become infamous as an embodiment of the spirit of authoritarianism. Elsewhere in his writings, however, he described the aims of Panopticon more attractively, and no less accurately, as 'the relief of human wretchedness' and 'the reformation of human wickedness' (145a.53).[65] His promises to the Pitt regime in connection with the enterprise included undertakings to keep the inmates of Panopticon clean, to 'fill up ... their time with either productive labour or profitable instruction,' and to 'ensure to them the means of livelihood at the expiration of their terms.'[66] In the case of Panopticon we see the most severe application of a principle which, in a milder shape, pervaded the theory of reward: the notion that in some instances 'it is necessary to put a constraint upon men's inclinations, that they may be at liberty to follow them.'[67] The most profoundly oppressive aspect of Panopticon was not the character of the punishments associated with it but the inexorable and inescapable quality of the remoulding process by which evil-doers were to be, too literally, re-formed into industrious and obedient utilitarian citizens. Given any natural inclination towards the ends advocated by Bentham on the part of the convict, the process of punishment could seem very enlightened indeed, as it did to the individual who, with Bentham's support on humanitarian grounds, sought to be transferred 'to the projected Penitentiary-House in Ireland, if such a thing can be done,' because it offered him hope of a new start.[68]

In defence of his principle of the universal admissibility of judicial evidence (i.e. his suggestion that all procurable evidence, of whatever quality, should be heard in open court in every case) Bentham employed an argument which would have served equally well as a response to charges of repressiveness levelled against Panopticon: 'Fatal to liberty? What means liberty? What can be concluded from a proposition, one of the terms of which is so vague? What my own meaning is, I know; and I hope the reader knows it too. Security is the political blessing I have in view: security as against malefactors on one hand – security as against the instruments of government, on the other.'[69] The characteristics which Bentham ceaselessly sought in his practical proposals regarding judicial evidence, procedure, and the promulgation of laws were those whose establishment would facilitate social systematization and control on the largest imaginable scale: simplicity, certainty, universality, and speed of operation.[70] It was in this area of Bentham's thought that the idea of human perfectibility became most evidently a limitation (and that an inescapable one) upon the sphere of actions within which human nature was to be permitted to develop.

If the principles applied to the Panopticon project seem to correspond *mutatis mutandis* with those employed in other phases of the judical-penal process, they also have their correlatives in the pages of Bentham's 'Poor Law' manuscripts. Indeed, Bentham was perfectly prepared to apply inspection-house principles to any institution for the remoulding of human behaviour. Workhouses, poor houses, madhouses, manufactories, lazarettoes, hospitals, and schools – all could be inspection houses.[71] In all such houses the 'comfortable-ness of the provision' would have to suit the class of inmates: 'it is very difficult to hit the proper medium. To fall short of the mark is inhuman: go beyond it and you give a bounty upon idleness in prejudice of industry.' Idleness was the omnipresent enemy, industry the constant goal; for 'Time must be filled up as well as existence kept alive. The good things of this life do not produce half the enjoyment when they are the usages of idleness, as when they are the price of industry' (87.80). In fact it was in his 'Poor Law' manuscripts that Bentham pronounced what can stand as his last word on the place of liberty in the conceptual framework of such projects as Panopticon: 'If security against everything that savours of tyranny be liberty, liberty, in the instance of this hitherto luckless class of human beings, can scarcely ever have yet existed in anything near so perfect a shape. But liberty, in a favourite sense of it, means lawless power: in this sense, it must be confessed, there will not only be little liberty, but in plain truth there will be none.'[72]

The essential structural principle of Panopticon, with most of its implications, was comprehensively articulated in the Panopticon letters written in 1787. These were published, with two postscripts, in 1791. Then began the long, frustrating, and ultimately tragic attempt to induce the government of the day to help finance and otherwise expedite the undertaking. In December 1792, however, Bentham turned aside from this most authoritarian and repressive of his enterprises to make a spirited defence of liberty in a pamphlet entitled *Truth versus Ashurst; or Law as it is, contrasted with what it is said to be.*[73] In it, he defended the right of every man to the law's protection, that is, to freedom from 'extortion, monopoly, useless formalities, law-gibberish, and law-taxes.' He denounced the unjust imposition of restraints on the poor, in the name of 'the safety and good order of the community at large,' for the sake of an uninterrupted flow of luxuries to the rich. He attacked restraints on the mobility of labour in the form of apprenticeship system and parish poor laws. He attacked the fallacy of virtual representation. He called, as in his essay on

'Indirect legislation,' for increased circulation of public knowledge of the laws and their grounds, and demanded that judicial proceedings be publicized so as to prefer their deterrent effect to their simply punitive one. These were the arguments of the man who was then immersed in the details of Panopticon. Clearly, his devotion to the principle of security for the law-abiding was no less complete than his dedication to the task of reforming evil-doers. Neither commitment, however, had the effect of mitigating the other. They were, to Bentham, complementary.

From 1791 onward, the Panopticon project made ever increasing demands on Bentham's time, energy and patience. By 1794 he was reduced to drafting letters to Pitt and Dundas so evocative of his pathetic and desperate plight that he could not send them. One of these read as follows: 'My fate will be a lesson to mankind: it will be a terror to well-doers. It shows the treatment that may be expected from the author of a plan ... which has been approved by Parliament ... My Brother ruined, my fortune wasted / my spirits sunk / my health consuming ... this is my reward.'[74] By October 1795, Bentham claimed to be wasting at least two-thirds of his time waiting for official word of Panopticon's fate. Convinced that success in this one enterprise would buy him leisure and means to pursue all his other objects, he deferred to a future time the completion of all the productions of his legislative 'workshop.' His book on penal legislation, he said, was no more complete than half a dozen others. The one most likely to be finished before or along with it was that on civil legislation.[75] Indeed, it was in the course of writing some introductory material for a civil code in this period that he was brought to consider how the French, in their Declaration of Rights, had gone wrong by granting to liberty and equality the pre-eminence in civil matters which was rightly due to the idea of security. The vital question of 'expediency' they had set aside altogether, replacing it with a 'crude allegation of the existence of equality,' a claim 'as notoriously as it is universally false.' Furthermore, 'Proceeding at the second step to liberty, property and security, they give them not as political blessings to be aimed at, but as rights, which they declare to be already in the possession of every human being, each in the highest conceivable degree of plentitude' (100.136). At this point in his career (1795), he was understandably inclined to see in French declarations based on natural rights theories the principal rivals and enemies of his own conception of civil law as the liquidator of individual rights. He was scornful of the French revolutionaries' explanations of the origins of civil rights. He asserted that in this case legislators and theorists should be guided by the 'principle of the abhorrence entertained by nature towards a vacuum' (ibid).

Bentham's theory of civil law tended to transform politics into economics in so far as it succeeded in turning the art of social policy-making into the distributive science of happiness: the economics of pleasure and pain. Art would never, he realized, cease to be an integral part of legislative practice, but science would increasingly provide the foundation for 'agenda,' while the principal arts required would be those of adroitness and restraint, the characteristics of a successful governmental policy of minimal intervention in domestic economic affairs. Dr Werner Stark's neat conclusion that the 'perfect synthesis' of 'the two great intellectual tendencies of the eighteenth century, empiricism and rationalism' in Bentham's writings resulted in a corresponding 'practical synthesis of the ideals of liberty and equality' is surely a questionable one. 'Bentham's psychology,' Stark tells us, 'is entirely empiricist ... [his] moral philosophy is entirely rationalist.' On the basis of the unqualified assumption that 'empiricism is thoroughly egalitarian' whereas 'rationalism is thoroughly libertarian,' Stark concludes that liberty and equality are 'not only the foundations of Bentham's Practical Philosophy, they are also the foundations of his Political Economy.'[76] The simple fact which interrupts and invalidates Dr Stark's chain of reasoning is that, as we have seen, Bentham's rationalism was not libertarian. It was utilitarian – even 'felicitarian' – but it did not posit liberty as a rational end-in-itself. The case was precisely the opposite. We can agree with Dr Stark's conclusion that the foundations of Bentham's practical philosophy are also those of his economics. The description of those foundations, however, especially as they relate to the idea of liberty, will have to be pursued further.

Elie Halévy also commented on the place of the idea of liberty in Bentham's economic writings, although mainly by implication. His distinction between the 'principle of the artificial identification of interests,' which he sees as governing Bentham's moral and political thinking, and the 'principle of the natural identity of interests,' which rules in the economic sphere, implies a more secure footing for liberty in the realm of economic activity than in morals and politics.[77] This implication can be accepted only so long as it is not thought to involve a theoretical duality in Bentham's system as a whole or in his concept of liberty. S.R. Letwin has rightly pointed out that the notion of 'natural harmony' or a 'natural identity of interests' has no real place in the thought of Bentham.[78] Nor, we may add, has any notion of a distinctive species of 'natural liberty' a place in the economic sphere.

The essential unity of Bentham's utilitarian thought as a whole and the undisturbed consistency of his ideas on liberty are displayed in his economic writings in various ways. Moreover, the circumstances surrounding the genesis and growth of his interest in political economy emphasize the closeness of the links between that field and other aspects of his work. We have thus far taken such phrases as 'hard currency' to be indicators of Bentham's propensity for using economic and financial terms in other contexts. Conversely, the influence (if that word is strong enough) of the principles of civil law upon Bentham's economic thinking is undeniable. We have seen that the ends of economic science were, as Bentham expressed them, those of civil law, modified only by the slightly narrower scope of economic science as compared with distributive law in its most general sense. Furthermore, it appears that Bentham's actual investigations into economic affairs received some practical stimulus from his work on 'The influence of place and time in matters of legislation,' where he observed that detailed maps, statistics of production, 'tables of the weights, measures and coins in use,' 'tables of ... population,' and the like would assist the legislator in gauging the nature and effect of local circumstances on policy.[79] After his initial enthusiasm over Panopticon had subsided, Bentham turned to the task of gathering just such information from his friend Arthur Young and the *Annals of Agriculture.*[80] Did he not then employ the basic data thus gathered in the construction of his economic theories?

The fears regarding the consequences of universal liberty and universal equality which coloured Bentham's legislative theories in *Of Laws in General* and the 'civil' manuscripts are readily apparent in the economic works as well. In his *Defence of a Maximum* he gave the lie in advance, as it were, to Professor Halévy's dissection of his system, and at the same time launched an attack on the use of 'natural liberty' arguments in the economic or any other sphere:

I have not, I never had, nor ever shall have, any horror, sentimental or anarchical, of the hand of government. I leave it to Adam Smith, and the champions of the rights of man (for confusion of ideas will jumble together the best subjects and the worst citizens on the same ground) to talk of invasions of natural liberty, and to give as a special argument against this or that law, an argument the effect of which would be to put a negative upon all laws. The interference of government, as often as in my humble view of the matter any the smallest ballance on the side of advantage is the result, is an event I witness with altogether as much satisfaction as I should its forbearance, and with much more than I should its negligence.[81]

In 'Supply without Burthen,' a work written, as Dr Stark has observed, 'under the shadow of the French Terror,' Bentham bemoaned the impotence of utilitarianism, though supported by 'the united powers' of Bacon, Locke, Hume, Smith, and Paley, in the face of 'one Danton bawling out natural rights.'[82] At several points in manuscripts preparatory to the writing of the 'Institute of Political Economy' he paused to attack theories of the rights of man (17.183-4), to criticize the 'want of correct and comprehensive views' in certain philosophers (Price, Paine, Rousseau, Montesquieu, Blackstone, Adam Smith) who had misguidedly attacked the idea of liberty in its correct form (17.169), and to inveigh once again against the complementary ideas of universal liberty and universal equality: 'Universal equality in respect of property and universal liberty in the sense in which it means universal equality in respect of political power, imply universal indigence and universal defencelessness. The rights of man are the right of being starved and conquered' (17.209-10).

The relationship between equalization of political power (i.e. 'universal liberty') and equalization of property was manifestly of great interest to Bentham. In chapter 16 of the *Introduction*, Bentham noted that 'even *liberty*' had at times been considered as one of the 'prodigious variety' of 'incorporeal objects of property' which could be objects of the 'operations of the law.' He was unable, however, from this perspective to define conclusively the relationship between liberty and property: 'though on so many occasions [liberty] is contrasted with property, yet on other occasions, being reckoned into the catalogue of possessions, it seems to have been considered as a branch of property.'[83] Bentham's invention of the category of 'incorporeal objects of property' constituted an adaptation to his own principles and purposes of John Locke's dictum that every man has a property in his own person.[84] Bentham finally came to approve mainly of those liberties which could be considered species of property and to renounce the idea of liberty as associated, particularly, with community of goods ('universal equality of property') and the overturning of the system of private property.

It is not surprising, given Bentham's invariable opposition to abstract organic or collectivist notions of political authority or public interests, and his firm advocacy of individualist and aggregative conceptions in their stead, that his idea of liberty was most intimately conjoined not with a broad or general notion of property but with the specific idea of *private* property. A passage in the 'Principles of the Civil Code' as printed by John Bowring asserted that 'there is no arrangement more contrary to the principle of utility, than community of goods, especially that kind of indeterminate community in which the whole belongs to every one.' Such an arrangement, it went on to say, produces unnecessary discord, stifles entrepreneurialism, and preserves an apparent equality which can only serve to hide a real inequality.[85] Equal treatment of unequal individuals begets only inequality. In a manuscript 'brouillon' on the subject of 'Civil equalisation,' Bentham expanded upon these arguments. 'What then is the institution of a community of goods? a contrivance for substituting punishment to reward, pain to pleasure, fear to hope, and servitude to liberty.' The 'extreme difficulty' of establishing 'a state of things so repugnant to the ordinary feelings and propensities of human nature,' Bentham claimed, 'is the best property attending it.' Community of goods, he cried, is institutionalized forced labour, a 'plan ... to subject the whole community for ever to the fate of criminals' (29.9). Elsewhere he denounced 'the levelling system' as destructive of security and 'opulence' (i.e. abundance) (88a.53-4). 'Inequality,' he maintained, 'is the natural condition of mankind' (88a.69).

It is not difficult to imagine the problems which would have beset Bentham's theories of the operations of civil law had the troublesome, 'indeterminate' notion of collective titles to property replaced the notion of individual title upon which Bentham's explanation of the very origins of property was founded. As early as the 1770s, he had argued that the first legal step toward 'constituting' property, public or private, was to 'restrain persons in general from meddling with the thing in question.' Next the law would 'repeal that restriction in favour of a certain person or persons of a particular description' (69.55). Moreover, in so far as his understanding of the relationship between liberty and property was an essential element in his conception of civil law, it was, as we have seen, central to his entire system of thought in the 1790s, and especially to his understanding of the structure of economic science.

The ends of economic art-and-science, as described by Bentham in his works on the subject, are *mutatis mutandis* those pursued by 'distributive' law throughout its broader sphere of activity. In a draft essay entitled 'National prospects, or a Picture of futurity' he listed the principal 'ends in view' in political economy as 'subsistence, security, opulence, equality i.e. maximum of opulence of the lower classes, liberty' (3.83). In the 'Manual of Political Economy' they were 'subsistence, enjoyment, security, and increase.' Equality was pronounced largely outside the pale of political economy, or, where within it, reducible to the pursuit of 'increase' or opulence. Bentham's belief was that the poor must be made less poor, not the rich less rich.[86] In his 'Institute of Political economy,' much as in the 'civil manuscripts,' he listed more than four ends (six in this case) in a preliminary draft, only to eliminate liberty, initially fifth of the six, from the list in its final form.[87] Lastly, in his 'Pannomion,' or 'all-comprehensive collection of law,' he listed the four ends, security, subsistence, abundance, and equality (subordinate as always to the principal end of happiness), together with some of the 'axioms' corresponding to them.[88]

With this reference to axioms we return yet again to Bentham's 'beginning': 'physical sensibility,' the 'ground of law' in every other sector of Bentham's system, was the ground of his theory of political economy as well. 'Government-legislation-political economy would be a study without an object, a labour without point but for their reference to, and influence on, human feelings.' To the variety of 'propositions ... serving to indicate the influence ... on those feelings [of] those events which government and legislation seek to regulate,' Bentham gave the name 'axioms of mental pathology': axioms because of their role, analogous to that of the axioms of mathematics, and mental as distinct from corporal (i.e. medical) pathology.[89] He referred elsewhere to axioms of 'moral' and 'political pathology,'[90] to axioms relevant to subsistence,[91] to abundance,[92] to 'Power, rank and reputation,'[93] etc. These axioms are crystallizations of the dictates of utility. They give a clinical tone to Bentham's interest in the study and control of human nature. From Bentham's definition of them, however, far from outlining a sphere of behaviour within which 'natural liberty' might flourish, they expose to view a fertile field for potential repression and/or manipulation.

Bentham considered human labour to be 'the source of wealth ... which gives birth to all the others.' Acknowledging that in some countries 'the human beings attached to the soil and sold with it constitute its principal value,' he nevertheless asserted that 'the value of human labour is not diminished, but considerably augmented by liberty,' and that 'the reason for considering the inhabitants of a country as constituting a portion of its productive capital will be the stronger, the more perfectly they are free from that undefined mass of obligations which is indicated by the word servitude or slavery.'[94] In the 'Institute of Political Economy,' Bentham advocated 'gradual abolition and intermediate modification of those personal obligations which come under the head of *slavery*.'[95] yet here as elsewhere his attitude was purely utilitarian, without a trace of regard for the intrinsic value of liberty. His condemnation of slavery involved not the slightest reference to dignity, humanity, or rights. It was based entirely on the superior capital value and productivity of free labour. He could see 'no reason for emancipating without indemnification even where actual slavery subsisted.' His dispassionate analysis of the slave's lot must surely constitute one of his most repulsive applications of the principle of security for expectations and the avoidance of disappointment: 'Whatever the condition [of slaves] was ... it was such as they had been bred under ... such as they had been accustomed to adjust to. To the eyes of free men it was a bad state to live in but to them it must have at least been much less bad, as experience had never shown them any other' (29.5). As a means to the chosen ends of security and stability, then, men must not only be enabled to get what they want: they must be taught to adjust – to want and accept what they get (25.14).

Bentham's writings in the field of political economy brought to full fruition the implications of his basic conception of civil law as distributive law. In other practical projects to which we have referred briefly, such as his voluminous writings on reforms required in the laws of judicial evidence and procedure, he applied himself to the problem of institutionalizing his theory of penal law. Certain projects, such as Panopticon and the Poor Law proposals, effected a synthesis of penal and distributive ideas. By roughly 1814 Bentham was prepared, for various reasons, to turn his attention once again to the two aspects of his systematic thought which had lain largely neglected throughout the almost thirty-year period dominated by penal reform, judicial reform, French fallacies, and Panopticon: his idea of 'Ethics in general' and the field of constitutional law.

The purpose of the present work has been largely to investigate certain ideas as propounded by Bentham before Benthamism. The phase in Bentham's career whose characteristics we are now to investigate occupies a chronological period well after Bentham's relationship with James Mill was initiated in 1807. The growth of a Benthamite circle, together with a wider circle of international admirers, must certainly have had its influence on Bentham's style. He now possessed an 'image' to cope with. The fact that in many eyes it was the image of a great servant in the cause of liberty must have struck him as ironic. If the image changed, however, the intellect did not. The most important theoretical development in the ideas of Bentham after the birth of Benthamism was a recurrence of the old desire, first noted by Bentham himself in 1772,[96] to go back to first principles before going forward to the completion of the ethical and constitutional aspects of his system. The encyclopedist in him underwent a renaissance. He began constructing the broadest possible conceptual maps of his system, patterning them after the old Encyclopedists' 'trees.' He systematized his axioms of mental, moral, and political pathology in a 'Table of the springs of action.' He embodied his vision of a complete *corpus juris* in the more overtly metaphysical framework of a 'Pannomion,' a complete body of names for all legal provisions and circumstances.[97] He approached his idea of a 'logic of the will' once again, this time from not the legal but the ontological point of view (14.44-141). He reiterated his critique of language and of 'fictions,' now as a branch of logic (14.166-173).[98] In sum, he redefined 'the art of invention' within the framework of a utilitarian logic and ontology.[99]

Much may remain to be discovered about the true significance of Bentham's efforts to produce a comprehensive deontology, or science of ethics. But pending the completion of an edition of the *Deontology* faithful to the arguments of the extant manuscripts[100] it is clear that this project, too, represents a formal reorganization of the ideas compactly presented in the last chapter of the *Introduction to the Principles of Morals and Legislation*: the division of the field into private and political, the employment of the categories of prudence, probity, and benevolence, and the basic conception, most germane of all to this discussion, of a man's duty to himself.[101]

The most substantial reconsideration of the idea of liberty involved in the resurgence of Bentham's ethical and ontological interest came in the course of his construction of a 'Table of the springs of action,' where he gave an analysis of the love of liberty as a motive for action. Under the heading 'Compound Pleasures exemplified,' he wrote:

Example IV. Love of liberty: *viz* constitutional liberty, or rather (to speak more distinctly) security — *component elements* —

1. *Desire of self-preservation* (No.13) *viz*. against *misrule* and its effects.

2. *Sympathy* (No.10) *viz*. that which has for its object the community at large, considered as liable to be made to suffer from the misrule.

3. Sympathy (No.10) towards this or that *individual*, considered as being ... or liable to be ... a particular *sufferer* from the misrule.

4. *Antipathy* (No.9) towards individuals, *viz*. in the character of lovers and supporters, creators or preservers of misrule; and partakers, actual or expected, in the fruits of it.

5. *Love of Power* (No.5) ex.gr. in respect of the influence exercised, — immediately or through the medium of the understanding, — on the wills of persons on the same side, or, in the way of intimidation, on the *wills* or *sensibilities* of persons on the opposite side.[102]

This was clearly the old wine of liberty as a fictitious and incorporeal entity served in an attractive new bottle. The compound pleasure called 'love of liberty,' however, was still a fiction, still resolvable into more substantial (if not strictly concrete), and less libertarian-sounding components.

One other preoccupation shaped the last major phase of Bentham's intellectual career: the ever-growing passion for codification. The later Bentham manuscripts are replete with references to renewals of work on 'Civil Code,'[103] 'Procedure Code,'[104] 'Penal Code,'[105] and above all 'Constitutional Code.'[106] Codification was the concrete polar opposite, and hence the structural complement, to the search for ontological premises. These two developments were to accomplish cumulatively the final, full extension of Bentham's utilitarian system. None of the projects implied or required substantial alterations or additions to Bentham's basic stock of theoretical concepts. Bentham's burst of interest in codification in the 1820s was probably not in the least due to any conceptual breakthrough, but rather to his expectation that he would be asked to produce, for example, a series of codes for Greece: 'Constitutional in the first place ... penal next as being the simplest, and lastly Distributive Code commonly called Civil' (12.219).[107]

In terms of relevance to the nature and development of Bentham's idea of liberty, the entire phenomenon of Bentham's late preoccupation with codification is less substantially significant than the contents of a single manuscript sheet of unestablished date, headed simply 'Constitution' (170.168).[108] Bentham there set down in a few succinct propositions his notion of the nature and basis of constitutional liberty:

1. Constitutional liberty depends upon and is proportional to the dependence of the possessors of efficient public power upon the will of the body of the people in virtue of the originative power they possess.
2. ... that dependence will be in proportion to the degree of facility which the will of the people has of manifesting itself.
3. The facility which the will of the people has of manifesting itself depends upon 1/ The liberty of speech. 2/ The liberty of assembling for the purposes of speech. 3/ The liberty of writing and printing. 4/ The liberty of communication for whatever is written or printed: under which is included not only the liberty of the post office but of every other channel of conveyance.
4. The knowledge of the occasions which call for it to manifest itself and of the grounds and propriety of the decisions it is called upon to form depends upon the publicity of state proceedings.

Under a fifth heading, Bentham advocated publicity for the acts of office-holders, the identities of individuals involved in them, and the data employed as a basis for decision-making in the case in view.

Even such a brief review as ours has been of the practical or theoretically formal enterprises which dominate the many years of application following Bentham's 'period of invention' clearly underlines the fundamental importance of his early devotion to the analysis of the basic linguistic elements of both the art of thought and the science of social theory.

It may seem, however, that in his description of constitutional liberty Bentham accorded to certain liberties a value and social priority greater than our examination of his thought in general would lead us to expect. In considering both the value of constitutional liberty and the nature of 'indirect legislation' he attached primary importance to publicity of government proceedings, freedom of the press, and freedom of public discussion. We now turn from the investigation of the good citizen's obligation to 'obey punctually' and focus on his right and duty to 'censure freely' to balance and complete our account of Bentham's thoughts on liberty.

12

Freedom of the press and public discussion

In reviewing some of Bentham's most important writings on freedom of the press and public discussion, it is useful to keep in mind B.R. Barber's observation: 'Socialization, advertising, propaganda, brainwashing, and even education may all contain elements of manipulation directed toward the reactive rather than the conscious person and designed to restrict rather than to enlarge conscious deliberation.'[1] It was characteristic of Bentham that he planned to make use of freedoms relating to the press and to public discussion in order to secure, in a seemingly paradoxical way, a more punctual and complete obedience on the part of citizens under a 'government of laws.' His purposes remained manipulative in spite of his endorsement of specific sorts of liberty. If he did not see himself as aiming to restrict conscious deliberation, that was because his real purpose was to redefine both consciousness and deliberation, and in so doing to define the conscious person in largely 'reactive' terms. Only within the boundaries established by his science of human nature would it be considered expedient to stimulate public discussion and debate.

In *On Liberty*, J.S. Mill wrote that 'Liberty, as a principle, has no application to any state of things anterior to the time when mankind have become capable of being improved by free and equal discussion.'[2] Bentham's belief was rather that the principle of utility could only achieve the universality of application appropriate to its nature in social conditions permitting a free circulation of public knowledge. For Mill the end and the means were one: participation in free and equal discussion was considered *intrinsically* important both as a necessary condition and as an implicit assertion of a principle of liberty. The relationship between means and ends in this context was different for Bentham. Freedom was for him a thing of relative and intermediate importance only. His advocacy of free public debate presupposed that the rules, the issues, and the very language of debate were framed in utilitarian terms. His object was not the preservation of free self-expression as an outlet for a uniquely human élan vital, but the mobilization of public opinion for the sake of security against misrule. He was still, as Mill saw it, attacking the evils of governmental tyranny while leaving the way open to a tyranny of the majority over the individual.

Bentham could see no intrinsic value in the freely expressed solitary dissent of the eccentric or the idiosyncratic individual. For him, all virtue lay in the utilitarian consequences of the argument, not in the manner or circumstances of its presentation. He did not suggest that the liberty to be mistaken was no liberty; he recognized it and denounced it as a mischievous species of liberty. He undertook to stamp out error, not by force, but by the transformation of disagreements of attitude into disagreements of belief.[3] This was the foundation upon which he based his claims that his system possessed universal applicability. The transformation was to be accomplished, not by means of unfettered discussion, but by the institutionalization of a fundamental set of utilitarian dictates. In the face of concrete, scientific demonstrations of the truths of utilitarianism, what would be the value of dissent grounded on feelings of sympathy or antipathy? Nowhere in the long list of his expressions of support for freedom of the press or public discussion does Bentham contradict, endanger, or qualify his commitment to the control of the frame of reference within which public debate is carried on – control by means of indirect legislation, scientific ethics, and a thoroughly programmed educational system.

A strictly libertarian view of freedom of the press and public discussion would see these kinds of liberty as fundamental to the preservation of privacy, of eccentricity, of non-conformity for its own sake – in short, of everything that distinguishes the libertarian individualism of J.S. Mill from the utilitarian individualism of Bentham. It would, for example, emphasize the importance of privacy as in some sense a necessary condition, physical or spiritual, of individual liberty. Bentham did not deny the practical value of privacy, but he could never have allowed his appreciation of it to override the clear utilitarian necessity for knowledge of individual behaviour on the legislator's part as the basis of political security. Defending his schemes for 'marking' (tattooing) individuals against the charge of being 'dangerous to liberty,' he showed no sympathy for any such liberties as would require a protective cloak of anonymity or secrecy for their enjoyment: 'The liberties of a country real or pretended are maintained not by the intrigues of a few but by the corroboration of the many: not in holes and corners but in the face of day: not by men whose shame it is, but whose glory it is to be known' (87.135). Just as publicity and free censure were to render rulers responsible to their subjects, so subjects would be expected to open their lives to an extraordinary degree to public or official inspection. The popular correlative of princely misrule was not crime, but delinquency. The citizen was expected to bear a heavy burden of moral and political duty, and given the character of Bentham's system it is difficult to discover any respect in which this burden could be lightened for the sake of the intrinsic value of liberty.

Bentham's proclamations of support for freedom of the press and of public discussion were confined largely within the boundaries of a specific context: the field of politics and of constitutional liberty as security against misgovernment. Only in a few brief passages did he make any reference to the private aspects of the problem: the need for security against libel and defamation as 'offences against reputation.'

In the Preface to his *Fragment on Government* (1776), Bentham devoted several pages to the argument that the laws 'ought to be scrutinized with freedom' in any properly functioning political society.[4] Free criticism of the laws, he maintained, should be the right − indeed the duty − not of the censorial jurist alone, but of every good citizen: 'I know not for what good reason it is that the merit of justifying a law when right should have been thought greater, than that of censuring it when wrong. Under a government of Laws, what is the motto of a good citizen? *To obey punctually; to censure freely.*'[5] In his study of sovereignty in the same work, he examined the distinction between free and despotic governments, and listed six criteria by which the degree of freedom permitted by a government could be measured.[6] The first three criteria pertained to the individual's opportunities for political participation and his chances of holding political power. These indices of political (or constitutional) liberty would fluctuate in accordance with changes in the distribution of power, the sources of entitlement to power, and the practicability of 'frequent and easy changes of condition between govern*ors* and govern*ed*.' Bentham was quite characteristically defining what was commonly called 'free' government as being more properly 'responsible' (i.e. representative and responsive) government. Certain liberties, however, were considered especially important as necessary conditions of the attainment and stability of responsible government. These were: the free publication of full descriptions and justifications of government actions, freedom of the press, and freedom of public discussion:

The *responsibility* of the governors; or the right which a subject has of having the reasons publicly assigned and canvassed of every act of power that is exerted over him ... The liberty of the press; or the security with which every man, be of the one class or the other, may make known his complaints and remonstrances to the whole community ... The liberty of public association; or the security with which malcontents may communicate their sentiments, concert their plans, and practise every mode of opposition short of actual revolt, before the executive power can be legally justified in disturbing them.

From this conception of the nature of these freedoms and this estimate of their importance Bentham never deviated in the entire course of his working life. He considered the unrestricted circulation of public information to be an indispensable link between rulers and ruled in political society, binding them together in a secure relationship based upon the conjunction of duty and interest on each side. Freedom of censure would provide subjects with their essential 'securities against misrule' by ensuring prompt exposure and elimination of government abuses and by making it the interest of governors to fulfil their duties. On the other hand, criticism would be as open to scrutiny as would legislative policy. Censure, like government, would be 'responsible.' Popular duty and interest would be harmonized by the achievement of the complementary goals of punctual obedience and free censure. The ultimate fruit borne by the seeds of liberty of the press and public discussion would be constitutional security.

Bentham's commitment to the unrestricted growth and continuing criticism of public knowledge testifies to his profound belief in the value of popular enlightenment in political and social affairs. In this sense he remained a *philosophe* to the last. Without a firm foundation of political knowledge and a tradition of free censure, the political impact of the moral sanction would be at best unpredictable and at worst persistently disutilitarian. Bentham's recurrent demand for the conversion of judge-made law into statute law, first explicitly stated in the *Comment on the Commentaries*,[7] was based on the belief that, to be validated by habitual obedience and improved by constructive criticism, that is, to be utilitarian, the law must be made accessible, understandable, and justifiable to as many citizens as possible. In *Truth vs Ashurst*, as we have seen, this position was vehemently reasserted.

Perhaps it was with this object in mind that Bentham in the 1770s put forward a 'plan for a government newspaper' (149.1-9),[8] later broadening his field of vision to include a study of the 'leading principles' of newspapers, 'professed universally' (107.24-7),[9] a glance at the idea of an encyclopedia (107.37),[10] a newspaper (the 'Indicator') designed to 'index the whole body of national intelligence' (108.2-14, 15-99),[11] and finally a 'prospectus of a morning family newspaper, "The Universalist" ' (149.282-311).[12] In the context of his work on 'Escheat' (1795), far removed from the political concerns of the *Comment* or *Truth vs Ashurst*, Bentham once again argued that 'liberty depends not upon the greater or less influence of the Crown with relation to the servants of the public and the representatives of the people, but on the spirit of the people itself.' He found 'a real source of danger to liberty' in 'the precarious tenure by which the right of the people to take cognisance in any shape of public measures is held under the subsisting laws: though, it must be confessed, it has never hitherto been held under any better.'[13]

We have seen that Bentham included in his 'Indirect' manuscripts an important series of arguments concerning the nature and significance of freedom of the press and public discussion. Some of the relevant manuscript passages eventually found their way into John Bowring's edition of the *Principles of Penal Law*.[14] One still extant passage, concerning the principles on which liberty of the press ought to be founded, has not yet been cited in the present discussion. In it Bentham asserts that 'the propriety of this institution [freedom of the press] depends upon two principles: that two heads are better than one: and that since human nature is not perfect those who have not the law should have the opinion of the world to check them' (99.130).[15] He goes on to claim that the English press is not free, principally because 'the laws against defamation' have not been defined. There is, he says, no more freedom for the press by law than there is toleration for religion. Thus legislatorial neglect is the source of 'the arbitrariness of the executive power' (ibid).

The claim that freedom of the press was the result, not of governmental policy, but of governmental negligence and inactivity, reappeared in the *Book of Fallacies,*[16] where Bentham observed caustically that

under favour of the contest between Whigs and Tories, the liberty of the press, the foundation of all other liberties, has been suffered to grow up and continue. But this liberty of the press ... what there is of it ... exists not by means but in spite, of law. It is all of it contrary to law: by law there is no more liberty of the press in England, than in Spain or Morocco. It is not the constitution of the government, it is not the force of the law; it is the weakness of the law we have to thank for it.[17]

Both Tories and Whigs, said Bentham, would willingly destroy liberty of the press, could they be assured that they would never thereafter have need of it. In their impotence without it lay the source of their support for it: 'Without this arm they could not fight their battles; without this for a trumpet, they could not call the people to their aid.'[18] Of the utility of a free press as an instrument of, and an incentive to, responsible government, he had more to say elsewhere in the *Book of Fallacies*. He dismissed the argument that no government could exist unprotected against public criticism with the reply that, on the contrary, 'No good government can exist without it.'[19] In Turkey, he observed, where freedom of the press and of public discussion had been extinguished, revolts and revolutions were more frequent and violent than anywhere else in the world.[20]

In his discussion in the *Book of Fallacies* of the 'sham distinction' between liberty and licentiousness as exhibited by the press,[21] Bentham put forward an unusual and broad definition of the press, equating it with every conceivable vehicle of public discussion. He took it to mean 'every instrument employed or employable for the purpose of giving diffusion to the matter of human discourse by visible signs.' Understood in these terms, the press has 'two distinguishable uses, – viz moral and political.' Its moral function is as a 'check ... to misconduct in private life.' Even a free press is thus an instrument of control in the ethical and psychological senses. Its political use is to 'check ... misconduct in public life,' which is to say, on the part of men employed or aspiring to be employed in 'the public service.' On one hand, freedom of the press by this definition is the principal extralegal source of control over the sort of political misconduct which is most likely to lead to 'power uncontroulable' in government hands and thence to 'arbitrary despotism.' On the other hand, a completely free rein for the press will result inevitably in the publicizing of a certain number of false imputations of private or public misconduct. To some extent, then, the price of liberty is the perpetuation of a degree of licentiousness.

How, in such a case, is the choice between censorship and a free press to be made? Bentham maintains that this choice is not as difficult as may at first appear. If 'just imputations' of misconduct be 'buried in utter silence' along with the 'unjust,' one can be sure that 'misconduct in every part of the field of action, moral and political, private and public, will range without controul which can be applied by the press, and not by anything else.' If, on the other hand, we provide for unjust imputations, along with the just, to have an 'unobstructed course ... through this channel,' 'personal suffering' is liable, but not by any means certain, to be the result. Moreover, 'open to accusation, that same channel is not less open to defence. He, therefore, who as truth on his side, will have on his side all that advantage which it is in the nature of truth to give.' Unless and until a means of barring unjust imputations without suppressing an equal proportion of just ones be found, 'the tendency and effect of all restrictions having for their object the abridging of the liberty of the press, cannot but be evil on the whole.' Until such time, moreover, the licentiousness of the press will remain interwoven (and confused) with its liberty, and the press will remain unable to fulfil completely its critical function. Powerholders will simply denounce and punish as licentious any troublesome manifestation of freedom of censure: 'Should that line [i.e. between liberty and licentiousness] ever have been drawn, then it is that licentiousness may be opposed without opposing liberty: while that line remains undrawn, opposing licentiousness is opposing liberty.' Full acceptance of Bentham's utilitarian social system would clearly enable such a line to be drawn. The object of this process, however, would be not the maximization of liberty, but its 'perfection,' that is, its complete subordination and adaptation to utilitarian ends.

It was not in the *Book of Fallacies* alone that Bentham discussed the problem of how to perfect liberty of the press in terms of maximizing the incidence of just imputations of misconduct and minimizing the incidence of unjust ones. In the course of an examination, in 1809, of the 'means employable by Jurymen for obtaining a Code of Libel law,' he recalled '[to obey] punctually, censure freely, J.B.'s Fragment motto. Not changed by Revolutions etc.' (26.43).[22] The problem of reconciling the right of free censure with the duty of punctual obedience, in the guise of the problem of distinguishing between just and unjust imputations of misconduct, formed a central obstacle to the definition of freedom of the press within the context of a code of libel laws. Similarly, within the wider framework of an effort to form a penal code, the definition of liberty of the press became an integral aspect of the analysis of 'offences affecting reputation,' (65.138-70).[23] The formulation in about 1810 of the idea of a 'Code of Defamation' was an expression of the same concern for a systematic evaluation of the justness of imputations of private or public misconduct (67.44-55).[24] If a legal framework could be provided for such a system, as Bentham argued in 1809, the 'disputable' claim voiced in the slogan 'Give us our rights' could be superseded by the 'indisputable' one, 'Give us our laws' (26.43).[25] The popular desire for liberty, however misguided, could be channeled into a path determined by utilitarian considerations: to serve as 'a remedy curative or preventive against misgovernment' (26.49).[26]

Towards 1820, Bentham began to frame his interest in the prevention of 'misgovernment' more exclusively and more vehemently in terms of his analysis of the nature and instruments of 'misrule' and the manifest need for 'securities' against it (111. passim).[27] In 1822, in his 'letters to Count Torreno,' he returned once again to the explicit defence of freedom of censure and, in one letter, even spoke of a class of 'Offences against the liberty of the people' (108.150).[28] Bentham corresponded with various Greeks and Englishmen interested or involved in the events of 1823-4 in Greece and the search for a new Greek constitution. Venerated by some Greeks as the 'genius of Greek liberty' and a servant of the 'cause of justice and liberty' (12.289, 322),[29] he was given a practical demonstration of the importance of freedom of the press by the varying fortunes of his works in the hands of publishers politically committed either to suppressing or circulating his ideas.[30] In a draft letter of 1823 to 'Greek legislators,' he took the wind out of the sails of would-be Greek libertarians even while advocating responsible government: 'Legislators! Let not words / names / let not vulgar errors deceive you. Not "independence," but "dependence," so it be rightly placed, is the great security for good government. Dependence, so it be rightly placed, can not be too strict. As for independence, supposing it to exist which it does not, it is anarchy. Dependence as it is your ... duty, so it is your only true glory — dependence on your constituents'

(21.309).[31] The foundation of such dependence, as we have seen, was to be provided by liberty of the press and of public discussion.

Bentham's most substantial expression of his position on freedom of the press and public discussion in these years, however, came in his four 'letters to the Spanish People' of 1820 (22.152-252).[32] There he attacked the prosecution of a Spanish newspaper editor for critical comments on the Madrid Police and a proposed Spanish law against political meetings. He was 'astounded' by the idea of such measures. He pointed to the absence of such provisions in the United States, 'that only seat of real and established good government,' where 'public tranquillity has not known what disturbance is.' He suggested that England as well as Spain should take a lesson from the United States, where no libel laws were in force, and where there had been prosecutions for political libel only during the brief reign of the Sedition Act from 1798 to 1801. 'Between one degree of disapprobation and another,' he asserted, 'it is not possible to draw a line.' Hence all criticism of government was liable to be treated as defamation or vituperation, and therefore as punishable. Bentham associated this problem with the established notion that repressive measures against personal attacks should increase in severity in direct proportion to the importance of the office held by the object of such attacks. He asserted the exact opposite: there should, above all, be no punishment for public attacks on public office-holders unless their intent be shown to be malicious and their allegations groundless and false: 'to place on any more advantageous footing the official reputation of a public functionary, is to destroy, or proportionably to weaken, that liberty, which, under the name of the liberty of the press, operates as a check upon the conduct of the ruling few.'

The benefits resulting from the 'security afforded for good government' by freedom of the press, he held, would be general in extent and immense in value, and would not be outweighed by any of its admitted inherent evils. Exposure to criticism, and even calumny, is the price of high public office. Moreover, as for cases where the public appeal is to a superior and the claim is that his subordinates have committed errors or injustices, 'without this liberty, the rulers in chief will not be sufficiently either disposed, or enabled to supply, so much as simple removal, much less punishment, for remedy against inaptitude on the part of their subordinates.' In short, then, the acceptance of the inherent evil of recurrent press licentiousness is a reasonable price to pay for the mitigation of the evils of despotism: 'In all liberty there is more or less of danger: and so there is in all power. The question is – in which there is most danger – in power limited by this check, or in power without this check to limit it?'

Bentham's espousal of liberty of the press and public discussion was no more profoundly liberal or libertarian than his endorsement of any other species of liberty. It was founded upon a purely utilitarian calculus of the good and evil consequences involved in the establishment and maintenance of those liberties. The most fundamental characteristic of the idea of liberty, here as elsewhere in Bentham's writings, is its employment as a means of obtaining security, and its repudiation as an end in itself.

13

Epilogue:
Philosophy, science, politics,
and Bentham's social thought

Jeremiah Bentham always hoped that his son Jeremy would become a brilliant and successful lawyer. It is therefore not surprising that the young Jeremy Bentham's first area of intellectual endeavour was legal theory. He might have gone on from there — no doubt his father fervently wished he had — to an active legal practice. He did not do so because even in youth he was, and knew himself to be, something other, and something perhaps greater, than a lawyer. He was a philosopher and a scientist. Aware of his own precocity, Bentham from an early age sought nothing less than 'the way of all others in which [he] might be of most service to his fellow creatures.' We have noted that it was Helvétius who convinced Bentham that this goal could best be attained, not by studies in botany, chemistry, or physical science, but by improving the 'science' of law rather than practising it as a profession.[1] From the combination of paternal influence and philosophical inclination Bentham thus became a legal scientist, which as he understood it meant a systematic legal expositer-cum-critic. He undertook the task of creating a scientific jurisprudence: hence his first proposed magnum opus, an exposition of the 'Elements of critical jurisprudence.' The sequence of development of his legal studies, from an initial interest in punishment to an analysis of penal law, then to an introductory study of morals and law-making and to a treatise on the idea of law in a very broad sense, transported him from what had at first seemed a circumscribed sphere of legalistic analysis to a boundless theatre of thought, the 'universal system of human actions.' This broadening of theoretical scope was both caused by and superimposed upon Bentham's commitment to 'science.' The enlargement of his sphere of interest, in turn, tended to increase Bentham's awareness of the close relationship between the theory and practice of law in a given society and the theory and practice of politics in the same society.

The study of law thus led to the study of politics and beyond it to the study of society as a web of human interaction. Why? Because Bentham's study of the law was, from the beginning, simply a focusing of his basic interest in the 'science of human nature.' From the beginning, when he determined to his satisfaction that physical sensibility was the ground of law, the enterprise of correlating an anatomy of human physical sensibility and a 'universal map of jurisprudence' beckoned to him.[2] However this could remain no simple exercise in legal theory. It constituted a systematic social theory, presupposing on one hand the discovery of a logic of human action and on the other an exhaustive analysis of the nature of law in its broadest sense as social imperation, a theory of politics, and more. It presupposed a systematic examination, of the traditional categories of philosophical inquiry as they applied to social phenomena: a metaphysics, an epistemology, a logic, and an ethics of human action and motivation. In short, the completion of Jeremy Bentham's grand intellectual enterprise presupposed the creation of a philosophy of social science. Yet in Bentham's day, unlike our own, it made sense to insist that this philosophy in turn must be scientific. Science was the measure of philosophy and not vice versa. Bentham's strongest intellectual commitment was to the idea of scientific method. His inspiration was derived from the success of physical scientists in mapping the world and analysing its constituent elements. His intention was to become the Newton of the moral (and social) sciences. One commentator has aptly described him as combining the roles of 'political inventor'[3] and 'social engineer.'[4] He was in fact a prototype of the social scientist in a time when the term *philosophe* characterized those who aspired to blend the best attributes of philosophy and science into a rich amalgam of inquisitive thought.

Bentham was therefore a philosophical radical long before he came to be considered a political radical. In the course of his career he embraced increasingly radical political creeds as means to the realization of the practical ends entailed by his radical social science (which was also, we have seen, a philosophy). Yet he never sought political involvement, political power, or political reform as an end in itself. Perhaps it is for this reason that attempts by recent commentators to show that Bentham was fundamentally a 'democrat'[5] or a 'liberal'[6] seem to miss the point. His political thought expressed more than a preference for a particular political ideology or party. Such terms were not even current in his formative years, and were certainly not the decisive categories of his thinking. He was not, on the whole, much fonder of politicians than of lawyers, which is not surprising since many of his contemporaries wore both hats. He could seek out a Lord Shelburne or a Catherine the Great precisely because the character and position of such individuals was thought to place them above, or simply outside, the mainstream of politics. Perhaps Bentham realized, whether consciously or not, that his social science, when fully developed, must constitute an implicit call for an end to political debate as such and its replacement by a utilitarian calculus of the societal consequences of prospective public policies.

Bentham never sought a reformed politics except as a manifestation of a reformed social philosophy and a means to an improved social and economic condition. The unhappy political career and the ultimate fate of his Panopticon proposal illustrate emphatically the unfortunate interaction of philosophical radical and practising politician.[7] Bentham's Burkean distaste for the Wilkesites, his passionate denunciations of the political philosophy of the American revolutionaries (mitigated in time only bn acknowledgment of the *economic* benefits of emancipating one's colonies[8] and his scornful dismissal of the French 'pandemonions' illustrate clearly the gap between political radicalism and Bentham's philosophical radicalism in the period 1775-90. Later, however, the political radicalism of Francis Place, of Burdett, of Edwin Chadwick, even of J.S. Mill (his protestations to the contrary notwithstanding, he owed much to Bentham in ideas as well as in method) was, or was at least meant to be, founded upon the principles of philosophical radicalism.[9] Since this study discusses only the activities of Bentham before the existence of Benthamites and Benthamism no attempt is made to specify the nature of the complex intellectual relationships which linked Bentham with his first and second generation political offspring.[10] The point is simply that, in so far as Bentham became a political radical or involved himself with any political movement or tradition, it was because he saw in it a means to the broad social ends entailed by his unwavering commitment to utilitarianism as a scientific social philosophy. He remained always 'the philosopher of Queen's Square Place.' At heart and in mind he was never anything more nor less.

In the last decade and more of his life, contented with (or perhaps unmoved by) the development of Benthamism as a political persuasion, he returned with a renewed and remarkable vigour to the essentially philosophical task of spelling out the first principles and mapping the final boundaries of his social science. The manuscripts of his last years are replete with references to the philosophical problems of nomography, ontology, and deontology and with efforts at codification – the conclusive delineation *in toto* of a radically reformed social structure as envisaged by Bentham. His studies of deontology, he now felt, should be the basis for a comprehensive work on the subject: in effect an ethical code, to be joined by a civil code, a criminal code, and constitutional code. These, together with a procedural code, the 'Institutes of Political Economy,' and a number of more specialized works such as the *Essay on indirect legislation* and *Chrestomathia*, would show to posterity, were it willing and able to avail itself of them, the shape of Bentham's ideal political society, the ultimate product of his initial decision to study the science of human nature.

In Bentham's view the physical sciences and the social sciences had a common mother in philosophy and a common object of study in Man. Certainly it would be difficult to overstate the influence exerted by Bentham's metaphysical and epistemological beliefs and theories on his political ideas. His was not, as is well known, a unique or basically original epistemological perspective. In his writings, however, as he himself felt, it was adhered to with a dogged rigour, based on a firm faith in its ultimately beneficial social implications. This rigour and consistency made those social and political implications, for better or for worse, strikingly clear in Bentham's writings. The roots of Bentham's explanations of the origins and justification of political society, of his concepts of political power and authority, and of his understanding of the rights and duties of the citizen are to be found in his initial epistemological and metaphysical principles. The present study has tried to demonstrate these roots by using the concept of liberty as a sort of intellectual prism. Some of what may have remained implicit throughout can perhaps now be made explicit by further analysis.

The sequence of developments with which we are to deal is not a chain reaction, there is nothing inevitable or automatic about it. Yet successive notions entertained by the young Bentham seem, in their logical inter-relatedness, to give coherence to his undertakings. At the beginning of the sequence we find metaphysics. Bentham's metaphysics is materialist, nominalist, and philologically oriented in a manner strikingly reminiscent of Hobbes. For Bentham, as for Hobbes, 'science' was essentially a matter of weaving correct definitions into a fabric of thought. Hobbes had argued in the *Leviathan* that science was essentially a well-ordered mode of discourse, proceeding from proper 'Definitions of Words' by 'Connexion of the same into general Affirmations, and of these again into Syllogismes,' leading to an 'End or last summe ... called the Conclusion.' Thus science became, in Hobbes's view, 'Knowledge of the consequence of words.' 'But if the first ground of such Discourse, be not Definitions; or if the Definitions be not rightly joined together ... there the End or Conclusion, is again *opinion*.'[11] Bentham, presumably unknowingly, echoed him with his judgment that an 'orderly, unbroken, well compacted chain of definitions' is 'the only sure ladder whereby a man can ... make his way up to ... the heights of science.' The universe of Bentham, as of Hobbes, is a universe of concrete objects and of names or words denoting those objects. The logic of individual behaviour in such a universe is the same for both men. Hobbes conceives of a variety of possible political masters having in common the single but decisive attribute of absolute and indivisible sovereign power. Bentham's 'sovereign masters,' pleasure and pain, also assume many forms but retain always and essentially, not by political necessity but in physiological fact, their absolute dominion over men.

A common belief in the impossibility of physically self-destructive behaviour is the key to the notion of natural law which is found explicitly in Hobbes's theory[12] and implicitly in Bentham's. The more we try to throw off the constraints imposed on us by our hedonistic sovereign masters, Bentham says, the more we do 'but confirm their dominion.' In Hobbes, what ultimately and inescapably proves the necessity of absolute political sovereignty is, likewise, our very physiological nature: the organism's instinct for self-preservation. In Hobbes, that instinct is seen as giving rise to an insatiable lust for power which finds expression in a war of each against all, terminated only by an agreement to place the powers of each in the hands of an absolute sovereign empowered to exact obedience from all.[13] In Bentham the 'habit of obedience' to one's hedonistic sovereign masters is pre-political even pre-social. The pre-political quest for power basic to the nature of Hobbesian man is in Bentham subordinated to a quest for equilibrium: for a stable and secure condition far removed from Hobbes's war of each against all. For Hobbes the original compact provides a sociopolitical remedy for the anarchic evils inherent in man's unvarnished nature. In Bentham's view human nature itself harbours a principle of behaviour that offers a solution to all problems of social disorder and at the same time denies the postulate of pre-social strife. For Bentham, man is a hedonistic animal in a more profound sense than that in which he is a political one. He is hedonistic by nature and political by habituation. His natural obedience to the sensory dictates of his own organism is simply regularized in the family and generalized in political society.

This verdict on the relationship between the individual and the sovereign power in political society flows directly from one crucial earlier step in Bentham's train of reasoning: the reduction of the social side of human psychology to a mere matter of physiology ('physical sensibility'). Here we come to the crux of the matter: for Bentham, human motivation was physical sensibility, given temporal extension by the human capacities for memory and anticipation. Observing that under most circumstances, on this analysis of the nature of a motive, the idea of pleasure or pain has the same motivating efficacy as its actual occurrence, Bentham quickly recognized the applicability of this insight to the sphere of government. Implicitly taking 'government' to mean the controlling of human behaviour by the manipulation of pleasures and pains and thence of human motives, he concluded that 'self-government' ought to mean, not the apotheosis of libertarian individualism, but the subjection of the unassisted individual to the dictates of his own isolated organism, adrift in an unorganized sea of 'inanimate or irrational' sources of sensory stimuli.[14] With such a jaundiced view of the lot of the self-governing individual as a point of comparison, the utility of government was clear to Bentham. Its indispensable function was to be the organization of the hedonistic social environment: the administration of pleasurable and painful things was to be the essence of the government of men.

Bentham's understanding of human motivation, of the 'springs of action,' the 'logic of the will,' or the 'axioms of mental pathology,' is the hinge upon which his whole social science turns. It assures him of the logic, of the ultimate malleability and predictability, of human actions. It allows him to design, to engineer, a structure of social and governmental authority to fit the known contours of the human personality. It enables him to entertain the notion of a configuration of sovereign power which channels human action but without, to his way of thinking, coercing the individual in any unacceptable sense. It allows him to claim that the internecine war between liberty and authority can be settled by the maximization of security.

Bentham's theory of motivation, the essence of his theory of human nature, had its roots in his epistemology. His epistemology, in turn, was derived directly from his metaphysics and his theory of language. From the study of what entities exist Bentham moved to an analysis of how knowledge of those things is conveyed, and thence to a description of how thought leads to action.

We have seen that Bentham, while giving qualified praise to John Locke's *Essay Concerning the Human Understanding*, denounced the contractual political theory of the *Second Treatise of Government*, committing in the process what must seem to twentieth-century eyes the theoretical abomination of preferring Sir Robert Filmer's analysis of political authority in some respects to the systems of Locke and Rousseau. He rejected Locke's contractual theory because he found it, quite rightly, to be incompatible with the epistemological principles of the *Essay*. He criticized the *Essay* because, as a materialist and a nominalist, he could not endorse the separation made in it between the logic of the understanding and that of the will. The *Essay* thus induced Bentham to crystallize his own conception of the relationship between thought and action. In producing his own logic of the understanding, Bentham modified Locke's dualistic ontology of ideas, discarding the category of ideas of reflection and retaining only ideas of sensation: hence his nominalism and his materialism. Here he was preferring Hobbes to Locke, apparently without knowing it. In adding to it a logic of the will, Bentham was extending Locke's *Essay* precisely into that area with which it had dealt least adequately, motivational theory. Bentham, dealing only with sensations as springs of action, and not with elusive and intangible abstractions, postulated for that reason a kinship of sensation and action (or reaction) much removed from anything in Locke's *Essay*. On that kinship he based the cohesion and coherence of his utilitarian view of the individual, government, and society as elements in a single systematic social science.

Bentham must have felt that Locke had glimpsed a basic truth in that moment of insight when he confessed that nature, by endowing men with the faculty of feeling pleasure and pain, had provided the inescapable and incessant 'innate practical principles' of human action. Seizing on this seeming truth of physiology – the same truth embodied in Bentham's initial 'proposition most obvious and incontestible' – 'physical sensibility the ground of law,' Bentham refused to take refuge in religion or abstraction when the time came to announce his political principles. He based his understanding of the duty of a good citizen, his concept of liberty, his notion of the origins of political society in man's 'habit of obedience,' his assessment of the utility of that society, and his conception of the appropriate form and extent of legal and political power, on his view that psychology means physiology, at least for the purposes of a political and social theory concerned ultimately with 'the universal system of human actions.'

Thus, the character of Bentham's 'science of human nature' determined the character of his political thought. His devotion to the principles implied by his original judgments as to the springs of action, the logic of the will, and the consequent dimensions and purposes of social control by the Legislator coloured his political prescriptions throughout his career. His elimination of abstract ideas from the realm of real entities, and hence from the list of springs of action, was the intellectual justification for his denial of the accuracy or utility of the conception of a hypothetical contract antedating both government and society. The kernel of his rejection of contract theory was expressed in his belief that 'it was contracts came from government, not government from contracts.' His attack on Locke's *Essay* may thus be seen as essentially an assertion that men derived their sense of obligation, of right, of duty, and of power, not from any abstract source such as a belief in liberty, democracy, a hypothetical original contract, or government, but from those internal springs of action known as motives, crystallized in the 'axioms of mental pathology' and decreed by the government of man's sovereign masters pleasure and pain.

Having established what seemed to him to be quasi-Newtonian laws outlining the logic of human action, Bentham naturally focused as well on the sociopolitical context in which such action would take place. Venturing first and foremost into the established realm of 'direct legislation,' he broadened his definition of the term 'law' so as to include every recognizable form of social 'imperation' (command). His logic of the will was by its nature a logic of imperation, and one sees in the juxtaposition of these two aspects and levels of imperation the essence of the cohesiveness of Bentham's system. Logically enough, Bentham thereafter broadened his view of the functions attributable to a lawmaker until they, in like manner, seemed to include every imaginable form of social control over the universe of human actions. Thought, in so far as it led to no action, not even by the most devious or convoluted of causal or logical sequences, could be left alone by the legislator. Action, however, and thought leading to or inspiring action, however indirectly, might be − in the end must be − controlled. It should come as no surprise to any attentive observer that Bentham eventually created the novel field of 'indirect legislation' and set out to chart the seemingly boundless oceans of deontology in this regulatory spirit. These enterprises, not the fervency of the later Benthamites, represent the apotheosis of that radicalism which is most truly Bentham's, as opposed to the radicalism whose real source and sustaining force was the fervour of a James Mill or the political ferment of the day. The prescience, the radical vision, and indeed some of the rather disturbing implications of Bentham's social theory were to be captured two hundred years later in the words of Frazer, the apostle of *Walden Two*:

We can achieve a sort of control under which the controlled, though they are following a code much more scrupulously than was ever the case under the old system, nevertheless *feel free*. They are doing what they want to do, not what they are forced to do. That's the source of the tremendous power of positive reinforcement − there's no restraint and no revolt. By a careful cultural design, we control not the final behaviour, but the *inclination* to behave − the motives, the desires, the wishes.

The curious thing is that in that case *the question of freedom never arises*.[15]

Beginning with the individual citizen, Bentham undertook to make plain the origins and extent of his duty to obey punctually and to justify the circumscription of his right to censure freely. The *primum mobile* of this chain of reasoning was Bentham's judgment that what is sought by men under the name of liberty is not truly mere liberty, the simple absence of coercion, but in fact security, the *assurance* of *right*. Bentham carried one important step further the 'thoughtful' Delolme's assertion, 'To live in a state where the laws are equal for all, and sure to be executed ... is to be free,' claiming that such a condition was wrongly referred to as freedom when it was in fact security. This step was a crucial one, for Bentham accepted the conventional judgment that liberty was *not* the 'child of law.' Unlike many of his contemporaries, however, Bentham, as a natural result of his view of the individual as a sensory organism, concluded that neither was liberty the true object of individual desires. If what humanity truly sought was security, the widely accepted judgment that politics was a battle between the individual defender of freedom and the state hungry for power must be rejected, for the state is the cradle of law, and 'the invaluable, the umivalled work of Law, is not liberty but security.' Moreover, it was Bentham's view that security would *not* be 'destroyed by unlimited Supremacy' (69.43): hence his view that the power of the sovereign must be seen as indefinite, if not infinite, in extent. Hence, too, Bentham's crucial distinction between 'political liberty entire' (complete absence of coercion) and 'liberty political in perfection,' an individual condition wherein 'the Laws and Institutions of the society he lived in were such as subjected him to no other coercion than the good of the society required him to be subjected to.' (69.209). By this point in the development of Bentham's political thought the idea of liberty as an end in itself has been removed from the political equation.

Yet we must in fairness keep in mind the obvious fact that Bentham was not, in the manuscript passages we have cited, expressing a hostility towards liberty or an unmitigated worship of power. His analyses of key political concepts convinced him that the power of governors and the security of citizens could and should rest equally firmly on the same foundation in law. His exposure of the grievous error involved in referring to a government as free, where what was truly at issue was the liberty (in fact the security) of its subjects, was accompanied by a clear endorsement of a government whose powers are fixed and publicly known at all times. He defined the State in strict terms of command and obedience, and yet continued to assert, as a consequence of the theoretical principles we have examined, that he was no advocate of slavery and no supporter of a 'slavish state.' He feared the enmity of 'men whose affections are warm on the side of liberty,' and remained always firmly convinced that he did not deserve it. As a result of the development of his views on human nature, social organization, and political power, he abandoned Hume's position that society must everywhere and always be the arena for 'a perpetual intestine struggle ... between authority and liberty.' He postulated instead a symbiotic relationship between individual security and governmental power, a relationship such that civil liberty need no longer be thought of as a subtraction from governmental power, but must instead be seen as part by-product and part residue: an essential constituent of the security provided for individual activities by legislative sovereignty and, less significantly to Bentham, a residual social vacuum, a peripheral area of activity subject to no direct regulation by government only because of the trivial social consequences of the actions involved. To determine how large the area of unregulated individual activities might be we need only ask ourselves what proportion of human thought is so private, what percentage of private action so inconsequential, that it results in no perceptible social consequences. Given the inevitable results of such a calculus, we should not be surprised to find that for Bentham the category of 'private self-regarding act' was virtually vestigial.

Long after Bentham's proposals for a fresh 'scientific' analysis of human motivation and a corresponding technology of environmental manipulation at the sociopolitical level had fallen on unreceptive ears, the cry for the creation of a 'science of human behaviour'[16] has in our own generation been raised once more. B.F. Skinner asserted in 1962 that what was missing from his contemporaries' discussions of human nature was an adequate 'treatment of the causes of behaviour.'[17] What was needed, he claimed, was 'a technology of behaviour ... a behavioural technology comparable in power and precision to physical and biological technology.'[18] In Skinner's view, the development of a behavioural science employing the 'strategy' of physics and biology would make it possible to abandon the concept of the 'autonomous agent' to which, as he put it, 'behaviour has traditionally been attributed.' Instead, social theorists would focus their attention upon 'the environment ... in which the species evolved and in which the behaviour of the individual is shaped and maintained.'[19] Functions previously seen as manifestations of individual autonomy are now seen as resulting from combinations of 'environmental contingencies' – and 'certain questions arise': 'Is man then abolished? Certainly not as a species or as an individual achiever. It is the autonomous inner man who is abolished, and that is a step forward. But does man not then become merely a victim or passive observer of what is happening to him? He is indeed controlled by his environment ... but ... it is an environment largely of his own making. The evolution of a culture is a gigantic exercise in self-control.'[20]

For both thinkers, recognition of the inescapable and inexorable character of the formative interplay between self and environment in social life was the *primum mobile* of social theory. Just as Skinner could refer to the inhabitant of Walden Two as living in an environment 'of his own making' and could identify self-control with the 'right' form of control of the many by a few, so Bentham equated self-government, not with freedom, but with a man's recognition of the proper nature and extent of his natural subjection to the dictates of pleasure and pain. Both thinkers were convinced that to accept the implications of these insights was to embrace the essential realities of social life. All that was thus to be abolished was merely myth, sentimentality, and escapism. Partisans of freedom, in the eyes of Bentham and Skinner alike, were the most profoundly deluded of social observers. Skinner summarized the case for environmental control in terms that Bentham would have endorsed: 'The literature of freedom ... has been forced to brand all control as wrong and to misrepresent many of the advantages to be gained from a social environment. It is unprepared for the next step, which is not to free men from control but to analyze and change the kinds of control to which they are exposed.'[21]

Bentham never provided posterity with a work analogous to Skinner's explicit assessment of the possibilities of a social condition 'beyond freedom and dignity.' We have seen no evidence to suggest that Bentham considered the concept of human dignity to be a particularly sinister fiction, although its categorization as a mere fictitious entity suggests it had been superseded epistemologically. What is much clearer and much more significant is that for Bentham, as for Skinner, in the context of a properly articulated view of man in society the problem of liberty simply did not arise in its traditional form. Bentham clearly regarded both the Lockean, contractual mode of thought (which has come to be associated in many minds with liberalism) and natural rights theories of democracy alike as manifestations of an ultimately counter-productive and romantic sentimentalism in politics. In their place he expounded a view of politics as a totally integrated segment of a comprehensive science of social action and organization, which was in turn simply the practical social manifestation of his theory of human nature. In the political sphere as elsewhere, his system of thought exhibits the comprehensiveness of the encyclopedist and the radicalism of a *philosophe*.

There is another sense in which, for Bentham, the problem of liberty did not arise: the philosophical sense. Bentham has become notorious for his airy dismissal of the free will versus necessity debate as an irrelevance, but the reasons for his attitude are little discussed. He espoused no interest in the question of free will and necessity because, like Hobbes,[22] he understood the human will as a determined thing, determined by an immanent logic which he hoped to expound. Moreover, what cannot be allowed in Bentham's system is the possibility that liberty – an absence, a negation of sensation, and an abstraction far removed from the concrete realities of pleasure and pain – might be an end-in-itself, a sufficient condition of happiness. As the absence of coercion, liberty was in Bentham's eyes the *sine qua non* of every pleasure and yet the essence of none. Anyone adopting such a view must presumably contend that those men who claim to seek liberty, to fight for it or defend it, and who say, with Professor Berlin, that what they desire is simply full freedom, freedom in both its negative and its positive sense,[23] are in fact pursuing something more than freedom. As Bentham sees it only 'negative' freedom is freedom pure and simple.

What others call positive freedom is, perhaps fairly enough, identified by Bentham as 'power' or 'right,' necessarily implying obedience or obligation on the part of others. A modicum of liberty is a condition of the exercise of every power as well as the enjoyment of every right. Every such exercise or enjoyment, however, inescapably entails restraint, and in some cases requires coercion. Whoever wishes to censure, or even to live, freely must accept his duty and obligation to obey punctually. Coercion, violent and painful restraint, can and should be minimized. Its minimization was a fundamental goal of Bentham's programme of social reform. Restraint as social control, however, is not thereby reduced in the least: to reduce social friction is not to abandon the constraints built into the social system by such frictionless, non-violent means as 'indirect legislation.' Clearly the extensive diversion of the currents of human desire and the cultivation and manipulation of the various non-physical social sanctions can be as effective as reliance on corporal punishment in directing social development. Modern experience tends to show that indirect means are by far the more effective. J.S. Mill was the first, but certainly not the last, to warn of the immense oppressive political potential of seemingly non-coercive manipulation of, or deference to, the social weight of public opinion. Bentham manifestly had no conception of the possibility of the suffocation of individuality under a blanket of social conformity.

Recalling for a moment Bentham's novel understanding of the meaning of self-government and the view of the relationship between the citizen and his governors implied by it, one may well ask: does not such a definition of what many would call the essence of individual freedom beg the essential question of the nature of the self at issue? If it does not, it certainly assumes the correctness of Bentham's utilitarian answer. It assumes that in a completely operative utilitarian society possessing an educational system, a code of ethics, a comprehensive legal framework, and a fully spun web of indirect legislation designed to cultivate, manage, or divert the individual's personal propensities, the essential self of each person remains intact. It assumes, then, that the nature of the self is exhausted by the comprehensive utilitarian analysis of pleasures and pains as springs of human action. For the social engineer who propagates such a view, human personality lies stripped of all essential mystery. No solace can be sought in spiritual sources. No reference to the 'soul' is permitted to confuse our understanding of the human organism. There is no ghost in the human machine.

Such a theory may be applauded or denounced for its 'scientific' nature or its secularism according to personal conviction. In Bentham's case, however, one cannot help but be struck by the courage of its candour, by its consistency, by its coherence, and, surprisingly often, by its timeless realism about politics in particular. Bentham was not possessed of Hobbes's intellectual adroitness, of Locke's capacity for invoking religious explanations and justifications for the basic characteristics of political society, or of that capacity for romanticism which enabled Rousseau, in the eyes of many, to rise above the logical contradictions of his arguments in the *Contrat Social*. Bentham, we know, published his work with a strange reluctance. His recalcitrance is not so difficult to fathom, however, if one accepts the fact that his science of social theory, once completed and promulgated, would have made his philosophical radicalism, his iconoclasm, and his architectonic aspirations all too clear to his contemporaries. He anticipated early in his career that he would have many critics and his expectation was correct. He could not decide whether to expound every one of his carefully constructed 'preparatory principles' at length for publication or to spare his readers a blow-by-blow account of his efforts to construct his own theoretical vocabulary. In the end he kept the details of his 'decisions concerning the construction of words' to himself. He took no pleasure in the 'voluminousness' of his system. Seeing that there was 'no end' to the process of terminological refinement, he abandoned the idea of acquainting all students of social thought with a complete logic of scientific discourse (69.36).

In an age of specialization and of technology, comprehensive knowledge of the kind sought by Bentham in its breadth and depth, is thought to be beyond the reach of any one man; a social system such as Bentham's, all-encompassing, final, and immutable because immanent, seems an archaism. Nonetheless, the development of clinical and social psychology, and especially of B.F. Skinner's theories of psychology, sociology, and politics has led to a new marriage of physiological and social studies in the 'social science' of behaviourism. Men now have the capacity to endow machines with knowledge in such quantities that it is not even possible to comprehend the extent, let alone weigh the implications, of such labyrinths of fact. Our age thus has good reason to reflect on the character and the implications of Bentham's 'science of human nature' and of the social science which grew out of it. Whether a social science based on Bentham's view of human nature is in principle unrealizable, or whether the concept of liberty as a necessary condition of every pleasure but never a sufficient condition of happiness is tenable or realistic, are questions of a kind that this study does not pretend to answer. We distrust the very comprehensiveness and conclusiveness of the kind of social theory Bentham constructed. We consider his understanding of liberty, as a necessary condition of every pleasure but never a sufficient condition of happiness, both unrealistic and unattractive. We explicitly deny the feasibility, while implicitly questioning the desirability, of such theorizing. We associate the pursuit of social order with 'rage,' violence, and the deliberate destruction of human liberty. An examination of Bentham's thought shows that order need not be sought in a state of rage. We distrust his confidence far more than we fear his rage.

Not a 'rage for order' but rather enthusiasm and optimism regarding the 'perfection of knowledge' explain Bentham's critique of the libertarianism of some of the political radicals of his day. Both rage and enthusiasm are passions, however, and it is clear that under the influence of the Enlightenment the pursuit of happiness and security through order became Bentham's passion. Moreover, he passed this intellectual legacy on to generations of utilitarians after him. The influence of utilitarian principles on modern social thought is consistently underestimated. Nowhere is this phenomenon more evident than in the field of political theory, where other 'isms' hold virtually exclusive sway. A study of Bentham as an eighteenth-century prototype of the modern social theorist may be important not only because an understanding of Bentham as a thinker is important, but also because an analysis of the roots and development of his passion for order can improve our comprehension of the nature of social theory both in his day and in our own.

Notes

PREFACE

1 See E. Halévy, *The Growth of Philosophic Radicalism*, transl. M. Morris, new ed., London, Faber and Faber, 1972, pp. 506-7
2 *The Correspondence of Jeremy Bentham*, vol. 1 (1752-76), ed. T.L.S. Sprigge, London, Athlone Press, 1968, pp. v-viii, esp. p. v
3 The name 'preparatory manuscripts' is not Bentham's. It is not found in the UCL manuscripts, except in so far as those manuscripts suggest that Bentham was then considering writing a work to be called 'Preparatory Principles.'

INTRODUCTION

1 See G. Wallas, *The Art of Thought*, London, Jonathan Cape, 1926.
2 Ibid, p. 10
3 Ibid
4 The evolution of Bentham's conception of his magnum opus on censorial jurisprudence is discussed below at the beginning of chapter 6. Works later published which began their careers as parts of this work include *An Introduction to the Principles of Morals and Legislation, Of Laws in General*, the *Essay on Indirect Legislation, The Influence of Place and Time in Matters of Legislation*, and others.
5 See Wallas, *The Art of Thought*, p. 10.
6 David Caute, *The Fellow Travellers*, London, Weidenfeld and Nicolson, 1973, cited in the *Observer*, 7 Jan. 1973, pp. 10-11
7 See S.R. Letwin, *The Pursuit of Certainty*, Cambridge University Press, 1965, especially the essays on Bentham and Beatrice Webb.

8 Phrases quoted are from a draft of *Was Bentham a Utilitarian?*, a paper by D. Lyons later condensed and published in Vol. 5 of the *Royal Institute of Philosophy Lectures, 1970-71*, London, Macmillan, 1972, pp. 196-221. In the text of the draft paper, they appear in fn. 52, pp. 32-3; in the published version these remarks do not appear.

9 G. Himmelfarb, 'The Haunted House of Jeremy Bentham,' in *Ideas in History. Essays presented to Louis Gottschalk by his former students*, ed. R. Herr and H.T. Parker, Duke University Press, Durham, North Carolina, 1965, p. 235.

10 See E. Halévy, *The Growth of Philosophic Radicalism*, transl. M. Morris, London, Faber and Faber, 1972, p. 506.

11 Ibid, p. 508

12 Ibid, p. 390

13 The passage quoted is from an early draft of 'Two concepts of power,' later published as Essay III, part 1, in *Democratic Theory: Essays in Retrieval* by C.B. Macpherson, Oxford University Press, 1973. In the published version these words do not appear.

14 Philip Rieff, *Freud: The Mind of the Moralist*, cited in G.B. Bantock, 'The Cultured Man: Eliot,' in *The Educated Man: Studies in the History of Educational Thought*, ed. Nash, Kazamias, and Perkinson, New York, J. Wiley and Sons, 1965, p. 338

15 B.R. Barber, *Superman and Common Men: Freedom, Anarchy and the Revolution*, Pelican, 1972, p. 67

16 Ibid, p. 43

17 Ibid, p. 61

18 See Barber's headnote to the discussion of this model (ibid, p. 49), which is from Sartre's *Existentialism and Humanism*.

19 Cited in *Agenda 1970: Proposals for a Creative Politics*, ed. T. Lloyd and J. McLeod, University of Toronto Press, 1968, pp. 26-7.

20 *Observer*, 2 June 1968

21 Bantock, 'The Cultured Man,' p. 338

22 H. Arendt, *Between Past and Future: Six Exercises in Political Thought*, London, Faber and Faber, 1954, p. 149

CHAPTER ONE: THE ENLIGHTENMENT

1 See the Preface to *A Fragment on Government* in *A Fragment on Government, with an Introduction to the Principles of Morals and Legislation*, edited and introduced by W. Harrison, Oxford, Blackwell, 1948, p. 3.

2 Bentham published the *Fragment* anonymously, knowing that anonymity would be more conducive to notoriety in a work of real quality than the revelation of the identity of an obscure author. Events proved him correct. When his authorship was revealed, sales of, and interest in, the *Fragment* dropped off. These are the facts as recollected by Bentham, prompted by Bowring, fifty-five years later. See *Works of Jeremy Bentham*, ed. J. Bowring, Vol. 10, *Memoirs*, pp. 77-9.

3 *Fragment on Government*, ed. Harrison, p. 112

4 Ibid, pp. 111-12

5 *Times Literary Supplement*, 31 Dec. 1925. 'Bentham, Blackstone, and the New Law'

6 François de Salignac de la Mothe Fénélon, *The Adventures of Telemachus, The Son of Ulysses*, transl., London, 1763, pp. 74-6

7 Ibid, p. 18

8 See C.W. Everett, *The Education of Jeremy Bentham*, New York, 1931; Leslie Stephen, *The English Utilitarians*, London, 1900, Vol. 1, 'Jeremy Bentham'; C.M. Atkinson, *Jeremy Bentham*, London, 1905; M.P. Mack, *Jeremy Bentham: An Odyssey of Ideas, 1748-1792*, London, 1963. See also *The Correspondence of Jeremy Bentham* (three vols published, covering period 1752-88, more vols in preparation), part of *The Collected Works of Jeremy Bentham*, General Editor J.H. Burns, London, Athlone Press. See bibliography for publication dates of various volumes (hereafter cited as CW *Correspondence*).

9 As early as 1771, 'Bentham's investigations in jurisprudence were diversified by experiments in chemistry' (CW *Correspondence* I, letter 92, Jeremy Bentham to Jeremiah Bentham, 3 Sept. 1771, p. 149, n. 1). See also ibid, 98, J.B. to Samuel Bentham, Aug. 1773, pp. 158-60, where Bentham instructs his brother in mathematics, and 101, Nov. 1773, pp. 164-70, also to Samuel Bentham, where the flippancy of Bentham's reaction to a legal query contrasts with his earnest enthusiasm for the latest 'mechanical inventions.'

10 In January 1774, Bentham was working on an 'abstract of Priestley on Airs' (CW *Correspondence* I, 105, pp. 175-6). Seven months later (July) he was still keenly working on 'Essence of Priestley' (112, pp. 187-9).

11 *Fragment on Government*, ed. Harrison, Preface, para. 2, p. 3

12 *Fragment*, ed. Harrison, Preface, para. 1, p. 3

13 Ibid, para 2, p. 3

14 Ibid

15 Ibid, para. 3, p. 3

16 Locke, too, acknowledged his 'masters' in the 'Epistle to the Reader' prefacing his *Essay Concerning Human Understanding* (abridged, edited, and

introduced by M. Cranston, Toronto, 1965), just as, we shall see, Bentham was to do. Locke referred to the scientists Boyle and Huygens, the physician Sydenham – and Isaac Newton. In relation to the objects and achievements of such men as these, Locke felt that it was 'ambition enough' to become 'an under labourer in clearing the ground a little,' clearing 'rubbish' from the path to 'knowledge,' combatting 'the learned but frivolous use of uncouth, affected, or unintelligible terms, introduced into the sciences, and there made an art of.'

17 *Fragment*, ed. Harrison, Preface, para. 16, p. 10

18 See Bacon, *Advancement of Learning*, Aphorism 129.

19 See the tale of Newton's apple and Fourier's apple in F. Manuel, *The Prophets of Paris*, New York, Harper and Row, 1965, p. 197

20 See UCL manuscripts, Box 32, p. 158. See also Mack, *Jeremy Bentham*, pp. 129-143, for evidence of Bentham's veneration of Bacon.

21 He displayed also a *philosophe*'s resistance to prejudice and conformity (UCL manuscripts, 73, p. 95, dated 1773, dealing with 'sexual noncon-formity'), impish sense of humour, and affection and admiration for Voltaire. (See his translation of *Le Taureau Blanc*, and especially his 'Preface which may just as well be read afterwards.' See also *Correspondence* I, 113, pp. 189-90, 20 July 1774, 'Pseudo-Voltaire' to J.B. Bentham's admiration for Voltaire pervades his draft letter to him of Nov. 1776: *Correspondence* I, 192, pp. 367-8.)

22 CW *Correspondence* II, 249, Spring 1778, pp. 115-18, J.B. to D'Alembert, p. 117. Bentham sent copies of the *Fragment* and his *View of the Hard-Labour Bill* to D'Alembert, L'Abbé Morellet (letter 250, pp. 118-20), and Chastellux (251, pp. 120-1). In 1789 Bentham wrote again to Morellet, in-dicating his belief that Morellet, Condorcet, D'Alembert, and Condillac were the four men he felt were most likely to understand and appreciate his work. (UCL mss, Box 169, pp. 164-7, dated 28 April 1789; also in CW *Correspondence* IV, in preparation).

23 See CW *Correspondence* II, 280, pp. 181-4, J.B. to Samuel Bentham, 27 Oct. 1778, p. 183. Helvétius is also referred to in the letters to d'Alembert and Chastellux cited in n. 22.

24 *Correspondence* II, 248, to the Rev. John Forster, April / May 1778, pp. 98-9.

25 See *Introduction to the Principles of Morals and Legislation*, ed. Burns and Hart, Preface, para. 35, pp. 8-9.

26 Ibid, p. 3

27 *Correspondence* II, 219, J.B. to Samuel Bentham, 3 June 1777, p. 57

28 Ibid, 336, J.B. to Jeremiah Bentham and Samuel Bentham, 9 Nov. 1779, p. 319. QSP was 'Queen's Square Place,' residence of Jeremiah Bentham.

When used as a noun by Samuel and Jeremy, 'QSPishness' referred to the sum total of their father's least endearing characteristics.

29 *Correspondence* IV (in preparation), J.B. to Reginald Pole Carew, 3 Oct. 1783

30 *Correspondence* II, 248, to the Rev. J. Forster, April/May 1778, p. 113

31 *Fragment*, ed. Harrison, Preface, para. 46, p. 22

32 *Introduction*, ed. Burns and Hart, chap. 16, fn. Y4 to para. 58, p. 273

33 Ibid

34 *Of Laws in General*, ed. H.L.A. Hart, London, 1970 (*Collected Works*, Gen. Ed. J.H. Burns), chap. 19, para. 1 (5), p. 232

35 Ibid, para. 1 (7), p. 233

36 E. Cassirer, *The Philosophy of the Enlightenment*, transl. F.C.A. Koelin and J.P. Pettegrove, Princeton, NJ, 1951

37 P. Gay, *The Enlightenment: an Interpretation*, 1, *The Rise of Modern Paganism*, Preface, p. xiii

38 See n. 1 above and P. Gay, 'The Enlightenment in the history of political theory,' in *Political Science Quarterly*, 69, 1954, p. 375. The headnote on the title page of Bentham's *Fragment* was a quotation from Montesquieu (*L'Esprit des Lois*, Livre 30, Chap. 15): 'Rien ne recule plus le progrès des connoissances, qu'un mauvais ouvrage d'un auteur célèbre: parce qu'avant d'instruire, il faut commencer par détromper.'

39 P. Gay, *The Enlightenment: an Interpretation*, 1, 'Bibliographical Essay,' p. 433

40 Ibid, Preface, p. xiii

41 Ibid, chap. 1, p. 3

42 Ibid, p. 121

43 Ibid. Vol. 2 is subtitled *The Science of Freedom*. There is, of course, a world of difference between liberated scientists and scientific libertarians, as Bentham was to demonstrate.

44 Diderot, *Oeuvres*, Vol. 3, p. 248, cited in Gay, *The Enlightenment*, 1, pp. 128-9

45 See D'Alembert to J.B., 26 June 1778, as appended to *Correspondence* II, pp. 133-6, J.B. to Samuel Bentham, 6 July 1778; see also letter 249, Spring 1778, J.B. to D'Alembert, pp. 115-18.

46 *Correspondence* I, 192, J.B. to F.M.A. de Voltaire, Nov. 1776 (?), pp. 367-8

47 *Fragment*, ed. Harrison, chap. 3, para. 21, p. 82

48 Beccaria, *Of Crimes and Punishments*, Introduction, p. 2, cited in *Fragment on Government*, ed. F.C. Montague (1891), Introduction, p. 27

49 This phrase forms the title of Claude Adrien Helvétius, *De L'Esprit: or, essays on the Mind*, transl. London, 1759 (1st edition in French, 1758), Essay 3, chap. 15.

50 Helvétius argued, in Essay 3, chap. 19 of *De L'Esprit*, that 'the air of liberty' and 'whole energy' derived from it, were the secrets of Tacitus's genius. (Ibid, p. 233, n. *h*)

51 Ibid, chap. 17, p. 194

52 Ibid, chap. 19, p. 198. This and the preceding chapter deal with 'Abject and submissive subjection' and 'Despotic power.'

53 Ibid, chap. 29, p. 229

54 F.J., Marquis de Chastellux, *An Essay on Public Happiness*, Transl. London, 1774, 2 vols. See esp. chap. 8, on 'The influence of the revival of learning upon the condition of Mankind.' The Greatest Happiness Principle is referred to on p. 112.

55 Chastellux, *Essay on Public Happiness*, chap. 8, pp. 141-2

56 Gay *The Enlightenment*, 1, pp. 132-3

57 Voltaire to le Cati, 15 April 1741, cited in Gay, *The Enlightenment*, 1, p. 135

58 Ibid, pp. 189-90

59 Ibid, pp. 25-6, where Gay cites the belief of Diderot and D'Alembert in the unity of all the sciences, and especially of politics and morals, which 'se tiennent par la main.'

60 Even in Bacon's famous Aphorism 129, nature is obeyed only in order that she may be commanded.

61 See Locke, *Essay Concerning Human Understanding*, ed. Cranston, Chap. 20, p. 144, and Chapter 21, p. 156. See also Holbach's 'Man is unhappy only because he does not know nature' (cited in Gay, *The Enlightenment*, 1, p. 184), and Gay's comment that for Condillac 'inquiétude, tourment, determines everything' (ibid, 2, p. 180). This sense of the motive power of uneasiness may be kept in mind as we observe the development of the relationship between liberty and security in Bentham's thought.

62 Cited in ibid, 2, p. 46

63 See Condillac, cited in Gay, *The Enlightenment*, 2, p. 165. Gay finds that Condillac's proposal for 'a reconstruction of philosophy on the model of the natural sciences' was 'at the heart' of Enlightenment thought.

64 Gay, *The Enlightenment*, 1, p. 321, n. 5

65 Condillac, *Essai sur L'Origine des Conoissances Humaines* (1746), cited in Gay, *The Enlightenment*, 2, p. 177. See also Locke *Essay Concerning Human Understanding*, ed. Cranston, pp. 25-7

66 Condillac, cited in Gay, *The Enlightenment*, 2, p. 177

67 Uneasiness and pain are prime motives for Bentham too.

68 See Gay, *The Enlightenment*, 2, p. 179

69 See *Introduction to the Principles of Morals and Legislation*, ed. Burns and Hart, Preface, p. 3.
70 David Hume, *Treatise of Human Nature*, ed. T.H. Green and T.H. Cerose, London, 1874, Vol. 1, p. 306
71 Ibid, esp. p. 307
72 Passages cited from H.S. Thayer, ed., *Newton's Philosophy of Nature* (1953), p. 117, by Gay in *The Enlightenment*, 2, p. 109
73 *Introduction to the Principles of Morals and Legislation,* Preface, p. 8

CHAPTER TWO: THE SCHOOL OF EXAMPLE

1 UCL mss, Box 27, pp. 148, 160. Page 160 includes some material headed 'Apol. for Limits,' which indicates a probable link with chap. 17, of the *Introduction*, 'Of the limits of the penal branch of jurisprudence.' See *Introduction to the Principles of Morals and Legislation*, ed. Burns and Hart, ed's introduction, pp. i-iii.
2 See M.P. Mack, *Jeremy Bentham: an Odyssey of Ideas, 1748-1792*, Chap. 3, p. 111.
3 Claude Adrien Helvétius, *De L'Esprit: or, essays on the Mind*, transl., London, 1759, Essay 3. Chaps. 17, 18, and 19 fulfil the promise, made in chap. 16 (p. 190 of Eng. transl.), to investigate the relationship between free and despotic governments.
4 Ibid, chap. 29, 'Of the slavery and allegorical genius of the Eastern nations' (Eng. transl. pp. 229-230)
5 Published 1764; translated from the Italian into English (1767) as *An Essay on Crimes and Punishments.*
6 Bonesana (Cesare) Marquis Beccaria,*Of Crimes and Punishments*, Chap. 1, 'Of the origin of punishments,' p. 5
7 Cf. especially *Of Law in General*, ed. Burns and Hart, appendix B, pp. 250-3
8 Beccaria, *Crimes and Punishments*, Chap. 1, pp. 5-6
9 Ibid, Introduction, p. 1
10 Ibid, chap. 2, 'Of the right to punish,' p. 7
11 *The Works of Jeremy Bentham*, ed. J. Bowring, Vol. 9, p. 123; see also E. Halévy, *The Growth of Philosophic Radicalism*, transl. M. Morris, London, 1952, p. 408
12 *Works*, ed. Bowring, Vol. 8, pp. 478, 481; see also Halévy, *Philosophic Radicalism*, p. 379.
13 *Fragment on Government*, ed. Harrison, Preface, para. 24, p. 13, n. 2

14 Ibid

15 Written in 1771, translated into English as *The Constitution of England: or an account of the English Government ...* (1775)

16 *The Constitution of England*, p. 221

17 *Fragment on Government*, ed. Harrison, chap. 3, 'The British Constitution', para. 21, p. 199

18 In chap. 1, pp. 22-3, for example, Delolme explains how liberty has 'taken root' in England but not in France.

19 See A. Hamilton, J. Madison, and J. Jay, *The Federalist, or the New Constitution*, edited with an introduction and notes by Max Beloff, Oxford, Blackwell, 1948, Introduction, p. lviii, p. lxiv, n. 2.

20 See CW *Correspondence* II, 199, J.B. to Samuel Bentham, 22-3 Jan. 1777, pp. 13-15. On pp. 13-14 Delolme is said to be doing a translation of Lind's 'answer,' and Delolme's *Constitution of England* is said to have 'great merit' and be 'well esteemed.'

21 *Correspondence* II, p. 12, n. 6

22 Ibid, 375, J.B. to Samuel Bentham, 6 Nov. 1780, p. 498

23 Delolme, *Constitution of England*, chap. 1, pp. 18, 22-3

24 Ibid, p. 18

25 Delolme, *Constitution de L'Angleterre*, Amsterdam, 1771, chap. 8, 'Liberté particulière,' p. 88

26 *Constitution of England*, chap. 5, 'In which an inquiry is made, whether it would be an advantage to public liberty that the laws should be enacted by the votes of the people at large,' p. 220

27 Ibid; see also n. *a* to p. 220: 'See Mr Rousseau's *Social Contract*, chap. 15.'

28 Ibid, pp. 221, 222-3, 226

29 The susceptibility of Rousseau to sophisms, in contrast to Marmontel's resistance to them, is the subject of a brief passage in UCL mss, Box 69, p. 207. Bentham's unsympathetic rendering of Rousseau's paradox of forced freedom is in UCL mss, Box 146, p. 1: 'Rousseau donne comme une proposition générale que, de la manière dont la société est formée il y a plus à gagner à nuir aux hommes, qu'à leur servir.' On the same page he adds a bitter condemnation of Rousseau as a thinker: 'Telle est l'association que font dans les idées l'ambition et l'envie unies à la pauvreté.'

30 *Introduction to the Principles of Morals and Legislation*, ed. Burns and Hart, chap. 1, para. 4, p. 12

31 *Fragment on Government*, ed. Harrison, chap. 1, para. 10, p. 38

32 The wheel has come full circle when a modern theorist can rediscover the fact that liberalism, or libertarianism, does not necessarily provide the best starting point for an explanation of the status of liberty in political society.

See B.R. Barber, *Superman and Common Man: Freedom, Anarchy and the Revolution*, Penguin Books, 1972, Essay 3, 'Forced to be Free: An Illiberal Defence of Liberty,' pp. 35-80, for an attempt to define liberty in a way that supersedes Bentham's approach: 'just as the Theory of Relativity encompasses but moves beyond Newtonian mechanism' (p. 37).

33 The use of a utilitarian calculus of mischiefs to determine the 'Juncture for resistence' was discussed in the *Fragment*, ed. Harrison, chap. 4, para. 21, p. 93.

34 See Robert Filmer, *Patriarcha: or, The Natural Powers of the Kings of England Asserted; and other political works of Sir Robert Filmer*, edited with an introduction and notes by Peter Laslett; Oxford, Blackwell, 1949, esp. pp. 3-4, 12.

35 Ibid, p. 13. See also *Observations upon Aristotle's Politiques Touching Forms of Government*, together with *Directions for Obedience to Governors in Dangerous and doubtfull Times*, London, 1652, ibid, pp. 203-4.

36 Filmer, *Observations upon Aristotle's Politiques*, ibid, p. 217

37 Ibid, p. 224

38 Filmer, *Directions for Obedience to Governors in Dangerous and doubtfull Times*, in *Patriarcha*, ed. Laslett, p. 232

39 Ibid, p. 231

40 Filmer, *Observations upon Aristotle's Politiques*, p. 225, original parentheses

41 David Hume, *A Treatise of Human Nature*, Book 3, 'Of Morals': part 2, chap. 2, 'Of the Origin of Justice and Property,' in *Hume: Theory of Politics*, ed. F. Watkins, London, 1951, p. 42

42 Ibid, chap. 8, 'Of the Source of Allegiance', p. 89. Cf. Bentham's portrait of the pre-political, pre-legal human conditions in *Of Laws in General*, appendix B, pp. 250-3.

43 David Hume, *Essays Moral, Political and Literary*, in *Hume*, ed. Watkins, part 1, essay 3, 'Of the Origin of Government,' p. 156

44 Ibid, pp. 156-7

45 See UCL mss, Box 96, p. 101 (headed 'Introd.'), where Locke's method was applauded as symptomatic of his 'great and original Genius.' See also ibid, p. 70, where Locke was nominated as 'the Father of intellectual science.' Locke, Bentham wrote, would 'live for ever,' unlike Montesquieu who would 'not outlive his century' (*Works*, ed. Bowring, Vol. 10, p. 143, from Bentham's Commonplace-Book for 1781-5). Locke's invaluable contribution to the arduous but essential task of defining leading ideas and principles was acknowledged, with special reference to the *Essay Concerning Human Understanding*, in *Correspondence* II, 122, J.B. to John Lind, 5 Oct. 1774, p. 205.

46 *Correspondence* II, 122, J.B. to John Lind, 5 Oct. 1774, p. 205

47 The relationship between Bentham's epistemological premises and his view of human nature and human freedom is further examined below in the Epilogue.

48 He compared Locke's achievement with those of Bacon (who 'proclaimed *fiat experimentum*' but was 'ignorant' of 'natural philosophy') and Newton (who 'threw light on one branch of science'). See *Works*. ed. Bowring, Vol. 10, pp. 587-8, 'conversations with Bentham in 1827-8' (age 79-80).

49 John Horne Tooke, *The Diversions of Purley*, London, 1786. See *Correspondence* II, 214, J.B. to Samuel Bentham, 6 May 1777, pp. 47-8. Bentham refers with obvious relish to the grammatical researches of 'Parson Horne' in another letter to brother Samuel, dated 27 Oct. 1778, ibid, pp. 181-4. Bentham and Horne Tooke, we are told, dined together in about 1803: *Works*, ed. Bowring, 10, p. 404. Other references to Horne Tooke are in ibid, 8, pp. 120, 185, 188.

50 See Locke's *Essay Concerning Human Understanding*, abridged, edited and introduced by M. Cranston, London, 1965, Book 2, 'Of Ideas,' chap. 12, 'Of complex ideas.'

51 Horne Tooke's arguments are discussed in Halévy, *Philosophic Radicalism*, p. 446.

52 Ibid

53 *Essay Concerning Human Understanding*, ed. Cranston, chap. 12, p. 101

54 Ibid, chap. 22, 'Of mixed modes,' p. 170

55 Halévy, *Philosophic Radicalism*, p. 446

56 Locke, *Essay*, Book 2, Chap. 1, 'Of ideas in general, and their original,' p. 61

57 Ibid, Book 1, 'Neither principles nor ideas are innate,' chap. 2, 'No innate practical principles,' p. 42

58 Ibid, p. 43

59 See *Works*, ed. Bowring, 10, p. 531 (an excerpt from Bentham's Memorandum-Book for 1821-2), and 5, p. 280 (in the 'Defence of economy against the Right Honourable Edmund Burke'). Locke's mistake was, said Bentham, to concentrate too exclusively on the pain of uneasiness as 'the cause of everything that is done' (10, p. 531), ignoring the important stimulus provided by the prospect of pleasure.

60 Locke, Essay, ed. Cranston, pp. 147-70

61 Ibid, Book 3, 'Of Words,' chap. 1, 'Of Words, or language in general,' pp. 229-31; chap. 9, 'Of the imperfection of words,' pp. 267-76; chap. 10, 'Of the abuse of words,' pp. 276-86

62 See, for the importance of the idea of 'fictions' in Bentham's thought, C.K. Ogden, *Bentham's Theory of Fictions*, London, 1932.

63 For the best of a considerable number of references by Bentham to his lack of interest in the problem of free will and determinism, see *Works*, ed. Bowring, 10, p. 216, where Bentham says, inter alia, 'I don't care two straws about liberty and necessity at any time.'

64 Locke, *Essay*, ed. Cranston, Book 2, chap. 21, 'Of power,' pp. 149, 151-2

65 Ibid, p. 161

66 See Halévy, *Philosophic Radicalism*, p. 6, n.1. For a fuller version, see *L'Origine du Radicalisme Philosophique*, Tome 3, p. 277, n. 6.

67 See ibid, p. 33, and Thomas Hobbes, *Leviathan*, edited with an Introduction by C.B. Macpherson, London, 1968, part 1, 'Of Man.'

68 Ibid, pp. 261-74

69 Ibid, p. 261

70 Ibid, p. 262

71 Ibid

72 Ibid, p. 264

73 Ibid, part 2, 'Of Commonwealth', chap. 21, 'Of the Liberty of Subjects,' p. 264

74 Ibid, chap. 20, p. 261

75 Ibid, chap. 21, p. 268

76 See Thomas Hobbes, *De Cive*, in *Works of Thomas Hobbes*, ed. Molesworth, 2, pp. 63, 65-6.

77 Hobbes, *Leviathan*, ed. Macpherson, Book 2, chap. 20, p. 261

78 See *Fragment on Government*, ed. Harrison, Preface, para. 16, p. 10.

CHAPTER THREE: THE SCHOOL OF EXPERIENCE

1 Joseph Preistley (DD), *An Essay on the First Principles of Government; and on the nature of Political, Civil and Religious Liberty* (1768), part 1, 'Of Political Liberty'; see p. 17.

2 Ibid, p. 16

3 See *Fragment on Government*, ed. Harrison, chap. 4, paras 23-5, pp. 94-5.

4 Priestley, *First Principles*, part 1, p. 15

5 See *Fragment*, ed. Harrison, chap. 4, paras 23-5, pp. 94-5.

6 Priestley, *First Principles*, pp. 15-16. For Bentham's distinction between political and civil liberty, see below, chap. 10.

7 Priestley, *First Principles*, pp. 21-22. For an exemplification of Bentham's feelings re universal suffrage, see *Jeremy Bentham's Economic Writings*, ed. W. Stark, London, 1954, Vol. 3, pp. 408, 411.

8 Priestley, *First Principles*, pp. 19-20
9 *Fragment*, ed. Harrison, chap. 4, para. 29, p. 96
10 Priestley, *First Principles*, pp. 45-46
11 Ibid, Part 2, 'Of Civil Liberty,' section 1, 'Of the nature of civil liberty in general,' p. 54
12 Ibid, p. 53
13 Ibid, p. 59
14 Ibid, p. 41
15 Ibid, p. 44
16 Ibid, Introduction, p. 12
17 Ibid, p. 13
18 Ibid, Part 1, 'Of Political Liberty,' p. 18
19 Ibid, pp. 18-19
20 CW *Correspondence*, II, 341, p. 336, J.B. to Samuel Bentham, 19-26 Nov. 1779: 'Faut-il que pour te faire plaisir, je souille ma plume législative en parlant de la misérable politique du jour?'
21 See *Correspondence*, III, 421, J.B. to Elizabeth Davies, 12-17 Oct. 1781, pp. 113-115.
22 See *Correspondence*, I, 60, J.B. to Jeremiah Bentham, 30 April 1765, pp. 86-87, esp. p. 87 and n. 6; see also ibid, 83, J.B. to Richard Clark, 16 Aug. 1768, p. 130.
23 Ibid, 83, p. 130.
24 See J.B. to John Bowring, 2 Feb. 1827, in *Works*, ed. Bowring, 10, p. 65, col. 2.
25 An account of the relevant events, and of John Glynn's role in support of Wilkes, can be pieced together from J.S. Watson, *The Reign of George III, 1760-1815*, Oxford, Clarendon, 1960, pp. 132, 133, 135, 140, 142, 143, 155-6, and 227. For the 1771 agitation, see p. 141.
26 Ibid, pp. 132, 133
27 Issues of the *Public Advertiser* and *The Gazetteer and New Daily Advertiser* for 1770 will be found in Vols 5 and 6, respectively, of the Burney Collection of Newspapers in the British Museum North Library. Passages hereinafter cited are from the correspondence columns of issues as indicated.
28 See the contributions of 'Advocate in the Cause of the People' to *Public Advertiser* for 6 and 29 Nov. 1770, for example.
29 Letter published in part in Ogden, *Jeremy Bentham*, p. 54, and in D. Baumgardt, *Bentham and the Ethics of Today*, Princeton, NJ, 1952, appendix III, pp. 552-3
30 For a note on John Lind see CW *Correspondence*, I, p. 23, n. 1.
31 Ibid, 12, John Lind to Jeremiah Bentham, 17 Nov. 1760, p. 23

32 See the additional note on Lind and his career in ibid, 99, p. 161, n. 2

33 See *Works*, ed. Bowring, 10, p. 56, col. 2.

34 J.B. to John Bowring, 30 Jan. 1827, ibid, p. 55

35 See *Correspondence*, I, p. 161, n. 2.

36 J.B. to John Bowring, 2 Feb. 1827, in *Works*, ed. Bowring, 10, p. 65, col. 1

37 Ibid, pp. 62-3

38 Ibid, p. 57, cols 1-2

39 In 1776

40 See *Correspondence*, I, 165, J.B. to Samuel Bentham, 9 May 1776, p. 332; 181, J.B. to John Lind, 12 Sept. 1776, p. 350.

41 *Works*, ed. Bowring, p. 57, col. 2

42 See *Correspondence*, I, 179a, J.B. to John Lind, 2 (?) Sept. 1776, pp. 341-4, ed. note; second sheet extant, headed 'Answ. to Declar. Preamble.'

43 See ibid, pp. 341-2, n. 1.

44 Ibid

45 *Correspondence*, I, pp. 342n, 341-3

46 See *Fragment on Government*, ed. Harrison, chap. I, 'Formation of Government', para. 9, p. 37 and para. 10, p. 38.

47 See *Correspondence*, I, 158, J.B. to John Lind, 27-8 March - 1 April 1776, pp. 309-10, n. 1.

48 Ibid, p. 310

49 Ibid, pp. 310-11

50 J. Lind, *'Three Letters to Dr. Price, containing Remarks on his Observations on the Nature of Civil Liberty, the Principles of Government, and the Justice and Policy of the War with America*, London, 1776, pp. 16-17n. For Lind's other works, see bibliography.

51 See *Correspondence*, I, p. 310n.

52 Joseph Priestley, LL D, FRS, *A Discourse on the Occasion of the Death of Dr. Price, delivered at Hackney on Sunday, May 1, 1791*, London, 1791, pp. 8-9

53 See UCL mss, Box 149, pp. 331-2 for Bentham's claim that Price had condemned all men to slavery by his definition of it in the *Observations*.

54 See *Introduction to the Principles of Morals and Legislation*, ed. Burns and Hart, chap. 1, para. 1, p. 11.

55 Ibid, chap. 2, para. 14, p. 28, n. *d*

56 Richard Price, *Observations on the Nature of Civil Liberty, the Principles of Government, and the Justice and Policy of the War with America*, London, 1776, p. 42

57 See *Correspondence*, I, p. 310n.

58 Price, *Observations on the Nature of Civil Liberty*, chap. 1, pp. 6-7.

59 Ibid, chap. 1, p. 3
60 Richard Price, (DD) *Additional Observations on the Nature and Value of Civil Liberty, and the War with America*, London, 1777, p.xv
61 *Fragment on Government*, ed. Harrison, chap. 4, para. 23, p. 94
62 Richard Hey, *Observations on the Nature of Civil Liberty, and the Principles of Government*, London, 1776. The *Dictionary of National Biography*, 43, p. 105, lists Hey as a Cambridge contemporary of William Paley, and as one of a group of Paley's sympathisers.
63 Hey, *Observations*, section 4, 'Principles of Civil Government,' para. 84, p. 47
64 Ibid, para. 80, pp. 44-5
65 Hey, *Observations*, pp. 53-8
66 Ibid, para. 98, p. 56, and para. 96, p. 55
67 Ibid, para. 93, p. 53; and cf. Bentham's sentiments in *The Rationale of Punishment*, transl. Richard Smith, London, 1830, Book 1, chap. 1, p. 1. (Cf., in turn, UCL mss, Box 141, p. 1).
68 Hey, *Observations*, paras 101 and 102, p. 58
69 Ibid, para. 8, p. 6
70 Ibid, para. 11, p. 7
71 Ibid, para. 13, p. 8
72 Ibid, para. 15, p. 9
73 Ibid
74 Ibid. The reader will note the reference to frequent discussions between Bentham and Lind of the ideas of property and restraint (i.e. coercion) as its basis. Liberty must surely, by definition, have been involved.
75 All quotations from UCL mss, Box 69, p. 59
76 Price's definition of slavery earned him a mild rebuke from Richard Hey and a venomous denunciation from Bentham. Hey quoted the controversial equation of liberty with self-government, by which standard so many were defined as slaves, in para. 39 of his *Observations*: 'As far as, in any instance, the operation of any cause comes in to restrain the power of self-government, so far slavery is introduced.' With the admirable intention of producing an objective distinction between civil restraint and abject slavery, Bentham linked slavery with constraint, and included constraint alongside restraint but distinct from it in his definition of coercion, and thence liberty.
77 Cf. Ogden, *Bentham's Theory of Fictions*

CHAPTER FOUR: FUNDAMENTAL WORDS

1 The sheet is headed 'C. Preface,' and the passage was probably envisaged as part of a preface to the 'Code of Criminal Law,' as Bentham called it in 1778,

to which, under the influence of the Berne Œconomical Society's announce-
ment of a competition for a 'Plan of Legislation on Criminal Matters,'
Bentham turned his attention in 1778. As such it is clearly related both to
Bentham's 'first major project as a writer,' the 'Elements of Critical Juris-
prudence,' and to the later *Introduction to the Principles of Morals and
Legislation*. For a detailed account of the chronology involved here, see
Introduction to the Principles of Morals and Legislation, ed. Burns and Hart,
London, Athlone Press, 1972, Editors' Introduction, p. ii.

2 Heading: 'PPI [Preparatory Principles Inserenda], p. 290, 699.' Marginal heading: 'Prefat. Definition. Utility of.' For an account of the relationship between PPI and 'Crit. Jur. Crim.' mss dealing also with the status of manuscript pages headed 'Key,' of which extensive use is made in this chapter,
see Preface.

3 He was convinced that the 'American dispute turns on words': see UCL mss,
Box 69, p. 177 (2), headed PPI 354.

4 For a specific reference to 'Locke's mischievous doctrine that by a violation
of the original compact the constitution is dissolved,' see UCL mss, Box 69,
p. 146, headed PPI 230, 563.

5 Headed 'Digest. Classification.' The page is crossed through in ink, perhaps
by Bentham, but, particularly in view of the compatibility of the sentiments
here expressed with those in other passages, this need not indicate that
Bentham did not endorse the ideas contained in this passage.

6 Headed 'Crit. Jurisp. Crim.' Marginal heading, 'Right Civil founded on
Natural − the notion exploded.'

7 John Locke, *Essay Concerning Human Understanding*, ed. M. Cranston,
Book 2, 'Of Ideas,' chap. 12, 'Of complex ideas'

8 Ibid, p. 101

9 Ibid, Book 2, chap. 30, 'Of real and fantastical ideas,' pp. 209-11

10 Ibid, chap. 22, 'Of mixed modes,' pp. 170-3

11 Ibid, chap. 12, 'Of complex ideas,' p. 101

12 Ibid,

13 Locke, *Essay*, p. 173.

14 CW *Correspondence*, II, 336, J.B. to Samuel Bentham, 9 Nov. 1779,
pp. 319-20

15 *The Diversions of Purley* was published in 1786. We are told that Bentham
'had considerable respect for this work' (*Correspondence*, II, p. 48, n. 7), but
a letter (280) to Samuel Bentham of 27 Oct. 1778 shows that Bentham had
great respect for Horne Tooke even then, crediting him with 'an important
discovery in Universal Grammar,' a 'Natural History and Chemical Analysis
[!] of *conjunctions*. It tears Harris's *Hermes* all to rags.' *Hermes* was published
in 1751.

16 See *Correspondence,* I, 127, J.B. to Samuel Bentham, 9 Dec. 1774, p. 221. In part of *Hermes*, Bentham said, the book's matter was 'drenched in a multitude of words.' Part of the book was 'Nonsense upon stilts.' Yet he admitted that he had 'wander'd in it a good while.'

17 *Correspondence,* I, 140, to Samuel Bentham, 12 Sept. 1775, p. 251

18 Locke, *Essay*, 'The Epistle to the Reader,' pp. 23-4

19 *Correspondence* I, 95, pp. 154-6, J.B. to Jeremiah Bentham, 14 Oct. 1772, pp. 154-5

20 Ibid, 192, J.B. to François Marie Arouet de Voltaire, Nov. 1776 (?), pp. 367-8

21 Ibid, III, 508, p. 293, J.B. to Jas Anderson, 12 July 1784

22 These manuscripts are described in the Preface.

23 (69.16-17). See *Introduction*, ed. Burns and Hart, chap. 3, 'Of the four sanctions or sources of pain and pleasure,' pp. 34-7.

24 Himmelfarb's comments are cited in my introduction to the present work. 'Panopticon' was Bentham's conception of an inspection-house for the housing or detention of criminals, paupers, the sick, and the jobless. Its circular design permitted constant scrutiny and supervision of any or all inmates by administrators located at its centre. For details, see *Panopticon; or, the Inspection House*, 2 vols, London, T. Payne, 1791; see also below, chap. 11

25 See E. Halévy, *La Formation du Radicalisme Philosophique*, Tome 3, p. 360, n. 86. The correct heading is 'Key': see UCL mss, Box 69, p. 59.

26 The marginal heading beside the last sentence is 'Liberty used improperly for Security.'

27 Halévy, *Radicalisme Philosophique*, Tome 3, p. 360, n. 68. See also UCL mss, Box 69, p. 59, headed 'Key.'

28 The reader may find interesting the comparison between Bentham's views on this point and Rousseau's feelings on the same subject. See *Social Contract*, Book I, chap. 6. Rousseau clearly felt, as did Bentham, that the law must protect the individual from his fellow citizens, securing his liberty by limiting theirs. It was by such exertions of legal sovereignty, indeed, that Rousseau imagined men might be forced to be free under the terms of a 'social contract.'

29 This is one of several statements under the marginal heading 'Liberty Defined.' This particular passage also carried the marginal heading 'Left free — left at liberty.'

30 *Introduction*, ed. Burns and Hart, chap. 1, para. 1, p. 11

31 *Fragment on Government*, ed. Harrison, Preface, para. 16, p. 10

32 UCL mss Box 69, p. 148, sheet headed 'Preparatory Principles. Inserenda,' Marginal heading 'The more Law, the more Liberty not true,' '574'

33 See UCL mss, 69, p. 31: 'That is a man's own [and not another's] which he has a *title* to possess / in other words which he has by *Law* an interest in. When he and he only has such title he is the person and the only person who stands exempted from the general Law which forbids property to be meddled with.' This passage should be compared with Bentham's examination of the 'fictitious' 'incorporal objects of property' in appendix B to *Of Laws in General*.

34 UCL mss, 69, p. 153: 'Possession'. 'Possession is liberty to use. Physical possession is physical liberty to use. Legal possession is Legal liberty to use accompanied with legal power, determinable however upon condition of legal disproval of legal right.' Cf. *Of Laws in General*, Bentham's remarks on 'possession' and 'occupation' in appendix B, para. 58, p. 273, where the nature of the distinction between 'physical' and 'legal' liberty is emphasized.

35 See *Introduction*, ed. Burns and Hart, Preface, p. 6.

36 The fact that this sheet has, at some time, been crossed over in ink need not suggest that Bentham retracted the opinions expressed therein. The mark may merely indicate that the material had served its purpose and been inserted into the argument of a full-fledged work. Cf. in this instance the argument concerning the 'Idea of political society' in the *Fragment on Government*, ed. Harrison, chap. 1, para. 10, p. 38.

CHAPTER FIVE: A 'COMMENT' AND A 'FRAGMENT'

1 Bentham, *A Comment on the Commentaries of Sir William Blackstone*, Book 1, Chapter 2, 'Law of Nature.' These are its final words. The edition published in 1928 under the editorship of C.W. Everett (Oxford, The Clarendon Press) has perforce been frequently cited. This writer has also, however, been allowed to read the manuscript of the forthcoming edition, edited by J.H. Burns, which is to be one of the volumes in the new *Collected Works*. In some cases manuscript references to the UCL collection have been supplied where material used is part of the substantial quantity of text which, while not included in the Everett edition, will be added to the Burns edition. In other cases reference is made to the pagination of the existing typescript of the forthcoming edition.

2 Sir Wm Blackstone, *Commentaries on the Laws of England*, 4th ed., 4 vols, Oxford, Clarendon, 1770, Introductory Section 2, 'Of the nature of laws in general,' pp. 40-1

3 See *Comment on the Commentaries*, ed. C.W. Everett, editor's introduction, pp. 43-4.

4 Ibid. The original passage from Blackstone's *Commentaries*, section II, p. 36, read as follows: 'This is the foundation of what we call ethics, or natural law. For the several articles into which it is branched in our systems amount to no more than demonstrating, that this or that action tends to man's real happiness, and therefore very justly concluding that the performance of it is a part of the law of nature; or, on the other hand, that this or that action is destructive of man's real happiness, and therefore that the law of nature forbids it.'

5 CW, *Correspondence*, I, 122, J.B. to John Lind, 5 Oct. 1774, p. 205

6 Headed 'Blackstone IX'

7 See *Comment*, ed. Everett, p. 61; see Blackstone, *Commentaries*, Section 1, p. 44.

8 *Comment*, ed. Everett, p. 62

9 Cf. *Of Laws in General*, ed. Burns and Hart, appendix B, para. 58, p. 273: 'Possession in general in a loose way of speaking may be said to be the absence of obstacles opposed to occupation: or in other words it is the liberty of occupation. As far as this liberty results from the situation which the thing is in, setting aside the interference of law, the possession may be termed physical: as far as it results from the aspect of the law, it may be termed legal.'

10 Quoted in part in *Comment on the Commentaries*, ed. Everett, p. 135; to be quoted in its entirety in Book 2, chap. 1 of the forthcoming edition of the *Comment*, ed. J.H. Burns

11 This passage is one of the additions to be made to Section 1.4 of the new edition of the *Comment*: 'Connection of Laws Natural, Divine and Municipal.'

12 The passage under attack is *Commentaries*, Book 1, p. 49.

13 *Comment*, ed. Everett, p. 79; see also editor's introduction, p. 17.

14 Delolme, J.L.; *Constitution of England*, London, 1775, p. 226: 'to concur by one's suffrage in enacting laws, is to enjoy a share, whatever it may be, of Power ... To live in a state where the laws are equal for all, and sure to be executed (whatever are the means by which these advantages are attained) is to be free.' Cf. Bentham on 'Government free' in chapter 4 above. Among the passages to be added to the forthcoming edition of the *Comment* is one (Section 2.1, 'Statute Law: Kinds of Statutes') in which Blackstone and Delolme are compared (cf. *Fragment*, Chap. 3, para. 21, p. 81): 'Foreigners are better furnished. They have Mr De L'Olme's short but excellent account of the British Laws, which contains the best of what our Author has said, with much that he should have said but has not.'

15 *Comment*, ed. Everett, p. 212, 'Common Law, how far consented to by the people'

16 Ibid, p. 212
17 Ibid
18 Blackstone, *Commentaries*, Book 1, p. 74
19 *Comment*, ed. Everett, p. 213
20 Ibid, p. 212
21 *Fragment*, ed. Harrison, Preface, para. 16, p. 10
22 This is one of the passages, drawn from the UCL mss, which will be added to the text of the new edition of the *Comment*. It will form part of Section 2.2.
23 See Chapter four above.
24 This passage will be used in the new *Comment*, ed. J.H. Burns, in Section 1.6 'Municipal Law.'
25 Ibid. The same chapter exhibits a statement of the principle that the determination of the 'juncture of resistance' (Cf. *Fragment*, ed. Harrison, chap. 4, para. 21, p. 93) consists of a calculation of the mischiefs of rebellion and submission respectively, which bears an interesting resemblance, in part, to Bentham's 'motto of a good citizen' (*Fragment*, Preface, para. 16, p. 10). The passage from the *Comment* refers to the 'calculation of mischiefs' principle: 'This is the only rule I can think of for submission and resistance. Does it fail of being explicit? I know of none that's more so. I see nothing in it that a good subject need be afraid, nor a good citizen ashamed to own.' The very important final sentence will appear in the forthcoming *Comment* edition, but was not included in the Everett edition.
26 This passage is to be added to the new *Comment* edition as part of Section 1.6, 'Municipal Law.' The section quoted from the *Commentaries* is Book 1, p. 53.
27 *Fragment*, ed. Harrison, Preface, paras 9 and 10, p. 6
28 Ibid, para. 10, p. 6
29 Ibid, para. 11, p. 6
30 *Fragment*, Preface, para. 11, p. 7
31 See supra text p. 146 and fn. 32, and text p. 145 and fn. 30.
32 *Fragment*, chap. 4, para. 13, p. 89
33 Ibid, para. 14, p. 89
34 Ibid, para. 15, p. 90. In paragraph 38 of the preface to the *Fragment* (ed. Harrison, p. 17) Bentham spells out for us the precise form taken by Blackstone's evasion of his task. Blackstone simply escapes into the 'everything is as it should be' fallacy. Bentham refers specifically to *Commentaries*, 1, p. 140, where, he says, 'he [Blackstone] commands us to believe, and that on pain of forfeiting all pretensions to either "sense or probity," that the system of our jurisprudence is, in the whole and every part of it, the very quintessence of perfection.' Bentham quotes Blackstone as saying that we enjoy all our 'rights and liberties' in society 'entire,' by 'birthright.' He interprets

240 Notes to pages 92-7

Blackstone as claiming that all the restraints imposed by 'the Laws of our country' are 1/ 'necessary' and 2/ 'so gentle and moderate ... that no man of *sense* or *probity* would wish to see them slackened.' And he quotes as follows (*Commentaries,* 1, p. 140): '*All* of us have it in our choice to do everything that a good man would desire to do; and are restrained from nothing, but what would be pernicious either to ourselves or our fellow citizens.' This is in Bentham's eyes sheer fantasy: total confusion of what is with what ought to be. Bentham immediately perceives and denounces the circular argument by which Blackstone supports his fantastic contention, and adduces the law enforcing a declaration of belief in the thirty-nine articles as a condition of worship as an example of a restraint which a man of sense and probity might well wish to see removed.

35 *Fragment*, ed. Harrison, Preface, para. 16, p. 10
36 Ibid, esp. paras 23-35, pp. 94-99
37 Ibid, chap. 4, para. 15, p. 90
38 Ibid, para. 23, p. 94
39 Ibid, para. 21, p. 93
40 Ibid, para. 22, p. 94
41 It will be recalled that, in a footnote to his definition of a 'state' Bentham maintained that 'what is called Liberty in a state does not depend upon any circumstance that will take it out of this definition,' although libertarian enthusiasts would find it a definition of a 'slavish state.'
42 *Fragment*, ed. Harrison, chap. 4, para. 23, p. 94
43 But see Bentham's remarks on the limits of sovereign power in *Of Laws in General*, chap. 9 'The generality of a law,' para. 25, p. 91.
44 *Fragment*, chap. 4, para. 24, pp. 94-5
45 Ibid, para. 25, p. 95
46 See D. Manning, *The Mind of Jeremy Bentham*, in the series *Monographs in Politics*, ed. J.W. Grove, London, Longmans, Green and Co., 1968, Introduction, p. 1.
47 *Fragment*, ed. Harrison, Preface, para. 32, pp. 15-16
48 Ibid, para. 33, p. 16
49 Ibid, chap. 5, para. 13, p. 111
50 Headed 'Free Government, Free Constitution. The expressions improper. Metonymical', Numbered 624 in the manner of the successive entries in the PPI manuscripts.
51 See CW, *Correspondence* I, 158, to John Lind, 27-8 March-1 April 1776, p. 311.
52 *Fragment*, ed. Harrison, chap. 3, para. 21, p. 81
53 Ibid

CHAPTER SIX: FUNDAMENTAL PROPOSITIONS

1 See CW, *Correspondence*, I, 160, J.B. to Samuel Bentham, 17 April 1776, p. 313.
2 Ibid, 186, J.B. to Jeremiah Bentham, 1 Oct. 1776, pp. 358-9. Subsequent quotations on this point are from p. 359
3 See *Introduction to the Principles of Morals and Legislation*, ed. Burns and Hart, chap. 16, 'Division of offences.'
4 *Correspondence*, I, 186, p. 395
5 *Introduction*, editor's introduction, p. ii.
6 Ibid
7 See *Rationale of Punishment*, transl. Richard Smith, London, 1830, Book 1, chap. 10, 'Popularity,' p. 73 (Cf. UCL mss, Box 141, p. 44, side 1).
8 Ibid, chap. 1, p. 1 (Cf. UCL mss, Box 141, p. 1)
9 Ibid, Chap. 10, p. 69 (Cf. UCL, Box 141, p. 43, side 1)
10 Ibid, p. 70. (Cf. UCL, Box 141, p. 43, side 2)
11 Ibid. Manuscript passage not extant. Gap exists in UCL mss between pp. 43 and 44 of Box 141. No continuity.
12 See *Introduction*, Preface, p. 1.
13 See CW, *Correspondence*, III, 405, J.B. to Jeremiah Bentham, 31 Aug. 1781, p. 69.
14 *Introduction*, chap. 1, para. 1, p. 11
15 Ibid, chap. 3, para. 1, p. 34
16 See *Introduction*, chap. 2, para. 14, n. *d*, p. 28.
17 See Bibliography for full titles of these works, which show that the *Constitutional Code* was 'for the use of All Nations and All Governments professing Liberal Opinions,' its leading principles were for the use of any state, and the *Deontology* was the guidebook to a general 'Science of Morality,' without reference to limitations of time or place.
18 *Introduction*, chap. 13, paras 1 and 2, p. 158
19 For precursors of the argument of the 'Cases Unmeet' chapter, see UCL Box 96, p. 76, where, under the heading 'Book I. Offences in General. Heads of the Book,' Chapter 5 is listed as 'Of exemptions from criminality,' and see also ibid, p. 99, where five cases are mentioned when 'the Law is simply and absolutely inexpedient — there ought to be no Law at all upon the Subject / matter.'
20 *Introduction*, chap. 13, para. 2, n. *a*, p. 158
21 Ibid, para. 3, p. 159
22 Ibid, paras 4-6, pp. 159-160. See ibid, Chap. 16, para. 35, n. 13, p. 231, for Bentham's interesting argument that usury involves free consent and thus cannot be an offence.

242 Notes to pages 103-9

23 Ibid, para. 17 (1), p. 164
24 Ibid, para. 3, p. 159
25 Ibid, para. 8 (2), p. 160
26 Ibid, paras 9 (3) to 12 (6), pp. 161-2
27 Ibid, para. 3, p. 159. Cf. Chapter 14, 'Of the proportion between punishments and offences,' pp. 165-74
28 Ibid, para. 13 (1), section 4, p. 163
29 Ibid, para. 14, p. 163
30 Ibid, para. 16 (2), pp. 163-4
31 CW, *Correspondence,* I, 95, J.B. to Jeremiah Bentham, 14 Oct. 1772, p. 155
32 See *Fragment,* ed. Harrison, Preface, para. 16, p. 10.
33 *Introduction,* ed. Burns and Hart, pp. 187-280
34 Ibid, pp. 281-300
35 Ibid, chap. 1, para. 4, p. 12
36 Ibid, chap. 16, paras 2-5, p. 188
37 *Introduction,* chap. 16, paras 6-9, pp. 188-90
38 See, for example, the analysis of public offences in *Of Laws in General,* ed. Hart, chap. 16, paras 16 (7) to 26 (17), pp. 205-8.
39 *Introduction,* chap. 16, para. 8, p. 189
40 On this point see the remarks of Prof. J.C. Rees, 'A re-reading of Mill on Liberty,' *Political Studies,* 8, 1960, p. 120.
41 *Introduction,* chap. 16, para. 15, pp. 195-6
42 Ibid, paras 33-7, pp. 225-34
43 *Introduction,* chap. 16, para 33, n. 72, p. 225
44 Ibid, para. 34, n. A3, p. 226
45 Ibid, para. 35, n. M3, p. 232
46 Ibid, para. 36, n. O3, p. 233
47 Ibid, para. 37, n. S3, p. 234
48 *Introduction,* chap. 16, para. 64, pp. 277-8
49 *Introduction,* chap. 16, para. 64, p. 278
50 See D. Lyons, 'Was Bentham a Utilitarian?' in *Royal Institute of Philosophy Lectures,* 5, 1970-1, London, 1972, p. 211, n. 2.
51 See *Introduction,* chap. 16, para. 11, pp. 191-193
52 *Of Laws in General,* ed. Hart, appendix B, pp. 251-88; see esp. p. 251.
53 *Introduction,* chap. 16, para. 27, p. 212
55 See ibid, chap. 16, para. 42, p. 241. Paras 38-55, pp. 234-70, cover 'offences against condition.' 'Domestic relations ... of legal institution' are dealt with in paras 40-3, pp. 236-44. Para. 42, p. 241, refers specifically to 'modes of servitude.'

56 Ibid, pp. 241-2
57 *Introduction*, chap. 16, para. 44, pp. 244-6
58 The two prevalent forms of deficiency are given as infancy and insanity (para. 44, pp. 244-5). There is also an interesting reference, however, in n. F4 to p. 245, to the placing of women in positions of 'perpetual wardship,' an act of tyranny which is itself responsibility for the creation of that inferiority (i.e. in women) by which it justifies itself. Shades of women's liberation!
59 See especially section *i*, 'Limits between private ethics and the art of legislation,' paras 1-20, pp. 281-93.
60 Ibid, p. 293
61 *Fragment*, ed. Harrison, chap. 5, para. 7, n. 1, part 4, p. 107
62 See *Introduction*, chap. 17, paras 2-4 (section *i*), pp. 282-3.
63 Ibid, para. 5, p. 283
64 See Lyons, 'Was Bentham a Utilitarian?' p. 217 and n. 1.
65 *Introduction*, chap. 17, section *i*, para. 6, pp. 283-4
66 Ibid, paras 7-8, pp. 284-5
67 Ibid, chap. 17, section *i*, para. 9, pp. 285-6. For 'indirect' interference, see below, chap. 8. In *Of Laws in General*, chap. 9, 'The generality of a law,' para. 25, pp. 91-2, Bentham asserts that 'the legislative power,' whether 'de classibus' or 'de singulis,' 'even though it be supreme, can never of itself be absolute and unlimited.' It does not even constitute 'the entire power of imperation,' falling short of it by 'so much as is contained in whatever powers of aggregation or disaggregation are established in the state' (p. 91). Whatever the purposes for which the sovereign attempts to interfere with individuals' actions, his 'intercourse' with 'particular persons' is limited, for 'Few will be the individuals whom he can find motives for selecting or the means for describing.'
68 Ibid, para. 10 (1), p. 286
69 Para. 11 (2), p. 286
70 *Introduction*, chap. 17, section *i*, para. 11 (2), p. 286-7
71 Ibid, para. 13, p. 287
72 Ibid, para. 15, pp. 289-90
73 Ibid, para. 16, pp. 290-1
74 Ibid, para. 19, pp. 292-3
75 Ibid, para. 18, p. 292
76 See ibid, chap. 13, para. 40, p. 236.
77 Ibid, chap. 17, section *i*, para. 18, p. 292. Subsequent quotations are from this paragraph until otherwise noted.
78 See ibid, preface, pp. 5-6.

79 Ibid, p. 1

80 Ibid

81 Lyons, 'Was Bentham a Utilitarian?' p. 211, n. 2

82 J.S. Mill, *Utilitarianism, Liberty and Representative Government*, introduction by A.D. Lindsay, Everyman's Library No. 482, London, Dent, 1964. 'On Liberty,' chap. 1, 'Introductory,' p. 65. As all quotations from Mill in this appendix are taken from this edition and this essay, the correct page number has simply been inserted in the text after the words quoted or referred to. All other quotations are footnoted in the ordinary way.

83 See Rees, 'A re-reading of Mill on Liberty,' p. 120

84 See UCL mss, Box 69, p. 89 (3 + 4). See also *Fragment on Government*, chap. 4, paras 23 and 24, pp. 94-5. The point is remade in a slightly different way in *Of Laws in General*, appendix B.

85 Bentham's commitment to this sort of programme is clear from the time of his interest in 'consent,' 'consultation,' and the franchise in the *Comment* to his later support, as a philosophical radical, for an enlarged and reformed electorate.

86 One of Bentham's two great failings, Mill found, was 'the incompleteness of his own mind as a representative of universal human nature.' This stemmed principally from his failure to grasp one 'great fact in human nature': he never recognised man as 'a being capable of pursuing spiritual perfection as an end; of desiring, for its own sake, the conformity of his character to his standard of excellence, without hope of good or fear of evil from other source than his own inward consciousness.' See J.S. Mill, 'Bentham,' in *Dissertations and Discussions*, 5 vols, Boston, 1865-75; 1, pp. 353, 359.

CHAPTER SEVEN: *OF LAWS IN GENERAL*

1 See *Of Laws in General*, ed. Hart, London, 1971 (a volume in the *Collected Works of Jeremy Bentham*, General Editor J.H. Burns), appendix E, pp. 304-11, for the text of a draft of this letter. See also UCL mss, Box 169, pp. 124-8, for the same and other draft letters, complete with deletions, insertions, and alternative readings, now printed as fully as possible in CW, *Correspondence*, III, 426, pp. 123-30.

2 *Of Laws in General*, ed. Hart, p. 304

3 Ibid

4 Ibid, p. 306

5 See ibid, pp. 306-8, for titles and brief descriptions of the work's chapters (except the first seventeen, which accompanied the letter in printed form),

and cf. 'Of Laws in General: Table of the Chapters,' which is appendix F. to ibid, pp. 312-13.

6 *An Introduction to the Principles of Morals and Legislation*, ed. Burns and Hart, London, 1970

7 *Of Laws in General*, ed. Hart, editor's introduction, p. 1

8 Ibid, appendix E, p. 308

9 Ibid

10 Ibid, appendix F, p. 312

11 Ibid, appendix E, p. 307

12 cw, *Correspondence*, III, 426, Jeremy Bentham to Lord Ashburton, 3 June 1782, p. 125

13 See *Of Laws in General*, ed. Hart, chap. 14, pp. 156-83.

14 Ibid, chap. 10, para. 16, pp. 119-20

15 A large X covers this page. It may indicate that these definitions have been superseded. In view of Bentham's employment of the concept of a general or universal law of liberty in *Of Laws in General*, however, they represent an important phase in Bentham's thought, whether abortive or not.

16 Cf. Delolme's conception of 'liberty of locomotion,' and note Bentham's attack on the Abbé Siéyès's 'doctrine of the liberty of locomotion,' in *Works*, ed. Bowring, 2, p. 532.

17 *Of Laws in General*, ed. Hart, chap. 10, para. 16, pp. 119-20

18 *Of Laws in General*, Appendix B, para. 7, p. 255.

19 See *Introduction*, ed. Burns and Hart, Preface, p. 8; cf. 'Concluding Note,' p. 301.

20 *Introduction*, ed. Burns and Hart, Preface, p. 1; cf. editor's introduction to *Of Laws in General*, ed. Hart, pp. 4-5.

21 *Introduction*, ed. Burns and Hart, Preface, p. 8

22 Ibid, 'Concluding Note,' p. 301

23 The only chapters in *Of Laws in General* whose titles do not refer to some particular characteristic of a law are 15, which deals with the whole class of 'customary laws,' 16 to 18, which examine the relationship between the penal and civil branches of law, and 19, 'Uses of the eighteen preceding chapters.'

24 *Of Laws in General*, chap. 10, 'Aspects of a law,' paras 9-10, pp. 98-100. These (and the latter part of para. 8, p. 98) show particularly clearly that Bentham attaches considerable practical importance to cases where the legislator remains indecisive and / or silent with regard to an action he has in view. The legislator may expressly decree that with regard to some act 'the subject shall have his choice' (para. 8, p. 98), or he may act positively to re-assure the subject who fears for his liberty (para. 10, head. 3, p. 99), by

issuing to him a permission based, in fact, upon the efficient force of a prohibition directed against those who might infringe upon the liberties in question. In this latter case, then, the efficacy of the permissive mandate is derived from coercion in prospect rather than in being.

In the same paragraph (p. 99), Bentham also refers to laws binding the sovereign himself, arguing that 'some of the most important laws that can enter into the code, laws in which the people found what are called their liberties, may be of this description.

25 *Of Laws in General*, chap. 10, para. 6, pp. 96-7
26 Ibid, Section ii, 'Primordial (Laws),' para. 3, p. 95
27 Ibid, Section iv, 'Alterative (Laws),' para. 16, p. 120
28 *Of Laws in General*, appendix B, para. 11, pp. 256-7
29 Ibid, para. 7, p. 255
30 The law so enacted is a 'non-commanding' or an 'originally-permissive provision,' a provision of the 'unobligative,' as distinct from the 'de-obligative' and 'obligative,' types (ibid, chap. 10, para. 16, p. 119). Such mandates will frequently fall into the 'undecisive' class of provisions.
31 See *Introduction*, ed. Burns and Hart, chap. 17, para. 8, p. 285.
32 Bentham sketched the tentative outlines of this discussion in ibid, chap. 16, para. 25, n. E2, pp. 205-7. See also *Of Laws in General*, ed. Hart, editor's introduction, pp. 6-8.
33 *Of Laws in General*, ed. Hart, appendix B, p. 251. All subsequent quotations are from this page until otherwise indicated.
34 Ibid, p. 252
35 Ibid, pp. 252-3
36 Ibid, para. 3, p. 253
37 Ibid.
38 See *Bentham's Theory of Legislation*, ed. C.K. Ogden, Book 2, 'Principles of the Civil Code,' Section *i*, 'Objects of the Civil Law,' chap. 1, 'Rights and Obligations,' pp. 94-5.
39 *Of Laws in General*, appendix B, para. 3, p. 254
40 See Thomas Hobbes, *Leviathan*, ed. Macpherson, Part 1, 'Of Man,' chap. 13, 'Of the *naturall condition* of Mankind, as concerning their Felicity, and Misery,' p. 185.
41 Ibid, chap. 11, 'Of the difference of Manners,' p. 161. There is a striking similarity between Hobbes's description of the 'Naturall Condition of Mankind' (ibid, chap. 13) wherein 'men live without other security, than what their own strength, and their own invention shall furnish them withall,' and wherein 'there is no place for Industry; because the fruit thereof is uncertain' (p. 186), and Bentham's evocation of a pre-political state wherein liberty

against the law is universal and is matched by universal anxiety and insecurity. Cf. also ibid, Part 2, 'Of Common-Wealth;' chap. 26, 'Of Civill Lawes,' p. 335: 'For to say all the people of a Common-wealth, have Liberty in any case whatsoever; is to say, that in such case, there hath been no Law made; or else having been made, is now abrogated.' See also the Epilogue below for further consideration of these points.

42 *Of Laws in General*, appendix B, para. 4, p. 254
43 Ibid
44 Paragraphs 4 to 11 cited here are ibid, pp. 254-7.
45 *Works*, ed. Bowring, 1, p. 341, 'Principles of the Civil Code,' Part 2, chap. 6, 'Community of Goods — its inconveniences.'
46 See John Locke, *Two Treatises of Civil Government*, Book 2, 'An Essay Concerning the True Original, Extent and End of Civil Government,' chap. 5, 'Of Property,' para. 27, p. 130 (Everyman).
47 *Of Laws in General*, appendix B, para. 7, p. 255
48 Ibid. Subsequent quotations are from paras 7 to 11, pp. 255-7, until otherwise indicated.
49 Ibid, para. 11, pp. 256-7

CHAPTER EIGHT: 'INDIRECT LEGISLATION' AND 'MATTERS OF PLACE AND TIME'

1 See *Introduction to the Principles of Morals and Legislation*, ed. Burns and Hart, Preface, p. 1; cf. *Fragment on Government*, ed. Harrison, chap. 3, para. 21, p. 81.
2 *Of Laws in General*, ed. Hart, chap. 19, para. 1 (7), p. 233
3 Ibid, para. 1 (2), p. 232
4 Ibid, para. 9, p. 245
5 Ibid, pp. 245-6
6 Ibid, p. 246
7 In chap. 14, 'Of the proportion between punishments and offences,' pp. 165-74.
8 Headed 'Indirect,' subheaded 'Plan'
9 See *Of Laws in General*, appendix E, J.B. to Lord Ashburton, 3 June 1782, p. 309. Bentham there proposed that he publish the *Introduction* and the 'book on Indirect Legislation' simultaneously, in order to capture at the same moment two contrasting types of readers. The *Introduction* would require 'strength of mind,' 'patience,' and a taste for 'metaphysics.' 'Indirect Legislation' (and with it the essay on 'Reward'), being 'full of propositions

of detail and illustrations,' would 'be somewhat less unpopular and less ill suited to the relish and the powers of the bulk of readers.'

10 Para. 11 (2), headed 'Indirect,' subheaded 'Devoting [i.e. diverting?] the Current of the Desires'. See also p. 13 (2), headed 'Indirect': '1. Institutions regarding criminal propensities in general. Such of these as regard the will, come under the head of education.'

11 See Bentham's analysis of liberty in his 'Table of the Springs of Action.'

12 Ibid. See also UCL mss, Box 87, pp. 18-19: 'The force of the moral sanction in as far as depends upon extent turns upon two great hinges, the *liberty of the press* and the *publicity of the proceedings in the courts of justice.*'

13 References to some of the numerous occasions, spread over the entire course of his intellectual life, on which Bentham reiterated his belief in the value of freedom of the press and of public discussion are given below in chap. 11.

14 Marginal heading to para. 6, p. 283, of chapter 17 of the *Introduction*, ed. Burns and Hart

15 Ibid. See also para. 15, p. 289: 'Of the rules of moral duty, those which seem to stand least in need of the assistance of legislation, are the rules of prudence.'

16 The reader will perhaps have noted that it is 'beneficience' that is given consideration in the *Introduction*, while 'benevolence' is considered in the 'Indirect Legislation' essay. The distinction is, of course, significant in view of the fact that beneficence, the performance of good *acts*, the object of *direct* legislation, is something quite different from benevolence, which is the propensity to perform such acts. To cultivate the propensity is feasible, even desirable. To use legislation to compel the performance of the acts themselves is for the most part unjustified: 'In many cases the beneficial quality of the act depends essentially upon the disposition of the agent,' which is to say, upon the question whether the actor's motives were 'such as denominate his conduct free and *voluntary*, according to one of the many senses given to those ambiguous expressions' (*Introduction*, chap. 17, para. 19, p. 292).

17 The maxims were: '1/ That no man is to be witness in his own cause. 2/ That no man is to be admitted to accuse himself. 3/ That no man's testimony who has any interest in the cause is to be heard. 4/ That no hearsay evidence is to be admitted. 5/ That no man is to be tried twice for the same offence.' Bentham planned to show the 'mistakenness' of these principles.

18 See UCL mss, Box 87, pp. 35, 188. The expression in quotation marks is not Bentham's, but the twentieth century's.

19 Ibid, p. 62.

20 Cf. *Fragment on Government*, ed. Harrison, chap. 4, para. 24, pp. 94-5

21 Headed 'Indirect Legislation – Misrule,' subheaded 'General.' See also ibid,

p. 112, where means for 'Narrowing the sphere of despotic influence' are discussed further.

22 This comment has been understood as referring not to the *de facto* reporting of parliamentary debates, which had been going on since 1771, but to the status of such reporting *de jure*.

23 Published in *Works of Jeremy Bentham*, ed. Bowring, 1, pp. 169-95. A new edition is in preparation, to be included as a volume in the forthcoming *Collected Works* series, general editor J.H. Burns.

24 See *Of Laws in General*, ed. Hart, appendix E, p. 308.

25 Both works were, in fact, intended to apply to their respective tasks principles already outlined in the *Introduction*. Specifically, Bentham asserted that the plan for the 'Place and Time' essay had been 'completely drawn' and described in the catalogue of 'Circumstances Influencing Sensibility' (*Introduction*, ed. Burns and Hart, chap. 6, pp. 51-73).

26 The full text of the manuscript passage includes four maxims whose guidance may be sought when the problem in view is one of a change in political or social institutions: '1/ No law should be changed, no usage at present observed in the exercise of authority should be abolished, without some specific reason: without some specific benefit to be got by it. 2/ The changing of a custom repugnant to our manners to one which is conformable to them for no other reason than such conformity, should not be reputed as a benefit. 3/ In all matters of indifference let the force of the political sanction remain neuter: and let the authority of the moral sanction take its course. 4/ The easiest innovation to introduce is that which is effected merely by refusing to a coercive custom the sanction of the law: by refusing to adopt customs which trench upon the liberty of the subject: especially where no individual reaps the profit of the coercion imposed upon another.'

27 See Jean-Jacques Rousseau, *Political Writings*, edited with introduction and notes by C.E. Vaughan, 2 vols, Oxford, Blackwell, 1962, vol. 2, Livre 1, 'Du Contrat Social,' chap. 6, 'Du pacte social,' p. 32.

28 Returning to his 'beginning' point, Bentham concluded that 'Sense, which is the basis of every idea, is so of every enjoyment; and unless man's whole nature be new modelled, so long as man remains man the stock of sense ... never can encrease.'

CHAPTER NINE: TWO BRANCHES OF THE LAW

1 See *Of Laws in General*, ed. Hart, chap. 19, para. 1 (2), p. 232.

2 Ibid, editor's introduction, p. 4

3 The most important passages in the *Introduction* are chap. 17, para. 29, pp. 298-300, 'Jurisprudence, civil-penal-criminal,' and the 'Concluding Note,' esp. paras 1-25, pp. 301-8, wherein 'the deplorable state of the science of legislation ... in respect of its form' is attributed to the absence of an adequate summary of 'all requisite expository matter,' (i.e. the lack of a civil code) (p. 308). The chapters in *Of Laws in General* relevant to the penal-civil distinction are referred to below.

4 See *Of Laws in General*, chap. 16, para. 13 (4), p. 204.

5 Ibid, appendix E, J.B. to Lord Ashburton, 3 June 1782, pp. 305-6

6 From the heading ('Introd. Criminal and Civil') it would appear that this is draft material for what is now *Of Laws in General*, chap. 17, 'Division of the laws into civil and criminal.'

7 Ibid, section *ii*, para. 4, p. 216. After employing the idea of a civil-criminal distinction for some time, Bentham came to realize (ibid, Section *i*, para. 9, p. 211) that 'the word criminal' did not refer to 'any branch of law as subsisting in contradistinction to 'the civil,' and that he must revert to the use of the term 'penal' instead. This cast no reflection on the nature or validity of the dichotomy itself. The term 'criminal' was simply set aside from this particular argument.

8 Ibid, chap. 19, para. 2, p. 234

9 Ibid, chap. 16, para. 11 (2), pp. 201-2

10 Ibid, para. 10 (1), pp. 200-1

11 Ibid, para. 12 (3), pp. 202-3

12 Ibid, para. 13 (4), pp. 203-4

13 Ibid, para. 12 (3), pp. 202-3

14 Ibid, chap. 18, para. 14, p. 227

15 Ibid, appendix A, 'Distinction Between Penal Law and Civil,' para. 4, n. *a*, and para. 8, n. b, pp. 248-9.

16 Ibid, appendix C, para. 5, p. 290

17 Ibid, appendix A, pp. 247 (para. 1), 248 (para. 4)

18 Ibid, chap. 19, para. 2, pp. 234-5

19 Ibid, para. 10, p. 246

20 Ibid, chap. 19, para. 10, p. 246

CHAPTER TEN: CIVIL LAW

1 See *Introduction to the Principles of Morals and Legislation*, ed. Burns and Hart, chap. 1, para. 1, p. 11.

2 See *Of Laws in General*, ed. Hart, appendix B, Part 1, para. 1, pp. 251-2.

3 See *Introduction*, ed. Burns and Hart, Preface, p. 6. The sequence of projected works there described is referred to below, in chap. 11. In the 'Projet' mss, where French equivalents for Bentham's English terminology had to be produced, civil law became 'droit distributif privé' (UCL mss, Box 99, p. 34) and constitutional law was rendered as 'droit distributif politique' (ibid, Box 32, p. 130).

4 See *Of Laws in General*, ed. Hart, chap. 16, 'Separation of the civil branch from the penal,' paras 10 (1) to 26 (17), pp. 200-8.

5 Ibid, para. 10 (1), p. 200

6 Ibid, para. 11 (2), p. 201

7 Ibid.

8 Ibid, para. 12 (3), p. 202. Subsequent quotations are from this paragraph and page until otherwise indicated.

9 Ibid, p. 203

10 Ibid, para. 13 (4), pp. 203-4

11 Ibid, para. 14 (5), p. 204

12 Ibid, para. 15 (6), pp. 204-5

13 Public offences are dealt with in paras 16 (7) to 26 (17) of chap. 16 in *Of Laws in General* (pp. 205-8). The public institutions which may be offended against include 'the preventive branch of the police' (para. 17, p. 205), the administrators of justice (para. 18, pp. 205-6), the army, described as 'the public force' (para. 19, p. 206), and the Sovereignty itself (para. 24, p. 207). More abstractly, he also lists such public 'institutions' as the external security of the state (para. 16, p. 205), the positive increase of the national felicity (para. 20, p. 206), the public wealth (para. 12, p. 206-7), population (para. 22, p. 13), the national wealth (para. 23, p. 207) and, finally, the national interest in general (para. 26, p. 208). None of these entities or cases is discussed in any detail. Bentham's point, reiterated in each successive paragraph, is that it is the task of the civil law, in its capacity as a fundamental aspect of the public or constitutional branch of the law (para. 19, p. 206), to define and distribute the rights and duties which provide the basis for all public institutions both concrete and abstract. What provides a thread of consistency running through these ten paragraphs is the involvement in each case of the security of the state (or, rather, of the community) in either its external or its internal aspect.

14 *Of Laws in General*, chap. 17, 'Division of the laws into civil and criminal,' Section *ii*, 'Limits between the criminal branch and the civil,' para. 4, p. 216

15 Ibid, chap. 18, 'Distinction between penal and civil procedure,' para. 1, p. 220

16 Ibid, appendix A, 'Distinction between penal law and civil,' para. 8, p. 249

17 Ibid, n. *b* to p. 249

18 Ibid, chap. 18, para. 4, p. 222
19 *Of Laws in General*, ed. Hart, appendix C, para. 4, p. 290
20 Ibid, para. 5, p. 290
21 Ibid, pp. 293-4
22 Headed 'Civil — beginning.' Box 99, p. 34, is headed 'Droit Privé Conts.' — 'Quatre buts du droit distributif privé.'
23 Box 32, p. 14, headed 'Civil — Proj. Matière — Beg. May 1786'
24 Box 99, p. 47, headed 'Civil Ordo, 12 Oct. 1795'
25 The only exception to his generalization is Box 99, p. 47, where he examines these priorities under headings which bear a discernible but imprecise resemblance to the latter chapters of Book 1 of the 'Principles of the Civil Code' in the *Theory of Legislation*, ed. Hildreth, pp. 96-148, entitled 'Objects of the Civil Law.' 'Bk. I, Ch. 19' deals with the 'Impossibility of doing any thing in the way of law but at the expense of liberty as against coercion by individuals, which may be regarded as one branch of security,' and 'Bk. I, Ch. 20' discusses 'How far Opulence ought to be and has been favoured without any sensible expense in the way of Liberty and thus of Security.' 'Bk. I, Ch. 21,' finally, relates 'How far Equality may be favoured in the same manner.'
26 See *Jeremy Bentham's Economic Writings*, ed. Stark, I, Introduction, p. 21.
27 CW, *Correspondence*, III, p. 424, J.B. to Jeremiah Bentham, 10-28 Dec. 1785
28 A very brief summary of the contents of these pages has been provided, probably by Richard Smith (who edited and translated *'The Rationale of Punishment,' by Jeremy Bentham*, London, 1830, and *The Rationale of Reward*, London, 1825), on the wrapper which surrounds folio 9 of UCL mss, Box 100.
29 A wrapper surrounding these sheets, dated 19 Nov. 1833 and initialled RS (Richard Smith?) bears the comment 'not used — consisting of distinctions and definitions.'
30 His endorsement of equalization of political power referred, as we have noted, to voting but not to 'equality in property', and not, as we have seen in our examination of *Of Laws in General*, to liberty as against the law. He could endorse equalization of liberty as a branch of security, but not as personal independence or political power.

CHAPTER ELEVEN: THE FRUITS OF INVENTION

1 CW, *Correspondence*, 3, 508, J.B. to Jas Anderson, 12 July 1784, p. 293
2 C.W. Everett, *The Education of Jeremy Bentham*, New York, Columbia University Press, 1931, p. 196

3 *Correspondence*, 3, 488, Samuel Bentham to J.B., 20/31 Jan.-22 Jan./2 Feb. 1784, p. 241

4 The 'Projet' mss are divided into 'projet forme' mss and 'projet matière' mss. An unpublished report on the structure and substance of them has been prepared by Dr M.H. James for the use of the Bentham Research Project at University College, London. With its help a decision will eventually be made as to the form in which the 'projet' mss are to be published as part of the new *Collected Works of Jeremy Bentham*. The most useful indication of their scope and contents which can be given to the general reader is the observation that Etienne Dumont's *Traités de Legislation* represents a drastic condensation of their substance.

5 *Correspondence* 3, 557, J.B. to Jeremiah Bentham, 10-28 Dec. 1785, p. 424

6 Ibid, 576, J.B. to Prince Dashkov, 19/30 July 1786, p. 483

7 See Everett, *Education of Jeremy Bentham*, p. 37.

8 *Correspondence*, III, 576, Geo. Wilson to J.B., 24 Sept. 1786, pp. 489-91. In 1785 the Rev. William Paley, archdeacon of Carlisle and former tutor of Christ's College, Cambridge, had published *The Principles of Moral and Political Philosophy*, a work based on lectures he had given at Christ's College between 1768 and 1776. It attracted much attention and was immediately adopted as the ethical textbook of Cambridge University. In George Wilson's eyes Paley seemed to be 'invading' Bentham's 'province as a reformer.' Wilson knew that Bentham's ideas on the subject covered in Paley's work had been arrived at and printed, although not published, long before 1785. His fear was that Bentham would be 'charged with stealing from [Paley] what you have honestly invented with the sweat of your own brow,' when in fact it was Paley whose ideas so resembled Bentham's that Wilson 'could almost suspect, if it were possible, that he had read [Bentham's] introduction.'

9 *Correspondence*, III, 592, J.B. to Geo. Wilson, 4/15 May 1787, pp. 544-6

10 Regarding that essay's advanced state of completeness in 1782, see *Of Laws in General*, appendix E, J.B. to Lord Ashburton, 3 June 1782, p. 309.

11 See *Jeremy Bentham's Economic Writings*, ed. Stark, London, Allen and Unwin, 1952, 1, p. 129. Regarding Bentham's advocacy of freedom of contracts and its significance, see Wm H. Alexander, *'Jeremy Bentham, Legal Philosopher and Reformer,' New York University Quarterly Law Review*. The first part, 'Life and Works' (7, 1929, pp. 141-55), includes an impressive list of reforms for which, it is argued, Bentham's advocacy of freedom of contract paved the way (see p. 154). The second part (7, 1929, pp. 465-73), deals with Bentham's 'Legal Philosophy' under the headings 'Theory of Punishment' and 'Extension of Individual Liberty.'

12 *The Rationale of Reward*, transl. Richard Smith, London, 1825, Book 1, pp. 117, 118

13 Ibid, Book 2, chap. 11, 'Of Trust and contract management,' p. 194

14 Ibid, Book 4, chap. 13, p. 279

15 Ibid

16 See W.H. Alexander, *Jeremy Bentham, Legal Philosopher and Reformer*, Part 1, p. 154. Alexander concludes that 'the extension of individual liberty is the second great principle which appears in the table of legislation traceable to his influence.'

17 See Everett, *Education of Jeremy Bentham*, p. 43.

18 J.B. to Lord Wycombe, 1 March 1789, in *Works of Jeremy Bentham*, ed. Bowring, 10, p. 196-7

19 Ibid

20 See British Museum Additional Manuscrips of Jeremy Bentham, Vol. 5, pp. 16-17, Mr White (Dublin) to J.B., 21 Feb. 1789.

21 J.B. to Lord Wycombe, 1 March 1789, *Works*, ed. Bowring, 10, 196-7.

22 Samuel Bentham to J.B., 12/23 Jan. 1791, British Museum Additional Manuscripts, Vol. 5, pp. 199-200

23 *Introduction to the Principles of Morals and Legislation*, ed. Burns and Hart, Preface, p. 3

24 Ibid

25 Ibid, para. 10, p. 3

26 Ibid, p. 5

27 The list is on p. 6, ibid.

28 See *Of Laws in General*, ed. Hart, pp. 220-31

29 *Introduction to the Principles of Morals and Legislation*, 'Concluding Note,' para. 27, p. 309

30 Ibid, pp. 309-10

31 See 'Draught of a New Plan for the Organization of the judicial establishment in France: proposed as a succedaneum to the draught presented, for the same purpose, by the Committee of Constitution, to the National Assembly, Dec. 21st, 1789, by Jeremy Bentham, March, 1790,' in *Works*, ed. Bowring, iv, pp. 285-406. See also the various French projects and interests suggested by UCL mss, Box 170, pp. 1-172, the most important of which was perhaps Bentham's essay on 'Representation' (pp. 87-121). See also *Essay on Political Tactics*, London, Payne, 1791.

32 See British Museum Additional Manuscripts, Vol. 5, p. 369: F. Chauvelin, 'Ministre plenipotentiaire De la République Française,' to J.B., dated London, 16 Oct. 1792.

33 Ibid

34 J.B. to Lord Lansdowne, 9-12 Aug. 1792, section headed 'Sun. Aug. 12/92'; to appear in CW, *Correspondence,* IV (in preparation)
35 Copies of the three letters referred to are presently held in the chronological file of material for ibid. They were originally taken from the Lansdowne mss. Regarding the parliamentary process, see especially J.B. to Lord Lansdowne, Wednesday 5, Sept. 1792.
36 J.B. to Lord Lansdowne, Monday 10 Sept. 1792
37 See Gallois to J.B., 15 Oct. 1792 (British Museum Additional Manuscripts, Vol. 5, 368), Beaumetz to J.B., 3 Nov. 1792 (ibid, 373), and Romilly to J.B., 5 Nov. 1792 (*Works,* ed. Bowring, 10, pp. 286-7).
38 J.B. to Lord Lansdowne, 10 Sept. 1792
39 J.B. to the minister of the interior of the French Republic, Oct. 1792, in *Works,* ed. Bowring, 10, 282-3
40 J.B. to H. Dundas, 20 May 1793, Public Record Office, Home Office 42/45, folder 121
41 J.B. to Philip Metcalf, 31 Oct. 1793; in *Works,* ed. Bowring, 10, pp. 295-6
42 J.B. to Samuel Bentham, 23 Sept. 1795, in British Museum Additional Manuscripts, Vol 6, pp. 107-8
43 J.B. to le Duc de Liancourt, 11 Oct. 1795, in *Works,* ed. Bowring, 10, pp. 312-13.
44 J.B. to Wilberforce, 1 Sept. 1796, in the Bodleian Library's Wilberforce Manuscripts, d. 13/35.
45 J.B. to Lord St Helen's, 12 [?] Sept. 1796, *Works,* ed. Bowring, 10, 320.
46 J.B. to W. Mitford, 25 March 1797; from New York Public Library, Manuscript Division, Miscellaneous papers, 'Bentham, J.'
47 J.B. to Wm Wilberforce, 1 Sept. 1796, Bodleian Library, Wilberforce mss, d. 13/35
48 J.B. to William Cobbett, 30 June 1801, (draft). UCL mss, Box 108, p. 114, contains several contemplated titles for Bentham's attack, the most grotesque of which is 'No French Nonsense: or A Cross-Buttock for the first Declaration of Rights: together with a kick of the A— for the Second ... by a practitioner of the Old English Art of Self-defence.'
49 *Works,* ed. Bowring, 2, p. 530, col. 2
50 See 'The Book of Fallacies: from the unfinished papers of Jeremy Bentham. By a friend,' ed. P. Bingham, London, 1824. Also in *Works,* ed. Bowring, 2, pp. 375-487. The mss are principally UCL, Boxes 103, 104, and 105.
51 See *Works,* ed. Bowring, 2, p. 389, also p. 388
52 Ibid, pp. 391-3
53 Ibid, p. 400
54 Ibid, p. 395

55 Ibid, pp. 400-1
56 Ibid, p. 420
57 Ibid, p. 423
58 *Correspondence*, III, p. 491; Geo. Wilson to J.B., 24 Sept. 1786
59 See 'Panopticon versus New South Wales,' in *Works*, ed. Bowring, 4, pp. 173-284. For various manuscript illustrations of Bentham's criticisms of the hulks, see A.T. Milne, *Catalogue of the Manuscripts of Jeremy Bentham*, 1962, p. 71.
60 See G. Himmelfarb, 'The Haunted House of Jeremy Bentham,' in 'Ideas in History. Essays presented to Louis Gottschalk by his former students,' ed. Herr and Parker, Durham NC, Duke University Press, 1965, p. 231.
61 See ibid, pp. 233, 236-8
62 Ibid, p. 235
63 J.B. to William Pitt, Jan. (?) 1791; among typescript copies of letters being prepared for inclusion in CW, *Correspondence*, IV
64 J.B. to J.P. Brissot, Nov. 1791, in *Works*, ed. Bowring, 10, p. 226
65 J.B. to Society of Agriculture, Sept. 1797, in UCL mss, Box 104 (a), p. 53
66 J.B. to Wm Pitt, Jan. 1791
67 See 'Rationale of Reward,' in *Works*, ed. Bowring, Vol. 2, pp. 197-8
68 J.B. to E. Nepean, 22 Feb. 1791, Public Record Office, H.O., 42/18, f. 34. To be included in CW, *Correspondence*, IV.
69 See 'Rationale of Judicial Evidence,' in *Works*, ed. Bowring, 7, p. 522
70 See 'Panopticon, Postscript, pt. 1,' ibid, 4, p. 85: 'Here may be observed ... that scene of clockwork regularity which it would be easy to establish ... Certainty, promptitude and uniformity are the qualities which may here be distinguished in the extreme.
71 The Panopticon letters of 1787 were intended to convey a structural principle 'applicable to any sort of establishment, in which persons of any description are to be kept under inspection.' See bibliography for the full title of the group of letters published in 1791, which includes the passage here quoted.
72 See 'Poor Law,' in *Works*, ed. Bowring, 8, p. 436, col. 1.
73 First published in 1823. See ibid, 5, pp. 231-8. Subsequent quotations are from pp. 233-5.
74 J.B. to Rt Hon. Wm Pitt. Not sent. 16 Sept. 1794. To be included in CW, *Correspondence*, IV.
75 J.B. to le Duc de Liancourt, 11 Oct. 1795, *Works*, ed. Bowring, 10, pp. 312-13
76 See W. Stark, 'Liberty and Equality, or, J.B. as an Economist. Part I, Bentham's Doctrine,' *Economic Journal*, 51, 1941, pp. 57-58

77 See E. Halévy, *Growth of Philosophic Radicalism*, transl. M. Morris, London, 1972, Part 1, chap. 1, pp. 17-18.

78 See S.R. Letwin, *The Pursuit of Certainty*, Cambridge, 1965, p. 146, n. 1.

79 See typescript for the text of the forthcoming edition of Bentham's 'Place and Time' essay, p. 6, in the Bentham Project Room, University College, London.

80 J.B. to Arthur Young, Sept. 1794, in *Works*, ed. Bowring, 10, pp. 302-3

81 See 'Defence of a Maximum,' in *Jeremy Bentham's Economic Writings*, ed. Stark, 3, pp. 257-8.

82 Ibid, 1, p. 336

83 *Introduction*, ed. Burns and Hart, chap. 16, para. 26, p. 212

84 See J. Locke, *Two Treatises of Government*, edited, with introduction, by Thos I. Cook, New York, 1947, 2nd treatise, para. 27, p. 134.

85 See 'Principles of the Civil Code,' Part 2, chap. 6, 'Community of goods — its inconveniences,' in *Works*, ed. Bowring, 1, p. 341.

86 *Economic Writings*, ed. Stark, 1, p. 226

87 Ibid, 3, 'Institute of Political Economy,' 'Introduction: Precognita and Precognoscenda,' p. 307

88 See *Works*, ed. Bowring, 3, pp. 211-13.

89 See *Economic Writings*, ed. Stark, 3, 'Institute of Political Economy,' pp. 308-9.

90 Ibid, 1, p. 93

91 Ibid, pp. 109-11

92 Ibid, pp. 111-12

93 Ibid, p. 117

94 Ibid, 3, 'The True Alarm,' p. 77

95 Ibid, 3, p. 339

96 See *Correspondence*, I, 95, J.B. to Jeremiah Bentham, 14 Oct. 1772, p. 155.

97 For references to a 'Pannomion' in the UCL mss, see Milne *Catalogue*, p. 89. See also *Economic Writings*, ed. Stark, 1, pp. 17-18.

98 Headed 'fictitious entities'; cf. Box 102, pp. 80-132 (re 'Terminology, language' etc.).

99 UCL mss, Box 101, pp. 385-405, 'Logic — Ch. X, Of the art of invention.' See also appendix C to M. Mack, *Jeremy Bentham, an Odyssey of Ideas*, London, 1965, and *Works*, ed. Bowring, 3, 285-95. Mrs Mack's appendix is headed 'Logical Arrangements, or Instruments of Invention and Discovery.'

100 The extant manuscripts are in UCL, Boxes 14 and 15. Bowring's edition has never been regarded by anyone as even substantially faithful to Bentham's mss since J.S. Mill and Francis Place, among others, denounced it. A new edition, a volume in the *Collected Works* series, is in preparation.

101 For the anatomy of the new formal framework, see Mack, *Bentham*, appendix A, p. 445, and *Economic Writings*, ed. Stark, 1, pp. 17-18 and p. 91. For references to chapter 17 of the Introduction, see chapter 6 above.

102 See *Works*, ed. Bowring, 1, p. 210, 'Table of the Springs of Action.'

103 Eg. UCL mss, Boxes 30, 31, and 111, all dating from between 1818 and 1829. For other examples, see Milne, *Catalogue*, p. 69.

104 Eg. UCL mss, Boxes 52 (b), 53-6, dating almost entirely from the 1820s. For further examples, see Milne *Catalogue*, pp. 95-6.

105 Eg. UCL mss, Box 67, pp. 1-18, 57-89, 114-163, 184-362, and Box 65, 171-236 and Box 68, pp. 3-9, 19-78, 115-381, dating mainly from 1818. For other examples, see Milne, *Catalogue*, pp. 91-2.

106 Eg. UCL mss, Boxes 34, 36 (including 'first lines' and 'first principles,' dated respectively 1821 and 1822), 37, 41 – dating predominantly from the 1820s. For further references see Milne, *Catalogue*, pp. 70-1.

107 J.B. to Lord Stanhope, ('in continuation') 14 March 1824

108 Cf. appendix E, pp. 453-7, to Mack, *Jeremy Bentham*, entitled 'On the Efficient Cause and Measure of Constitutional Liberty,' taken from UCL mss, Box 126, pp. 8 ff.

CHAPTER TWELVE: FREEDOM OF THE PRESS AND PUBLIC DISCUSSION

1 See B.R. Barber, *Superman and Common Men*, chap. 3, 'Forced to be free: an illiberal defence of liberty,' p. 66.

2 J.S. Mill, *On Liberty*, 'Introductory,' p. 73, in *Utilitarianism, Liberty and Representative Government*, ed. A.D. Lindsay (Everyman)

3 Cf. C.L. Stevenson, *Ethics and Language*, New Haven, Yale University Press, 1944, Part 1, chap. 2, pp. 2-8

4 See *Fragment on Government*, ed. Harrison, Preface, paras 15 to 24, pp. 8-13.

5 Ibid, para. 16, p. 10

6 Ibid, chap. 4, para. 24, pp. 94-5

7 See *Comment on the Commentaries*, ed. Everett, chaps 10 ('Statute Law: kinds of statutes'), 12 ('Construction of statutes'), and 13 ('Common Law.); cf. UCL mss, Box 49, pp. 291-6 (1804, 1805), on the 'Practicability of the conversion of jurisprudential law into statutory.'

8 See UCL mss, Box 149, pp. 1-9; dated c. 1775 by A.T. Milne in his *Catalogue of the Manuscripts of Jeremy Bentham*.

9 Dated c. 1794 by Milne, *Catalogue*

10 Dated 1775

11 Dated 1796-1803

12 Dated 1831

13 See *Jeremy Bentham's Economic Writings*, ed. W. Stark, 1, 'Supply without Burthen or Escheat vice Taxation' (1795), p. 339.

14 See, for example, *Works of Jeremy Bentham*, ed. Bowring, 1, p. 538, on the superiority of freedom of the press to a state of censorship, and p. 563 on the efficacy of a free press in directing public opinion. These passages formed part of the 'Principles of Penal Law, Part Four, Indirect Means of Preventing Offences' in the same volume.

15 Headed 'Penal Code — Indirect.' Cf. *Works*, ed. Bowring, 1, pp. 574-5.

16 Prepared from manuscripts dating from 1806 to 1821: see Milne, *Catalogue*, pp. 66, 75.

17 See 'The Book of Fallacies,' in *Works*, ed. Bowring, 2, Part 4, chap. 3, the fallacy of the 'Matchless Constitution,' p. 443.

18 Ibid, pp. 443-4

19 Ibid, Part 2, chap. 4, 'Official Malefactor's Screen: Attack us, you attack Government,' p. 424

20 Ibid, pp. 423-4

21 Ibid, Part 4, chap. 6, 'Sham Distinctions.' 'Exposure — Example 1,' pp. 451-3. Subsequent quotations are from these pages until otherwise indicated.

22 Headed 'Press — Ch. 2. Compulsory Means — 1. Code Desirable.' We have dealt above with Bentham's moderating, and eventually hostile, advice to the French revolutionaries. If he expected punctual obedience to accompany free censure in their case, however, he also expected governing authorities such as Necker to refrain from 'stopping the mouths' of critics. See J.B. to Geo. Wilson, 16 May 1789, in *Works*, ed. Bowring, 10, pp. 200-1.

23 Dated 1810, 1817, 1818

24 Dated c. 1810 by Milne

25 March 1809

26 Headed 'Press — Libel Law as it ought [to be],' dated 6 April 1809

27 See UCL mss, Box 111, pp. 60-137, 151-206, and 207-54, for Bentham's analysis of the nature and instruments of misrule and the need for radical reform, dated 1818-1820.

28 'To Torreno — Letter V,' 22 Sept. 1821; see also C. Kenny, 'A Spanish View of Bentham's Spanish Influence,' *Law Quarterly Review*, 2, 1895, p. 60.

29 Mavrocordato to J.B., 6 June 1824. See also Orlando, Luriottis and Zaimi to J.B., dated 1823-4

30 Leicester Stanhope informed Bowring (20 Dec. 1823) that the government of the day was 'slyly acting as censor over the Press, and attempting to suppress the thoughts of the finest genius of the most enlightened age, the thoughts of the immortal Bentham' (UCL mss, Box 12, pp. 164-7).

31 J.B. to Greek Legislators, 24 Feb. 1823
32 See also *Works*, ed. Bowring, Vol. 2, pp. 277-97. All subsequent quotations are from ibid, 2, pp. 277-80.

EPILOGUE

1 Correspondence II, 248, J.B. to Rev. J. Forster, April/May 1778, pp. 98-9 Cited above in Chapter 1.
2 'Map of Jurisprudence' appears frequently as a marginal heading in Bentham's 'preparatory manuscripts.' For example, see UCL mss, Box 88a, p. 141, where Bentham envisages a work to be entitled 'A Map of Jurisprudence as it is and as it ought to be,' complete with an epigraph taken from the *Esprit des Lois*.
3 See H.L. Beales, 'Bentham as political inventor,' *Contemporary Review*, 129, 1926, pp. 308-19.
4 See H.L. Beales, 'Jeremy Bentham, social engineer,' in *The Listener*, 3 Aug. 1932, pp. 143-50.
5 In *Jeremy Bentham: An Odyssey of Ideas*, London, 1963, M.P. Mack shows much interest in the question of when Bentham became a democrat; see especially p. 438.
6 The intention of C.I. Smith, 'Bentham's Second Rule,' *Journal of the History of Ideas*, 31, 1970, pp. 462-3, seems to be to claim that Bentham can be shown to have held one principle (to wit: that in any utilitarian social calculus of pleasures and pains each individual shall count as one, and none as more than one) compatible with some forms of liberalism. This, however, does not mean that he was altogether, or even fundamentally, a liberal theorist.
7 See supra, Chapter 11, p. 314, fn. 88 and text. The proposal was eventually allowed to become a dead letter, and Bentham did not receive compensation for his immense sacrifices for a good twenty years, (until 1812). On this point see C.W. Everett, *Jeremy Bentham*, London, 1966, p. 44.
8 See UCL mss, Box 8, pp. 92, 10-62, and Box 162 for drafts of a work entitled 'Emancipate Your Colonies.' See also *Works*, ed. Bowring, 4, 407-19.
9 See, for one source, E. Halévy, *Growth of Philosophic Radicalism*, London, 1972, p. 263 ff.
10 Ibid
11 Thomas Hobbes, *Leviathan*, ed. C.B. Macpherson, London, 1968, Book 1, chap. 7, p. 131
12 Ibid, Book 1, chaps 14 and 15, sets out Hobbe's understanding of the character of the 'Laws of Nature.' In UCL mss, Box 69, p. 126, headed

'Preparatory Principles Inserenda,' Bentham described 'Natural Law' as a 'contradiction in terms,' referring to 'such laws as exist in a state of things where there are none.' Yet in Bentham's theory there are clearly certain physiological imperatives which shape human behaviour in the absence of 'artificial' laws, and these might reasonably be considered neo-Newtonian laws of human nature in form and effect.

13 Hobbes, *Leviathan*, ed. Macpherson, Book 2, chap. 18, p. 228 ff.

14 UCL mss, Box 69, p. 55. Cited above in Chapter 1.

15 B.F. Skinner, *Walden Two*, New York, Macmillan, 1962, p. 262

16 B.F. Skinner, *Beyond Freedom and Dignity*, New York, Knopf, 1962, p. 5

17 Ibid, p. 7

18 Ibid, p. 5 Bentham put forward a somewhat narrower, and therefore perhaps more easily tenable, conception of the 'field of technology' as it related to human actions in his notes on *Chrestomathia* (a course of educational instruction 'conducive to useful learning'). There he defined general technology as 'the aggregate body of the several sorts of manual operations directed to the purposes of art, and having, for their common and ultimate end, the production and preparation of the several necessaries and conveniences of life.' See *Works*, ed. Bowring, 8, p. 148. Bentham here identifies technology with art, which in this case means practice (see ibid, p. 27). He clearly felt, however, that an adequate social theory or an adequate educational programme must include both art (practice) and science (knowledge). Indeed, he asserted (ibid) that 'in the very nature of the case' these two 'will be found so combined as to be inseparable.' Hence it would be unfair to Bentham to suggest that his social theory was nothing more than a 'technology' in *his* meaning of that term.

19 *Works*, ed. Bowring, 8, p. 184

20 Skinner, *Beyond Freedom and Dignity*, p. 215. Note that chap. 8 of the same work is entitled 'The Design of a Culture.'

21 Ibid, p. 43

22 See Hobbes, *Leviathan*, ed. Macpherson, Book 1, chap. 6, pp. 127-8.

23 I. Berlin, *Four Essays on Liberty*, London, Oxford University Press, 1969

Bibliography

PRIMARY SOURCES

Writings of Jeremy Bentham

1 / Manuscripts

Catalogue of the Manuscripts of Jeremy Bentham in the Library of University College, London, compiled by A. Taylor Milne, 2d ed., London, Athlone Press, 1962
The Bentham Manuscripts in the Library of University College, London
[Footnote references to this material take the form 'UCL mss,' and refer to box number and page, i.e. 69.53 means Box 69, page 53.]
British Museum Additional Manuscripts, Vols 33537 to 33564
[These volumes contain the main body of Bentham mss and correspondence in the British Museum; they are numbered from 1 to 28, beginning with vol. 33537 as vol. 1.]

2 / Collections of works

The Collected Works of Jeremy Bentham, General editor, J.H. Burns (cited in notes as CW)
Part I / *The Correspondence of Jeremy Bentham*, 1 / *1752-76*, and 2 / *1777-1780*, edited by Timothy L.S. Sprigge, London, Athlone Press, 1968; 3 / *1781-1788*, edited by I.R. Christie, London, Athlone Press, 1971. Further volumes in preparation
Part II / *Principles of Legislation*, 1 / *An Introduction to the Principles of Morals and Legislation*, ed. J.H. Burns and H.L.A. Hart, London, Athlone Press, 1970;

2/ *Of Laws in General*, ed. H.L.A. Hart, London, Athlone Press, 1970. Further volumes in preparation

The Works of Jeremy Bentham. Published under the Superintendence of his Executor, John Bowring, 11 vols, Edinburgh, William Tait, 1838-43

Œuvres de J. Bentham, Translated by P.E.L. Dumont, 3 vols, Brussels, Hauman, 1829-30

Jeremy Bentham's Economic Writings, critical edition based on his printed works and unprinted manuscripts by W. Stark, 3 vols, London, Allen and Unwin, 1952

Works

Bentham's Theory of Fictions, edited by C.K. Ogden, London, Kegan, Paul, Trench, Trubner and Co., 1932

Chrestomathia: being a collection of papers, explanatory of the design of ... the Chrestomathic Day School ... [with part II, being] an essay on nomenclature and classification: including a critical examination of the encyclopedical table of Lord Bacon, as improved by D'Alembert; and the first lines of a new one ... London, Payne and Foss and R. Hunter, 1816-17 [Also published in *Works of Jeremy Bentham*, ed. Bowring, vol. 8]

Codification proposal, addressed by J.B. to all nations professing liberal opinions; or Idea of a proposed all-comprehensive body of law, with an accompaniment of reasons, applying all along to the several proposed arrangements ... Also, intimation, from the author, to the competent authorities in the several nations and political states, expressive of his desire and readiness to draw up, for their use respectively, the original draught *of a body of law, such as above proposed*, London, I. McCreery, 1822

A Comment on the Commentaries: a criticism of William Blackstone's Commentaries on the Laws of England ... Now first printed from the author's manuscript, with introduction and notes by Charles Warren Everett, Oxford, The Clarendon Press, 1928

Constitutional Code: for the use of all nations and all governments professing Liberal opinions, Volume 1, London, R. Howard, 1830

Deontology; or the Science of Morality: in which the harmony and coincidence of Duty and Self-Interest, Virtue and Felicity, Prudence and Benvelolence, are explained and exemplified. From the manuscripts of Jeremy Bentham, arranged and edited by John Bowring, 2 vols, London, Longman, Rees, Orme, Brown, Greene and Longman, 1834

A Fragment on Government and An Introduction to the Principles of Morals and Legislation, by Jeremy Bentham, edited with an introduction by Wilfrid

Harrison, professor of politics, University of Warwick, Oxford, Basil Blackwell, 1967

A Fragment on Government, edited with an introduction by F.C. Montague, Oxford, Clarendon Press, 1891

'Leading principles of a constitutional code, for any state, by Jeremy Bentham,' *The Pamphleteer*, 22, 1823, No. 44, pp. 475-86

'Panopticon'; or, the Inspection House: containing the idea of a new principle of construction applicable to any sort of establishment, in which persons of any description are to be kept under inspection: and in particular to Penitentiary-houses, Prisons, Houses of industry, Workhouses, Poor Houses, Manufactories, Madhouses, Lazarettos, Hospitals, and Schools; with a plan of management adopted to the principle: in a series of letters, written in the year 1787, from Crecheff in White Russia, to a friend in England, 2 vols, Dublin, printed, London, reprinted, T. Payne, 1791

The Rationale of Punishment, by Jeremy Bentham, translated and edited from the French of Dumont by Richard Smith, London, Robt. Howard, 1830

The Rationale of Reward, by Jeremy Bentham, [Translated and edited by R. Smith], London, J. and H.L. Hunt, 1825

Théorie des peines et des récompenses, par M. Jérémie Bentham, jurisconsulte anglois, rédigée en français d'après les mss, par Ét. Dumont, 2 vols, London, 1811

Theory of Legislation, by Jeremy Bentham, translated from the French of Etienne Dumont by R. Hildreth, London, Kegan, Paul, Trench, Trubner and Co., 1896

The Theory of Legislation, by Jeremy Bentham, edited with an introduction and notes by C.K. Ogden, London, Kegan, Paul, Trench, Trubner and Co., 1931

Traités de Législation civile et pénale, Précédés de Principes Généraux de Législation, et d'une Vue d'un Corps complet de Droit: Terminés par un Essai sur l'influence des Tems et des Lieux rélativement aux Lois, par M. Jérémie Bentham, jurisconsulte anglois, publiés en François par Ét. Dumont, de Génève, d'après les Manuscrits confiés par l'Auteur. 3 vols, Paris, Bossange, Masson et Besson, 1802

Writings of other authors

Bacon, Francis, Viscount St Albans, *The Works of Francis Bacon*, 5 vols, London, A. Millar, 1765

Beccaria Bonesana (Cesare), Marquis, *Dei delitti et delle pene* (1764), translated from the Italian as *An Essay on Crimes and Punishments*, with a commentary, attributed to Monsieur de Voltaire, translated from the French, London, J. Almon, 1767

Blackstone, Sir William, *Commentaries on the Laws of England*, 4th ed., 4 vols, Oxford, Clarendon Press, 1770

Bonnot de Condillac, Étienne, *Essai sur l'origine des connoissances humaines*, 2 vols, 1746

- *Traité des Systèmes, où l'on en démèle les inconvenients et les avantages*, Amsterdam, 1771

Chastellux (François Jean), Marquis de, *De la félicité publique, ou Considérations sur le sort des hommes dans les différentes époques de l'histoire*, 2 vols, 1772; translated into English as *An Essay on Public Happiness*, 2 vols, 1774

Delolme: see Lolme.

Filmer, (Sir) Robert, *Patriarcha: or, the Natural Powers of the Kings of England Asserted, and other political works of Sir Robert Filmer*, edited with an introduction and notes by Peter Laslett, Oxford, Blackwell, 1949

Harris, James, *Hermes: or a Philosophical Inquiry concerning Language and Universal Grammar*, London, 1751

Helvétius, Claude Adrien, *De L'Esprit* (1758), translated into English as *De L'Esprit, or, Essays on the Mind, and its several faculties*, translated from the edition printed under the author's inspection, London, 1759

Hey, Richard, *Happiness and Rights, a dissertation upon several subjects relative to the Rights of Man and his Happiness*, London, 1792

- *Observations on the Nature of Civil Liberty and the Principles of Government*, London, 1776

Horne Tooke, John, *E Π EA Π TEPOEVT ∝, or, the Diversions of Purley*, London, 1786

Hobbes, Thomas, *Leviathan, or the Matter, Forme, and Power of a Commonwealth Ecclesiasticall and Civill*, edited with an introduction by C.B. Macpherson, London, Pelican Books, 1968

[Hume, David], *The Philosophical Works of David Hume*, 4 vols, London, 1875-8

Hume: Theory of Politics, containing *A Treatise of Human Nature*, Book III, Parts I and II, and thirteen of the *Essays, Moral Political and Literary*, edited by Frederick Watkins, London, Thos Nelson and Sons, 1951

Lind, J., *Remarks on the Principal Acts of the Thirteenth Parliament of Great Britain*, London, 1775

- *Three Letters to Dr Price, containing remarks on his Observations on the Nature of Civil Liberty ... by a member of Lincoln's Inn, FRS, FSA*, London, 1776

- *An Answer to the Declaration of the American Congress*, London, 1776

Locke, John, *An Essay Concerning Human Understanding*, abridged, edited, and introduced by Maurice Cranston, London, Collier-Macmillan, 1965
- *Two Treatises of Government*, with a supplement, *Patriarcha*, by Robert Filmer, edited with an introduction by Thomas I. Cook, New York, Hafner Publishing Co., 1947
Lolme, Jean Louis de, *La Constitution de l'Angleterre* (1771), translated into English as *The Constitution of England: or an account of the English government* ... London, 1775
Mill, John Stuart, *Dissertations and Discussions; political, philosophical and historical. Reprinted chiefly from the Edinburgh and Westminster Reviews*, 4 vols, London, J.W. Parker, 1859-75
- *Utilitarianism, Liberty and Representative Government*, introduction by A.D. Lindsay, London, Dent, 1964
Price, Richard (DD), *Observations on the Nature of Civil Liberty, the Principles of Government, and the Justice and Policy of the War with America*, London, 1776
- *Additional Observations on the Nature and Value of Civil Liberty* ... London, T. Cadell, 1777
Priestley, Joseph (LL D, FRS), *A Discourse on the Occasion of the death of Dr Price; delivered at Hackney on Sunday, May 1, 1791*, London, 1791
- *An Essay on the First Principles of Government, and on the Nature of Political, Civil and Religious Liberty*, London, 1768
Rousseau, J.J., *Du Contrat Social, ou Principes du droit politique* (1762), in vol. 2 of *The Political Writings of Jean Jacques Rousseau*, edited from the original mss and authentic editions, with introduction and notes by C.E. Vaughan, 2 vols, Oxford, Basil Blackwell, 1962
Salignac de la Mothe Fénélon, François de, *Les Avantures de Télémaque, fils d'Ulysse, ou suite du quatrième livre de l'Odyssée d'Homère*, 3 vols, The Hague, 1699; translated into English as *The Adventures of Telemachus, the Son of Ulysses ... in French and English* ... 2 vols, London, 1742

SECONDARY SOURCES

Books

Arendt, H., *Between Past and Future: Six Exercises in Political Thought*, London, Faber and Faber, 1954
Atkinson, C.M., *Jeremy Bentham: his life and work*, London, Methuen, 1905
Barber, B.R., *Superman and Common Men: Freedom, Anarchy and the Revolution*, Pelican Books, 1972

Baumgardt, D., *Bentham and the Ethics of Today*, Princeton, NJ, Princeton University Press, 1952

Berlin, Isaiah, *Four Essays on Liberty*, London, Oxford University Press, 1969

Brinton, C., *English Political Thought in the Nineteenth Century*, New York, Harper and Row [Harper Torchbook], 1962 [first published by Harvard University Press, Cambridge Mass., 1949]

Burns, J.H., *Jeremy Bentham and University College*, London, Athlone Press, 1962

Cassirer, Ernst, *The Philosophy of the Enlightenment*, transl. by Fritz C.A. Koelin and James P. Pettegrove, Princeton NJ, Princeton University Press, 1951

Cobban, A., *Rousseau and the Modern State*, London, 1934

Cohen, V., *Jeremy Bentham*, Fabian Tract No. 221, 'Biographical Series' No. 11, April 1927

Cooper, David (ed.), *The Dialectics of Liberation*, Penguin Books, 1968

Cranston, M., *Freedom: a New Analysis*, 3d ed. London, Longmans, 1967

Davidson, W.L., *Political Thought in England: the Utilitarians from Bentham to J.S. Mill*, London, Williams and Norgate, 1915

Dicey, A.V., *Lectures on the Relation between Law and Public Opinion in England during the nineteenth century*, London, MacMillan, 1905

Everett, C.W., *The Education of Jeremy Bentham*, New York, Columbia University Press, 1931

‒ *Jeremy Bentham*, London, Weidenfeld and Nicolson, 1966

Fédération Internationale des Sociétés de Philosophie, *Enquête sur La Liberté*, [a collection of essays on liberty in several languages, some in English] Paris, Hermann et Compagnie Éditeurs, 1953

Gay, P., *The Enlightenment: An Interpretation*. 2 vols, 1/ *The Rise of Modern Paganism* (1967), 2/ *The Science of Freedom* (1970), London, Weidenfeld and Nicolson

Halévy, E., *La Formation du Radicalisme Philosophique*, 3 vols, Paris, 1901-4, translated by Mary Morris as *The Growth of Philosophic Radicalism*, with a preface by John Plamenatz, London, Faber and Faber, 1972 [first published in England in 1928]

James, M.H. (ed.), *Bentham and Legal Theory*, Belfast: Northern Ireland Legal Quarterly, 1974. [originally published in Northern Ireland Legal Quarterly, 24, 1973]

Keeton, G.W. and George Schwarzenberger (eds), *Jeremy Bentham and the Law*, London, Stevens and Sons, 1948

Laski, H.J., *Political Thought in England: Locke to Bentham*, London, Oxford University Press, 1920

Letwin, S.R., *The Pursuit of Certainty*, Cambridge University Press, 1965

Lloyd, T. and J. McLeod (eds), *Agenda 70: Proposals for a Creative Politics*, Toronto, University of Toronto Press, 1968

Lyons, D., *In the Interest of the Governed: A Study in Bentham's Philosophy of Utility and Law*, Oxford, Clarendon Press, 1974

MacCunn, J., *Six Radical Thinkers: Bentham, J.S. Mill, Cobden, Carlyle, Mazzini, T.H. Green*, London, Edward Arnold, 1910

Mack, M.P., *Jeremy Bentham: An Odyssey of Ideas*, London, Heinemann, 1963

Macpherson, C.B., *Democratic Theory: Essays in Retrieval*, Oxford, Clarendon Press, 1973.

– *The Political Theory of Possessive Individualism, Hobbes to Locke*, London, Oxford University Press, 1962

– *The Real World of Democracy*, Toronto, Canadian Broadcasting Corporation, 1965

Manning, D.J., *The Mind of Jeremy Bentham*, London, Longmans, Green and Co., 1968

Marcuse, Herbert, *An Essay on Liberation*, Pelican Books, 1972

– *Reason and Revolution*, 2nd ed. with supplementary chapter, London, Routledge and Kegan Paul, 1969

Mitchell, W.C., *Bentham's Felicific Calculus*, published by the Academy of Political Science, New York, 1918 [reprinted from *Political Science Quarterly*, 33, 1918]

Nash, P., A.M. Kazamias, and H.J. Perkinson, *The Educated Man: Studies in the History of Educational Thought*, New York, John Wiley and Sons, 1965

Ogden, C.K., *Jeremy Bentham, 1832-2032*, with notes and appendices, London, Kegan, Paul, Trench, Trubner and Company, 1932

Parekh, B. (ed.), *Bentham's Political Thought*, London, Croom Helm, 1973

– *Jeremy Bentham: Ten Critical Essays* London, Frank Cass, 1973

Phillipson, Coleman, *Three Criminal Law Reformers: Beccaria, Bentham, Romilly*, London, J.M. Dent and Sons, 1923

Plamenatz, J., *The English Utilitarians*, Oxford, Basil Blackwell, 1958

– *Man and Society*, 2 vols, London, Longmans, 1963

– *Consent, Freedom and Political Obligation*, 2nd ed. Oxford Paperbacks, Oxford University Press, 1968

Pringle-Pattison, A. Seth, *The Philosophical Radicals, and other essays*, London, Wm Blackwood and Sons, 1907

Randall, J.H. jr, *The Career of Philosophy*, 2 vols, 2/ *From the German Enlightenment to the Age of Darwin* New York, Columbia University Press, 1965

Skinner, B.F., *Beyond Freedom and Dignity*, New York, Knopf, 1962

- *Walden Two*, New York, MacMillan Paperbacks, 1962 [originally published 1948]
Stephen, (Sir) Leslie, *The English Utilitarians*, 3 vols, London, Duckworth & Co., 1900 [Volume I is a biography of Bentham.]
Watson, J. Steven, *The Reign of George III, 1760-1815*, Oxford, at the Clarendon Press, 1960
Wheeler, H. (ed.), *Beyond the Punitive Society*, San Francisco, W.H. Freeman and Co., 1973
Wolin, S.S., *Politics and Vision: continuity and innovation in western political thought*, Boston, Little, Brown and Co., 1960

Articles

Alexander, W.H., 'Jeremy Bentham, Legal Philosopher and Reformer,' *New York University Quarterly Law Review*, 7, part 1, 'Life and Works,' No. 1, Sept. 1929, pp. 141-55, Part 2, 'Legal Philosophy,' No. 2, Dec. 1929, pp. 465-73
Ayer, A.J., 'Man as a Subject for Science,' in *Philosophy, Politics and Society*, 3rd ser., edited by P. Laslett and W.G. Runciman, Oxford, Basil Blackwell, 1969
- 'The Principle of Utility,' in *Philosophical Essays*, London, MacMillan, 1954
Beales, H.L., 'Jeremy Bentham, Social Engineer,' *The Listener*, 3 Aug. 1932, pp. 148-50
Blaunt, Charles, 'Bentham, Dumont and Mirabeau,' *University of Birmingham Historical Journal*, 3, 1951-2, pp. 153-64
Burns, J.H., 'Bentham and the French Revolution,' *Transactions of the Royal Historical Society*, 5th ser., 16, 1966, pp. 95-114
- 'Du côte du Chez Vaughan: Rousseau Revisited,' *Political Studies*, 12, 1964, pp. 229-34
- 'J.S. Mill and Democracy,' *Political Studies*, 5, 1957, pp. 158-75, 281-94
Coing, H., 'Bentham's "Interessenjurisprudenz," ' *The Irish Jurist*, 2, 1967, pp. 336-51
Crick, Bernard, 'Freedom as Politics,' *Philosophy, Politics and Society*, 3d ser., edited by P. Laslett and W.G. Runciman, Oxford, Basil Blackwell, 1969
Dinwiddy, J.R., 'Bentham's Transition to Radicalism, 1809-10,' *Journal of the History of Ideas*, 35, 1975, pp. 683-701
Friedman, R.B., 'New Explorations of Mill's Essay "On Liberty," ' *Political Studies*, 14, 1966, pp. 281-304
Gagnebin, B., 'Jeremy Bentham et Étienne Dumont,' lecture delivered at University College, London, Tuesday, 8 June 1948, printed in *Jeremy*

Bentham Bicentenary Celebrations: Bicentenary Lectures, London, H.K. Lewis and Co., 1948

Gay, Peter, 'The Enlightenment in the history of political theory,' *Political Science Quarterly* 69, 1954, pp. 374-89

Gunn, J.A.W., 'Jeremy Bentham and the public interest,' *Canadian Journal of Political Science* 1, 1968, pp. 398-413

Hart, H.L.A., 'Bentham,' *Proceedings of the British Academy*, 48, 1962, pp. 297-320

- 'Bentham on sovereignty,' *Irish Jurist*, 2, 1967, pp. 127-55

Himmelfarb, Gertrude, 'Bentham's Utopia: The National Charity Company,' *Journal of British Studies*, 10, 1970, pp. 84-117

- 'The Haunted House of Jeremy Bentham,' in *Ideas in History: essays presented to Louis Gottschalk by his former students*, edited by R. Herr and H.T. Parker, Durham NC, Duke University Press, 1965, pp. 199-238

Holdsworth, Sir Wm, 'Bentham's Place in English Legal History,' *California Law Review*, 28, 1940, pp. 568-91

Hume, L.J., 'Bentham and the nineteenth century revolution in government,' *Historical Journal*, 10, 1967, pp. 361-75

Hutcheson, T.W., 'Bentham as an economist,' *Economic Journal*, 66, 1956, pp. 288-306

Kort, F., 'The issue of a science of politics in Utilitarian thought,' *American Political Science Review*, 46, 1952, pp. 1140-52

Lundin, H.G., 'The influence of Jeremy Bentham on English democratic development,' *University of Iowa Studies in the Social Sciences*, 7, no. 3

Lyons, D., 'Was Bentham a Utilitarian?' in *Reason and Reality, the Royal Institute of Philosophy Lectures*, 5, 1970-1, London, St Martin's Press, 1972

Macpherson, C.B., 'Democratic theory: ontology and technology,' in Spitz (ed.), *Political Theory and Social Change*, New York, 1967

- 'Post-Liberal democracy?' *New Left Review*, 33, Sept.-Oct. 1965, pp. 3-17

Muirhead, A., 'A Jeremy Bentham Collection,' *The Library: Transactions of the Bibliographical Society*, 5th ser., 1, 1946, pp. 6-27

Parris, H., 'The nineteenth century revolution in government: a reappraisal reappraised,' *Historical Journal*, 3, 1960

Peardon, T.P., 'Bentham's ideal republic,' *Canadian Journal of Economics and Political Science*, 18, 1951, pp. 184-203

Pratt, R.C., 'The Benthamite theory of democracy,' *Canadian Journal of Economics and Political Science*, 21, 1955, pp. 20-9

Rees, J.C., 'A phase in the development of Mill's ideas on liberty,' *Political Studies*, 6, 1958, pp. 33-44

- 'A re-reading of Mill on liberty,' *Political Studies*, 7, 1960, pp. 113-29

Robbins, L. (Lord), *'Bentham in the Twentieth Century': An address to the Assembly of Faculties, University College London, 16 June 1964*, London, Athlone Press, 1965

Roberts, Warren jr, 'Behavioural factors in Bentham's conception of political change,' *Political Studies*, 10, 1962, pp. 163-79

– 'Bentham's conception of political change: a liberal approach,' *Political Studies*, 9, 1961, pp. 254-66

Shackleton, Robert, 'The greatest happiness of the greatest number: the history of Bentham's phrase,' *Studies on Voltaire and the Eighteenth Century*, 90, 1972, pp. 1461-82

Shapiro, J.S., 'J.S. Mill: pioneer of democratic liberalism in England,' *Journal of the History of Ideas*, 4, 1943, pp. 127-60

Sidgwick, H., 'Bentham and Benthamism,' *Fortnightly Review*, new ser., 21, 1877, pp. 647 ff

Smith, C.I., 'Bentham's second rule,' *Journal of the History of Ideas*, 31, 1970, pp. 462-3

Stark, W., 'Liberty and equality, or Jeremy Bentham as an Economist,' *Economic Journal*, Part 1/ 'Bentham's doctrine,' 51, 1941, pp. 56-79, Part 2/ 'Bentham's influence,' 56, 1946, pp. 583-608

Tarlton, C.D., 'The overlooked strategy of Bentham's *Fragment on Government*,' *Political Studies*, 20, 1972, pp. 397-406

Ten, C.L., 'Mill on liberty,' *Journal of the History of Ideas*, 30, 1969, pp. 47-68

– 'Mill on self-regarding actions,' *Philosophy*, 48, 1968, p. 29

Viner, J., 'Bentham and J.S. Mill: the Utilitarian background,' *American Economic Review*, 39, 1949, pp. 360-82

Wallas, G., 'Bentham as political inventor,' *Contemporary Review*, 129, 1926, pp. 308-19

– 'Jeremy Bentham,' *Political Science Quarterly*, 38, 1923, pp. 45-46

Newspapers

The Gazetteer and New Daily Advertiser for 1770

The Public Advertiser for 1770

Times Literary Supplement, 31 Dec. 1925, 'Bentham, Blackstone, and the New Law,' p. 1

Index

Works by Bentham to which significant reference is made in the text of this book are listed alphabetically by title under the heading Bentham, Jeremy (works of).